DIALOGUE ON THE ERRORS AND

The Getty Research Institute
Los Angeles
Texts & Documents

DIALOGUE ON THE ERRORS AND ABUSES OF PAINTERS

GIOVANNI ANDREA GILIO

Edited by

MICHAEL BURY, LUCINDA BYATT, and CAROL M. RICHARDSON

Translated by

MICHAEL BURY and LUCINDA BYATT

THE GETTY RESEARCH INSTITUTE PUBLICATIONS PROGRAM
Thomas W. Gaehtgens, *Director, Getty Research Institute*
Gail Feigenbaum, *Associate Director*

Published by the Getty Research Institute, Los Angeles
Getty Publications
1200 Getty Center Drive, Suite 500
Los Angeles, California 90049-1682
www.getty.edu/publications

Laura Santiago, *Manuscript Editor*
Hespenheide Design, *Designer*
Jim Drobka, *Cover Designer*
Amita Molloy, *Production Coordinator*
Stuart Smith, *Series Designer*

Distributed in the United States and Canada by the University of Chicago Press
Distributed outside the United States and Canada by Yale University Press, London

Printed in China

Type composed in Minion and Trade Gothic

Library of Congress Cataloging-in-Publication Data
Names: Gilio, Giovanni Andrea, -1584, author. | Bury, Michael, 1947- editor, translator. | Byatt, Lucinda, editor, translator. | Richardson, Carol M., 1969- editor. | Getty Research Institute, issuing body.
Title: Dialogue on the errors and abuses of painters / Giovanni Andrea Gilio ; edited by Michael Bury, Lucinda Byatt, and Carol M. Richardson ; translated by Michael Bury and Lucinda Byatt.
Other titles: Dialogo secondo, nel quale si ragiona degli errori, e degli abusi de' pittori circa l'historie. English | Texts & documents.
Description: Los Angeles : Getty Research Institute, [2018] | Series: Texts & documents | "This volume translates Giovanni Andrea Gilio, Dialogo secondo, nel quale si ragiona degli errori, e degli abusi de' pittori circa l'historie, which is the second dialogue in Gilio, Due dialogi [di M. Giovanni Andrea Gilio da Fabriano] . . . (Camerino: Antonio Gioioso, 1564)."—ECIP galley. | Includes bibliographical references and index.
Identifiers: LCCN 2017035968 | ISBN 9781606065563
Subjects: LCSH: Painting—Early works to 1800. | Painting, Italian. | Painting, Renaissance—Italy.
Classification: LCC ND615 .G48513 2018 | DDC 759.5—dc23
LC record available at https://lccn.loc.gov/2017035968

Front cover: Michelangelo Buonarroti, *Last Judgment* (detail), 1535–41. See p. 158. Vatican Museums and Galleries, Vatican City / Artothek / Bridgeman Images
Back cover: Raphael, *Transfiguration,* 1516–20. See p. 120. Vatican Museums and Galleries, Vatican City / De Agostini Picture Library / Bridgeman Images

This volume translates Giovanni Andrea Gilio, *Dialogo secondo, nel quale si ragiona degli errori, e degli abusi de' pittori circa l'historie,* which is the second dialogue in Gilio, *Due dialogi [di M. Giovanni Andrea Gilio da Fabriano]* . . . (Camerino: Antonio Gioioso, 1564).

CONTENTS

MICHAEL BURY, LUCINDA BYATT, AND CAROL M. RICHARDSON

INTRODUCTION

The text presented here in translation—*Dialogo secondo, nel quale si ragiona degli errori, e degli abusi de' pittori circa l'istorie* (Dialogue on the errors and abuses of painters)—was written in the early 1560s by an obscure cleric from Fabriano, Giovanni Andrea Gilio.[1] It takes the form of a dialogue in which six people, five of whom are identifiable as real individuals, discuss issues that have arisen from the contemporary practice of painting.[2] One of the individuals is himself an ecclesiastic, and the others are a mixed group consisting of several lawyers, a medical doctor, and a cultivated gentleman. In life, all of them were probably friends of the author. The only place where Gilio speaks in his own voice is in a brief preface where he outlines his intentions; otherwise, he uses the voices of the different participants to raise issues and present different points of view. The discussions between them cover all kinds of subject matter, sacred and profane, but the primary concern is with questions about errors and abuses to be found in paintings of sacred subjects.

A particular strength of Gilio's text is that the ideas put forward are exemplified by reference to actual paintings, especially works by or connected with Michelangelo Buonarroti. Gilio's text is known today in large part because it contains an extended critique of Michelangelo's fresco of the *Last Judgment*. Unveiled in 1541, this painting had elicited an unparalleled response. There were many who proclaimed it the absolute pinnacle of pictorial achievement, while others condemned it as quite inappropriate to and even subversive of the purposes it was meant to serve. Stimulated by this case, various writers of Gilio's time had explored the idea that, in the field of contemporary sacred painting, a fault line existed between, on the one hand, the professional skills and imagination of the painter and, on the other, the requirements of the subject matter he was to represent. In a famous letter to Michelangelo in 1545, Pietro Aretino criticized the painter for having wanted to show "an impiety of irreligion only equaled by the perfection of his painting" in his *Last Judgment*;[3] and Giorgio Vasari, in the context of his life of Fra Angelico, published in 1550, wrote of how religious works might be praised for their artistry and power (*artificio e virtù*) but simultaneously condemned for their indecency or immodesty (*disonesto*) because they failed to communicate devoutness.[4] Both of those writers concentrated on the insistent presence of naked figures as the most important sign of the disjunction of the artist's skill and the requirements of the subject matter. What Gilio does through his dialogue is to extend that critique to show how, more generally, prevailing attitudes and priorities among painters were potentially in conflict with the validity and function of sacred painting and that a resolution, accommodating both, needed to be found. Michelangelo was the particular target because, Gilio writes, he was the prince of painters and whatever he did was imitated by everyone.[5]

Gilio's writing presents a distinct challenge to modern understanding because of the way he uses certain terms. Most problematic is his use of the term *arte.* It is only too easy to think that this might be translated as "art" and thus integrated with what we now understand by that word. But in line with the common usage of the period, what Gilio means is the art or craft of painting: the knowledge, methods, and techniques that the painter learned from his teachers and from the works he saw around him. Alongside the acquired art of painting, the painter brought to bear on any task his own powers of mind and intellect, for which Gilio uses the word *ingegno.* As for the tasks of the painter, the subjects of central focus in the *Dialogo* are histories (*istorie*). The word *istorie* has two meanings in Gilio's writing. He sometimes uses it to mean any painting representing an event or action (a story), but he also uses it to mean any subject that is true—and it is the latter sense that for Gilio is the important one. A history in that sense is a subject that is true and real (*vero*), as opposed to something made up to seem true (*finto*) or something fabulous or mythic (*favoloso*). While a poetic painter (*pittore poetico*) handling made-up or fabulous material was entitled to develop his own personal ideas, a historical painter (*pittore istorico*) was required to suppress personal conceptions and remain faithful to the approved sources: he should see himself as a translator from words into images. The Bible, the lives of the saints, and other sacred writings recounted true history, and it was essential for painters to understand the specific demands that these texts placed upon them. Gilio's diagnosis of the underlying cause of error and abuse in sacred painting was the failure to distinguish between the true (*vero*), truthlike (*finto*), and fabulous (*favoloso*) subject matter and the different requirements of each.

Gilio's text reveals a wide cultural frame of reference: theology, law, and ancient and modern history and literature, as well as an acquaintance with great works of modern Roman painting. The ideas expounded are founded in ancient rhetoric and the theory of poetry: prominent among the texts he uses are Aristotle's *Poetics* and especially Horace's *Ars Poetica.* Horace's influential concept "as is painting so is poetry" (*ut pictura poesis*) justifies the application of literary theory to the criticism of painting.[6] These ideas are interwoven with ideas derived from contemporaneous writing on painting, particularly Lodovico Dolce's *Dialogo della pittura intitolato l'Aretino* (Dialogue on painting, entitled the *Aretino*), published in 1557. And Gilio's awareness of the theological literature on images played a fundamental part in the way he wrote. His objective was not the justification of holy images in the face of radical Protestant challenges to their legitimacy, as was the case with many of his contemporaries. However, he does draw on ideas developed by Catholic apologists, such as Konrad Braun and Ambrogio Catarino, and deploys them for his own purposes. Gilio is fascinated by painting and wants to purify it. In his view, that requires thoughtfulness and discrimination. Gilio may not have been a profound thinker, but he had a clear objective and amassed an impressive range of supporting material to pursue it.

In the first essay of this volume, Michael Bury assembles the evidence that can be discovered about Gilio, his text, and the scope of that text. He then discusses in depth the debates between the speakers in Gilio's *Dialogo* about the errors committed by painters in dealing with the subject matter of sacred painting, the reasons for those errors, and what might be done to remedy them. The second essay, by Carol M. Richardson, considers the general treatment of Gilio's *Dialogo* by recent art historians, especially the ways in which the text has been related to the Council of Trent and Catholic Reform. She suggests that Gilio's *Dialogo* is a rich indication of the issues at stake in the period for both artists and churchmen. The third essay, by Lucinda Byatt, examines the text in its own right and highlights its most significant challenges. She discusses some key problems raised by the translation and looks in more detail at the setting of the *Dialogo* and other aspects relating to the patronage and printing of the book.

It is the hope of this volume's editors that this first-ever English translation of Gilio's *Dialogo . . . degli errori e degli abusi de' pittori* will open up this fascinating text—and the important questions it raises—to as wide an audience as possible. Gilio's text will stimulate and enrich debate about art in its historical, religious, and intellectual settings, and it will contribute to a more nuanced understanding of differences that, sadly, tend to be exaggerated, especially in the context of religious polemical exchange.

We shall not cease from exploration
And the end of all our exploring
Will be to arrive where we started
And know the place for the first time.
(T. S. ELIOT, "LITTLE GIDDING," LINES 239–42)[7]

Notes

1. Giovanni Andrea Gilio's *Dialogo secondo, nel quale si ragiona degli errori, e degli abusi de' pittori circa l'istorie* is the second of two dialogues published together in a single volume. The full title of the volume is *Due dialogi [di M. Giovanni Andrea Gilio da Fabriano]. Nel primo de' quali si ragiona de le parti morali e civili appertenenti a' letterati cortigiani, et ad ogni gentil'huomo, e l'utile che i prencipi cavano dai letterati. Nel secondo si ragiona degli errori de' pittori circa l'historie. Con molte annotationi fatte sopra il Giuditio di Michelangelo, et altre figure, tanto de la vecchia, quanto de la nova cappella. Et in che modo vogliono esser dipinte le sacre imagini. Con un discorso sopra la parola Urbe, Città, Colonia, Municipio, Prefettura, Foro, Conciliabolo, Oppido, Terra, Castello, Villa, Pago, Borgo, e qual sia la vera città* (Camerino: Antonio Gioioso, 1564).
2. See "Dramatis Personae," this volume, 79–82. Francesco Santi is the only one of the participants who cannot be independently identified outside the text.
3. Lodovico Dolce uses Aretino as a character in the dialogue and has him articulate that point at some length; see Dolce, *Dialogo della pittura intitolato l'Aretino* (Venice: G. Giolito de' Ferrari, 1557), in *Trattati d'arte del Cinquecento: Fra manierismo e controriforma,* vol. 1, ed. Paola Barocchi (Bari: Laterza, 1960), 141–206, 343–47, 433–93. Originally written in November 1545 and addressed to Michelangelo, Aretino's letter was published in 1550 and readdressed to Alessandro Corvino with some verbal differences; see Pietro Aretino, *Il quarto libro de le lettere* (Venice: Bartolomeo Cesano, 1550), 83r–84, in *Il Carteggio di Michelangelo,* vol. 4, *1553–1552,* ed. Giovanni Poggi, Paola Barocchi, and Renzo Ristori (Florence: Sansoni, 1979), 215–19.
4. See Vasari, *Le vite de' piu eccellenti architetti, pittori, et scultori italiani . . . nell'edizione per i tipi di Lorenzo Torrentino Firenze 1550,* ed. Luciano Bellosi and Aldo Rossi (Turin: Einaudi, 1986), 344.
5. Gilio, this volume, 145.
6. Horace, *Ars Poetica,* line 361, in *Satires; Epistles; The Art of Poetry,* trans. H. Rushton Fairclough, Loeb Classical Library 194 (Cambridge, MA: Harvard University Press, 1926), 480–81.
7. T. S. Eliot, "Little Gidding," in *Four Quartets* (1943; Boston: Mariner, 1971), 59.

MICHAEL BURY

GILIO ON PAINTERS OF SACRED IMAGES

The Author and His Work

Giovanni Andrea Gilio, the author of *Dialogo secondo, nel quale si ragiona degli errori, e degli abusi de' pittori circa l'istorie* (Dialogue on the errors and abuses of painters), is a slightly shadowy figure; very little biographical information about him has come to light.[1] Nothing is known directly about his birth, but because he is always referred to as from Fabriano, it is supposed that he was born there. He was a cleric: a canon and then, from 1567, prior of the chapter of San Venanzio, the principal church at Fabriano.[2] As an old man, Gilio retired to the hermitage of San Vicino, near Frontale and not far from Fabriano, where he died in 1584.[3] He wrote various books on devotional and literary subjects. Among the devotional texts is a life of Saint Athanasius, and also two treatises.[4] One of these, titled *Trattato de la emulatione che il demonio ha fatto a Dio* (On the Devil's emulation of God), is directed against idolatry and superstition and is accompanied by lengthy discussions of the true nature of God. The other, *Le persecuzioni della Chiesa* (Persecutions of the Church), is a history of the martyrs and of those who suffered in defense of Catholic orthodoxy.[5] Gilio's final book, *Topica poetica,* is concerned with poetics and includes a dictionary of rhetorical figures of speech.[6]

The *Dialogo* that concerns us here was probably written between 1561 and 1562.[7] It was published as one part of a rather miscellaneous collection of elements in a single volume printed at Camerino in 1564, under the title *Due dialogi* (Two dialogues).[8] In addition to the *Dialogo . . . degli errori e degli abusi de' pittori* (the second dialogue), this volume contains another dialogue (the first dialogue), on the subject of the qualities appropriate to educated courtiers and the benefits these courtiers could bring to the princes they serve.[9] There is also a brief discourse arguing that Fabriano be granted the dignity of being called a city. All three texts were dedicated to Cardinal Alessandro Farnese, and it has been plausibly suggested that the volume was conceived as an appeal to him for patronage.[10] It is probably significant that *Trattato de la emulatione che il demonio ha fatto a Dio* was dedicated to Vittoria Farnese, Duchess of Urbino, who was Alessandro's sister.

Although the dating of *Trattato de la emulatione che il demonio ha fatto a Dio* is not absolutely clear, it seems most probable that it was first published in 1563. The copy in the Biblioteca Casanatense at Rome lacks a printed title page but has in its place a handwritten one with the date 1550.[11] However, this is unique; all other existing copies have printed title pages dated either 1563 or 1564, so there is strong reason to discard the earlier date and to suppose that it was written at very much the same time as the *Due dialogi.*[12] If 1563 is correct, then it can be asserted with some confidence that Gilio had been in Rome at some point before that year. In *Trattato de la emulatione che il demonio ha fatto a Dio,* he describes having witnessed a street performance there, when a Spaniard performed a card trick before a crowd, and he also recalls coming across a "hermaphrodite" who claimed prophetic powers.[13] In addition, there is evidence in the *Dialogo de le parti morali appertenenti a' letterati cortigiani* (Dialogue on the moral qualities befitting educated courtiers), which is set in Rome, of a detailed knowledge of the local topography, personalities, and customs.[14]

Given this evidence, the question immediately arises of whether Gilio had resided in Rome for any great length of time. If he had, it would probably have been in the household of an established figure, yet there is little to link Gilio to any such person or network.[15] The only clues to a possible patron are a number of allusions, direct and indirect, to the archbishop of Siena, Francesco Bandini Piccolomini, and to the Sienese Accademia degli Intronati, of which the archbishop was one of the founders.[16] Bandini had been in voluntary exile at Fabriano in 1552, when he was recalled to Siena on the orders of Pope Julius III; we know that Gilio had contact with the archbishop then, because Gilio's long poem, quoted at the beginning of the *Dialogo . . . degli errori e degli abusi de' pittori,* was composed for him.[17] In 1559, Gilio dedicated to him his life of Athanasius. Bandini held various significant positions in Rome during the pontificate of Paul IV, between 1555 and 1559, and he seems to have maintained a certain prominence under the next pope, Pius IV.

However, it seems unlikely that Gilio found a position in the archbishop's Roman household. In the *Dialogo de le parti morali appertenenti a' letterati cortigiani,* Gilio says that Bandini wanted to become a Maecenas but because of circumstances was unable to fulfill his ambition; perhaps Bandini had not given Gilio the support he had hoped for.[18] By the early 1560s, Farnese patronage may have seemed to hold out better prospects. Cardinal Alessandro was of course a dominant figure in the patronage of learning and of the visual arts in Rome from the pontificate of his grandfather, Paul III, until Alessandro's death in 1589.[19] But unfortunately, we know nothing of his response to Gilio's work. If it is correct to think that Gilio aimed for Farnese support, it is remarkable that in the *Dialogo . . . degli errori e degli abusi de' pittori,* major Farnese commissions are subject to condemnation, in particular Michelangelo Buonarroti's Vatican frescoes for Paul III. Gilio's censure of these commissions does, however, fit with Alessandro's new reforming zeal, noted by contemporaries in the 1560s.[20] One of Gilio's reasons for adopting such a critical stance could have been to show that he was an upright man who could be turned to for honest advice, not a flatterer. In short, that he, Gilio, was an example of the moral and educated courtier that he had written about in the first of the *Due dialogi.*

The *Dialogo* displays an extensive and well-informed acquaintance with modern Roman painting more or less up to the moment Gilio would have begun writing it around 1561. Particularly striking are references to works in progress: the Cesi and the Sforza Chapels in Santa Maria Maggiore.[21] Cardinal Guido Ascanio Sforza had commissioned the latter from Michelangelo around 1560.[22] Additionally, on three occasions in the text, firsthand visual knowledge of the Roman paintings being discussed is explicitly claimed by participants in the *Dialogo.* The first is a remark made by Francesco Santi about the inappropriate movement of an angel (see fig. 16): "I can't help laughing when I am in Rome and I walk through the Minerva and see . . . an angel acting like a dove when, folding its wings as they sometimes do, it seems to plunge headfirst downward, or as if released from a sack, it falls out of the sky."[23] The second is Pulidoro Saraceni's positive response when asked whether he has actually seen the frescoes in the hall of the Palazzo della Cancelleria (see figs. 5, 29).[24] The third is Vincenso Peterlino's comment on the Madonna in the Cesi Chapel in Santa Maria della Pace: "Receiving the annunciation from the angel, she makes a movement turning round that makes me laugh whenever I see her."[25]

What Gilio himself may have seen remains an open question. Those works that were in churches, like the *Annunciation* in the Cesi Chapel, were completely public and readily accessible to anyone. However, the frescoed hall of the Cancelleria and (most importantly for the *Dialogo*) the paintings by Michelangelo in the great papal chapels—the Sistine and the Pauline—were another matter (see figs. 14, 19, 26). The evidence available suggests that to enter them required permission.[26] Nonetheless, someone with Gilio's clerical status would probably have easily obtained access to the Sistine, either when services were being held or when they were not.[27] There is plenty of evidence that artists wanting to study and draw the Sistine Chapel encountered few difficulties. There is less information about visitors to the smaller Pauline Chapel, which had a role in several different rituals of the Vatican Palace. But again, for someone like Gilio, access would probably have been quite straightforward if he had wanted it.[28]

In any case, the flourishing print-publishing industry in Rome meant that by the early 1560s, printed copies of a great number of paintings were available for purchase, including many of those discussed in the text. There is an explicit acknowledgment of the importance of prints within the text itself: when the discussion turns to Michelangelo's fresco of the *Last Judgment,* a print of the fresco is brought out and we are told specifically that the group gathered around it.[29] Whatever he had or had not seen for himself, Gilio may well have made quite extensive use of prints to assist him when he was writing; this would help to explain the confident engagement with specific works, which is such a significant element in his text generally.

Gilio's preparation for writing on the errors of painters depended upon his familiarity with ancient and modern published works on the history and theory of painting. Thus he regularly refers to Pliny's *Naturalis Historia* and Vitruvius's *De architectura;* and he evidently knew Leon Battista Alberti's *De pictura,* the first edition of Giorgio Vasari's *Le vite de' più eccellenti pittori, scultori, e architettori,* and Lodovico Dolce's *Dialogo della pittura intitolato l'Aretino.*[30] Interestingly, Gilio also alludes to an unpublished (and now untraceable) treatise on painting being prepared by the Fabrianese painter and draftsman Francesco Agostini, who is known to have worked in Rome as well as Fabriano; he was, no doubt, a friend.[31]

Even more important was Gilio's knowledge of poetics and rhetoric. He constantly cites Horace's *Ars Poetica,* which, with its famous simile "as is painting so is poetry," gave strong support to the idea that literary theory could be transferred for use in the discussion of painting.[32] He knew Aristotle's *Poetics* and also works of ancient and modern rhetoric. Significantly, alongside these secular works of history and criticism, Gilio also knew the theologically directed literature on images: the thirteenth-century *Rationale divinorum officiorum* (Rationale for the divine offices) of Durandus and also sixteenth-century texts that had been produced to counter the iconoclastic arguments of the Protestant reformers.[33] Prominent among the latter were the works of Konrad Braun (Conradus Brunus) and Ambrogio Catarino (Politi).[34] In important ways, it is Gilio's merging of secular and theological traditions of criticism that gives his text much of its value.[35]

In its own time, Gilio's *Due dialogi* had a certain success.[36] This can primarily be measured by the response it provoked in subsequent writing about painting; there is unfortunately very little direct evidence about sales.[37] Among later secular writers, the *Dialogo . . . degli errori e degli abusi de' pittori* was cited—in an extremely positive way—by Raffaello Borghini in his dialogue *Il Riposo,* published at Florence in 1584; Borghini's close reading of Gilio is evident throughout.[38] And it was almost certainly consulted by Giovanni Paolo

Lomazzo for his *Trattato dell'arte della pittura, scoltura, et architettura* (Treatise on the art of painting, sculpture, and architecture) of 1584, and by Giovanni Battista Armenini for his *De' veri precetti della pittura* (*On the True Precepts of the Art of Painting*) of 1586. Although neither writer explicitly acknowledges his debt, there are unmistakable echoes of Gilio's *Dialogo* in each of their treatises.[39] In a religious context, the *Dialogo* was recommended by the Jesuit Antonio Possevino in his bibliography of recommended books, the *Bibliotheca selecta* of 1593—that remarkable mirror image of the *Index librorum prohibitorum* (Index of prohibited books).[40] And Federico Borromeo's book on sacred art, *De arte sacra,* exhibits at several points the influence of Gilio. Although not completed and published until 1624, it has plausibly been argued that it was first drafted in the 1590s.[41]

The Scope of the *Dialogo*

What kind of work is the *Dialogo?* Scholars usually include it among the art treatises of the sixteenth century, and in a sense that classification is correct, despite it being very different from any of the other treatises by virtue of being a reforming tract. Neither Gilio himself nor any of the interlocutors who participate in the discussion he invents lay any claim to having professional knowledge of painting.[42] No apology is offered for that. They are ecclesiastics, lawyers, doctors, and gentlemen, engaging with the treatment of subject matter in contemporary painting. What they bring is knowledge of literature, history, law, philosophy, and theology, as well as of earlier writing about painting, which they apply to the works chosen for discussion. When Gilio briefly outlines his intentions in the address to Alessandro Farnese that prefaces the *Dialogo,* he writes of his concern about the abuses and errors in subject matter that the "ignorant" painters of the time had allowed to proliferate.[43] Implicitly, Gilio and his well-educated interlocutors can provide the knowledge the painters lack and ensure that what is conveyed to the spectator is appropriate to the subject matter. Although Gilio believes that contemporary painters often failed in their handling of subject matter, he accepts the idea that the art of painting, by which he means all the craft skills and methods learned and put into practice by painters, had been restored to its full capacity by Michelangelo, Raphael, and other contemporary masters.[44]

In many modern interpretations of Gilio's *Dialogo,* what has been sought, and found, is an aesthetic point of view. This has led to serious misunderstandings. Enormously influential in this regard was Rensselaer Lee, whose article in the *Art Bulletin* of 1940, titled "*Ut pictura poesis:* The Humanistic Theory of Painting," lays out a rather complex argument. Lee writes that Gilio's criticisms of Michelangelo demonstrate a complete failure of comprehension in the face of the profundity of that artist's subjective imagination but that Gilio was, through those criticisms, giving expression to a real aesthetic dislike: a hostility to "the general tendency in Mannerist art to sacrifice meaning to empty aestheticism."[45] Paola Barocchi sets Gilio against "mannerism" as well, claiming, for example, that his attacks on strained, unnatural poses in the works of Michelangelo and his contemporaries were an expression of a dislike of "formalism."[46] Emphasizing style, John Shearman later generalizes the point: in his view, "a natural antipathy" exists between the aestheticism of "mannerism," which he names the stylish style, and the serious religious content of the kind demanded by the Catholic Church of the Counter-Reformation period; and he cites Gilio as a witness.[47] These and many other modern writers not only have seen Gilio as developing a particular aesthetic but also have interpreted his criticisms in terms of their own aesthetic preferences.[48] Thus, Lee approves of the attack on "empty aestheticism," and Barocchi, who herself clearly disapproves of "formalism," co-opts Gilio to her cause. What all of these writers did was to interpret Gilio as presenting and building on a theory that polarized form and content, style and meaning, in which his focus on errors and abuses was the consequence of his narrow concerns with content and his inability to appreciate fully the artistic values of form and style.[49] But the dichotomies of form/content and style/meaning in the modern senses of these terms are not in play here.

To understand what Gilio wrote, it is essential to concentrate on his treatment of subject matter, and especially on his use of the critical principle of decorum as the criterion for what was appropriate in its representation. Failure to observe decorum was, in Gilio's view, a fundamental aspect of what was wrong with the painting of his own time. Vincenso Peterlino, one of the interlocutors in the *Dialogo,* notes at the heart of the problem a failure to understand that subjects fall into different categories, each requiring its own distinctive treatment. Painters had to be taught to classify them, for only then would they have a correct sense of purpose. He identifies three genres of subject: the true (*il vero*), the fictive (*il finto*), and the fabulous (*il favoloso*), each with its own rules.[50] In the category of the true, Vincenso argues, historical subjects, including above all sacred subjects, have to be represented with the most careful attention to the texts and to the most authoritative interpretations of them; the fictive are poetic subjects that, although not historically true, require the appearance of truth to be observed, so they have to be rendered in a lifelike way; and fabulous subjects, such as the metamorphoses of the ancient gods, are those that are neither true nor lifelike.

This system of classification could have come from various sources, but the most probable is the very widely circulated commentary on Horace's *Ars Poetica* (1500, and many subsequent editions) by Josse Bade (Iodocus Badius Ascensius).[51] Dealing with subject matter (*materia*), Bade writes:

> The matter is threefold: either altogether true, something that actually occurred, as in histories; or not true, but truth-like, something that could have occurred, like the plots in comedies; or neither true nor truth-like, such as many poetic fables, for example Virgil's ships changing to nymphs, and many of the metamorphoses in Ovid.[52]

This scheme ultimately derived from that much-used ancient text on rhetoric, believed at the time to have been written by Cicero: the *Rhetorica ad Herennium.*[53]

In addition to this classification of the genres of subject matter, Vincenso Peterlino also distinguishes three different types of painter, defined in terms of the nature of the material they undertook to present: the historian (*istorico*), the poet (*poeta*), and the mixed (*misto*). Confusingly, the distinctions are not coterminous with those used for the genres of subject matter.[54] Those responsible for the sacred histories in the Sistine and Pauline Chapels in the Vatican are painter-historians; Raphael was a pure poet when he painted the Feast of the Gods in the loggia of the Farnesina (see fig. 4); and Vasari and Francesco Salviati, as painters respectively of rooms in the Cancelleria and in the Palazzo Farnese, are in the mixed category (see figs. 5, 6, 29).[55] The source for the three types of painter seems to have been Aristotle's classification of writers in his *Poetics.* The distinction between the historian and the poet is expounded by Aristotle in a passage in which he asserts the greater significance and value of the poet.[56] While Aristotle's value judgment is rejected, the basis of the classification is accepted. The essential difference between these two types is that "the one [the historian] tells us what has happened and the other [the poet] the sort of thing that might happen."[57] The third category, that of the mixed painter, is derived from Aristotle's characterization of epic poets, especially Homer. Considering the similarities and differences between history and epic, Aristotle shows how, in the latter, there are rich possibilities for deploying the irrational and the false alongside the true.[58] It is this classification of painters (rather than subjects) that provides the principal thematic divisions of Gilio's text.[59]

Making use of the dialogue form, Gilio assigns to different voices the lead in expounding different aspects of his subject. As has been seen, Vincenso, a lawyer, is given the task of setting out the different classes of subject and of painter;

he then goes on to discuss the poetic painter.[60] Consideration of the historical painter follows. This is the central preoccupation of the *Dialogo* and occupies by far the most space: significantly more than half of the whole text. Although supposedly all types of historical painting are in question, it rapidly becomes clear that the painter of religious subject matter is the main concern. Beginning with general considerations of what kinds of knowledge such a painter should have, the lead is taken by another lawyer, Silvio Gilio, who emphasizes in particular the errors that follow from a lack of knowledge about and understanding of the subjects themselves and from inadequate preparation.[61] Troilo Mattioli, presumably a lawyer too, leads the discussion of abuses, with examples of the failures by historical painters to represent their subjects correctly.[62] Then Francesco Santi, who is characterized as an educated gentleman, addresses the question of what historical painters should bear in mind when they prepare the figures they intend to introduce into their works.[63] Finally, Ruggiero Coradini, an ecclesiastic, takes on Michelangelo's *Last Judgment.*[64] In this very lengthy section of the *Dialogo,* the fresco is given an exemplary status as the culmination of what the art of painting can achieve, but it is also subjected to rigorous critical examination, with questions about how faithful it is to authoritative theological opinion and how truthful it is to its subject matter. The discussion takes the form of an exposition of what would actually happen on the last days of the world, followed, at each point, by a discussion of the adequacy of Michelangelo's painting as a representation of the events. The last part of the *Dialogo,* with the medical doctor Pulidoro Saraceni leading, focuses on the theme of the mixed painter.[65]

Sacred Painting: The Invention of the Subject Matter

In the *Dialogo,* the subject (*materia*) is the major issue, and within that discussion Gilio makes his most important contribution. He is addressing an area that, in contemporary rhetorical theory and poetics, was considered under the heading of "invention" and had already been deployed for the criticism of painting by writers such as Paolo Pino and Lodovico Dolce.[66] What Gilio's interlocutors add is an insistence on the importance of attending to the different types of subject and to the different demands they make of painters. In the case of historical and, in particular, sacred subjects, the primary problem had been a failure to appreciate the importance of their truth value; according to M. Ruggiero, citing Horace, painters had been wrong to believe that the grant of artistic license gave them complete freedom.[67] Earlier Vincenso Peterlino had pointed out that Horace had carefully qualified the freedom of license permitted to painters and poets. Even the painter of poetic subjects or fables, who could legitimately represent much that his imagination dictated, was constrained by decorum and, with qualifications, the requirement of lifelikeness (*il verisimile*).[68] But the painter of history was subject to much more severe constraints: there was no excuse for confusing history with poetry.[69] Historical subject matter has to be carefully distinguished from fiction, argues Silvio Gilio, "because to mix it with the poetic and the fictional is nothing other than to disfigure truth and beauty and to produce something false and monstrous."[70] And sacred subjects needed even more care than other kinds of historical material, as Ruggiero points out when criticizing Michelangelo's inclusion of Charon ferrying the damned in his *Last Judgment:*

> A historian should imitate theologians rather than poets. And this is how Michelangelo should have behaved, because if in the secular field the poetic corrupts historical subjects, could we say that it enhances spiritual subjects in the case of sacred things of such importance?[71]

In the *Dialogo,* the idea that Christian subjects have an absolute truth that needs to be accurately preserved when they are represented by painters is tied to the famous pronouncement of Gregory the Great justifying religious paintings as the Bible of the illiterate.[72] For Gilio, the historical painter is nothing other than a translator from one language into another, from writing into painting.[73] Konrad Braun is explicitly cited in corroboration of this idea.[74]

With sacred subjects, it was essential not only to pay the closest attention to the written texts but also to identify the correct ones: sources had to be canonical, not apocryphal.[75] When there were competing texts, they had to be correctly ranked. An especially significant example of failure on this count is provided by Michelangelo's choice of Ezekiel as the source for visualizing the events of the Last Judgment.[76] The lawyer Silvio Gilio defends Michelangelo's treatment of the resurrection of the dead in the lower left section of the fresco by citing Ezekiel.[77] This defense elicits the following response from Ruggiero, the authoritative ecclesiastic: "As for the prophecy of Ezekiel, I would reply that to the Prophet was shown only the mystery and not the actual way it would happen. Paul tells us that it [the Resurrection] will be in an instant, in the twinkling of an eye."[78] The full truth of the New Testament was to be preferred to the partial truth of the Old. Michelangelo, like other painters, was not free to choose a text at will simply because it suited his own imagination.

The discussion of Michelangelo's representation of Christ standing in judgment reveals that it was not just the choice of text but its proper interpretation that mattered. The participants in the dialogue discuss whether the reference in the Gospel according to Saint Matthew to Christ being seated "upon the throne of his glory" should be taken literally or allegorically.[79] Ruggiero pronounces that in general the literal meaning should be preserved, as long as it does not result in absurdity or in something that contradicts other Christian beliefs. He argues that in this particular instance there is no reason not to accept the literal meaning.[80] Michelangelo was therefore wrong to show Christ standing (see fig. 21).[81]

In the final section on painters of mixed subjects, the proposal that the painter should, wherever possible, observe the simple truth and not allegorize is made forcefully by the medical doctor Pulidoro Saraceni. The issue in question is the representation of the Cross in the form of a tree (see fig. 28): "showing one thing and meaning another should never happen, because the Cross alone, simply represented, will carry these meanings and many others. One can make much fuller interpretations of the simple truth than of the fictional and adulterated."[82] And simplicity brought with it greater intelligibility. Even paintings intended for the learned should be intelligible without great effort, while an ignorant audience needed straightforward representations of the sacred texts because they would be unable to distinguish between what was true and what was allegorical or metaphorical.[83]

However, deviation from literal truth in the representation of an event was permissible in certain circumstances. Troilo Mattioli argues that it is acceptable for a painter to introduce variations in nonessential aspects of a subject, although Silvio counters with the warning that what might appear to be accidents are often closely bound up with the substance, and the painter needs a very good knowledge of the subject in order to discriminate correctly between the essential and the nonessential.[84] Additionally, and very significantly, deviation from strict truth could be allowed if it helped communicate the fundamental qualities of the figures involved. Thus, Michelangelo's representation of the Virgin shrinking from the vision of punishment in his *Last Judgment* is defended by the lawyer Vincenso Peterlino on the grounds that the Virgin was being characterized as the Madonna of pity (see fig. 21).[85] Ruggiero, who argues strongly that at the moment of judgment the time for pity would be over and the Madonna would be in full agreement with the decisions of her Son, nevertheless concedes that if the fiction demonstrably informs spectators about the Virgin's essentially compassionate nature, then it is acceptable.

The same type of argument is used when it comes to the question of whether the martyrs should be represented carrying the instruments of their martyrdom (see figs. 21, 22). Ruggiero insists that they would not in fact be carrying such instruments, in opposition to Francesco Santi's argument that on the day of judgment there would be some identifying sign to amplify the glory of the individual martyrs. Ruggiero does admit that in this case a fiction is permissible for the sake of uneducated spectators.[86] Still, such concessions had to be very carefully considered. Especially revealing is the argument between the interlocutors about whether it was acceptable for Michelangelo to show the blessed being helped to ascend into heaven. (The men are discussing the groups of figures to the left of the trumpeting angels in the fresco.) Pulidoro contends that such representations, while not strictly truthful, do enable the painter to teach his audience about the different ways in which they might achieve salvation. However, Pulidoro's argument is rejected by Ruggiero.[87] Not only do the striving figures fail the test of truth, according to Ruggiero, but they also provoke derision rather than devotion.[88] Even worse, he argues, was the rosary being used to haul people up into heaven—in his view, such a representation expresses contempt for religious devotion. The transformation of sacred objects into visual metaphors undermined the respect they were due. On the other side of Michelangelo's fresco, the representation of angels struggling with devils is equally objectionable to Ruggiero. While Michelangelo may have intended to demonstrate how evil spirits are always tempting us, in Ruggiero's opinion it was not acceptable to show them fighting, because it was ridiculous to imply that salvation might be determined by physical force.[89] This is the decisive point: anything that provoked derision had to be avoided. As we shall see, the issue of decorum was paramount.[90]

Sacred Painting: The Invention and Design of Figures (Decorum)

Subjects required more from painters than the knowledge and understanding of stories and concepts. If the truth of the subject (*la verità dei soggetti*) depended on the choice of sources and their correct interpretation, then that truth also depended on the visual invention through which it was expressed. Central to Gilio's sense of what the painter himself brought to the creation of the subject was the invention of figures: they were the primary instruments for the visual articulation of the subject matter. This idea—that figures and their actions were the means to convey thoughts and emotions and thus were key to the relationship between the painting and the story being told—had been put forward by Leon Battista Alberti in the fifteenth century, in his treatise *De pictura*.[91] According to Alberti, the challenge for the painter was to design figures whose qualities, movements, gestures, expressions, and dress were appropriate to the characters and thoughts of the people they were supposed to represent. And it was the concept of decorum (*decoro* in Gilio; Dolce had used the term *convenevolezza*) that provided the criterion to assess the match between the representation and the person represented.[92]

The way writers in the mid-sixteenth century perceived the interrelationship between the story as it was told in words and the visual invention of figures is illustrated by the humanist Annibale Caro's account of his program for the fresco decoration of Cardinal Alessandro's bedroom at Caprarola. In a letter to the chosen painter, Taddeo Zuccaro, Caro writes:

> It is not enough for me to give you the subjects for the paintings at the palace of Caprarola in verbal terms, because besides the invention we need to include the arrangement, poses, colors, and many other considerations.[93]

As Clare Robertson remarks in her analysis of Caro's letter, if we think about this in terms of contemporary ideas of rhetoric, we seem to move from the domain of finding the subject (*inventio*) into that of expressing what had been found (*elocutio*)—the rhetorical category that in the verbal arts meant the use of appropriate words for the concepts devised.[94] Caro thinks that, in order to present the painter with an adequate program, he needs to concern himself with movements, gestures, dress, and other visual features that might be thought to belong to the sphere of design.

What emerges very clearly from Caro's letter is the ambiguity that results from the attempt to apply rhetorical categories to the painter. The painter's process of invention necessarily involved design; therefore, in the figural arts it was extremely difficult to distinguish invention from design.[95] Dolce, whose *Dialogo della pittura intitolato l'Aretino* Gilio knew well, understood this, describing two sources of invention:

> Invention originates from two quarters, the subject matter [*historia*] and the painter's intellect [*ingegno*]. Subject matter simply supplies the painter with his material [*materia*]. From his intellect, over and above the elements of disposition [*ordine*] and propriety [*convenevolezza*], there come the poses, the variety and again (so to speak) the dynamism of the figures; but this aspect is shared with design.[96]

Primarily interested in what was contributed by the painter's mind or intellect (*ingegno*), Dolce had passed over subject matter without going into any detail. Gilio brought very different priorities to the issue and found, in this idea of the two sources of invention, a means to express his concerns about the errors that afflicted contemporary painting. He was working with a concept of decorum that allowed him to judge whether invention—and those aspects of design that overlap with invention—succeeded or failed in finding appropriate ways to convey the subjects; in the case of historical subjects, this meant especially how to convey their truth (*la verità dei soggetti*).[97]

In the preface, Gilio expresses regret that no book or set of rules existed that laid out for painters how to treat every type of figure they might be called upon to invent.[98] And over the course of the *Dialogo,* there are frequent complaints about the indecorousness or unsuitability of painted figures when compared to the persons described in the Bible or the lives of saints that the figures purported to represent.[99] In many cases, the objections to what painters had done are very specific, factual ones, as for example the age of Paul in Michelangelo's *Conversion of Paul* in the Pauline Chapel (see fig. 14). Francesco Santi accuses Michelangelo of having showed Paul as about sixty years old, when he could have been only eighteen or twenty.[100] But contemporary painters are also accused of offending decorum in religious subjects in other, more general ways. In his prefatory address to Alessandro Farnese, Gilio criticizes contemporary painters for their practice of twisting their figures into strained or forced poses, without due consideration for the subjects they were supposed to be representing—even though in some cases, such poses legitimately, and very effectively, serve their purpose. Examples of good practice given in the *Dialogo* are the possessed boy in Raphael's *Transfiguration* altarpiece (see fig. 10) and the fallen Saul in Michelangelo's *Conversion of Paul* (see fig. 14). But this kind of strained pose is often condemned by Gilio's interlocutors as quite inappropriate. According to Francesco Santi, the straining movements of the angels carrying the instruments of the Passion in the upper parts of Michelangelo's *Last Judgment* are inappropriate because such divine beings would not need to expend great effort on the task (see figs. 21, 22). But the movements are wrong also because they make them "look more like acrobats or jugglers than angels."[101]

The movements invented for a figure had to be appropriate not just to the immediate action in which they were involved but also to the type of person who performed them.[102] Francesco further argues that these strained poses are harsh and unnatural, proposing that painters should create movements that are not only fitting but graceful and natural too; he advocates the normative, not the idiosyncratic or the artificial.[103] The section of the *Dialogo* in which these remarks about movements are made is led by Francesco—and in line with Gilio's practice elsewhere, it is the leader's arguments that carry authority. It may be supposed that the arguments about decorum put forward by Francesco essentially correspond with Gilio's own views.

Closely connected with this way of thinking is the condemnation of modern painters' propensity to represent nude figures in religious compositions. When it was a matter of representing saintly people, this was profoundly indecorous. Ruggiero condemns the practice: "a saint would not only have avoided displaying his private parts to others but would not even have looked at them himself.

So if we venerate the saints for a sanctity that abhors this behavior, why should the painter, against the laws of sanctity, decency, and decorum, try to force them so inappropriately to behave in the opposite way?"[104]

The condemnation of nudity reveals that there is another crucial dimension to decorum, apart from the matching of representation to action and to person: the need to elicit from the audience an appropriate response. This emerges most clearly in the discussions around the resurrected dead in Michelangelo's *Last Judgment*. It is agreed by all the participants in the *Dialogo* that the approved sacred texts make it absolutely clear that the dead will be resurrected without clothes.[105] Ruggiero, who leads this part of the discussion, is then asked by Troilo: "If they are all to be resurrected naked and you approve of paying attention to the accuracy of even the smallest detail, do you seriously blame this representation of what will actually happen?" In response, Ruggiero argues that because mankind is in a fallen state, showing the resurrected naked will arouse shame and scandal, not devotion, in the spectator; it risks inducing laughter and mockery, which must at all costs be avoided.[106]

The traditional theory to justify Christian sacred images, used from the thirteenth century, throws light on this argument. Three valuable functions were attributed to sacred images: teaching, edifying, and making active in the memory.[107] What emerges from the argument in the *Dialogo* about Michelangelo's representation of the resurrected dead is a conflict between teaching and edification. Edification should be given priority over the truth-telling appropriate for teaching. Paintings had to convey a "sense of the reverent propriety due to the mysteries of the faith"—and nudity compromised propriety.[108]

A similar consideration underlies many of the judgments about the poses and movements invented for figures. For example, the clinching point in the case against Michelangelo's representation of Christ in the *Conversion of Paul* (see fig. 14) is the likely effect on the spectator. Silvio argues that Christ's plunging movement demonstrates the freedom of his divine body from the physical constraints that affect ordinary people. But Francesco replies that what Christ may be physically capable of is not the issue: "Even if from Christ's point of view these are not matters of consideration, they must be from ours, because we perceive devotion or scandal depending on how the figures are represented."[109] Shown falling from the heavens, Christ lacks dignity. A sacred figure should be respected and venerated, and must be represented in such a way as to elicit that veneration.[110] If a painter wants to give his figures strained positions, he must ensure that the movements are of a kind consistent with the arousal of devotion.[111]

That the poses and movements, as well as the nudity of the figures, in Michelangelo's *Last Judgment* did provoke mockery and ridicule was not

Gilio's invention. In Dolce's *Dialogo della pittura,* the leading participant, Pietro Aretino, had remarked that were it not for the ridiculous things (*cose ridicole*) to be seen in the *Last Judgment,* he might have been prepared to believe that it was full of the most profound ideas hidden behind the surface.[112] At very much the same time as Gilio was writing, the Milanese painter Giovanni Paolo Lomazzo reported on reactions to the *Last Judgment* in his unpublished book, *Il libro dei sogni:* "It is said that he had the idea of depicting on that wall a crowd or rabble of rough laboring types and actors who would go jumping up and down."[113] In a brilliantly subversive joke, found in a pasquinade of the time, the nakedness of the figures is linked to the sexual immorality of the papal court:

> O you who criticize the Florentine [Michelangelo], think about the painting a bit. You will see that every figure is entirely appropriate within the chapel of the divine Jesus. There is Saint Catherine, with bowed head, naked as nature made her, and other saints standing there soberly, showing their arses to don Paolino.[114]

Don Paulino was the pope, Paul III.

A strength of the dialogue structure as deployed by Gilio is that, at least at moments, it allows real differences of opinion to be expressed. In the debate over the way the dead were depicted emerging from their tombs in the lower left part of the *Last Judgment,* Ruggiero is very critical of their ridiculous appearance, likening them to "a crowd of slugabeds." By contrast, the very same invention is praised by Silvio for its didactic and expressive effectiveness:

> But it seems to me that this is one of the most appealing and beautiful mysteries to be found in the whole of this history, because it shows clearly that each person must come forth at the time of the Resurrection, wherever they are buried. . . . As for the man who lifts himself up and surveys the heavens . . . he doesn't know whether he deserves pity or justice; he behaves thus because he is in doubt.[115]

What is in contention is sacred visual rhetoric. The representation of the Last Judgment should move the audience to gasp, tremble, and repent, but, according to Ruggiero, Michelangelo had provoked laughter, mockery, and derision.[116] It was every preacher's worst nightmare—an audience sniggering at and ridiculing his sermon. Gilio uses the dialogue form to demonstrate that there is disagreement over the matter; however, he allows dissent only up to a point, for it is Ruggiero's voice and opinions that are made to prevail.

The Causes of and Remedies for Errors and Abuses

Why, in Gilio's opinion, had the truth of the subject matter (*la verità dei soggetti*) so often been compromised and distorted in contemporary sacred painting, and what could be done about it? Gilio sought the answers in what his contemporaries defined as the different sources of "invention."[117] First, successful invention required knowledge, and no one contests Ruggiero's characterization of modern painters as ignorant people of low social status. Lacking in education, they did not understand the subjects they had to treat and were thus led into significant error.[118] This disadvantage could be overcome if they gave themselves the time needed to master the subject matter and if they consulted those who had relevant knowledge to help them. Painters needed to plan their inventions by making drawings and then correcting and altering them in the manner of a poet drafting a poem.[119] In his *Dialogo della pittura,* Dolce had discussed the need to make drawings, recommending that for each subject the painter make several; he had thought of them as alternative inventions, from among which a choice could be made.[120] For Gilio, by contrast, a drawing provided the platform for learning about and adjusting the figures—their characters, their clothes, their movements, and their interactions—to achieve the required decorum.[121]

Apart from knowledge and understanding of the subjects, a major source of invention lay in the powers of mind or intellect possessed by the painter; this is the faculty labeled by Gilio as *ingegno.* Significant errors resulted from the desire of painters to display their powers of mind—to invent new things and to develop their own subjective notions of the subject matter—without regard for the truth. A painter with an active, lively mind or intellect will be full of imaginative ideas (*capricci*), and Silvio claims that it had become a dominant practice among contemporary painters to prefer such personal inventions to the truth.[122] No authoritative sets of rules existed to challenge the legitimacy of this method of invention, and Silvio advises that such a code ought to be drawn up, for these abuses could then be brought under control.[123]

Ingegno as a source of painterly invention was very closely interwoven in Gilio's mind with his ideas about the art of painting itself. The recurrent use of the term *arte* in the *Dialogo* is potentially very misleading for a reader brought up with modern ideas of "Art." What Gilio meant by *arte* is what we would call the craft of painting: the skills and methods learned by the painter. The common pairing of *arte* and *ingegno* was intended to convey a combination of learned and natural abilities.

Of Michelangelo, whose erroneous and abusive inventions were identified as so significant, Pulidoro asserts:

> I don't think there is a painter, even the most stupid, who does not know that Michelangelo wished to satisfy the art [of painting] rather than the historical truth. What he has failed to do [in the *Last Judgment*] came not from ignorance but from the desire to show posterity the excellence of his mind [*ingegno*] and the excellence of the artistic skill [*arte*] that he possesses.[124]

What Pulidoro means is illustrated by the discussion of Michelangelo's representation of the dead rising from their tombs. Ruggiero argues that Michelangelo was quite wrong to show the risen dead only half awake and apparently confused about where they are meant to go. If Michelangelo justified this personal invention (*capriccio*) to himself on the grounds that he believed people in that situation would be confused, then he was wrong, for the resurrected dead would know where they were going, whether it was to heaven, purgatory, or hell. Ruggiero sees the error as a consequence of Michelangelo's desire "to embellish his brush and satisfy the art [of painting] rather than the truth": it was not that he did not know the truth, it was that he preferred to show off his skill.[125] Michelangelo created a "fable" that gave him the opportunity to invent a variety of active figures and remarkable movements.[126] Indeed, the way that he embellished his brush and satisfied the art of painting was above all through his invention of figures that displayed "every possible movement and pose that the human body can gracefully adopt."[127] Both Ruggiero and Pulidoro agree that it was Michelangelo's complete command of all the skills (*arte*) of painting that enabled him to exhibit such invention.

It is within the context of this argument that the *Dialogo* articulates what Gilio saw as a major source of error among contemporary painters. Examining the print of Michelangelo's *Last Judgment,* Francesco Santi pronounces that the painter had restored the art of painting to its *decoro.*[128] By this he means that Michelangelo's command allowed him to represent whatever might make a fine artistic effect. Troilo presents this in entirely positive terms: painting needs its own *decoro* and freedom.[129] If the poet or painter has no freedom to find appropriate forms by making use of the qualities and powers of his respective art, then there can be no glory or *decoro* of poetry or painting.[130] The need for painting to have its own *decoro* is not contested within Gilio's text; even the hard-line Ruggiero accepts this—with, however, the very significant caveat that it could be achieved only when art is subordinated to nature and personal imagination to truth.[131] Problems arise because judgments of what is appropriate come to be determined solely from within the conventions and practices of the art of painting. Michelangelo's achievement was thus simultaneously the most praiseworthy fulfillment of the art of painting (he restored painting to its true image)[132] and the most dangerous encouragement to error. Ruggiero argues that Michelangelo had achieved such mastery of the art of painting—which offered him abundant options for creating figures of great beauty and immense power—that he had mistakenly come to believe that pictorial invention should be built around that mastery alone. In Ruggiero's contribution to the *Dialogo,* the art of painting takes on an almost living presence; painters, out of love for their art and a desire to project their own abilities, are seen as complying with its promptings.[133]

There are two significant points in the text where this issue is brought into the foreground. The first comes in the discussion of the appropriate ways to represent scenes of martyrdom and, in particular, the Passion of Christ. Sebastiano del Piombo's *Flagellation of Christ* in San Pietro in Montorio at Rome is used as the point of reference (see fig. 12).[134] Pulidoro reports the praise it has received: in its anatomical command, the supremely beautiful nude body of Christ displays the power of painting. But Troilo, who leads the discussion at this point, criticizes the painting for concealing the terrible violence and suffering that characterized the event itself; Sebastiano has made it appear merely a game. Troilo says that he has heard painters argue that to show Christ's body wounded and broken would offend the decorum (*decoro*) of painting. But how could that be the case, for the aim of painting was to imitate nature; surely that meant representing the ugly as well as the beautiful? For Troilo, there is no contradiction between the demands of the art of painting and the demands of the subject. It is the artist's choice to make beauty his objective: the vanity of painters is at fault, not the art of painting.[135] Troilo ends the discussion by pointing out that there are many subjects that do require beautiful figures, as well as many that do not.[136]

The second example occurs in the discussion of the appropriate representation of the blessed at the time of the Judgment. The subject was what theologians called the beatific vision: all the blessed would be enraptured and their senses so engaged when they had a direct, unmediated experience of Christ that they would turn toward him with complete attentiveness. Ruggiero argues that Michelangelo's representation of the blessed looking here and there, this way and that, completely fails in this regard. Silvio objects that it would be absurd to paint things in the way Ruggiero suggests; without introducing variety of movement, gesture, and expression the painter would appear ignorant. Ruggiero counters with the argument that at the basis of the painter's art lies the intention to express the inner states of mind of his figures through their outward movements. Michelangelo, inventing for the blessed a diversity of freely moving figures, failed to convey their inner state of beatitude.[137]

What is significant about each of these examples is the assertion that painters have choices. Beautiful figures, the power of muscular bodies, and the variety of movement, gesture, and expression were the glories of the art of painting; however, to seek appropriate forms from within those parameters, with little regard for the goal and purpose of the task at hand, was to fall into serious error. It even offended common ideas of good practice. Silvio himself had earlier asserted that the painter who adapted his art to the task deserved higher praise than he who adapted the task to his art.[138] A painting is to be judged by its effect, not by its display of qualities supposedly essential to the art of painting itself, which, as Ruggiero would point out, may be appreciated only by a few connoisseurs.[139]

The simple truth could have the greatest effect. Ingenuity and artifice, introduced in an attempt to amplify the subject, might make that subject less effective.[140] Pulidoro explicitly makes this point when he compares a wooden cross found in a rustic hermitage with a cross made of silver or gold and decorated with jewels, found in a city. The elaborate cross distracts him from thoughts of devotion and makes him think about "richness and ornament, about the nobility of the materials and the excellence of the craftsman." Pulidoro insists on "the power and efficacy that truth has in itself."[141] Natural, dignified representations of the subject were needed, both for didactic and devotional reasons. In concluding his account of the Last Judgment and Michelangelo's representation of it, Ruggiero says:

> This beautiful and holy story . . . should be painted in a faithful, pure, simple, true, and chaste way; just as it should be faithful, pure, simple, true, chaste, and complete if written or preached about. It should be full of fear, terror, and wonder so that the spectators gasp, tremble, and repent rather than laugh and make fun of it, treating it as a thing of little importance.[142]

At the end of the *Dialogo,* Ruggiero sets out his ideas about how sacred paintings should be handled, and he gives particular emphasis to the importance of tradition. Earlier painters, perhaps following now-lost rules laid down by the Church, had represented the holy figures with respect and decorum, giving them gravity in their poses and using certain valuable conventions, such as providing angels with wings and saints with halos (see fig. 34). Ruggiero argues that to the moderns these traditional ways have come to seem "base, uncouth, plebeian, old-fashioned, and humble" and that this perception has led modern painters to invent naked, strained figures that are neither decent nor devout.[143] In behaving like this, modern painters replaced ancient custom—a holy practice (*santo uso*) that from centuries of use had the force of law—with subjective conceptions (*capricci*).[144]

It is important to remind ourselves that Gilio does not contest the importance of the art of painting, its methods and skills, in themselves. In the preface, he celebrates the acquisition of skills that in recent times had restored the art of painting to the level it had once enjoyed in antiquity. These skills and a lively and active *ingegno* were essential, and their absence led to awkward and ridiculous work. Silvio says quite directly that painters of an earlier time "were coarser, and since they were neither intellectually alert nor inventive, they relied on the past; they could only produce clumsy work."[145] And later in the *Dialogo,* Pulidoro, mentioning the early painted cycles of the Old and New Testaments at St. Peter's in Rome, remarks that the "figures look like *baronci,* or were made by Goths," meaning that they were ugly and clumsy.[146] In contrast, modern painters were able to create figures that were triumphantly successful in communicating the most difficult things, such as the thoughts and characters of their protagonists. Silvio exemplifies this by referring to the possessed boy in Raphael's altarpiece of the Transfiguration and to the figure of Saul in Michelangelo's *Conversion of Paul* (see figs. 10, 14).[147]

Yet unlike modern painters, the earlier painters had truly pious intentions. According to Ruggiero, they might have been lacking in lively intellect and skills, producing clumsy and even absurd results, but their works did not display vanity or show off the power of the art of painting. They did not fall into the errors of the moderns, who, with all their abilities, followed their own personal imaginations and displayed their great skills, without proper attention to the purpose of what they were doing.[148]

Gilio was probably influenced by the Dominican polemical writer Ambrogio Catarino, who identifies the problems raised by images that displayed either too much or too little artistry and insists, like Gilio, on the need for decorum: the need to properly respect the persons represented. Catarino writes that

> certain images are so lacking in art that they scarcely represent the appearance of men, but, rather, of monsters. However, others, on the contrary, are made with such art that, with certain unsuitable gestures, they sometimes do not preserve decorum in the figures, and having no dignity, they do not excite devotion.[149]

In Gilio's *Dialogo,* Ruggiero argues this case, giving a historical dimension to Catarino's proposition: "And it appears to me that the artists who came before Michelangelo paid more attention to truth and devotion than to ostentation."[150] Ruggiero, faced by Silvio's objection that the lack of intellectual capacity and skill of earlier painters had produced errors and abuses, resolves the issue by saying that if the painters before Michelangelo had erred in minor ways, the moderns erred in major ones: "and it would be best to make a regulated mixture [*regolata mescolanza*] of the two to produce a mean that compensates for the defects of each, so that the works have a proper correspondence [*debite proporzioni*] with the type of subject."[151] In sacred histories, the commitment to truth and devotion would be accompanied by the intellect and skill necessary to achieve it.

Positioning Gilio

Gilio positions the speakers in the *Dialogo* as learned viewers of painting. With respect to sacred painting, their principal concern, they discuss how the forms and meanings of certain paintings are or are not appropriate to the subject matter of scripture or of the other sacred texts that they are intended to represent. The dominant argument is that sacred texts are true by definition, and although they may need interpretation, that interpretation must be acceptable to theologians and to the Church; it is not acceptable for painters to replace that truth with private, subjective ideas (*capricci*). The absolute need is to communicate that truth and to arouse devout reverence for it in the audience. Instead, many paintings convey erroneous information and provoke derision among those who see them.

The belief in and insistence on the fundamental importance of the objective truth of sacred story is where Gilio's arguments from secular notions of decorum meet, rather uncomfortably, his theological ideas. It is revealing to compare the way that Gilio constructs his arguments with the deployment of many of the same concepts by a secular writer like Vasari. In Vasari's life of Raphael (1550), he comments on Raphael's Vatican fresco of the Repulse of Attila:

> Raphael introduced into this scene Saints Peter and Paul in the sky, with swords in hand, as they come to defend the Church. And although this is not what the history of Leo III tells us, nevertheless Raphael, following his own personal conception [*capriccio*], wanted to represent it in this way; for it often happens with paintings, as with poems, that one digresses in order to embellish the work, without departing from the main idea in an inappropriate way.[152]

Vasari does not distinguish clearly between poetry and history; he sees painters of sacred subjects as little different from poets in the license they have to invent. The constraint he implicitly places on personal invention (*capriccio*)—not to digress from the substance of the subject in a way that is inappropriate—is loose. And he evidently regards embellishment (*ornamento*) as an acceptable justification for a painter making alterations to the written history he was meant to be depicting.

What is argued in Gilio's *Dialogo* is that such attitudes result in sacred paintings that fail to perform their function because they introduce subjective elements that distort and even subvert truth and devotion. The criticism of the invention of figures whose poses and movements are strained (*sforzato*) should be seen in this light, as should the discussion of nudity. For Gilio, the motivation behind the design of such figures might be the painter's desire to display his skill and intellect. This facet of Gilio's thought picks up the old theological idea that complex displays of skill in religious painting can distract the attention of the viewer away from the subject represented to the painting itself, although this is not an argument that is pursued.[153] The display of skill and intellect in twisted or naked figures is primarily condemned by some of Gilio's interlocutors when the result is the creation of figures whose expressive meanings fail to meet the interlocutors' definitions of truth and decorum.

Interpretations of Gilio's *Dialogo* that identify the target as painters who cultivated style at the expense of expressive function or who were guilty of the empty aestheticism said to characterize so-called mannerist painting of the mid-sixteenth century rather miss the point.[154] They impose anachronistic modern polarities of form and content, of style and meaning, onto the arguments of the text. John Shearman himself, reflecting on the attack on Michelangelo's *Last Judgment* in which the painter is accused of favoring displays of his own skills at the expense of devotion, felt impelled to say that Michelangelo's expressive intention "cannot seriously be denied."[155] And yet Michelangelo was Gilio's prime exhibit of what had gone wrong with sacred painting.

Describing his intentions in writing the *Dialogo* in his prefatory letter to Alessandro Farnese, Gilio says he wants to provide the means for thinking about the representation of subjects in painting. He concludes with an address to the cardinal: "And when you happen to go into the Sistine Chapel you can consider whether the *Last Judgment* and the ceiling, as well as the other figures, observe historical truth."[156] Michelangelo's religious paintings, and in particular the *Last Judgment,* lie at the heart of Gilio's work. From the moment of its unveiling in 1541, the *Last Judgment* provoked unprecedented attention: both extravagant praise and strong condemnation. Gilio's *Dialogo* was part of a considerable literature.[157] His critical approach takes its energy from an issue that had already been signaled by Aretino and others in relation to Michelangelo: the tension between, on the one hand, his extraordinary skills and intellect, and, on the other, the nature and value of the subject matter he represented. Seeking a resolution accomodating both, Gilio's wide-ranging *Dialogo* brings to bear artistic, literary, and rhetorical theory and, woven together with those, significant theological arguments. The points of view set out in the *Dialogo* are those of the audience of painting, not those of the painter.

As we have seen, the *Dialogo* was probably written between 1561 and 1562, but it was not published until 1564, by which time the context had changed. The twenty-fifth and final session of the Council of Trent, in December 1563, had issued a decree on relics and sacred images.[158] The decree asserted the value of sacred images against the iconoclastic ideas developed by Protestant reformers, but warned that they must not be the occasion "of dangerous error to the unlettered" and that they must avoid "all sensual appeal . . . so that [they] are not painted or adorned with seductive charm."[159] After the end of the Council, the decrees were submitted to the pope for his approval and he in turn formed a commission to prepare a confirmation of the Council's decisions and to consider the best means of carrying them out. There were thirty-three items regarded as being of particular urgency; it was decided that eleven of them should be acted on immediately.[160] One of these concerned the need to eliminate whatever was obscene or manifestly false in painting in churches, and the paintings in the Sistine Chapel were explicitly mentioned. The order of the commission issued on 21 January 1564 specified that in the case of the paintings in the Sistine Chapel, such elements were to be covered up.[161] This was a sentence of expurgation, not cancellation—remarkable because all other paintings deemed obscene or false were apparently to be destroyed.[162] The censorship corrections that were made, by Daniele da Volterra, were exclusively concerned with covering up the offending parts of the naked figures and removing anything obscene.[163]

Compared to Gilio's ideas, the extremely limited objectives of the censors acting within the context of the pronouncements of the Council of Trent are striking. In his *Dialogo,* Gilio is concerned with a whole visual rhetoric. He interweaves secular critical theory with theological notions of the functions of sacred images to develop a critique of the practice of contemporary sacred painting. And he uses the dialogue form to reveal the different dimensions that such a critique requires. By these means he wanted to show patrons (and their painters) the processes of thought that they needed to adopt when they considered pictorial invention. Gilio's work offers something entirely consistent with, but far richer than, the schematic statements of Trent.

Notes

1. Giovanni Andrea Gilio, *Dialogo nel quale si ragiona degli errori e degli abusi de' pittori circa l'istorie,* in *Trattati d'arte del Cinquecento: Fra manierismo e controriforma,* vol. 2, ed. Paola Barocchi (Bari: Laterza, 1961), 1–115. The present translation was made from this edition. A useful compilation of what is

known about Gilio is provided in Michele Di Monte, "Gilio, Giovanni Andrea," *Dizionario Biografico degli Italiani* [*DBI*], 54 (2000). Modern interest in Gilio's *Dialogo* really can be said to begin with Julius von Schlosser's survey of writing about art from the Middle Ages to the eighteenth century: *Die Kunstliteratur.* First published in 1924, the survey was translated into Italian as *La letteratura artistica* and revised in 1964. See Julius von Schlosser, *Die Kunstliteratur: Ein Handbuch zur Quellenkunde der neueren Kunstgeschichte* (Vienna: Anton Schroll, 1924); and Julius von Schlosser, *La letteratura artistica: Manuale delle fonti della storia dell'arte moderna*, trans. Filippo Rossi, ed. Otto Kurz (Florence: Nuova Italia, 1964). Paola Barocchi's publication of Gilio's original text, in the second volume of her *Trattati d'arte del Cinquecento,* was accompanied by learned notes and commentary. But it was Charles Dempsey who first directed attention to the particular value and originality of the writing in his essay, "Mythic Inventions in Counter-Reformation Painting," in *Rome in the Renaissance: The City and the Myth; Papers of the Thirteenth Annual Conference of the Center of Medieval & Early Renaissance Studies,* ed. P. A. Ramsey (Binghamton: State University of New York at Binghamton, Center for Medieval & Early Renaissance Studies, 1982), 55–75.

2. Bonita Cleri and Giampiero Donnini, eds., *La Cattedrale di Fabriano* (Fabriano: Cassa di Risparmio, 2003), 17. San Venanzio became the Fabriano Cathedral only later, when Fabriano gained its own bishop; in Gilio's time the town was part of the diocese of Camerino.
3. Filippo Vecchietti and Tommaso Moro, *Biblioteca picena, o sia notizie istoriche delle opere e degli scrittori piceni . . .* (Osimo: D. A. Quercetti, 1790–96), 5:91–93; Gilio was "prior of the Hermitage of Suavicino (San Vicino) or rather of the church which is today called San Domenico Loricato" (91). Unless otherwise indicated, all translations are mine. The sources for this information were the written acts of the 1579 visitation of Alfonso Maria Binarini, bishop of Camerino.
4. Giovanni Andrea Gilio, *La vita di s. Atanasio patriarca di Alessandria . . .* (Venice: Pietro Bosello, 1559).
5. Giovanni Andrea Gilio, *Trattato de la emulatione che il demonio ha fatto a Dio* (Venice: Francesco de' Franceschi, 1563; reprint, 1564). This volume consists effectively of three treatises: one on the Devil's emulation, one on the names used in scripture to refer to God, and one on what was meant when God was described in physical terms. Giovanni Andrea Gilio, *Le persecuzioni della Chiesa* (Venice: Gabriele Giolito de' Ferrari, 1573).
6. Giovanni Andrea Gilio, *Topica poetica* (Venice: Oratio de' Gobbi, 1580; facs. reprint, Munich: W. Fink, 1970). See also Carlo Ossola, "La 'Topica Poetica' di G.A. Gilio da Fabriano," in *Retorica e poetica: Atti del III Convegno Italo-Tedesco,* ed. Daniela Goldin and Gianfranco Folena (Padua: Liviana, 1979), 259–83.
7. For the conversations that constitute the *Dialogo,* Gilio sets the scene in the spring of 1561; Gilio, this volume, 88. From the course of a discussion about the date of the end of the world, it may be inferred that 1562 was the year in which that part of the text was written; Gilio, this volume, 162. A very tenuous hint that it might have been started earlier is provided by the mention of the count, rather than the duke, of Maddaloni, the latter of which he became in 1558; see this volume, 93n22.

8. Giovanni Andrea Gilio, *Due dialogi. Nel primo de' quali si ragiona de le parti morali e civili appertenenti a' letterati cortigiani, et ad ogni gentil'huomo, e l'utile che i prencipi cavano dai letterati. Nel secondo si ragiona degli errori de' pittori circa l'historie* (Camerino: Antonio Gioioso, 1564; facs. reprint, Florence: S.P.E.S., 1986). The reprint is accompanied by a brief introduction by Paola Barocchi.
9. *Dialogo de le parti morali appertenenti a' letterati cortigiani, et ad ogni altro gentil'huomo* has been published in a modern edition: Giovanni Andrea Gilio, *Dialogo del letterato cortigiano,* ed. Paolo Cherchi (Ravenna: Longo Editore, 2002). (Page references are to the Cherchi edition.) In the original volume, it was placed first, before *Dialogo . . . degli errori e degli abusi de' pittori.* It is set in Rome, and the kind of courtier that is envisaged is one who might serve in and bring dignity to a cardinal's establishment. The requirements for such a courtier are laid out: a command of all the liberal arts and of philosophy, theology, and law, along with virtuous and decorous behavior. The date of writing is not clear. As Cherchi notes (17), Michelangelo is referred to as still alive, which would make 18 February 1564 a terminus ad quem. The mention of Cardinal François de Tournon as dead (168–69) establishes 22 April 1562 as a terminus a quo. Although the reference to the new cardinal of Mantua (59) could mean Francesco Gonzaga, who was created cardinal in February 1561, it is more likely that Federico Gonzaga, whose elevation to the cardinalate occurred in January 1563, was intended. On the evidence we have, it is reasonable to suppose that at least parts of the text were composed in 1563. Cherchi's claim that the Council of Trent is described as an event of the past is not correct (58).
10. Clare Robertson, *"Il gran cardinale": Alessandro Farnese, Patron of the Arts* (New Haven: Yale University Press, 1992), 205. Farnese had apparently visited Fabriano and was said to have defended the right of the town to be considered a city, even though it had no bishop; see the text titled *Discorso sopre la Città, l'Urbe, Colonia, Municipio, etc.,* in Gilio, *Due dialogi,* 123r.
11. The existence of the copy in the Biblioteca Casanatense at Rome (see library call number ee XIII 21) had been noted by Vecchietti and Moro, *Biblioteca picena,* 5:92. In the Casanatense's copy, all the preliminary printed matter, including the title page and the dedication, is missing. A handwritten title page, with the date 1550 and with Venice as the place of publication, is inserted at the beginning.
12. There are passages in *Trattato de la emulatione che il demonio ha fatto a Dio* that relate very closely to what was written in the *Dialogo.* See, for example, the discussion of the representation of the angels carrying the instruments of the Passion at the Last Judgment (72r–v); cf. Gilio, this volume, 146–48.
13. See Gilio, *Trattato de la emulatione che il demonio ha fatto a Dio,* 31v: "While I was in Rome, I remember having seen a Spaniard. . . ." For the mention of the *hermafrodito,* see 35r.
14. Gilio's *Dialogo de le parti morali appertenenti a' letterati cortigiani* (titled *Dialogo del letterato cortigiano* in Cherchi) opens with one of the two interlocutors, Giovan Maria Gilio, visiting the Villa Giulia (45); his route back into Rome is confidently and accurately described. Familiarity with the cardinals and other high ecclesiastics in Rome around 1561–63 lies behind assessments of their attitudes toward educated men (58–61). Particularly revealing of an

intimate acquaintance with the city are passing comments on such subjects as the preachers active in the city (79), and the displays of oratory in the church of Sant'Eustachio, when students received their doctorates (125).

15. One of the two interlocutors in the first of the *Due dialogi* is a certain Giovan Maria Gilio, who came from Fabriano and who was in all likelihood a relative of Giovanni Andrea's. He is described by Giuseppe Colucci as a lawyer (*legista*) and as a most trusted legal expert in Rome (*giurista accreditatissimo in Roma*). For this information, see Giuseppe Colucci, "Uomini Illustri di Fabriano," in *Antichità picene dell'abate Giuseppe Colucci patrizio camerinese*, vol. 17, *Delle antichità del Medio e dell Infimo Evo,* vol. 2 (Fermo: Dai torchi dell'autore, 1792), 168.
16. For references to Francesco Bandini Piccolomini, see Gilio, this volume, 89–90, 122; on the Sienese Accademia degli Intronati, see Gilio, this volume, 150–51. Bandini was archbishop of Siena from 1529 until his death in 1588. For further biographical information, see Giuseppe Alberigo, "Francesco Bandini Piccolomini," *DBI,* 5 (1963), http://www.treccani.it/biografie/.
17. Giovanni Antonio Pecci, *Memorie Storico-Critiche della Città di Siena* (Siena: Pazzini Carli, 1755–60; reprint, Siena: Cantagalli, 1988), 4:13. For Gilio's poem and its genesis, see Gilio, this volume, 89–92.
18. Gilio, *Due dialogi,* 8r–v.
19. Gilio, *Due dialogi,* 7r–v. Gilio constructed an elaborate eulogy of Alessandro's magnanimity and the liberality of his patronage in the first of the dialogues. It is cited in part by Robertson, *"Il gran cardinale,"* 13.
20. Alessandro Farnese's personal commission, the decoration of the hall of the Cancelleria, known as the Hall of the Hundred Days (Sala dei Cento Giorni), painted by Vasari and assistants in 1546, is not exempt from criticism, but it is handled with more tact; Gilio, this volume, 212. Clare Robertson has discussed what she calls "an almost ostentatious increase in [Farnese's] piety" in the 1560s, when he embarked upon an impressive program of religious reform in the churches under his jurisdiction. His aims were to eliminate abuses in the performance of divine worship and to materially improve the churches themselves. The great change in his spiritual commitment was a subject of comment at the time; see Robertson, *"Il gran cardinale,"* 158–62.
21. Gilio, this volume, 235, 237. When Gilio was writing, Cardinal Federico Cesi (d. 1565) was overseeing the construction and decoration of the chapel, which had been founded much earlier; see Francesco Colalucci, "Le pitture della cappella di S. Caterina in S. Maria Maggiore: I Cesi, Vasari, Siciolante e la Controriforma," *Bollettino dei Monumenti Musei e Gallerie Pontificie* 14 (1994): 114.
22. See Giulio Carlo Argan and Bruno Contardi, *Michelangelo Architect,* trans. Marion L. Grayson (New York: Harry N. Abrams, 1993), 348 (no. 29).
23. Gilio, this volume, 144–45. The painting being referred to was probably the *Adoration of the Shepherds* in the Gabrielli Chapel in the church of Santa Maria sopra Minerva, in Rome, painted by Battista Franco in 1550; Walther Buchowiecki, *Handbuch der Kirchen Roms: Der römische Sakralbau in Geschichte und Kunst von der altchristlichen Zeit bis zur Gegenwart* (Vienna: Hollinek, 1970), 2:704–5. See also this volume, 144n173.
24. Gilio, this volume, 212. See also note 20 above.

25. Gilio, this volume, 235. Michelangelo designed an Annunciation for the altarpiece of the chapel; the now-lost painting was executed after his designs by Marcello Venusti, probably in the late 1540s. See Johannes Wilde, *Italian Drawings in the Department of Prints and Drawings in the British Museum: Michelangelo and His Studio* (London: British Museum, 1953), 110–13.
26. Gilio's knowledge of the Cancelleria frescoes may have been largely literary, for nothing he wrote goes beyond what he could have learned from Anton Francesco Doni's detailed description and interpretation, which Gilio cited; Gilio, this volume, 212. See Anton Francesco Doni, *Foglie della Zucca* (Venice: Francesco Marcolini, 1552), 133–49.
27. John Shearman suggests that a visitor to Rome with connections might even gain access to the presbytery or inner area of the Sistine Chapel for a service. John Shearman, *Raphael's Cartoons in the Collection of Her Majesty the Queen, and the Tapestries for the Sistine Chapel* (London: Phaidon, 1972), 21–22.
28. Margaret Kuntz, "Designed for Ceremony: The Cappella Paolina at the Vatican Palace," *Journal of the Society of Architectural Historians* 62, no. 2 (2003): 231–32, 242–43.
29. Gilio, this volume, 156–57, 159.
30. This volume uses the following editions of these works: Pliny the Elder, *Natural History,* trans. H. Rackman, W. H. S. Jones, and D. E. Eichholz, 10 vols., Loeb Classical Library 330, 352–53, 370–71, 392–94, 418–19 (Cambridge, MA: Harvard University Press, 1938–63); Vitruvius, *On Architecture,* vol. 1, *Books 1–5,* and vol. 2, *Books 6–10,* trans. Frank Granger, Loeb Classical Library 251, 280 (Cambridge, MA: Harvard University Press, 1931, 1934); Leon Battista Alberti, *On Painting and On Sculpture: The Latin Texts of "De pictura" and "De statua,"* ed. and trans. Cecil Grayson (London: Phaidon, 1972); Giorgio Vasari, *Le vite de' più eccellenti pittori, scultori, e architettori: Nelle redazioni del 1550 e 1568,* 6 vols., ed. Rosanna Bettarini and Paola Barocchi (Florence: S.P.E.S., 1966–87); and Lodovico Dolce, *Dialogo della pittura intitolato l'Aretino* [Venice: G. Giolito de' Ferrari, 1557], in *Trattati d'arte del Cinquecento: Fra manierismo e controriforma,* vol. 1, ed. Paola Barocchi (Bari: Laterza, 1960), 141–206.
31. Gilio, this volume, 238–39. Agostini is also mentioned in the first of the *Due dialogi;* see Gilio, *Dialogo del letterato cortigiano,* 47. For further information, see "Francesco Agostini," *DBI,* 1 (1960).
32. The phrase *ut pictura poesis* is from Horace, *Ars Poetica,* in *Satires; Epistles; The Art of Poetry,* trans. H. Rushton Fairclough, Loeb Classical Library 194 (Cambridge, MA: Harvard University Press, 1926), 480–81 (line 361).
33. William Durandus, *The Symbolism of Churches and Church Ornaments: A Translation of the First Book of the "Rationale Divinorum Officiorum" Written by William Durandus,* ed. and trans. John Mason Neale and Benjamin Webb (Leeds: T. W. Green, 1843); and Guillaume Durandus [Gulielmus Durandus], *Rationale divinorum officiorum,* vol. 1, books 1–4, ed. Anselme Davril and Timothy M. Thibodeau (Turnhout: Brepols, 1995).
34. Konrad Braun (Conradus Brunus), *De imaginibus,* in *Opera Tria* (Mainz: Franz Behem, 1548). Ambrogio Catarino, *Disputatio . . . de cultu et adoratione imaginum* [Rome, 1551], in *Enarrationes* (Rome: A. Blado, 1552), 144. Ambrogio Catarino

was his religious name as a Dominican monk; his secular name had been Lancellotto Politi. Sometimes the two names are conflated and he is referred to as Catarino Politi.

35. Giuseppe Scavizzi, *The Controversy on Images from Calvin to Baronius* (New York: Peter Lang, 1992), 93–99.
36. *Censimento nazionale delle edizioni italiane del XVI secolo* (EDIT16: http://edit16.iccu.sbn.it/web_iccu/ihome.htm). The online census records the existence of three copies of the *Due dialogi* with the date 1574 on the title page, but with the 1564 date in the colophon. There are two possible explanations for this: either the date 1574 was a typographical error, corrected after a certain number of copies were printed, or an attempt was made to relaunch the book in 1574. The latter possibility is given support by the observation that the typesetting of the title page with the date 1574 eliminates many of the word breaks that are to be seen on the title page with 1564.
37. Bartolomeo Ammannati bought a copy of the *Due dialogi* soon after it was published. See Victoria Kirkham, "Creative Partners: The Marriage of Laura Battiferra and Bartolomeo Ammannati," *Renaissance Quarterly* 55 (2002): 527, 553. Ammannati refers to Gilio as "Gioan Andrea Lilio."
38. Raffaello Borghini cites Gilio's book twice. See Raffaelo Borghini, *Il Riposo* (Florence: Marescotti, 1584; reprint with introduction and analytical index by Mario Rosci, Milan: Edizioni Labor, 1967), 53, 82. Published in English as Borghini, *Raffaello Borghini's "Il Riposo,"* ed. and trans. Lloyd H. Ellis (Toronto: University of Toronto Press, 2007).
39. Lomazzo reveals the influence of Gilio in a number of places; see, for example, Giovanni Paolo Lomazzo, *Il libro dei sogni* (ca. 1563), in *Scritti sulle arti,* ed. Roberto Paolo Ciardi (Florence: Marchi and Bertolli, 1973), 1:105, 113, 145, 255. Armenini's debt is especially clear in his discussion of inventions: Giovanni Battista Armenini, *De' veri precetti della pittura,* ed. Marina Gorreri (Turin: G. Einaudi, 1988), 87–88 (book 1, ch. 9). Published in English as Giovanni Battista Armenini, *On the True Precepts of the Art of Painting,* ed. and trans. Edward J. Olszewski (New York: Burt Franklin, 1977). In his *Il Figino* from 1591, Gregorio Comanini implicitly refers to Gilio when he has the priest Ascanio Martinengo defend Michelangelo's handling of the beatific vision in the *Last Judgment;* Gregorio Comanini, *Il Figino: Overo del fine della pittura* [Mantua, 1591], in *Trattati d'arte del Cinquecento: Fra manierismo e controriforma,* vol. 3, ed. Paola Barocchi (Bari: Laterza, 1962), 353–54. For Comanini's knowledge of Gilio, see also Eugenio Battisti, *Rinascimento e Barocco* (Turin: Einaudi, 1960), 207–9.
40. Antonio Possevino, *Bibliotheca selecta* (Rome: Domenico Basa, 1593), 2:315–18 (book 17, ch. 24). In chapter 24, Possevino devotes some pages to Gilio (to whom he refers as Lilio, as did Ammannati; see note 37 above).
41. Federico Borromeo, *Sacred Painting, Museum,* ed. and trans. Kenneth S. Rothwell, introduction and notes by Pamela M. Jones (Cambridge, MA: Harvard University Press, 2010). On the ages of the Magi, see Gilio, this volume, 146; and Borromeo, *Sacred Painting, Museum,* 84–85 (2.4.2). On the limits of Horatian license, see Gilio, this volume, 132–33; and Borromeo, *Sacred Painting, Museum,*

118–19 (2.10.6). On the representation of Christ's wounds, see Gilio, this volume, 134–35; and Borromeo, *Sacred Painting, Museum,* 118–19 (2.10.7). On the argument against the nakedness of figures in Paradise, see Gilio, this volume, 182–84; and Borromeo, *Sacred Painting, Museum,* 120–21 (2.10.10).

42. Vincenzo Caputo, "Ragionando di pittura tra artisti e letterati," *Quaderni di italianistica* 31 (2010): 43–60. Caputo notes that Troilo Mattioli does at one point say that he has spoken to painters (55, citing Gilio; see this volume, 136). Although the *Dialogo,* with its elaborately set conversation on the banks of the Giano, is evidently a fiction, the existence in Fabriano of a group of intellectuals who exchanged ideas about painting is attested to by a group of poems celebrating Gentile da Fabriano's Saint Mary Magdalene from the altarpiece he painted in the early fifteenth century for the church of Santa Maria del Val di Sasso (now in the Pinacoteca di Brera; see fig. 34). Among the contributors to the collection of poems—one of whom was Gian'Andrea Gilio—were some of the interlocutors in the *Dialogo:* Silvio Gilio, Vincenso Peterlino, and Troilo Mattioli. Unfortunately, the poems are impossible to date; they had remained in manuscript, unpublished until 1850. See Romualdo Sassi, "Sonetti di poeti fabrianesi in onore di Gentile da Fabriano," *Rassegna marchigiana* 2 (1923–24): 273–83.

43. Gilio, this volume, 85–86.

44. Gilio, this volume, 85–87. Positioning the writing as conceived from the point of view of spectators, not painters, marks the work out from earlier texts used by Gilio. Pietro Aretino, presenting the three parts of painting in Lodovico Dolce's dialogue, *Dialogo della pittura intitolato l'Aretino,* explicitly says he will speak as a painter, not as a philosopher ("Ma ragionerò da pittore, e non da filosofo"); Dolce, *L'Aretino,* in Barocchi, *Trattati,* 1:164. The English translation of the Dolce is in Mark W. Roskill, ed. and trans., *Dolce's "Aretino" and Venetian Art Theory of the Cinquecento* (Toronto: University of Toronto Press in association with the Renaissance Society of America, 2000), 118–19. In an early published collection of poetry, Aretino had described himself as a painter; Pietro Aretino, *Opera nova del fecundissimo Giovene Pietro Pictore Aretino* (Venice: Zoppino, 1512).

45. Rensselaer W. Lee, *"Ut pictura poesis": The Humanistic Theory of Painting* (New York: Norton, 1967), 40. First published in *Art Bulletin* 22, no. 4 (1940): 197–269. Page references are to the 1967 volume.

46. Barocchi, *Trattati,* 2:525–26, 2:581–82n5 for Gilio p. 33; and 2:592nn1–2 for Gilio p. 55. Federico Zeri, *Pittura e Controriforma: L'arte senza tempo di Scipione da Gaeta* (Turin: Einaudi, 1957), 30, has judged Gilio's treatise the "first open reaction to Mannerism, and in particular to its special Michelangelesque sense."

47. John K. G. Shearman, *Mannerism* (Harmondsworth: Penguin, 1967), 177–78. Shearman characterizes "mannerism" as the cultivation of style at the expense of its expressive function; he acknowledges a certain paradox here, for only with difficulty can Michelangelo be accused of not aiming at expression (164). For Gilio and the so-called Counter-Reformation, see the essay by Carol M. Richardson in this volume.

48. For a brief discussion of the term *mannerism* and its various meanings, see Michael Bury, "Mannerism," in *The Oxford Companion to Western Art,* ed. Hugh

Brigstocke (Oxford: Oxford University Press, 2001), 446–47; and Jeroen Stumpel, "Speaking of Manner," *Word and Image* 4, no. 1 (1988): 246–64.

49. Barocchi, *Trattati,* 2:526. A valuable critique of many modern interpretations of Gilio's text is provided by Robert Gaston, "How Words Control Images: The Rhetoric of Decorum in Counter-Reformation Italy," in *The Sensuous in the Counter-Reformation Church,* ed. Marcia B. Hall and Tracey E. Cooper (Cambridge: Cambridge University Press, 2013), 85–87.
50. Gilio, this volume, 100.
51. Ann Moss, "Horace in the Sixteenth Century: Commentators into Critics," in *The Cambridge History of Literary Criticism,* vol. 3, *The Renaissance,* ed. Glyn P. Norton (Cambridge: Cambridge University Press, 1999), 68–69.
52. "Est autem ut praelibavimus materia triplex. Primo quia aut omnino vera est et revera gesta ut in historiis: aut non vera est sed verae similis et quae geri potuit: ut argumenta comica. Aut necque vera neque verae similis ut multae fabulae poeticae: qualis est apud virgilium afferens naves aeneae mutatas in nymphas, et multae transformationes apud Ovidium: quibus tamen aut ad naturam aut ad historiam aut ad mysticam rem respiciendum est." Josse Q. Bade, ed., *De arte poetica libellus* (Paris: Jean Petit and Denis Roce, 1503), 4v–5r. The English translation is in Moss, "Horace," 68–69. Gilio uses the example of Virgil's ships; see Gilio, this volume, 216.
53. [Cicero], *Rhetorica ad Herennium,* trans. Harry Caplan, Loeb Classical Library 403 (Cambridge, MA: Harvard University Press, 1954), 22–25; see also this volume, 100–101n46.
54. Malcolm Bull, *The Mirror of the Gods* (London: Allen Lane, 2005), 392–93.
55. Gilio, this volume, 101–4. Vasari's room in the Cancelleria is known as the Hall of the Hundred Days (Sala dei Cento Giorni) and Salviati's in the Palazzo Farnese is known as the Sala dei Fasti Farnesiani; see this volume, n52 on pp. 102 and 104.
56. Aristotle, *Poetics,* trans. Stephen Halliwell, in Aristotle, *Poetics;* Longinus, *On the Sublime;* Demetrius, *On Style,* Loeb Classical Library 199 (Cambridge, MA: Harvard University Press, 1995), 58–59 (1451b).
57. Aristotle, *Poetics,* 58–59 (1451b).
58. Aristotle, *Poetics,* 120–25 (1460a–1460b); the heroic measure of epic is said to accommodate metaphor readily, 120–21 (1459b). Lee notes the connection with epic; see Lee, *"Ut pictura poesis,"* 39.
59. Gilio, this volume, 100–104. On the *pittore poetico,* see Gilio, this volume, 104–14; on the *pittore istorico,* see Gilio, this volume, 114–20; and on the *pittore misto,* see Gilio, this volume, 198–221, 237–39.
60. Gilio, this volume, 104–14.
61. Gilio, this volume, 114–21.
62. Gilio, this volume, 121–37.
63. Gilio, this volume, 140–57. Francesco Santi is the only participant in the *Dialogo* whose existence cannot be independently verified.
64. Gilio, this volume, 157–97.
65. Gilio, this volume, 198–225.
66. Paolo Pino, *Dialogo di pittura* [Venice: Paolo Gherardo, 1548], in *Trattati d'arte del Cinquecento: Fra manierismo e controriforma,* vol. 1, ed. Paola Barocchi (Bari:

Laterza, 1960), 93–139; and Dolce, *L'Aretino,* in Barocchi, *Trattati,* 1:141–206. In his later book, the *Topica poetica* of 1580, Gilio asserted that nothing was more important for a written composition than the "invention." Gilio, *Topica poetica,* 4v–5r.

67. Gilio, this volume, 183, citing Horace, *Ars Poetica,* 480–81 (line 373); see also Gilio's prefatory letter to Alessandro Farnese in Gilio, this volume, 85–87. As Schlosser points out, the search for historical truth links Gilio to the contemporary growth of interest in archaeological investigation: Schlosser, *La letteratura artistica,* 428. A leading figure in the development of Christian archaeology was Onofrio Panvinio, whose principal patron was Alessandro Farnese. Panvinio had returned to Rome with his patron following the death of Paul IV in 1559, and devoted himself to the study of Christian cult buildings (Stefan Bauer, "Panvinio, Onofrio," *DBI,* 81 [2014]).
68. Gilio, this volume, 100–104, 105–7, following Horace's *Ars Poetica,* 450–51 (lines 9–13).
69. Such distinctions were commonplace at the time. Titian, in a letter to Philip II dated 28 July 1563, distinguishes between mythological paintings, described as "di fabulosa invention" (he refers to them elsewhere as *poesie,* for example in his letter of 2 April 1561) and a Last Supper described as a "materia historica di devotione"; Matteo Mancini, *Tiziano e le corti d'Asburgo: Nei documenti degli archivi spagnoli* (Venice: Istituto Veneto di Scienze, Lettere ed Arti, 1998), 269–70 (doc. no. 149), 291–92 (doc. no. 173). See Charles Hope, *Titian* (London: Jupiter, 1980), 125–26.
70. Gilio, this volume, 132.
71. Gilio, this volume, 195; see Dempsey, "Mythic Inventions," 65. Benedetto Varchi had viewed Michelangelo's use of Dante as giving his works grandeur and majesty and stimulating him to extraordinary invention; he uses Charon as an example. Benedetto Varchi, *Lezzione: Nella quale si disputa della maggioranza delle arti e qual sia più nobile, la scultura o la pittura* [Florence: Lorenzo Torrentino, 1549], in *Trattati d'arte del Cinquecento: Fra manierismo e controriforma,* vol. 1, ed. Paola Barocchi (Bari: Laterza, 1960), 57.
72. Gilio, this volume, 116. See also the discussion of this issue in Richardson, this volume, 53.
73. Gilio, this volume, 132. Aristotle, near the beginning of *Poetics* (28–29 [1447a]), asserts the equivalence of painting and poetry as arts of imitation, but notes that each deploys different means to achieve the representation of things: one "colours and shapes," the other "rhythm, speech and harmony." See Donald Andrew Russell and Michael Winterbottom, *Classical Literary Criticism* (Oxford: Oxford University Press, 1972), 51.
74. Gilio, this volume, 196, 229–30 (Braun, *De imaginibus,* 144). It may or may not be significant that Konrad Braun's *De imaginibus* (see note 34 above), cited more than once by Gilio in his *Dialogo,* had been dedicated to Alessandro Farnese. Braun's work belonged to the tradition of writing in defense of images against the Protestant iconoclasts.
75. Gilio, this volume, 140–41.
76. Ezekiel 37:1–10.

77. Ascanio Condivi, in his 1553 biography of Michelangelo, had identified Ezekiel as Michelangelo's source; see Ascanio Condivi, *Vita di Michelangelo Buonarroti*, ed. Giovanni Nencioni (Florence: S.P.E.S., 1998), 49; and Asciano Condivi, *The Life of Michelangelo*, trans. Alice Sedgwick Wohl and ed. Hellmut Wohl (University Park: Pennsylvania State University Press, 1999), 84.
78. Gilio, this volume, 167; on Paul, see 1 Corinthians 15:52.
79. Matthew 25:31 (Vulgate 32).
80. Gilio, this volume, 179–80. Augustine, *De doctrina Christiana* (book 3, §33, §84, §91), had proposed these criteria for distinguishing between literal and metaphorical meaning; see idem, *De doctrina Christiana*, ed. and trans. R. P. H. Green (Oxford: Clarendon, 1995), 165, 169, 173.
81. Issues of biblical interpretation exercised Gilio in his *Trattato de la emulatione che il demonio ha fatto a Dio* of 1563; for example, 87r: "not everyone is given the spirit of wisdom enabling them to interpret scripture, but each person must be content with what the Holy Church thinks, in order to be sure not to fall into error" (non è dato ad ogn'uno lo spirito de la Sapienza, e d'interpretare la scrittura, ma a ciascuno dee essere contento di quanto tiene la Santa Chiesa, che sarà sicuro di non potere errare).
82. Gilio, this volume, 210. On the iconography of the *Arbor Vitae*, see this volume, 209n374.
83. Anton W. A. Boschloo, *The Limits of Artistic Freedom: Criticism of Art in Italy from 1500 to 1800* (Leiden: Primavera Pers, 2008), 41. On paintings for the learned, see Gilio, this volume, 213–14. Gilio makes the point about the ignorant in the context of his discussion of Michelangelo's introduction of Charon into the *Last Judgment*; see Gilio, this volume, 194.
84. Gilio, this volume, 116–17. The distinction between substance and accidents, between essential and nonessential qualities, is a fundamental concept of Aristotelian thought. See Howard Robinson, "Substance," in *The Stanford Encyclopedia of Philosophy* (spring 2014), ed. Edward N. Zalta, http://plato.stanford.edu/archives/spr2014/entries/substance/.
85. Gilio, this volume, 192.
86. Gilio, this volume, 189–92. Later in the *Dialogo*, Ruggiero positively advocates the representation of saints with their attributes; Gilio, this volume, 234. In the latter case he was talking about single figures of saints, while in the present passage the issue was the history of the Last Judgment.
87. Gilio, this volume, 174–76.
88. Gilio, this volume, 174–75.
89. Gilio, this volume, 175. Horace, from the very beginning of his *Ars Poetica*, identifies derisive laughter as the consequence of failure to write good poetry; see idem, *Ars Poetica*, 450–51 (line 5), for example.
90. Schlosser had identified the concept of decorum as fundamental to Gilio's text; see Schlosser, *La letteratura artistica*, 426–28.
91. Leon Battista Alberti, *De pictura*, in Alberti, *On Painting and On Sculpture: The Latin Texts of "De pictura" and "De statua,"* ed. and trans. Cecil Grayson (London: Phaidon, 1972), 81–85 (book 2, esp. §41–44). On this point, see Svetlana Alpers,

"*Ekphrasis* and Aesthetic Attitudes in Vasari's *Lives,*" *Journal of the Warburg and Courtauld Institutes* 23 (1960): 199–200. See also this volume, 87n10.

92. Horace had expounded this; idem, *Ars Poetica,* 462–65 (lines 153–78) and 458–61 (lines 99–127). For its implications, see Weinberg, *History of Literary Criticism,* 2:801. Later Gabriele Paleotti, the archbishop of Bologna, specifically defined decorum as the "dignity of the person" (*dignità della persona*), as he discussed inept painting; see Paleotti, *Discorso intorno alle imagini sacre e profane,* in *Trattati d'arte del Cinquecento: Fra manierismo e controriforma,* vol. 2, ed. Paola Barocchi (Bari: Laterza, 1961), 372. The English translation is in *Discourse on Sacred and Profane Images,* trans. William McCuaig (Los Angeles: Getty Research Institute, 2012), 227 (book 2, ch. 27).
93. The letter is dated 2 November 1562. Annibale Caro, *De le lettere familiari del commendatore Annibal Caro* (Venice: Bernardo Giunti, 1581), 2:180: "I soggetti . . . ch'io vi dia per le dipinture del Palazzo di Caprarola, non basta che vi dicano a parole, perche oltre l'inventione, ci si ricerca la dispositione, l'attitudini, i colori, et altre avertenze assai."
94. Clare Robertson, "Annibal Caro as Iconographer: Sources and Method," *Journal of the Warburg and Courtauld Institutes* 45 (1982): 172–73.
95. David Summers, *Michelangelo and the Language of Art* (Princeton, NJ: Princeton University Press, 1981), 74.
96. Dolce, *L'Aretino,* in Barocchi, *Trattati,* 1:171 (Roskill, *Dolce's "Aretino,"* 128–29; the last words of Roskill's translation have been slightly modified). For the translation of *energia* as "energy," see John K. G. Shearman, *Only Connect: Art and the Spectator in the Italian Renaissance* (Princeton, NJ: Princeton University Press, 1992), 209, where he links *energia* to the idea of a *pictura heroica,* as used by Andrea Fulvio in 1527 to characterize Michelangelo's Sistine ceiling. See also Dolce, *L'Aretino,* in Barocchi, *Trattati,* 1:164 (Roskill, *Dolce's "Aretino,"* 116–17), where Dolce writes: "The invention is the fable or history which the painter chooses on his own, or others present him with, as material for the work he has to do."
97. Gilio, this volume, 85–86.
98. Gilio, this volume, 86.
99. Gilio, this volume, 146–47.
100. Gilio, this volume, 144–45.
101. Gilio, this volume, 146.
102. Gilio, this volume, 148–50. The importance of taking account of the type of person represented was an absolutely key element in theories of decorum. Horace, *Ars Poetica,* 462–65 (lines 153–78). See Lee, *"Ut pictura poesis,"* 34–36; and note 92.
103. Gilio, this volume, 148–49. Francesco sets himself against Paolo Pino's *Dialogo di pittura,* in Barocchi, *Trattati,* 1:115; see this volume, 87n10. Pino makes no suggestion that this figure should be appropriate to the subject matter. Quintilian may also have been a target of Francesco's, for he had written of the "twisted [*distortum*] and elaborate [*elaboratum*]" pose of Myron's *Discobolos,* the novelty and difficulty of which was praiseworthy. See Quintilian, *The Orator's Education,* vol. 1, *Books 1–2,* ed. and trans. Donald A. Russell, Loeb Classical Library 124

(Cambridge, MA: Harvard University Press, 2002), 342–43 (2.13.9–10); and Quintilian, *Institutio Oratoria,* trans. Ernst H. Gombrich, "The Leaven of Criticism in Renaissance Art: Texts and Episodes," in idem, *Studies in the Art of the Renaissance,* vol. 3, *The Heritage of Apelles* (Oxford: Phaidon, 1976), 122 (2.13.10).

104. Gilio, this volume, 184.

105. Ruggiero had earlier cited Job 1:21: "Naked came I out of my mother's womb and naked shall I return thither." Gilio, this volume, 167. Unless otherwise noted, direct quotations from the Bible are from the Douay-Rheims translation undertaken at the English College of Douay-Rheims and printed in two parts: New Testament (1582) and Old Testament (1609–10).

106. Gilio, this volume, 183–84.

107. Michael Baxandall, *Painting and Experience in Fifteenth-Century Italy: A Primer in the Social History of Pictorial Style* (Oxford: Oxford University Press, 1972), 40–41. The functions of teaching and moving an audience had, of course, also been part of the office of the orator as defined in ancient rhetorical theory. See Brian Vickers, *In Defence of Rhetoric* (Oxford: Clarendon, 1998), 357.

108. Lee, *"Ut pictura poesis,"* 38. See Gilio, *Dialogo... degli errori e degli abusi de' pittori,* in Barocchi, *Trattati,* 2:80; and Gilio, this volume, 185–86: [Ruggiero]: "Tenga per fermo il pittore che far si diletta le figure de' santi nude, che sempre gli leverà gran parte de la riverenza che se li deve. Però compiacciasi più tosto de l'onestà e del convenevol decoro, che de la vaghezza de l'arte, la quale a pochi dilettarà; perché non mi pare che in quelle poche parti vergognose sia tal secreto di natura ascosto o tant'arte, che, non le mostrando, l'artefice n'aggia da esser riputato ignorante e goffo." Stuart Lingo argues that Gilio used the phrase *vaghezza de l'arte* to mean sensual beauty; Lingo, *Federico Barocci: Allure and Devotion in Late Renaissance Painting* (New Haven, CT: Yale University Press, 2008), 6, 130–31. But these beauties of *arte* were explicitly said to give pleasure only to the few, implying as elsewhere (Gilio, this volume, 132–33) that the *vaghezza de l'arte* lies in all the alluring qualities that are specific to the art of painting itself, qualities that might tempt the artist to neglect his subject. One of them was mastery of the representation of the nude.

109. Gilio, this volume, 144.

110. Lee found in Horace a notion of decorum meaning "a specific conformity to what is decent and proper in taste and even more in morality and religion"; Lee, *"Ut pictura poesis,"* 37. Moral improvement was certainly, for Horace, one possible function of poetry; see Horace, *Ars Poetica*, 478–79 (lines 333–37) and 482–83 (lines 399–401). Dolce, in writing of *convenevolezza* in Michelangelo's *Last Judgment,* condemns the nudes as no stimulus to devotion; Dolce, *L'Aretino,* in Barocchi, *Trattati,* 1:188–89 (Roskill, *Dolce's "Aretino,"* 162–63).

111. Gilio, this volume, 235.

112. Dolce, *L'Aretino,* in Barocchi, *Trattati,* 1:190 (Roskill, *Dolce's "Aretino,"* 164–67). Aretino mentions in particular the blessed kissing, the beardlessness of Christ, and the devil pulling a man down to hell by his testicles.

113. Lomazzo, *Il libro dei sogni,* 1:101–2: "Dicesi che egli aveva pensato di fare in quella facciata una gabbia overo ciurma de fachini e de istrioni che andassero

saltellando di la su." Lomazzo's laborers and actors derive from advice about the movements of the body inappropriate for orators in [Cicero], *Rhetorica ad Herennium,* 200–203 (3.15.26).

114. Valerio Marucci, Antonio Marzo, and Angelo Romano, *Pasquinate romane del Cinquecento* (Rome: Salerno, 1983), 1:498 (no. 462): "O voi che riprendete 'l fiorentino, / considerate un poco la pittura: / vedrete che sta ben ogni figura / nella capella di Gesu divino. // Sta santa Caterina a capo chino, / nuda si come fecce la natura, / ed altri santi stanno con misura / a mostrar i lor culi a don Paulino." There may be an allusion to a notorious episode involving the pope's son, Pier Luigi Farnese, who, in 1537, raped Bishop Cosimo Gheri of Pistoia. According to Melinda Schlitt, the pasquinade is to be dated 1544; see Schlitt, "Painting, Criticism, and Michelangelo's *Last Judgment* in the Age of the Counter-Reformation," in *Michelangelo's "Last Judgment,"* ed. Marcia B. Hall (Cambridge: Cambridge University Press, 2005), 119.
115. Gilio, this volume, 166.
116. Gilio, this volume, 196–97.
117. Alessandro Lionardi, for example, identifies three major sources of poetic invention: first, in the poet's knowledge (what he had heard, read, and seen); second, in his mind or intellect (*ingegno*); and third, in the art of poetry itself. See Alessandro Lionardi, *Dialogi dell'invenzione poetica* (Venice: Plinio Pietrasanta, 1554; facs. reprint, Munich: Wilhelm Fink, 1970), 10–11. Lionardi's passage is noted by Ulrich Langer, "Invention," in *The Cambridge History of Literary Criticism,* vol. 3, *The Renaissance,* ed. Glyn P. Norton (Cambridge: Cambridge University Press, 1999), 138. Gilio was very aware of how valuable the theory of poetry was to the understanding of the visual arts.
118. Gilio, this volume, 95–97.
119. Gilio, this volume, 119–21, 125, 149–50.
120. Dolce, *L'Aretino,* in Barocchi, *Trattati,* 1:170 (Roskill, *Dolce's "Aretino,"* 128–29).
121. Gilio's attitude to drawing is similar to Caro's when Caro recommended to Vicino Orsini that the painter—employed to make a fall of the giants at Bomarzo following his invention—might make and show Caro a drawing. If this were done prior to the execution of the final work, Caro could suggest improvements. See letter of 12 December 1564 in Caro, *De le lettere familiari,* 2:238 (see note 93 above).
122. "and in my view the worst thing is to abandon truth in response to some subjective idea [*capriccio*] that abuses it. This has become dominant to such an extent these days that few are seen doing the opposite" (e pessima cosa io stimo lasciar la verità per ubidire al capriccio et al abuso; il quale oggi ha di maniera preso il dominio, che a pochi si vede fare il contrario). Gilio, this volume, 121; and Gilio, *Dialogo . . . degli errori e degli abusi de' pittori,* in Barocchi, *Trattati,* 2:29. Baldinucci defines the word *capriccio* as meaning a personal idea and invention ("proprio pensiero e invenzione"); see Filippo Baldinucci, *Vocabolario toscano dell'arte del disegno* (Florence: Franchi, 1681), 28.
123. "Rules and specifications should be drawn up by someone who has the knowledge, so that it would not be permissible for everyone to follow their own personal conceptions but only to do what they ought" (e si facessero, da chi sa, regole e determinazioni tali, che non fusse lecito ad ognuno fare secondo che gli detta il

capriccio, ma come far si deve). Gilio, this volume, 131; and Gilio, *Dialogo . . . degli errori e degli abusi de' pittori,* in Barocchi, *Trattati,* 2:38.

124. "Non penso che sia niuno, quanto si voglia goffo pittore, che non sappia o non pensi che Michelagnolo più tosto compiacer voluto sia de l'arte, che de la verità istorica, e quello che egli non ha fatto non sia da ignoranza proceduto, ma dal voler mostrare ai posteri l'eccellenza del suo ingegno e la eccellenza de l'arte che è in lui." Gilio, *Dialogo . . . degli errori e degli abusi de' pittori,* in Barocchi, *Trattati,* 2:55; and Gilio, this volume, 160.
125. "più tosto ha voluto abbellire il pennello e compiacere a l'arte che al vero." Gilio, *Dialogo . . . degli errori e degli abusi de' pittori,* in Barocchi, *Trattati,* 2:68; and Gilio, this volume, 173.
126. Gilio, this volume, 172–73. The suggestion that Michelangelo invents a "fable" might be a reference to Paul's second letter to Timothy (2 Timothy 4:3–4), where Paul predicts a time when men "will indeed turn away their hearing from the truth, but will be turned unto fables (*ad fabulas*)."
127. Gilio, *Dialogo . . . degli errori e degli abusi de' pittori,* in Barocchi, *Trattati,* 2:54: "perché egli [Michelangelo] più s'è voluto compiacere de l'arte, per mostrar quale e quanta sia, che de la verità del soggetto, et ha fatto come l'innamorato, il quale, per sodisfare a la sua favorita, ogni cosa stima lecita e bella; e ciò penso che da altro proceduto non sia, che, vedendosi innanzi sì largo campo da mostrare, in tanta moltitudine di figure, tutto quello che vagamente può fare un corpo umano per via di sforzi e d'altri posamenti, non ha voluto perdere l'occasione di non lasciare a' posteri memoria del suo mirabile ingegno." See also Gilio, this volume, 159. Horace had warned the poet against the temptation to introduce "glittering purple passages" quite inappropriately; Horace, *Ars Poetica,* 450–51 (lines 14–19).
128. Gilio, this volume, 157.
129. Gilio, this volume, 172.
130. Gilio, this volume, 104.
131. Gilio, this volume, 157.
132. Gilio, this volume, 85.
133. Gilio, this volume, 157.
134. Dolce had asserted the centrality of beauty in *disegno;* Dolce, *L'Aretino,* in Barocchi, *Trattati,* 1:171–72 (Roskill, *Dolce's "Aretino,"* 130–31). Roskill points out that Dolce avoids confronting the difference between imitating nature and surpassing nature. See Giorgio Vasari, preface to part 3 of the *Lives:* "Design is the imitation of what is most beautiful in nature when [designing] all the figures" (Il disegno fu lo imitare il più bello della natura in tutte le figure), in *Le vite de' più eccellenti pittori, scultori, e architettori: Nelle redazioni del 1550 e 1568,* vol. 4, ed. Rosanna Bettarini and Paola Barocchi (Florence: S.P.E.S., 1976), 4.
135. Gilio, this volume, 136–37.
136. Gilio, this volume, 134–35. Francesco asks: "Can [painters] not show the power of the art [*forza dell'arte*] in all [different subjects]?" This elicits from Troilo a comparison with Horace's painter, who knew how to paint cypress trees well and introduced them everywhere (*Ars Poetica,* 450–53 [lines 19–21]). The issue of the painter's art concealing the truth emerged in contemporary discussions

of scientific illustration—for example, in Leonhart Fuchs, *De historia stirpium commentarii insignes* (Basel: Michael Isengrin, 1542). The English translation is in Fuchs, *The Great Herbal of Leonhart Fuchs,* trans. Frederick Meyer, Emily Trueblood, and John Heller (Stanford, CA: Stanford University Press, 1999), 1:213: "Over and over again, we have purposely and deliberately avoided the obliteration of the natural form of the plants lest they be obscured by shading and other artifices that painters sometimes employ to win artistic glory (*artis gloriam*). And we have not allowed the craftsmen so to indulge their whims as to cause the drawing not to correspond accurately to the truth." See also Sachiko Kusukawa, *Picturing the Book of Nature: Image, Text, and Argument in Sixteenth-Century Human Anatomy and Medical Botany* (Chicago: University of Chicago Press, 2012), 109.

137. Gilio, this volume, 179–82. As with the discussion of beauty, this may be directed against Dolce, who had proposed "variety" as an essential aspect of *disegno,* although he had warned against excess; see Dolce, *L'Aretino,* in Barocchi, *Trattati,* 1:179 (Roskill, *Dolce's "Aretino,"* 144). Ironically, Gilio is recommending what Dolce had condemned as "maniera"; see Dolce, *L'Aretino,* in Barocchi, *Trattati,* 1:196 (Roskill, *Dolce's "Aretino,"* 176–77).
138. Gilio, this volume, 132–33.
139. Gilio, this volume, 186.
140. Painters who mix the true and the fictional with the aim of amplifying their subjects are discussed toward the end of the *Dialogo* (Gilio, this volume, 199–212). Pulidoro, who leads in this section, judges such an approach inappropriate for sacred painting. Gilio's arguments are analyzed by Charles Dempsey, who gives the name "ornamented epic style" to the mixed pictorial genre; see Dempsey, "Mythic Inventions," 64–65.
141. Gilio, this volume, 210, 212. Unease about the appropriateness of using ingeniously wrought and precious materials for ecclesiastical purposes has a long history within the Catholic Church. Saint Bernard's twelfth-century *Apologia for Abbot William* expresses this in various ways; see *The Cistercian World: Monastic Writings of the Twelfth Century,* trans. and ed. Pauline Matarasso (Harmondsworth: Penguin, 1993), 55–58 (xii.28). Religious images made with elaborate artifice were criticized because men were thereby distracted from proper devotion; such criticism was found among Catholic theologians of the early sixteenth century. See, for example, Hieronymus Emser, *Das man der heyligen bilder in den kirchen nit abthon, noch unehren soll* [Dresden, 1522], in *A Reformation Debate: Karlstadt, Emser, and Eck on Sacred Images; Three Treatises in Translation,* ed. and trans. Bryan D. Mangrum and Giuseppe Scavizzi (Toronto: Centre for Renaissance and Reformation Studies, 1991), 86; and this volume, 132–33n142. It is cited by Alexander Nagel, *Michelangelo and the Reform of Art* (Cambridge: Cambridge University Press, 2000), 13–14.
142. Gilio, this volume, 196–97.
143. Gilio, this volume, 231. It is interesting to notice that in a poem celebrating the Saint Mary Magdalene of Gentile da Fabriano (see fig. 34), Gilio stresses Gentile's *arte* and *ingegno;* implicit is his recognition of these qualities in this exceptional image, which does not include the invention of complex movements and subjective conceptions. See Sassi, "Sonetti," 275.

144. See Ingo Herklotz, "*Historia sacra* und mittelalterliche Kunst während der zweiten Hälfte des 16. Jahrhunderts in Rom," in *Baronio e l'arte: Atti del Convegno Internazionale di Studi, Sora, 10–13 ottobre 1984*, ed. Romeo De Maio, et al. (Sora: Centro di Studi Sorani Vincenzo Patriarca, 1985), 60.
145. "non avendo l'ingegno desto né vivo; non potevano far le loro opere se non goffe." Gilio, *Dialogo . . . degli errori e degli abusi de' pittori*, in Barocchi, *Trattati*, 2:55; and this volume, 161. Inadequate command of the skills could lead to error too—as shown in Silvio's example of the early representations of the Crucifixion with four nails, supposedly the result of a lack of *ingegno* that led painters simply to repeat Byzantine models.
146. Gilio, this volume, 227. On the word *baronci*, see this volume, 227n441. Vasari had referred to the "Greek" (Byzantine) paintings admired in Italy before the revival of the arts around 1250 as *baroncesche*. See Giorgio Vasari, *Le vite de' piu eccellenti architetti, pittori, et scultori italiani . . . nell'edizione per i tipi di Lorenzo Torrentino Firenze 1550*, ed. Luciano Bellosi and Aldo Rossi (Turin: Einaudi, 1986), 99.
147. Gilio, this volume, 119. See Nagel, *Michelangelo*, 14–15.
148. Gilio, this volume, 160–61.
149. Ambrogio Catarino (see note 34 above), *Disputatio*, 144, wrote about the abuse represented by paintings that were not faithful to their archetypes: "Est et tertius nec dissimulandus abusus, quam Imagines non repraesentant decenter archetypon, eo quod ipsae turpes sunt et ab artificibus imperitis fabricatae, nescientibus per artem imitari naturam. Vidi enim ego quasdam Imagines ita inconditas ut vix humanam speciem referrent, sed potius monstrosa membra. Alias autem econtrario tanta arte compositas, ut quibusdam importunis gestibus interim personarum decorem non servent, nihil gravitatis habentes, nihil devotionis excitantes." Scavizzi suggests that Catarino's argument had been important for Gilio; see Giuseppe Scavizzi, *Arte e architettura sacra: Cronache e documenti sulla controversia tra riformati e cattolici (1500–1550)* (Reggio Calabria: Casa Editrice del Libro, 1982), 201. There are other passages in Gilio's *Dialogo* where a knowledge of Catarino seems to be displayed: in one, Francesco seems to pick up Catarino's condemnation of too much art (Gilio, this volume, 142), while Pulidoro echoes Catarino's statements about incompetent painters (Gilio, this volume, 116). Horace had briefly discussed the problems of too little and too much art; see Horace, *Ars Poetica*, 452–53 (lines 24–31).
150. Gilio, this volume, 160. The argument that modern painters produced less satisfactory religious images than had their predecessors can be found in the writings of sixteenth-century theologians; take, for example, Hieronymous Emser (*Das man der heyligen bilder*, 86), who had identified as an abuse the artifice to be seen in modern religious images. In his 1522 defense of images, Emser claimed that earlier paintings in churches had been simple images (*schlechte bild*); this was not because of any lack of skill, but a deliberate decision to have less costly images and ones that did not distract viewers from devout contemplation.
151. Gilio, this volume, 161. Earlier in the text (116), the phrase "*debita proporzione*" had been used to describe the proper correspondence between the type of subject matter and its treatment in a painting, and that is what is alluded to here.

152. Vasari, *Le vite,* 4:183: "Fece Raffaello in questa storia San Pietro e San Paolo in aria con le spade in mano che vengono a defender la Chiesa: e se bene la storia di Leon III non dice questo, egli per capriccio suo volse figuraralla forse cosí, come interviene molte volte che con le pitture come con le poesie si va vagando per ornamento dell'opera, non si discostando però per modo non conveniente dal primo intendimento."
153. See note 141 above.
154. The cultivation of style was the argument of Shearman, *Mannerism,* 164; and empty aestheticism was the argument of Lee, *"Ut pictura poesis,"* 40.
155. Shearman, *Mannerism,* 164.
156. Gilio, this volume, 87.
157. Paola Barocchi, "Schizzo di un storia della critica cinquecentesca sulla Sistina," *Atti dell'Accademia Toscana di Scienze e Lettere "La Colombaria"* 21 (1956): 194–212. Francesco had warned that "a small error committed by Michelangelo is much more significant than a large error made by anyone else, for he is the prince of all painters and none of the others has such high standing, nor is held in such high regard as he is; in the past he set, and he still sets, the standard for all painters, both those living now and those to come"; see Gilio, this volume, 145–46.
158. Hubert Jedin, *Crisis and Closure of the Council of Trent: A Retrospective View from the Second Vatican Council,* trans. N. D. Smith (London: Sheed & Ward, 1967).
159. *Decrees of the Ecumenical Councils,* vol. 2, *Trent to Vatican II,* ed. and trans. Norman P. Tanner (Washington, D.C.: Georgetown University Press, 1990), 775, 776.
160. Romeo De Maio, *Michelangelo e la Controriforma* (Florence: Sansoni, 1990), 39.
161. "Picturae in capella Apostolica coperiantur, in aliis autem ecclesiis deleantur, si quae obscenum aut evidenter falsum ostendant, juxta decretum secundum in Sess. 9 sub Pio." See Ludwig von Pastor, *The History of the Popes from the Close of the Middle Ages: Drawn from the Secret Archives of the Vatican and Other Original Sources,* vol. 12, *Paul III (1534–1549),* ed. Ralph Francis Kerr (London: Kegan Paul, Trench, Trubner, 1923), 618n1. On the appointment of the commission, 30 December 1563, see Hubert Jedin, *Geschichte des Konzils von Trent* (Freiburg: Herder, 1975), 4:226–27. Among the members of the commission were Carlo Borromeo and Gabriele Paleotti. For Paleotti's papers, see Paolo Prodi, *Il Cardinale Gabriele Paleotti (1522–1597),* vol. 1 (Rome: Edizioni di Storia e Letteratura, 1959), 196n9.
162. Fabrizio Mancinelli, "The History, Execution Technique, First Censorship and Restoration Intervention," in Francesco Buranelli et al., *The Last Judgement: I, The Restoration* (New York: Rizzoli, 1999), 28. See also J. Martinez De Bujanda, *Index des livres interdits,* vol. 8, *Index de Rome: 1557, 1559, 1564; Les premiers index romains et l'index du Concile de Trente* (Quebec: Centre d'études de la Renaissance, 1990), 54, 84–85, where there is a discussion of the formulation, in the early 1560s, of ideas of expurgating books that contained objectionable material, rather than completely suppressing them as Paul IV's index of 1559 had done.
163. The payment (15 December 1567) to the heirs of Daniele da Volterra for his work on the *Last Judgment* specifies that it was "for covering the shameful parts of the

figures in the chapel of pope Sixtus" (in tegendis partibus pudendis figurarum cappelle pape sixti); see *Michelangelo e la Sistina: La tecnica, il restauro, il mito,* exh. cat. (Rome: Fratelli Palombi, 1990), 286 (no. 182). Francesco Buranelli et al. identify the censorship interventions of the sixteenth century; see Buranelli et al., *The Last Judgement,* 132–37, 275–78. Apart from his covering up of offensive nudity, Daniele repainted the figures of Saints Catherine and Blaise, whose poses in relation to each other had been thought obscene (see fig. 22).

CAROL M. RICHARDSON

GILIO'S POINT OF VIEW

> "Now," said M. Francesco, "consider what Lutheran churches must be without paintings. And indeed all Lutherans have shown how they have erased completely from their hearts the memory that they stripped from the churches."[1]

Written in the early 1560s, Giovanni Andrea Gilio's *Dialogo secondo, nel quale si ragiona degli errori, e degli abusi de' pittori circa l'istorie* (Dialogue on the errors and abuses of painters) is essential reading for anyone interested in the issues that concerned artists and patrons in the sixteenth century. The text provides a vivid insight into the challenges facing artists who wanted to paint pictures for sacred spaces. During this period, the Protestant Reformation had raised questions about the role of art in churches: whether altarpieces and statues should appear at all was open to debate. At the same time, in the Roman Catholic world there was renewed interest in personal spirituality and the Church's teaching, and the role of art in the edification and inspiration of the faithful was part of this.[2] For Catholics, as I will argue here, art had the potential to represent the continuity and persistence of Catholicism itself, not least because Protestants had rejected its power in precisely these areas. Gilio writes about the errors of painters because it mattered all the more in a church concerned with the education of Catholic Christians and the representation of common purposes rooted in a shared past.

Art historians have tended to associate Gilio with a particular point of view regarding art for the Church. In publishing Gilio's text in 1961, the art historian Paola Barocchi revivified the discussion about images in this period, upsetting assumptions that art produced after the Council of Trent was somehow intellectually and psychologically debased.[3] Whether or not the period in which Gilio was writing was one of Catholic "reform" or "Tridentine Catholicism," and the extent to which this affected artistic production, is still subject to debate.[4] Art historians have suggested links between the art and the history of the period—we might even call it a zeitgeist—in the shape of mannerism, Counter-Maniera, and Counter-Reformation style, even though the works of art produced in Italy in the second half of the sixteenth century surely can be characterized only by their wonderful diversity.[5] The value system of a contemporary cleric such as Gilio was entirely different from the spirit of the age so far identified. There is, I would argue, a mismatch between Gilio's point of view and that of the art historians who have mined his text for clues.

To judge from its prevalence in secondary texts concerning sixteenth-century art, the *Dialogo . . . degli errori e degli abusi de' pittori* seems at times to do little more than broadcast Gilio's disappointment at Michelangelo's *Last Judgment* fresco (see fig. 19). As a result, Gilio has been characterized as "a conservative ecclesiastic" whose treatise represents a "rigid system" and whose "severe morality is notable."[6] He stands accused of "severity of judgement" and "theological pedantry."[7] Others have been more measured, although they still undermine Gilio as a mere clerical critic. David Summers praises Gilio's lucidity as "he often sets forth the errant position with a clarity outstanding in Cinquecento writing, the more visibly to demolish it."[8] Alexander Nagel makes the important point that "it would be wrong to depict Gilio, and several other Counter-Reformation writers, simply as conservative critics of innovation in art."[9] So what is Gilio's point of view if he is not simply a "conservative critic"? Crucial to the formation of these assumptions, and what has led to regular if usually passing reference to Gilio's *Dialogo,* is his relationship with the Council of Trent: the Council's decrees were promulgated in 1564, the same year that Gilio's *Dialogo* was published.

In this chapter I will explore the idea that Gilio was somehow channeling the views of the Council of Trent for a broader public interested in art. I will then suggest that, while there are indeed links, those links are not to the Council's decree concerning sacred images but rather to the authority and persistence of the Roman Catholic Church itself explored in the Council's first sessions.

Gilio, the Council of Trent, and the Decree Concerning Art

How accurate then is it to characterize Gilio as "an art lover, who supported the Trent decree," who even "provided the kind of guidelines that were lacking in the decree"?[10] To what extent was Gilio "speaking with the voice of Catholic Reform"?[11] Marcia Hall pinpoints his separation of sacred from secular art as introducing "the essence of the reform of painting that the Counter-Reformation called for."[12] The *Dialogo* has been received as a definitive statement by a cleric in the context of Tridentine reform, which uses Michelangelo's *Last Judgment* as its main case study. But the issues of what artists could offer the Church, and how they might do it, were complex and multifaceted and ultimately not resolvable, at least not by Gilio—who, in fact, seems to avoid definitive conclusions. This first section will look for the presumed connections between Gilio and the Tridentine decree directly concerning art. It will ask if it is possible to draw any connections between Gilio, the *Dialogo,* and the Council of Trent. The answer is yes, but not in the way that art historians have identified to date. The second section will therefore broaden this search to parts of the Council that had concluded before Gilio was writing.

A general council of the Church was mooted and convened in Mantua in 1537, but it disbanded shortly after. The Council of Trent finally began in 1545 and then met in three separate periods: the first ran from 1545 to 1547, the second from 1551 to 1552, and the third from 1562 to 1563. In 1561, when Gilio was writing, the Council had not met since 1552 and would not reconvene for its final period until 18 January 1562. The Council did not deal with the issue of sacred images until its very last session, in December 1563.[13] Therefore the most important point to make concerning the relationship between Gilio's *Dialogo* and the Council of Trent is this: even though the publication date is 1564 and the Council's decrees were promulgated in 1564, the dialogue was planned without any anticipation of the Council, given that Gilio must have been writing in 1561. Gilio could possibly have been writing with the knowledge that art in churches would be discussed, though even this seems unlikely.

Historians such as Simon Ditchfield have carefully established the chronology of events and ideas at the time, warning that "the image of the Council of Trent as a monolith that symbolizes the fundamental coherence and rigidity of the Roman Catholic counterattack on Protestantism is very much a retrospective one." It was "an event which unfolded in space as well as time."[14]

The final months of the Council of Trent, from July to December 1563, were by far its busiest, as session twenty-three, session twenty-four, and the last, session twenty-five, dealt with everything from the residence of bishops in their diocese to marriage, visitations, indulgences (the issue that had proved most divisive with Lutherans), and, among it all, sacred images.[15] John O'Malley has argued that the main reason images in churches were dealt with at all was the eventual participation of the French in the Council at this third and final period.[16] Until that point King Francis I of France had been more concerned with his resistance to the power of the Holy Roman emperor, Charles V, who exerted considerable influence over the Council. By the end of 1562 Francis was dead, and increasing success for the Protestant Huguenots overshadowed national tensions. A major point of difference for the Catholic and Huguenot sides in France was the role of art in churches—and tensions had escalated to the point of violent iconoclasm.[17] But in the end, at Trent the decree concerning relics and images was rushed through without any discussion at the last session on 2 December, as the Council headed for its agreed closure on 9 December.[18] The news that the pope, Pius IV, was ill and possibly at death's door (he survived) increased the sense of urgency. By simply reasserting the declarations of the Second Council of Nicaea (787) against the heresy of iconoclasm, the Tridentine decree contradicted the Protestant nihilism of iconoclasm (as Gilio might have seen it) in the same way that the earlier council had done, while at the same time stressing the historical continuity of Catholic practice.[19]

However, the decree that would in the long run have the most effect on art and architecture was not the one directly concerning relics and sacred images.[20] Instead it was the important and hard-won reassociation of bishops with their dioceses: bishops were no longer free agents but shepherds of a flock of parishes and priests gathered around a specific locale (sixth session, 13 January 1547).[21] In the assertion of episcopal authority, Trent referred, as it often did, to the decrees of the Council of Sens convoked in 1527 to stop Lutheran ideas from seeping into France. There, the issue had been not images per se but who was in control: "because of the sensuality of some images and their deviation from the truth of Scripture, in the future none be placed in the churches unless the bishop or his vicar approve beforehand and visit the church."[22]

It took several decades for evidence to emerge of the direct intervention of the bishops, now resident in their dioceses, in the creation of sacred spaces. Published in 1577, *Instructiones fabricae et supellectilis ecclesiasticae* (Instructions on church furnishings and buildings) by Carlo Borromeo, archbishop of Milan from 1560 to 1584, was first mentioned in the acts of the Fourth Archdiocesan Provincial Council of 1573. Such councils or synods were the result of Trent and a direct response to its decrees.[23] The *Instructiones* resonated with the published series of the synod conclusions, the *Acta Ecclesiae Mediolanensis* (1566–83; Acts of the Church of Milan), which soon set the pattern for reformed dioceses across Europe, gaining renewed momentum in 1599 with the publication of the second edition and in 1610 with Borromeo's canonization.[24] The quick and efficient adoption of the Tridentine spirit in Milan set an important precedent elsewhere.

This is the context that explains Gabriele Paleotti's *Discorso intorno alle imagini sacre e profane* (1582; *Discourse on Sacred and Profane Images*), which, despite its influence, was left unfinished. Bishop of Bologna from 1567 to 1597, and an associate of Cardinal Giovanni Morone, the papal legate who brought the Council to a close, and Carlo Borromeo, Paleotti was enacting his post-Tridentine role as a resident bishop to govern the physical fabric and decoration of the religious buildings under his jurisdiction. Another important ecclesiastic, Federico Borromeo (Carlo Borromeo's young cousin and ward) owed much to Gilio and is arguably a culminating figure in this chronology.[25] As archbishop of Milan from 1607 until 1620, Federico founded the Ambrosiana—comprising a diocesan library, art museum, and art academy—as a place to focus on the reform of art and scholarship in the context of the Tridentine decrees. Like Gilio, he was primarily concerned with figurative arts: Federico carefully established both general and specific guidelines in the two books of his *De pictura sacra* (published in 1624).[26]

Although there was an awareness among diocesan clergy of the Council of Trent taking place in the background, and although some of its decrees had been published, Simon Ditchfield notes that "to imagine that the likes of Gilio, writing in the early 1560s, would be aware that there was even a nascent 'Tridentine aesthetic' is to put the cart before the horse."[27] It took Borromeo and Paleotti, who were directly engaged in the Council and its immediate aftermath, ten and twenty years, respectively, to produce manuals designed to guide other bishops and clergy. Even then, these texts do not delimit Tridentine values. As Ditchfield memorably puts it, "devotion to the cult of saints was a kinetic, multimedia experience, a mobile *gesamtkunstwerk* in which art, architecture, sculpture, work, music, and print were deployed to move heart and soul through eye and ear."[28] The process of defining how these elements might come together continues to this day.

Giovanni Andrea Gilio was a provincial priest based in Fabriano. He had visited Rome at some point before 1550, though we do not know if he did so subsequently. As a diocesan cleric, Gilio was on the periphery of Tridentine reform and, like most of his peers, not directly engaged with it. But rather than undermining the significance of the *Dialogo,* this looser association makes that text all the more insightful. Gilio was also a talented writer keen to attract the attention of an influential patron who could draw him into the life of a courtier in the papal court in Rome. Paolo Cherchi, in his 2002 introduction to the *Dialogo del letterato cortigiano* (Dialogue on educated courtiers)—the dialogue that Gilio wrote alongside the *Dialogo . . . degli errori e degli abusi de' pittori*—describes Gilio as an aspiring member of the third generation of courtier: one who serves.[29] The first kind of courtier was defined by Baldessar Castiglione as a cultivated man of good taste and judgment, reflecting but also refining the raw power of the prince. The second type was the learned man who left behind the temptations of the solitary life to put his gifts to the use of princes or states, with the potential of attaining the heights of his profession, as ambassador—known as a legate or nuncio in the case of the Church. This type of courtier was more than a mere servant; his status derived from the honor and power of that which he served—the state or the Church, for example. While the purpose of these first and second generations of court functionary receded with the rise of bureaucratic roles such as chamberlain or secretary, Gilio had in mind the third kind of courtier, whose domain remained the world of letters. This is where the potential power and usefulness of Gilio's *Dialogo* resides.

At the Council of Trent, the princes of the Church, especially the bishops and cardinals, could fix the boundaries of Catholic doctrine. Men such as Gilio were poised to fill out the necessary detail in the form of practical rules of application and engagement.

Despite this broader context, Gilio's *Dialogo . . . degli errori e degli abusi de' pittori* is often used more narrowly as an "attack on Michelangelo's *Last Judgment*."[30] Although the *Dialogo* evidences aspects of the reaction to Michelangelo's fresco in the middle of the sixteenth century, Gilio's text was not written as a direct attack: it is a dialogue in which points of view are put forward about Michelangelo's fresco as well as other works. The text's structure is as significant as its content, as Puterbach notes: "Dialogue, as a literary form, spoke eloquently to Catholics, Protestants, and Puritans engaged in these controversies primarily because Dialogue can disguise the source of controversial opinion."[31] Perhaps the most famous example of this was when Galileo Galilei, in 1623, chose the dialogue form to consider the Copernican system as hypothesis, not fact—even if he ultimately failed to hide his views.[32]

The dialogue mode allows Gilio to present different points of view without necessarily drawing a definite conclusion.[33] More specifically, Gilio employs the doctrinal or instructive dialogue form associated with Socrates. This was structured to enable "learned men seeking for truth among men of learning" to gradually whittle away at a topic, bringing in and throwing out examples as they went along, until only relevant detail was left.[34] (In contrast, in his *Dialogo della pittura intitolato l'Aretino,* Lodovico Dolce uses a different kind of dialogue—the declamatory—to establish a single viewpoint according to the model of Lucian.) The conversational dialogue allows the author to question and disprove opposing arguments, all the more deliberately to ridicule them.[35] As Gilio tells his dedicatee, Cardinal Alessandro Farnese, in the preface, his aim is "to have a field marked out in which they [poets and painters] can run in any direction." The interlocutors then wander through an actual meadow in search of this virtual one, reciting poetry, playing, and singing before musing on various topics such as the seasons—"some praising one, some another."[36]

The example of the *Last Judgment* enables the group to deepen its discussion through a specific instance, "to plow the greatest and deepest ocean that there is" because Michelangelo has there "shown what the art [of painting] is capable of. He has done this in such a way that it amazes not only those who see it but everyone in the world who hears about it."[37] The lively discussion that Gilio constructs makes the subject of the fresco—a unique combination of both Last Judgment and Resurrection—seem even richer. The focus of this part of the discussion, however, is largely the subject and contemporary understanding of the resurrection of the body, not Michelangelo's depictions per se.[38] It serves to emphasize the achievement of the artist in even beginning to represent such an allusive narrative. "I think you are splitting hairs. Painting too needs its own decorum and freedom," Troilo eventually declares, in exasperation at Ruggiero's theological pedantry that inevitably finds Michelangelo lacking.[39]

Overall the discussion highlights the challenges and choices that Michelangelo faced in the depiction of a difficult subject, as well as the difficulties the Church had in working with artists to ensure there was no ambiguity in their uniquely powerful contribution. Ruggiero closes the section on the historical painter by agreeing that if men are without sin, then they can be trusted, but as most are tainted and inconsistent "this beautiful and holy story . . . should be painted in a faithful, pure, simple, true, and chaste way."[40] This truth, however, is relative, not absolute—and throughout the *Dialogo* it is the effect of the artwork on the viewer that matters most. Therefore, what is true also has to be appropriate according to the cumulative experience and expectation of viewers, whether those viewers are informed or illiterate. The effect on the spectator is cited in the case of the plunging Christ in the *Conversion of Paul* (see fig. 14)—"Even if from Christ's point of view these are not matters of consideration, they must be from ours, because we perceive devotion or scandal depending on how the figures are represented."[41] Painters are therefore central in communicating the Church's message, and they must know what they are doing and why. They articulate the Church community visually, fixing its identity in space by capturing ideas that have formed through time. But it is an ongoing process of negotiation and clarification that sometimes even involves the invention of fictions. This is an important corrective to the kind of imperious "thought control" of which art historians are suspicious in the relationship between art and the Church.[42]

The assertion of fixed or unambiguous meaning was fraught with difficulties in the sixteenth century. In the end, the *Dialogo* fails to establish a set of "rules or methods of procedure" because, I would suggest, that is not Gilio's purpose. Gilio was writing in, and contributing to, an uneasy period in which ideas and assumptions were being scrutinized. Indeed, the process of debate itself is as much the focus of the text as the subject of painters' mistakes and misjudgments. As a cleric himself, Gilio would have been well aware of the limits of his own authority to dictate which potential answers might be acceptable. Ecclesiastical hierarchy put these decisions in the hands of the Church as a collective whole. Coevally, in the 1560s, Gilio and the clerics at Trent were thinking about art, and both raised the importance of art's effects on viewers. This shared endeavor ensured the continued relevance of Gilio's text over the fifty years it took for the ideas it vivifies to filter through to the handbooks of Gabriele Paleotti and Federico Borromeo.[43] The active, constant, and organic process Gilio's text represents was important enough to be the subject of one of the first decrees of the Council of Trent. Gilio's Tridentine context is therefore to be found much earlier in the Council's proceedings.

History, Tradition, Authority

Works of art, Gilio states, reach a vast audience, greater than any other kind of teaching. But whereas a text, which exists on a page or in a spoken moment, can easily be corrected, an artist has one chance with his painting.

> M. Silvio said: "Indeed the painter has much more impact than the teacher, because the latter teaches a hundred, while the [work of the] former is seen by ten thousand. The latter can be corrected whenever he is revealed as wrong, while the former's work cannot be amended without erasing it from the wall. Who could be so obstinate (unless he be a Lutheran) that, on seeing the image of our Lord crucified, scourged, and bleeding, he would not feel some remorse in his conscience and would not wish to honor him and pay him reverence?"
>
> "That shows," said M. Vincenso, "how saintly, holy, and necessary the work of the Church has been in allowing paintings, by means of which both learned and ignorant men are aroused to devotion, challenged to imitation, and provoked into penitence every time they see them."
>
> "Now," said M. Francesco, "consider what Lutheran churches must be without paintings. And indeed all Lutherans have shown how they have erased completely from their hearts the memory that they stripped from the churches."[44]

As well as offering inspiration to proper devotion, painting equates to the Church's "memory" (*memoria*). Stripped from Lutheran churches, these effaced images left a void in the Protestant concept of church. In dramatic contrast, this memory was for Catholics the manifestation of the collective, shared experience of community, its history and identity: it was, in Rome's view, the very source of ecclesiastical authority. When in 1566 Pius V embargoed documents recording discussions at Trent, it was because of the Catholic understanding of the continuity of history, of "the power of the past to disturb the present."[45] But, unlike texts, images in churches are public in nature. Paintings are designed with an audience in mind. They cannot be censored or hidden, as doing so requires their destruction. Gilio makes it clear that images are also integral to the Church's memory. What was at stake from Gilio's perspective was no less than the unity of the Church, a problem that had been inconceivable before

Protestant dissension. On the Roman Catholic side, Gilio shows that artists had an important role to play in maintaining a consistent and coherent message through what they chose to remember and what was forgotten. They were guardians of the most evident form of the Church's memory, hence the repeated emphasis of Gilio's interlocutors on the effect art has on its audience.

Slightly later, in his *Discorso intorno alle imagini sacre e profane* (1582), Paleotti stressed the links between vision and memory: he quotes from the prayer used at the dedication of images in churches that refers to the "eyes of memory" with which the devout meditate on the example of the saints depicted in paintings or sculptures.[46] Paleotti underlines the proximity of the sense of sight to memory. Unlike information from books, which is hard-won but quickly forgotten,

> images sculpt what they teach into the panels of memory so firmly that it remains stamped there for many years. That is not all: images encompass the broadest and gravest concepts in a confined space . . . revealing the greatness of the potency, wisdom, justice, and mercy of God and the sum of all celestial virtues in a single point.[47]

The relationship of art to memory had a long history. Gilio quotes the fourth-century mystic Gregory of Nyssa, who wrote of art's "affective power."[48] An important source used to counter Protestant literalism in the sixteenth century, Gregory of Nyssa had warned that "if we remain with the mere facts of the text, the historical narrative of the Scriptures does not provide examples of a good life . . . unless there is something behind the letter."[49] Gilio also refers to the ubiquitous sixth-century letter of Gregory the Great to Bishop Serenus, a text that had retained its currency over the years in describing art as the Bible of the illiterate.[50] Mary Carruthers and other scholars, however, have stressed the complexity of the seemingly straightforward assertion that images illustrate words. They urge a recognition of "the richly networked memory" of biblical, theological, and other kinds of texts and cultures that combine together in the religious experience of both educated cleric and poor illiterate.[51] Memory, therefore, is more than a simple process of bringing to mind or reimagining. The Church's shared experience is its institutional memory, and the reconstitution of its history as image (or text) both asserts and validates its continuity.

One of the earliest sessions at the Council of Trent dealt with the problem of defining the relationship between scripture and tradition. While Martin Luther had asserted that scripture alone was sufficient, his original, narrower aim to exclude Aristotelian philosophy had, by the 1540s, expanded in the Protestant mind. The Catholic aberration was now represented by all of the customs, ideas, and liturgical enactments that, over one and a half millennia, had come to elucidate and embellish the Christian message in the Roman Church. Where were the boundaries of Christian faith, and how far could these comfortably be established beyond the Bible—and the New Testament in particular?[52] Luther's insistence on the primacy of text, and especially scripture, provoked the decree on the "acceptance of the sacred books and apostolic traditions," promulgated during the fourth session of the Council of Trent on 8 April 1546:

> The council clearly perceives that this truth and rule [that the purity of the gospel, purged of all errors, may be preserved in the church] are contained in written books and in *unwritten traditions* which were received by the apostles from the mouth of Christ himself, or else *have come down to us,* handed on as it were from the apostles themselves at the inspiration of the holy Spirit. . . . [T]he council accepts and venerates with a like feeling of piety and reverence all the books of both the old and the new Testament, since the one God is the author of both, as well as the traditions concerning both faith and conduct, as either directly spoken by Christ or dictated by the holy Spirit, which have been preserved *in unbroken sequence in the catholic church.*[53]

Hubert Jedin, one of the first modern historians of the Council of Trent, stressed the continuity of manifold traditions that externalize Catholicism's endurance and therefore its legitimacy. This sense of tradition as collective memory was the principle underlying all Tridentine reform. The 8 April decree also reinforced the idea of the Church as a bureaucracy whose role was to maintain and police this cumulative identity and common purpose.[54] The Church's traditions were, in turn, upheld and maintained by the bishops, including the bishop of Rome.[55] To this end, the constitutions published at the conclusion of the Third Provincial Synod of the Archdiocese of Milan in 1573 affirmed the responsibility of bishops in preserving and promoting the history of their patrimony, specifically because they embodied the apostolic succession:

> The bishop [as holder of] an office instituted at the very beginning of the history of the Church should diligently collect together the names, pastoral character and pastoral activities of his predecessors, and should make certain that all these things are written down, arranged in order and put into a certain book so that the memory [*memoria*] be conserved of those things which have been done or instituted by those bishops and so that they [the books] may be of perpetual use and assistance in the good governance of that church.[56]

In Gilio's *Dialogo,* it is precisely this underlying system of tradition and authority to which Ruggiero, the cleric, refers when asked to explain how sacred images should be painted:

> It is a difficult matter to construct a correct and infallible argument that it should be like this and could not be otherwise, since we have no law or rule about this matter, except the evidence of what was the custom among painters prior to Michelangelo (which, as you lawyers know, is law), and except what Gulielmus Durandus wrote about it in his *Rationale divinorum officiorum*. . . . I think painters were given rules or methods of procedure, but, in the same way that many, many books have perished, so too these [rules] have been lost. But custom is enough for us, since, as I mentioned, it has the force of law, given that it lasted for so many years before being altered and ruined by the subjective conceptions of modern painters.[57]

Custom (*consuetudine*) consists of precedent, "rules or methods of procedure," and, in the case of art, "evidence of what was customary among painters prior to Michelangelo." Custom embraces the concepts of history, tradition, and authority, which remain central to Roman Catholic collective identity and which were defined in the sixteenth century in opposition to Protestant ideas. Key to this is the idea of continuity, of "unbroken sequence in the Catholic Church" as it was phrased in the decree, which, as John O'Malley points out, "persists as a recognizable Catholic trait even to the present."[58]

By the middle of the sixteenth century, history per se had acquired very different implications for Protestants and Catholics.[59] Eric Cochrane, whose work in the twentieth century alerted subsequent scholars to history's active rather than passive status in the period, stressed that history post-Trent became "an autonomous and indispensable element in the ongoing process of the clarification of doctrine."[60] Simon Ditchfield has extended and deepened these ideas to show that "an engagement with the past . . . allowed for particular as well as universal narratives to be constructed," which could authorize or discredit claims to orthodoxy.[61] For Protestant reformers, history was something that seemed to stand between their rediscovered True Church and the first centuries, before the Apostolic Church was tarnished by time. For Catholics, history represented no less than the enduring continuity of Christ's commission to Saint Peter, the model of the first martyrs and Church Fathers, through to the present.[62] These mutually exclusive concepts of history explain the very different approaches that would lead to the Protestant *Magdeburg Centuries* (1559–74) and to the Catholic *Annales Ecclesiastici* (1588–1607) by Cesare Baronio.[63]

As a historian in the sixteenth century, Baronio was not responsible for constructing a new narrative or testing an old one: it was his job to demonstrate the continuity of the apostolic tradition, its authority rooted in Rome—an authority that was perpetually reasserted and reenacted by the bishops. Indeed, the direct riposte to the *Magdeburg Centuries*—published in 1565 by Konrad Braun, the canonist and theologian to whom Gilio refers on several occasions in the *Dialogo*—criticized the *Centuries'* thematic arrangement, arguing that it was the historian's job to tell the story, not critique the narrative.[64] The principle behind the *Annales* was that "the defense of the truth [is] . . . synonymous with Catholicism."[65] The history constructed by Baronio showed that the Roman Catholic Church was *semper eadem* (ever the same).[66] In his address to the reader in the first volume, Baronio stresses the role of the continuity of history in supporting the continuity of the one Holy, Catholic, and Apostolic Church—personified in the person of the pope based in Rome.

> We shall demonstrate for every age that the visible monarchy of the Catholic Church was instituted by Christ our Lord and founded upon Peter and his true and legitimate successors, the true Roman pontiffs, and that it is preserved inviolate, religiously guarded neither broken nor interrupted but continuous, for ever.[67]

Francesco Panigarola, in his Italian compendium to the *Annales,* puts it more directly, by quoting Eusebius: "The Church of God has always been one and the same in all times: one faith, one Christ, and one God."[68] This idea lies behind Gilio's criticism of artists who diverge from tradition. Catholic history "emphasized pattern over detail and authority over argument" because continuity, not change, is the issue.[69]

Authority as a recurring theme underlies much Catholic polemical writing from the second half of the sixteenth century, and for good reason. The English Jesuit Robert Persons identified the "self-authorization of (Protestant) discourse" as the primary cause of religious division.[70] Mutually exclusive versions of authority made dialogue impossible. For Protestants, authority resided in Scripture alone; for Catholics, the Bible was part of the Church's magisterium, the *ecclesia docens.*[71] That teaching, however, can be difficult to detect except in censorious pronouncements. The papacy, John Henry Newman later observed, hardly took the initiative—it "only served as a brake . . . in the development of doctrine," reacting to the collective initiatives of individuals.[72] He saw this brake in action in two ways: "in direct statements of truth, and in the condemnation of error."[73] This is why, then, the collective exercise of control over ideas in the

Roman Catholic Church might be characterized as "the suspicious conservatism of ecclesiastical authority."[74] It is this unwillingness to differentiate between the Catholic and the Protestant exercise of authority that has resulted in the suspicion that Gilio is merely a conservative cleric. The alternative Gilio puts forward here is an example of an individual within the nascent Tridentine Church taking the initiative, contributing to the debate, but not expecting to have the last word. It is therefore particularly misleading to characterize Gilio's sense of *vero,* or truth, as "the literal truth to Scripture."[75] This is a decidedly Protestant worldview that would have been foreign to Gilio. What is truth in the context of mid-sixteenth-century debates about art? More crucially, who decides, and therefore what role is Gilio expecting to play? Gilio is not so much "a critic alert to the symbolic implications of images" but a cleric well aware of the power of images, informed about the complexities of the issue—and also alert to his own position within the Church's evolving magisterium.[76] Therefore, Gilio declares through his dialogue that "no one should let himself be carried away by the false belief that painters can do anything, as if there were neither reasons nor rules to constrain them within due and appropriate limits."[77]

Conclusion

This discussion of the Roman Catholic Church's exclusive ownership of truth and history, and its ultimate authority, is not designed to sideline Gilio as a mere cleric. Instead it has been my aim to refocus attention in the history of art on the vital significance of the issues Gilio was highlighting. Painters could not simply be left to their own devices. They too had to play their part in the new determination and focus on communicating the crucial message of ecclesiastical unity that characterizes the last four decades of the sixteenth century.

At the very end of the *Dialogo,* following the discussion of the "mixed" painter, Francesco asks Ruggiero "how the sacred images should be painted."[78] The theologian refers to the importance of custom, which "has the force of law." This is a very Roman Catholic answer. "What is this ancient custom?" asks Troilo. Ruggiero refers to the continuity of shared experience and tradition that is owned and therefore has to be regulated by the Church. This, I propose, is why the dialogue ends with the prompts to Cardinal Cesi and Cardinal Santa Fiore: it is they who must dictate what is appropriate in the painted decoration they have commissioned for their chapels in Santa Maria Maggiore in Rome.[79] There is no outward measure of artistic success: it resides in the collective authority of the Church. In the same way, Gilio's initial dedication to Cardinal Farnese does not mean that he wishes to offer a potential patron an implementable guide to ensuring appropriate images in church. Instead Gilio offers up considerations to the cardinal, whose share in the papal imperium gave him the right to dictate "whether the *Last Judgment* and the ceiling, as well as the other figures, observe historical truth."[80]

Notes

1. Gilio, this volume, 229.
2. See John O'Malley's opening address to the conference on Federico Borromeo in November 2003, where he discusses "the need more deeply and pervasively to integrate the history of spirituality with cultural history"; John O'Malley, "Patronage, Spirituality, and the Power of the Beautiful: Some Historiographical Considerations," in *Federico Borromeo Principe e Mecenate: Atti delle giornate di studio, 21–22 novembre 2003,* ed. Cesare Mozzarelli (Milan: Biblioteca Ambrosiana, 2004), 28.
3. Robert W. Gaston, "How Words Control Images: The Rhetoric of Decorum in Counter-Reformation Italy," in *The Sensuous in the Counter-Reformation Church,* ed. Marcia B. Hall and Tracey E. Cooper (Cambridge: Cambridge University Press, 2013), 85.
4. See the warnings in Simon Ditchfield, "Of Dancing Cardinals and Mestizo Madonnas: Reconfiguring the History of Roman Catholicism in the Early Modern Period," *Journal of Early Modern History* 8, no. 3 (2004): 386–408.
5. On the issue of mannerism as style, period of time, or working method, see Hessel Miedema, "On Mannerism and *maniera,*" *Simiolus: Netherlands Quarterly for the History of Art* 10, no. 1 (1978–79): 19–45; and Marcia B. Hall, "A Note on Style Labels," in *After Raphael: Painting in Central Italy in the Sixteenth Century* (Cambridge: Cambridge University Press, 2001), xii–xv.
6. Bette Talvacchia, "The Word Made Flesh: Spiritual Subjects and Carnal Depictions in Renaissance Art," in Hall and Cooper, *The Sensuous in the Counter-Reformation Church,* 54.
7. Discussed in Gaston, "How Words Control Images," 76, 85–86, as quoted in Rensselaer W. Lee, *"Ut pictura poesis": The Humanistic Theory of Painting* (New York: Norton, 1967), 40, first published in *Art Bulletin* 22, no. 4 (1940): 197–269. But, as Gaston points out, Gilio's "listing of 'errors' . . . is only with difficulty seen by the modern art historian as a component of a program of religious reform." Gaston, "How Words Control Images," 87.
8. David Summers, *Michelangelo and the Language of Art* (Princeton, NJ: Princeton University Press, 1981), 80.
9. Alexander Nagel, "Art as Gift: Art and Religious Reform in the Renaissance," in *Negotiating the Gift: Pre-Modern Figurations of Exchange,* ed. Gadi Alzazi, Valentin Groebner, and Bernhard Jussen (Göttingen: Vandehoeck & Rupprecht, 2003), 345.
10. Gaston, "How Words Control Images," 86; and Marcia B. Hall, *The Sacred Image in the Age of Art: Titian, Tintoretto, Barocci, El Greco, Caravaggio* (New Haven, CT: Yale University Press, 2011), 122.

11. Morten Steen Hansen, *In Michelangelo's Mirror: Perino del Vaga, Daniele da Volterra, Pellegrino Tibaldi* (University Park: Pennsylvania State University Press, 2013), 25; Marcia Hall (*After Raphael,* xv) describes him as one of the "spokesmen for the Counter-Reformation."
12. Hall, *After Raphael,* 190; and Hall, *Sacred Image,* 7, 94.
13. For an excellent overview of the Council of Trent, see John W. O'Malley, *Trent: What Happened at the Council* (Cambridge, MA: Belknap, 2013).
14. Simon Ditchfield, "Trent Revisited," in *La fede degli italiani: Per Adriano Prosperi,* ed. Guido Dall'Olio, Adelisa Malena, and Pierroderto Scaramella (Pisa: Edizioni della Normale, 2011), 1:357.
15. Ditchfield, "Trent Revisited," 361.
16. John W. O'Malley, "Trent, Sacred Images, and Catholics' Senses of the Sensuous," in Hall and Cooper, *The Sensuous in the Counter-Reformation Church,* 33–35.
17. See Olivier Christin, "L'iconoclasme huguenot: 'Praxis pietatis' et geste révolutionnaire," in "Usages de l'image," special issue, *Ethnologie française* 24, no. 2 (1994): 216–25; and, for a very useful view of recent historiography, Judith Pollmann, "Countering the Reformation in France and the Netherlands: Clerical Leadership and Catholic Violence 1560–1585," *Past & Present,* no. 190 (2006): 83–120.
18. O'Malley, *Trent,* 36.
19. On the historical context for the Second Council of Nicaea, see Thomas F. X. Noble, *Images, Iconoclasm, and the Carolingians* (Philadelphia: University of Pennsylvania Press, 2009), 75–81.
20. O'Malley, "Trent, Sacred Images," 32.
21. Francesco C. Cesareo, "The Episcopacy in Sixteenth-Century Italy," in *Early Modern Catholicism: Essays in Honour of John W. O'Malley, S.J.,* ed. Kathleen M. Comerford and Hilmar M. Pabel (Toronto: University of Toronto Press, 2001), 73.
22. O'Malley, "Trent, Sacred Images," 32, quoted and translated from Giovanni Domenico Mansi, *Sacrorum conciliorum nova et amplissima collectio* (Florence: Zatta, 1759–98; reprint, Graz: Akademische Druck- und Verlagsanstalt, 1960–62), 32:1200. See also O'Malley, *Trent,* 261: "the bishops at Trent . . . turned their most severe discipline against themselves."
23. Robert Sénécal, "Carlo Borromeo's *Instructiones fabricae et supellectilis ecclesiasticae* and Its Origins in the Rome of the Time," *Papers of the British School at Rome* 68 (2000): 241–67.
24. O'Malley, *Trent,* 260; Enrico Cattaneo, "La singolare fortuna degli 'Acta Ecclesiae Mediolanensis,'" *La Scuola Cattolica* 111 (1983): 191–217; and Simon Ditchfield, "Thinking with Saints: Sanctity and Society in the Early Modern World," *Critical Inquiry* 35, no. 3 (2009): 576.
25. Pamela Jones, *Federico Borromeo and the Ambrosiana: Art Patronage and Reform in Seventeenth-Century Milan* (Cambridge: Cambridge University Press, 1993), 31, 101–2.
26. Federico Borromeo, *Sacred Painting, Museum,* ed. and trans. Kenneth S. Rothwell Jr. (Cambridge, MA: Harvard University Press, 2010), 3–143.
27. Simon Ditchfield, email to the author, 19 August 2015. I am very grateful for his personal insights into this issue.

28. Ditchfield, "Thinking with Saints," 576.
29. Giovanni Andrea Gilio, *Dialogo del letterato cortigiano,* ed. Paolo Cherchi (Ravenna: Longo, 2002), 11–15. Cherchi discusses in particular Giovanbattista Cinzio Giraldi's *Discorso intorno a quello che si conviene a giovane nobile et ben creato nel servire un gran principe* (Pavia: Girolamo Bartoli, 1569), which was written in 1565 and published in Pavia in 1569.
30. Marcia B. Hall, "Introduction," in Hall and Cooper, *The Sensuous in the Counter-Reformation Church,* 11.
31. Joseph Puterbach, "'Truth Hath the Victory': Dialogue and Disputation in John Foxe's *Actes and Monuments,*" in *Printed Voices: The Renaissance Culture of Dialogue,* ed. Dorothea Heitsch and Jean-François Vallée (Toronto: University of Toronto Press, 2004), 137.
32. William Shea, "Galileo's Copernicanism," in *The Cambridge Companion to Galileo,* ed. Peter Machamer (Cambridge: Cambridge University Press, 1998), 227, 233; Maurice A. Finocchiaro, *The Routledge Guidebook to Galileo's Dialogue* (New York: Routledge, 2014), 46; and Ernan McMullin, "Galileo on Science and Scripture," in Machamer, *The Cambridge Companion to Galileo,* 324–25.
33. One of only a few authors who draws attention to this important point is Hall, *Sacred Image,* 122–23.
34. Quintilian, *Institutio oratoria,* 2:365, as quoted in D. R. Edward Wright, "Structure and Significance in Dolce's *L'Aretino,*" *Journal of Aesthetics and Art Criticism* 45, no. 3 (1987): 275.
35. Wright, "Structure and Significance," 275.
36. Gilio, this volume, 93.
37. Gilio, this volume, 156.
38. The subject is discussed in Marcia B. Hall, "Michelangelo's *Last Judgment:* Resurrection of the Body and Predestination," *Art Bulletin* 58, no. 1 (1976): 85–92. See, more recently, Marcia B. Hall, "Introduction," in *Michelangelo's "Last Judgment,"* ed. Marcia B. Hall (Cambridge: Cambridge University Press, 2005), 1–50.
39. Gilio, this volume, 172.
40. Gilio, this volume, 196.
41. Gilio, this volume, 144.
42. Julian Gardner, review of *Federico Borromeo and the Ambrosiana,* by Pamela Jones, *Journal of Ecclesiastical History* 45, no. 1 (1994): 179–80.
43. Jones, *Federico Borromeo,* 31.
44. Gilio, this volume, 229.
45. Simon Ditchfield, "What Was Sacred History? (Mostly Roman) Catholic Uses of the Christian Past after Trent," in *Sacred History: Uses of the Christian Past in the Renaissance World,* ed. Katherine Van Liere, Simon Ditchfield, and Howard Louthan (Oxford: Oxford University Press, 2012), 96–97.
46. Gabriele Paleotti, *Discourse on Sacred and Profane Images,* trans. William McCuaig (Los Angeles: Getty Research Institute, 2012), 128.
47. Paleotti, *Discourse,* 115, also 117, 217. Paolo Prodi, in his introduction to the English translation of the *Discourse* (16), points to the "tension . . . in Paleotti's work toward a conception of painting as the visual narrative, both rational and

critical, of sacred history, as the interpretation of both the Bible and the tradition," which comes from his collaboration with the historian Carlo Sigonio.

48. Gilio, this volume, 228. On Gregory of Nyssa in the sixteenth century, see Giuseppe Scavizzi, *The Controversy on Images from Calvin to Baronius* (New York: Peter Lang, 1992), 85, 97n129.
49. Gregory of Nyssa, "Prologue," *Commentary on the Song of Songs*, translated and discussed in Michael Azkoul, *St. Gregory of Nyssa and the Tradition of the Fathers* (Lewiston, NY: Edwin Mellen Press, 1995), 172.
50. Gilio, this volume, 116. Celia Chazelle, "Memory, Instruction, Worship: 'Gregory's' Influence on Early Medieval Doctrines of the Artistic Image," in *Gregory the Great: A Symposium,* ed. John C. Cavadini (Notre Dame, IN: University of Notre Dame Press, 1995), 181–215.
51. Mary Carruthers, *The Craft of Thought: Meditation, Rhetoric, and the Making of Images, 400–1200* (Cambridge: Cambridge University Press, 1998), 165–66.
52. O'Malley, *Trent,* 93.
53. My emphasis. *Decrees of the Ecumenical Councils,* vol. 2, *Trent to Vatican II,* ed. and trans. Norman P. Tanner (Washington, D.C.: Georgetown University Press, 1990), 663; Tanner references 2 Thessalonians 2:14: "hold the traditions which you have learned, whether by word, or by our epistle."
54. Hubert Jedin, *A History of the Council of Trent,* vol. 2, *The First Sessions at Trent 1545–47,* trans. Dom Ernest Graf (St. Louis, MO: B. Herder Book Co., 1961), 92: "Instead of defining the content of the current of Tradition by listing individual traditions, the decree connects it with the uninterrupted succession of the officials of the Church (*continua successione*) whilst its authority . . . was given parity with that of Scripture." O'Malley (*Trent,* 97) reminds us that it is important to note that the Council "spoke not of Tradition, that is, of some global category of transmission, but only of traditions, in the plural." See also Joseph Ratzinger, "On the Interpretation of the Tridentine Decree on Tradition," in Karl Rahner and Joseph Ratzinger, *Revelation and Tradition,* trans. W. J. O'Hara (Freiburg: Herder, 1966), 50–66.
55. Richard R. Gaillardetz, "The Reception of Doctrine: New Perspectives," in *Authority in the Roman Catholic Church: Theory and Practice,* ed. Bernard Hoose (Aldershot: Ashgate, 2002), 95.
56. *Acta Ecclesiae Mediolanensis,* 2 Colossians 278, quoted and discussed in Ditchfield, "What Was Sacred History?," 87.
57. Gilio, this volume, 230.
58. O'Malley, *Trent,* 98.
59. Simon Ditchfield, *Liturgy, Sanctity, and History in Tridentine Italy: Pietro Maria Campi and the Preservation of the Particular* (Cambridge: Cambridge University Press, 1995), 273.
60. Eric W. Cochrane, *Historians and Historiography in the Italian Renaissance* (Chicago: University of Chicago Press, 1981), 463.
61. Simon Ditchfield, "'Historia Magistra Sanctitatis'? The Relationship between Historiography and Hagiography in Italy after the Council of Trent (ca. 1564–1742)," *Studies in Medieval and Renaissance History* 3 (2006): 160.

62. In 1522 the Benedictine monk and future cardinal Gregorio Cortesi had recommended history over theology because the Lutherans were attacking that which to Catholics had "consistently been received and passed on, obviously with divine inspiration." Discussed in Cochrane, *Historians and Historiography,* 457.
63. Simon Ditchfield (*Liturgy, Sanctity, and History,* 277–78) points to the lack of popular success of the *Magdeburg Centuries:* it was "the Lutheran indifference to history and its corresponding emphasis on scripture" that led to only two editions, whereas Cesare Baronio's work was still being reprinted in the nineteenth century; see also Cochrane, *Historians and Historiography,* 462.
64. Ditchfield (*Liturgy, Sanctity, and History,* 282) discusses Konrad Braun, *Adversus novam historiam ecclesiasticam quam Mathias Illyricus et eius Collegae Magdeburgici per centurias nuper ediderunt . . . admonitio Catholica* (Dillingen: Sebald Mayer, 1565).
65. Cyriac K. Pullapilly, *Caesar Baronius: Counter-Reformation Historian* (Notre Dame, IN: University of Notre Dame Press, 1975), 166.
66. Ditchfield, *Liturgy, Sanctity, and History,* 283–85.
67. Cesare Baronio, *Annales Ecclesiastici,* vol. 1 (Antwerp: Plantin, 1589), 33; the translation is in Ditchfield, *Liturgy, Sanctity, and History,* 283. See also the essays in Romeo De Maio et al., eds., *Baronio e l'arte: Atti del Convegno Internazionale di Studi, Sora, 10–13 ottobre 1984* (Sora: Centro di Studi Sorani Vincenzo Patriarca, 1985).
68. "La Chiesa di Dio, la quale altro non è, che la congregatione di quelli, che hanno la vera fede di Christo; cosi è sempre state la medesima, e in ogni tempo una sola, come una sola è la fede, un solo è Christo, e un solo è Dio": Francesco Panigarola, *Il compendio de gli Annales ecclesiastici del Padre Cesare Baronio* (Rome: Gigliotto, 1590), 1, translated in Cochrane, *Historians and Historiography,* 461.
69. Ditchfield, *Liturgy, Sanctity, and History,* 285.
70. Ronald Corthell, "Robert Persons and the Writer's Mission," in *Catholicism and Anti-Catholicism in Early Modern English Texts,* ed. Arthur F. Marotti (London: Macmillan, 1999), 35.
71. A tricky term, *magisterium* before the nineteenth century referred to *magistri* (masters) and the many parts of the Church, including the universities, that made up its collective authority, embodied by the pope *in capite et in membris.* See Hugh Lawrence, "Spiritual Authority and Governance: A Historical Perspective," in *Authority in the Roman Catholic Church: Theory and Practice,* ed. Bernard Hoose (Aldershot: Ashgate, 2002), 52.
72. John Henry Newman, *Apologia pro vita sua* (London: Longmans, Green & Co., 1929), 265; discussed in Lawrence, "Spiritual Authority and Governance," 54.
73. John Henry Newman, *A Letter Addressed to His Grace the Duke of Norfolk on Occasion of Mr. Gladstone's Recent Expostulation* (London: B. M. Pickering, 1875), 121. Newman was primarily concerned with the implications of papal infallibility declared at the first Vatican Council in 1870, discussed in Paul Parvis, "Guardian Angels and Carrotburgers: Two Views of the Role of the Magisterium," *New Blackfriars* 71, no. 841 (1990): 368–69: "Newman's two kinds of statements bind in very different ways. A negative statement—a condemned proposition, an anathema—tells the theologian what he must not say. A positive statement, however,

does not tell him what he *must* say; it only tells him what he *may* say. It provides a model, a pattern, of an appropriate way of talking. It supplies a vocabulary or commends a style."

74. Lawrence, "Spiritual Authority and Governance," 56.
75. Hellmut Wohl, *The Aesthetics of Italian Renaissance Art: A Reconsideration of Style* (Cambridge: Cambridge University Press, 1999), 58.
76. Wohl, *Aesthetics of Italian Renaissance Art,* 210.
77. Gilio, this volume, 156.
78. Gilio, this volume, 230.
79. Gilio, this volume, 235.
80. Gilio, this volume, 87.

LUCINDA BYATT

GILIO'S TEXT AND THE ENGLISH TRANSLATION

There are well-charted reefs to be navigated regarding the translation of historical texts, and the decision of which bearing to follow is usually dictated by its intended purpose and its readership. Having agreed that Giovanni Andrea Gilio's *Dialogo secondo nel quale si ragiona degli errori, e degli abusi de' pittori circa l'istorie* (1564; Dialogue on the errors and abuses of painters) would primarily be a university teaching text, Michael Bury and I also assumed that the readership would be broadly concerned with Gilio's *Dialogo* not as a literary work or for philological analysis but rather for its art-historical significance. Nonetheless, a balancing act is required to produce a readable text that also respects the original and that in some instances retains some of the characteristics of the dialogue, not to mention the voices of the individual speakers.

Dictionaries Used in the Translation

For the translator, dictionaries form the basic tools of the trade. One of the earliest bilingual Italian-to-English dictionaries was compiled by the Italian exile John Florio. It was printed twice in London: at the end of Elizabeth's reign, in 1598, under the title *A Worlde of Wordes;* and again in 1611 with a new title that reflects the dynastic change and the specific, and innovative, nature of the volume: *Queen Anna's New World of Words; or, Dictionarie of the Italian and English Tongues.*[1] Offering a rich variety of definitions, Florio is enlightening, often entertaining. Both editions of his work have been made available online. A critical edition, with an introduction by Hermann W. Haller, was also published in 2013.[2] Another key resource for translators, the Accademia della Crusca portal, offered us a range of tools, including first, second, and third editions of the *Vocabolario* (1612, 1623, and 1691), the monolingual dictionary compiled by academicians.[3] One subject-specific dictionary was also used for this translation: Filippo Baldinucci's *Vocabolario toscano dell'arte del disegno,* published in 1681.[4] Baldinucci became well known as a connoisseur, writer, and member of the Accademia della Crusca, and it is to that institution that his dictionary is dedicated.[5] Overlooking the fact that Baldinucci describes his own work as a "wretched, unformed product of my pen" (misero aborto della mia penna), the *Vocabolario toscano* provides useful definitions of specialized terms.[6] Two later dictionaries proved particularly useful because of the broader range of literary sources cited, including occasionally Gilio's *Due dialogi.*[7] The first of these is the *Dizionario della lingua italiana,* largely the work of Niccolò Tommaseo, whose first volume appeared in Turin in 1861—significantly, the year of Italy's unification.[8] The second and undoubtedly most complete reference instrument is the *Grande dizionario della lingua italiana,* or *GDLI,* founded by Salvatore Battaglia and published in twenty-one volumes between 1961 and 2002. Both works are often referred to by their lead author's name: the Tommaseo is available online through the Accademia della Crusca portal, while the Battaglia volumes are in major libraries.[9] Lastly, it is worth mentioning the collaboration between the present-day Accademia della Crusca and various institutions, including the Fondazione Memofonte. That collaboration has produced a valuable monolingual corpus of the terminology used in a range of art treatises written during the sixteenth century, including Gilio's *Dialogo.*[10]

The Printed Text

Our source text is the transcription made by Paola Barocchi from the editio princeps of Giovanni Andrea Gilio's second dialogue, *Dialogo . . . degli errori e degli abusi de' pittori,* printed in Camerino, in the Marches, by Antonio Gioioso in 1564, and dedicated to Cardinal Alessandro Farnese.[11] In a philological note, Barocchi comments on the "modest typographical skill" demonstrated by the Camerino editors of Gilio's work, who lacked the support of correctors who were well trained in grammar, such as those who might have worked on the text had it been printed in Venice or Florence.[12] All the "errori," or *errata corrige,* noted on folios 143v–144r of the 1564 edition, were corrected by Barocchi.[13] Likewise, where the misspelled *Crucifisso* and *sustanza* appeared in the original, Barocchi amended them to *Crocifisso* and *sostanza.* Barocchi also introduced modern orthography (*abbiamo* instead of *habbiamo,* for example).

However, other oddities commented on in the 1564 text have remained: on folio 144r, the printer refers to errors of "transposed and substituted letters" (traspogitione e mutatione di lettere). Here the error is compounded, since the word used to point out that letters have been transposed is itself misspelled (*traspogitione* instead of *traspositione*).[14] This example may reinforce the notion that the printer used local typesetters who were possibly careless or influenced by the local Marchigiano dialect. Equally, mistakes of this kind may have been caused by the typesetters' misreadings of Gilio's manuscript: *propogito* instead of *proposito* is the most frequent; additional examples are *indivigibile* instead of *indivisibile* and *compogitione* instead of *compositione.* Other errors, like *fengi* or the past participle *fento* (instead of *fingi* and *finto*), or *debbe* for *dovette,* may have been introduced by Gilio himself.[15] Dialectal forms appear as either the aspirates of the Tuscan dialect or the softer pronunciation of *falzo, consienza,* and even Messer "Vincenso" (in our translation, this spelling has been retained instead of Vincenzo). Another proper name that is possibly influenced by dialectal pronunciation is Pulidoro. Polidoro would be the normal form of this name, but in the 1564 edition the simple vowel *o* becomes a *u,* a dialectal usage remarked on by Wilhelm Meyer-Lübke.[16] The Roman emperor's name Augusto is misspelled as "Agusto," and the well-known late fifteenth-century literary text is referred to as *Hipernotomachia* rather than *Hypnerotomachia.*[17] What the learned Gilio made of such blunders is not known. His opinion regarding the written supremacy of the Tuscan language is expressed in the first of the *Dialogi,* although, as Brian Richardson adds, he did concede that spoken versions of Italian varied from region to region.[18] Notwithstanding this, typographical errors abound, despite the fact that Gilio warned his printers, in a roundabout way, to pay attention, by making Messer Silvio, the cautious lawyer, quote Horace's insistence on rewriting one's work ten times: "I do not place the painter in any better position than the writer, who, according to Horace, should not publish his work without having made many corrections [*cassature*] and changed it ten times."[19] *Cassatura,* according to John Florio (1598), means "a crossing out of any writing, a casheering."[20]

Little is known of the printing works that produced these texts. The owner, Antonio Gioioso, was himself a native of Camerino and returned there from Naples in June 1550 to run the printing press, a position he held for the next twenty-seven years.[21] A relatively small number of works emerged from the press in Camerino prior to Gioioso's death in 1577, and the most successful may have been Gilio's *Due dialogi.*[22] On the frontispiece of several of the existing copies of the text appears Gioioso's printing device: a six-pointed comet whose sparks fall onto a burning fire from which two upright branches emerge, one an olive and the other a palm, the whole within a figured frame with anthropomorphized horned heads.[23]

Nothing has emerged to explain why Gilio decided to send the book to Gioioso. Was it indicative of the pride that Gilio took in his native Marche, and more particularly Fabriano? Was it a question of convenience, since a local printer might have been cheaper and quicker? In his letter to the reader, Gioioso makes a point of stating that the book has been printed to "please the many gentle spirits (who urged me to do so)"—so were friends of Gilio, rather than

Gilio himself, instrumental in arranging the publication?[24] Whatever the reason for using Gioioso, Gilio's work was indeed printed by a "local" printer—albeit from Camerino—rather than a larger publisher elsewhere, despite all Gilio's aspirations and despite his dedication to the powerful Farnese cardinal.

The significance of the choice of Cardinal Alessandro as the dedicatee remains intriguing, and although discussed further by Michael Bury and Carol M. Richardson in their essays in this volume, nothing is known about whether Gilio ever asked permission to dedicate the *Due dialogi* to him, or indeed where, when, and how the book was eventually delivered to the cardinal. It seems virtually impossible that Gilio would have presented it in person; the work may simply have been dispatched, or presented by a third party, possibly one of those "gentle spirits" or someone known to them. Would the book have arrived as a single copy, or were two or three presented in the hope of further patronage? Brian Richardson notes that it was normal to request permission and subsequently to send dedicatees and other favored recipients a copy, often specially bound.[25] Indeed, at least one copy of Gilio's *Due dialogi* does appear to have reached the Farnese library. In 1567, two years after Fulvio Orsini had been appointed to the post of Cardinal Alessandro's librarian, he ordered the preparation of an inventory of the books then in the library.[26] This inventory includes a section on the vernacular books (the *vulgari stampati*), but disappointingly, Gilio's work is not included.[27] Its absence may not be significant: copies of books dedicated to Cardinal Alessandro may have been stored separately (or given away), considering the significant numbers of donated copies that were received. Proof that Gilio's book was present in the Farnese library eventually emerges in a later inventory of the library, dated 1653, in which it is listed as "Gilio Due dialoghi sopra la parola urbs, citta, colonie, Camerino 1564."[28] It would appear that this is the copy now in the Biblioteca Nazionale of Naples; there, the catalog records its provenance as from "Casa Farnese."

Issues of Language

Returning to a closer examination of the *Dialogo,* it does not take long for a reader of the original to realize that Gilio's word order differs significantly from modern Italian. This strongly Latinized construction takes the form of strings of subordinate clauses, as well as syntactical inversion that often places the verb at the end of the clause.[29] Examples can be found throughout the text, but the dedicatory letter to Cardinal Alessandro offers an example of this stylistic inversion combined with use of the subjunctive:

Perché quasi tutti confidano nel detto d'Orazio che al pittore et al poeta ogni cosa lecita *sia,* per mostrar loro quanto innanzi questa licenza stender *si deggia* ho fatto questo discorso, acciò chi più di me *ne sa* abbia per l'innanzi campo da currerci per ogni verso.[30]

Because nearly everyone trusts in the saying of Horace that to painters and poets everything is permitted, I have written this dialogue in order to show them how far that license should be extended, so that those who know more than me will in the future have a field marked out in which they can run in any direction.

The use of this strongly Latinized style poses the problem of how to translate this and other passages into readable English, retaining a little of the somewhat solemn—or, as Barocchi would have it, patristic—style of the dedicatory letter.[31]

Once the dialogue proper begins, this Latinized construction fades away to a degree, and the tenses return to a more normal pattern of past absolute (or preterit) in the narrative parts; and present, imperfect, and conditional (all indicative) in the passages of direct speech.

Passing from syntax and tense to vocabulary, an early consideration was whether to use a single English word to translate each of Gilio's key terms (the three types of painting—*misto, poetico,* and *istorico;* not to mention the significance of key terms like *favoloso, arte, artefice, capriccio,* and *decoro,* to name a few). A compromise solution was adopted: the categories of painting were always translated using the same term for consistency, but other key words were given varying translations to reflect a range of meanings. For readers with a particular interest in the translation, a glossary that identifies these variations has been added. However, one or two examples of problematic words may prove instructive. Using the dictionaries by Florio, Tommaseo, and Battaglia mentioned earlier, it was usually possible to tease out a solution. The following passage, in which Messer Silvio is talking about his professional activities as a lawyer, helps illustrate this.

"Voi mi darete un carico non convenevole a le mie forze, e molto meglio di me M. Francesco ve lo potrebbe dipingere e dechiarare, dilettandosi egli de l'istorie e di simili galanterie; ché la mia professione è più di gire per i palazzo sollecitando le cause, formare i libelli, sbolgettar paragrafi e leggi, che studiar Plinio e gli altri che di ciò hanno scritto."[32]

"You place on me a burden unsuited to my powers, and M. Francesco could set it out and explain it much better, because he delights in histories and other such elegant things. My profession is to go round the palaces pleading cases, drawing up summonses, and proffering articles and laws, not studying Pliny and those others who have written on the subject."

Two phrases are worth singling out: "galanterie" and "sbolgettar paragrafi e leggi." Tommaseo, for *galanteria,* cites Benedetto Varchi's definition: "Elegance, or fineness, because this word gallantness [*galantería*] is not yet used by good writers."[33] In short, although not used by "good" writers, the term was synonymous with "elegance, refinement" or what Florentines termed, in common parlance, *galante,* the essence of a *galantuomo.* Florio suggests this translation: "gallantnesse, handsomnesse, propernesse, gracefulnesse, decencie."[34] Our translation opted for "elegant things" to pair up with "histories." As for the second phrase, "sbolgettar paragrafi e leggi": a *bolgia* may mean bag or pocket, so *sbolgettare* can signify, according to Florio, "to pull out of one's pocket." Used here by Messer Silvio, *sbolgettare* becomes "proffering articles and laws," which retains an idea of to pull out, or to "shew foorth," as Florio puts it.[35]

In other instances, some idiomatic expressions—such as "non ci date più martello" and "a voi tocca questa fava"—have undoubtedly lost something in translation, but a more idiomatic rendering might have sounded forced or too anachronistic. "Don't bang on" might have worked for the former and "you've pulled the short straw" for the latter, but accusations of anachronism would probably have swiftly followed. The translations ultimately adopted are more subdued; perhaps they lose color and association, but they seem more appropriate and identify more specific meanings. For "non ci date più martello," the translation "don't torment us further" preserves what is arguably the original sense of the phrase, with reference to the Passion. Two slightly different meanings were identified for the phrase "a voi tocca questa fava," meaning—as Florio points out—"it falles to your lot."[36] Other words and expressions have been included in the glossary if they appear more than once or if they merit particular explanation.

Setting the Scene

Details about the setting of the *Dialogo* can be gleaned by looking at some of the ways in which Gilio sets the scene for the discussion between his six characters. In this respect, the question of the timing of the discussion and above all the sequence of the meals mentioned offers an insight into the context of the dialogue. The six young men meet outside Fabriano, close to the river Giano, at the paper mills (referred to as the *valchiere*), belonging to Messer Giovan Bernardino Santi (possibly related to one of the participants, Francesco Santi). Having decided to enjoy the long-awaited fine weather, the young men order the servants to prepare supper (*cena*).[37] That this is an evening meal becomes clear from the fact that, before going out, the group proceeds to eat lunch (*desinare*). Having eaten at around eleven in the morning, the whole of the afternoon would then have been at their disposition for the discussion. We are informed at the start of the *Dialogo* that the sun is nearing the end of Aries; therefore, by, say, mid-April, the days would already have been quite long.[38] Much later in the *Dialogo,* Messer Francesco refers to the height of the sun in the sky as an indication that there is still some time before the evening meal.[39] This clarifies the amount of time spent outside and the order of meals—first lunch and then the evening meal. Sadly, though, there is no further description of any food, whether actually eaten, or even any mention of what might be on the menu for dinner. The end of the *Dialogo* is disappointingly abrupt and the discussion breaks off with no hint of anticipation of the evening meal, let alone a suggestion that they all enjoy a glass of wine after all that talking.

Another comment might be made on the setting and in particular on Gilio's numerous descriptions of the plants and trees. After a long and exceptionally severe winter, the worst in living memory, spring had finally arrived. At the start of the *Dialogo,* the red, white, and green of the valley drew many of the citizens outside, including Gilio's group of six young men. The men leave the paper mills and go out into what is described as a garden (*giardino*), where they admire the red and white roses. The author seems at pains to emphasize the pleasure given to the senses: the sound of the birds and the river, as well as the sight, smell, and touch of the flowers.[40] (Taste is missing, but the group has already eaten and, as mentioned earlier, nothing more is said about food and drink.) While in the garden, Messer Pulidoro—the doctor of medicine—uses the roses and other perfumed flowers as visual prompts to refer to the classical author Dioscorides and to Pietro Andrea Mattioli's commentaries on the latter. On leaving this garden, the men stroll into a fine meadow (*bel prato*) where they sit down by the river, in the shade of oaks and other trees.[41]

The allusion to classical and bucolic settings is manifest. Gilio refers to a wide range of classical authors, but the actual quotations he gives are usually in Italian. This poses a problem. For example, *Ars Poetica,* by Gilio's most cited author, Horace, had been translated into Italian by Lodovico Dolce in 1535. However, the verses quoted by Gilio do not follow Dolce's translation, suggesting that he was either translating from his own remembered version of Horace or translating afresh from an actual copy of Horace's text that he had at hand. Moreover, Gilio's translation into Italian is more sober than Dolce's, but he too cannot resist adding an extra adjective on occasion (here, *orridi*):

Horace
Scimus, et hanc ueniam petimusque damusque vicissim; sed non
ut placidis coeant immitia, non ut serpentes avibus geminentur,
tigribus agni.[42]

Dolce
"E l'istesso perdono hor l'uno hor l'altro
Chiedemo a concedemoci a vicenda:
Ma non però, che facciam gir di pari
Le cose, che son'aspre e fiere a quelle,
che fierezza e asprezza in se non hanno:
Non, ch'agli Uccei si giungono i Serpenti:
E a le Tigri i mansueti Agnelli."[43]

Gilio
"Lo sappiamo ancor noi e diamo spesso
Questa licenza ad altri e per noi stessi
La dimandiamo; non ch'i mansueti
Animai si congiungan coi feroci
E con gli augelli gli orridi serpenti
S'accompagnano, e i tigri con gli agnelli."[44]

In our translation, in all cases where Gilio quotes in Italian from classical sources, and in order to retain the idiosyncrasy of his own phrasing,[45] we have followed his Italian translation instead of using published English translations of the classical passage.

Gilio's own verses are interesting. This *Dialogo secondo* contains a *canzone,* or song, in the form of a love poem or eulogy of the river Giano on whose banks the discussion takes place.[46] Gilio attributes the work to himself—and Messer Francesco Santi, who is described as "a well-mannered young person, both man of letters [*letterato*] and merchant"—happens to have a copy in his pocket.[47] Santi gives it to Messer Silvio Gilio, who proceeds to read it aloud. We are informed that the *canzone* was written for the archbishop of Siena, Francesco Bandini Piccolomini, on the occasion of a visit to Fabriano, possibly in 1552.[48] Whether it was sung on that occasion, or again read, is not stated. However, all those present remembered the poem and remarked on not having heard it for some time. Moreover, as noted above, Santi had a copy of the *canzone* in his pocket. All these details support the idea that the personages named in the group were known to Gilio and were occasional, if not regular, companions.

Some years after the publication of the *Due dialogi,* Gilio's *Topica poetica* (1580) was produced in Venice, printed by Oratio de' Gobbi.[49] It was dedicated to another influential figure, Giacomo Buoncompagni, Duke of Sora and son of the reigning pope, Gregory XIII, indicating that Gilio was still seeking to give the widest scope to his views—as he had done by dedicating the *Due dialogi* to Cardinal Alessandro. In the dedication Gilio praises the classical poets, of course, but also the Tuscans: Dante Alighieri and Petrarch, as well as Pietro Bembo ("true father of the Tuscan language" [*vero padre della Toscana lingua*]), Ludovico Ariosto, Giulio Camillo, Lodovico Dolce, Girolamo Ruscelli, Francesco Sansovino, Jacopo Sannazzaro, and Claudio Tolomei. The reliance on Horace's *Ars Poetica* has already been noted with regard to the *Dialogo,* but in *Topica poetica* Gilio seems to make an independent claim for the compelling power of verse: "There is no doubting that verse has great power to move."[50] Somewhat pretentiously, Gilio claims that although the poets "of our time" (*a tempi nostri*) have written quite well (*assai bene*) about the power of poetry, his aim in *Topica poetica* is to go further and show the link between poetry and place.[51] Indeed, at the end of *Topica poetica,* Gilio includes a series of sonnets written by three female poets from the Marches (contemporaries of Petrarch), which he compares to the sonnets of greater perfection and beauty written by Vittoria Colonna, marchioness of Pescara.[52]

The Art of Translation

It is illuminating to note that Gilio compares the artist to the translator on numerous occasions in the *Dialogo.* In doing so, he is guided, again, by Horace and by two Christian translators, Saint Jerome, who had much to say on the activity, and Saint Isidore.[53] At a key point in the *Dialogo,* Gilio sets the "historical" painter in parallel to Horace's precept that "He lies who mixes the false and the true." In the words of Messer Silvio, Gilio then extends this to the translator, stating that "the historical painter is nothing other than a translator who translates history from one language into another; that is, from the language of the pen into that of the brush, from writing into painting."[54] This form of artistic translation, from the written to the visual, must be faithful, or else it runs the risk of being derided or causing somnolent boredom: "And if one does not translate faithfully, blame follows and one becomes worthy of derision—or of sleep, as Horace said."[55]

However, when dealing with nonfactual, unhistorical events, a different technique is required. Messer Silvio also backs this point of view and is even more specific when he points out that, unlike a faithful interpreter for whom retaining trust and delivering a precise oral message was often a matter of life or death, a translator may, like the artist, take more license. Here, Messer Ruggiero appears to contradict the view that a translator may take more license. He gives the more prescriptive view and states that "Horace did not mean to say that the translator should pay attention to the intention of the author rather than to his words, because imitation is one thing, translation something else."[56] In this sense, the translator should not slavishly translate the work word for word, a precept that reflected the modus operandi adopted by both Saint Jerome and Saint Isidore,[57] "[f]or while the altering of unimportant nonessential elements is of no significance, to infect the substance is an inexcusable error."[58]

This brings me back to the difficulties of translating historical texts—or, one might say, translation tout court. A literal translation, albeit plodding, would allow readers to understand the individual words, but it would struggle to convey a fuller sense of the overall text. Instead, this translation has endeavored to render Gilio's more subtle meanings by following Pulidoro's advice that "[w]hat is not understood cannot be reflected on, and what is not reflected on cannot be judged."[59] In doing so, like the artists whom Gilio chastens with the words of Horace as they move from quill to brush, from ink to paint, the translator must be equally cautious moving from one language to another. Working alongside Michael Bury on the translation of Gilio's second dialogue has been an immense privilege. I hope that our translation will come as close as possible to that elusive and balanced goal of a "regulated mixture" (*regolata mescolanza*)[60] and succeed in conveying the original spirit of the text while at the same time bringing a readable English version of this important work to a wider audience.

Notes

1. John Florio, *A Worlde of Wordes; or, Most Copious and Exact Dictionarie in Italian and English* (London: Printed by Arnold Hatfield for Edw. Blount, 1598); and John Florio, *Queen Anna's New World of Words; or, Dictionarie of the Italian and English Tongues* (London: Printed by Melch. Bradwood, for Edw. Blount and William Barret, 1611).
2. John Florio, *A Worlde of Wordes: A Critical Edition,* ed. Hermann W. Haller (Toronto: University of Toronto Press, 2013).
3. For the "Scaffali digitali" portal, see http://www.accademiadellacrusca.it/it/scaffali-digitali/. The editions of the *Vocabolario* are available at http://www.lessicografia.it/.
4. Filippo Baldinucci, *Vocabolario toscano dell'arte del disegno* (Florence: Santi Franchi al Segno della Passione, 1681).
5. See Sergio Samek Ludovici, "Baldinucci, Filippo," *Dizionario Biografico degli Italiani* [*DBI*], 5 (1963), http://www.treccani.it/biografie/.
6. Baldinucci, dedication to the academicians of the Crusca, in *Vocabolario toscano,* vi. Unless otherwise indicated, all translations are mine.

7. Salvatore Battaglia cites Gilio, for example, in the description of Saint Francis, dressed in a cowl that is described as being made "di finissimo panno tutta falduta," all pleated. Salvatore Battaglia, *Grande dizionario della lingua italiana* [*GDLI*], vol. 5, ed. Salvatore Battaglia and Giorgio Bárberi Squarotti (Turin: Unione tipografico-editrice torinese, 1968), 590, citing Giovanni Andrea Gilio, *Dialogo nel quale si ragiona degli errori e degli abusi de' pittori circa l'istorie,* in *Trattati d'arte del Cinquecento: Fra manierismo e controriforma,* vol. 2, ed. Paola Barocchi (Bari: Laterza, 1961), 33. See also Giovanni Andrea Gilio, *Due dialogi . . . Nel primo de' quali si ragiona de le parti morali e civili appertenenti a' letterati cortigiani, et ad ogni gentil'huomo, e l'utile che i prencipi cavano dai letterati. Nel secondo si ragiona degli errori de' pittori circa l'historie* (Camerino: Antonio Gioioso, 1564; reprint, Florence: S.P.E.S., 1986).
8. Niccolò Tommaseo and Bernardo Bellini, *Dizionario della lingua italiana,* 8 vols. (Turin: L'Unione, 1861–74).
9. *Tommaseo Online,* http://www.tommaseobellini.it/.
10. *Trattati d'arte del Cinquecento,* http://memofonte.accademiadellacrusca.org/index.asp.
11. Gilio, *Dialogo . . . degli errori e degli abusi de' pittori,* in Barocchi, *Trattati,* 2:1–115. Barocchi's text is also available online through the Fondazione Memofonte; http://www.memofonte.it/trattati/giovanni-andrea-gilio.html.
12. Paola Barocchi, "Nota filologica," in *Trattati d'arte del Cinquecento: Fra manierismo e controriforma,* vol. 2, ed. Paola Barocchi (Bari: Laterza, 1961), 545. Another work by Gilio was indeed published in Venice, in 1563: *Trattato de la emulatione che il demonio ha fatto a Dio* (Venice: Francesco de' Franceschi, 1563). This work was dedicated to Cardinal Alessandro's sister, Vittoria Farnese, Duchess of Urbino.
13. I have referred to the digitized copy of Gilio's *Due dialogi* from Österreichische Nationalbibliothek, Vienna, which is available online. See http://digital.onb.ac.at/. The *Dialogo secondo nel quale si ragiona degli errori, e degli abusi de' pittori circa l'historie* can be found on fols. 69r–122v.
14. In the second half of the sixteenth century, orthography continued to be a focus of bitter debate. The Tuscans abandoned the Latin nexus *-ti* followed by a noun (examples of which are still present here: *transpositione, mutatione, compositione, gratia*) and instead adopted the use of the phonetic <*ts*>/*-z* (as in *tranposizione,* etc.). See Bruno Migliorini, *Storia della lingua italiana* (Florence: Sansoni, 1960), 383.
15. See Francesco Bruni's excellent note on the linguistic aspects of Gilio's work; Bruni, "Nota linguistica," in Giovanni Andrea Gilio, *Dialogo del letterato cortigiano,* ed. Paolo Cherchi (Ravenna: Longo, 2002), 23–35 (esp. 27).
16. Francesco D'Ovidio and Wilhelm Meyer-Lübke, *Grammatica storica della lingua e dei dialetti italiani,* trans. Eugenio Polcari (Milan: Tipografia Umberto Allegretti, 1906), 193.
17. Francesco Colonna, *Hypnerotomachia Poliphili* (Venice: Aldo Manuzio, 1499).
18. Giovanni Andrea Gilio, *Dialogo de le parti morali appertenenti a' letterati cortigiani, et ad ogni altro gentil'huomo,* in his *Due dialogi* (Camerino:

Antonio Gioioso, 1564; reprint, Florence: S.P.E.S., 1986), fol. 40r, cited by Brian Richardson, "The Concept of a *Lingua Comune* in Renaissance Italy," in *Languages of Italy: Histories and Dictionaries,* ed. Anna Laura Lepschy and Arturo Tosi (Ravenna: Longo, 2007), 11–28, esp. 23–24 and 23n46.

19. Gilio, this volume, 120. For the Italian, see Gilio, *Dialogo . . . degli errori e degli abusi de' pittori,* in Barocchi, *Trattati,* 2:29.
20. Florio, *Worlde of Wordes* (1598), 62.
21. Dennis E. Rhodes, "Notable Acquisitions *1975–1985: Italian Books 1501–1600,*" *The British Library Journal* 12, no. 1 (1986): 95. See also Vittorio Emanuele Aleandri, *La stampa degli statuti di Camerino e il tipografo Antonio Gioioso* (Camerino: Tipografia Savini, 1902); and Michele Santoni, "L'arte della stampa in Camerino: Appendice a Bibliografia storica marchigiana," *Atti e memorie della R. Deputazione di storia patria per le Marche* 6 (1903): 95–102.
22. On Antonio Gioioso, see Carla Casetti Brach, "Gioioso, Antonio," *DBI,* 55 (2001). Gioioso also published a work by the renowned Veronese polymath Girolamo Fracastoro titled *De temperatura vini sententia* (Camerino: Antonio Gioioso, 1553).
23. *CERL Thesaurus,* s.v. "Gioioso, Antonio," http://thesaurus.cerl.org/record/cni00020925. Of the numerous existing copies, those at the Biblioteca Nazionale Centrale of Florence, the Biblioteca Universitaria Alessandrina in Rome, the Biblioteca Nazionale of Naples, the British Library, and the Österreichische Nationalbibliothek in Vienna have been examined.
24. "ho volute a compiacenza di molti gentili spiriti (che accio pregato m'hanno) mandare a le stampe questa opera di M. Giovanni Andrea..." Giovanni Andrea Gilio, "Antonio Gioioso stampatore, À li lettori," in *Due dialogi,* unfoliated preliminary verso page.
25. Brian Richardson, *Manuscript Culture in Renaissance Italy* (Cambridge: Cambridge University Press, 2014), 219–20. I would like to thank the author for his advice on this point.
26. This is cited in Paul Oskar Kristeller, *Iter italicum: Accedunt alia itinera; A Finding List of Uncatalogued or Incompletely Catalogued Humanistic Manuscripts of the Renaissance in Italian and Other Libraries,* vol. 6, *(Italy 3 and alia itinera 4), Supplement to Italy (G–V), Supplement to Vatican and Austria to Spain* (London: Warburg Institute, 1992), 99. For Fulvio Orsini, see Raphaële Mouren, "La Bibliothèque du Palais Farnèse avant Fulvio Orsini," *Mélanges de l'École française de Rome: Italie et Méditerranée* 107, no. 1 (1995): 7–14; and Federica Matteini, "Orsini, Fulvio," *DBI*, 79 (2013).
27. "Inventario autografo di F. Orsini di manoscritti e libri farnesiani consegnati al suddetto Fulvio orsini nel 1567 e 1589," *Carte Farnesiane* busta 1853/1, fols. 36r–79r (vernacular books, 77r–79r), Archivio di Stato, Naples.
28. François-Charles Uginet et al., *Le Palais Farnèse* (Rome: École française de Rome, 1981), vol. 1, pt. 2, p. 418.
29. Bruni, "Nota linguistica," 31–32.
30. Gilio, *Dialogo . . . degli errori e degli abusi de' pittori,* in Barocchi, *Trattati,* 2:3 (my italics); and Gilio, this volume, 86.
31. Barocchi, *Trattati,* 2:570, n2 to Gilio p. 4.

32. Gilio, *Dialogo . . . degli errori e degli abusi de' pittori,* in Barocchi, *Trattati,* 2:23–24; and Gilio, this volume, 114.
33. "Eleganza, ovvero leggiadria, poichè questo vocabolo galantería non è usato ancora dai buoni scrittori." Niccolò Tommaseo and Bernardo Bellini, *Dizionario della lingua italiana* (Turin: L'Unione, 1869), vol. 2, pt. 2, pp. 987–88.
34. Florio, *Queen Anna's New World of Words* (1611), 202. In the earlier edition, a shorter definition is given for *galanteria:* "gallantnes, bravenes, handsomnes, decencie, a good grace" (Florio, *Worlde of Wordes* [1598], 142).
35. Florio, *Queen Anna's New World of Words* (1611), 467.
36. Florio, *Worlde of Wordes* (1598), 423.
37. Gilio, this volume, 89, 89n14.
38. Gilio, this volume, 88.
39. Gilio, this volume, 198.
40. Gilio, this volume, 88–89.
41. Gilio, *Dialogo . . . degli errori e degli abusi de' pittori,* in Barocchi, *Trattati,* 2:6; and Gilio, this volume, 89.
42. Horace, *Ars Poetica,* in *Satires; Epistles; The Art of Poetry,* trans. H. Rushton Fairclough, Loeb Classical Library 194 (Cambridge, MA: Harvard University Press, 1926), 450 (lines 11–13).
43. Lodovico Dolce, trans., *La poetica d'Horatio tradotta per Messer Lodovico Dolce* ([Venice], 1535), n.p.
44. Gilio, *Dialogo . . . degli errori e degli abusi de' pittori,* in Barocchi, *Trattati,* 2:18. For the English, see Gilio, this volume, 106.
45. Another example where Gilio quotes more freely in Italian from classical sources occurs in the quote from Horace, *Ars Poetica,* 452 (lines 29–30), where, based on Horace's image of dolphins among the trees and pigs in the surf, Gilio ridicules such a painter further by adding his own description of "fish in the skies and birds in the waves." Gilio, *Dialogo . . . degli errori e degli abusi de' pittori,* in Barocchi, *Trattati,* 2:18–19; and Gilio, this volume, 107.
46. Gilio, this volume, 90–92.
47. "giovine garbato, letterato e mercatante." Gilio, *Dialogo . . . degli errori e degli abusi de' pittori,* in Barocchi, *Trattati,* 2:6; and Gilio, this volume, 89.
48. See Gilio, this volume, 90n17, 150–51n188.
49. Giovanni Andrea Gilio, *Topica poetica* (Venice: Oratio de' Gobbi, 1580; facs. reprint, Munich: W. Fink, 1970). Orazio (de') Gobbi's name appears with various spellings, including, in this case, Oratio de' Gobbi.
50. "Non si può negare, che il verso non habbia gran forza a m[u]overe." Giovanni Andrea Gilio, dedication to Signor Iacomo Buoncompagno [Giacomo Buoncompagni], Duke of Sora, in Gilio, *Topica poetica,* n.p.
51. Gilio, dedication in *Topica poetica,* n.p.
52. Mercedes Arriaga Florez, "Le scrittrici marchigiane: Un giallo litterario," *Studi umanistici piceni,* 28 (2008): 161–62.
53. See, for example, Jerome, *Liber de optimo genere interpretandi (Epistula 57),* ed. G. J. M. Bartelink (Leiden: E. J. Brill, 1980); and Megan Hale Williams, *The Monk and the Book: Jerome and the Making of Christian Scholarship* (Chicago: University of Chicago Press, 2006).

54. Gilio, this volume, 132.
55. Gilio, this volume, 132.
56. Gilio, this volume, 167.
57. Gilio, this volume, 167.
58. Gilio, this volume, 167.
59. Gilio, this volume, 214.
60. Gilio, this volume, 161; and Gilio, *Dialogo . . . degli errori e degli abusi de' pittori,* in Barocchi, *Trattati,* 2:56.

DRAMATIS PERSONAE

The six interlocutors in Gilio's *Dialogo* are listed here in the order given by Gilio **[89]**.[1]

Messer Ruggiero Coradini (Corradini), Canon and Doctor

Ruggiero is the only person among the company identified as an ecclesiastic (although Vincenso Peterlino may also have been in holy orders). He is mentioned in Giuseppe Colucci's "Uomini Illustri di Fabriano."[2]

In the *Dialogo,* Ruggiero praises the artists who came before Michelangelo **[160–61, 185]**. He is invited to speak about the *Last Judgment* because the matter is ecclesiastical and theological **[157–97]**. He argues that in interpretation of subject matter, the literal meaning is to be accepted unless there are strong reasons for preferring an allegorical one **[179–80]**. Toward the end of the *Dialogo,* he is entrusted with the task of explaining how sacred paintings should be painted **[230]**: "That is a matter for men of religion, but M. Ruggiero, who reads the sacred texts, will be able to tell you." He believes rules governing sacred painting did once exist, but now are lost **[230]**.

Messer Vincenso Peterlino (Vincenzo Petrolino), Doctor of Law

Colucci mentions Vincenso in "Uomini Illustri di Fabriano": "This is that Vincenzo Petrolino, doctor of law, who Giovanni Andrea Gilio records in the second book of his dialogues on page 70."[3] Colucci gives him the title Monsignore. Vincenso was a doctor of both canon and civil law, and podestà of San Ginesio (1555). Gregory XIII appointed him bishop of Muro Lucano in the Basilicata.[4] Vincenso had a reputation for being a good lawyer and being interested in poetry. He died at Fabriano in 1606 and was buried in the church of Santa Lucia. He, along with Giovanni Andrea Gilio himself, contributed to a group of poems celebrating the Magdalene of Gentile da Fabriano.[5] Romualdo Sassi, who published these poems, spells his name "Petrollini."[6]

In the *Dialogo,* Vincenso distinguishes the different types of painting **[100–104]**. He takes on the task of describing the poetic painter **[104–14]**, admitting license for the poetic painter [101] but with limits of verisimilitude [106–7]. He approves of the regulation of painters [104; 107; 112]. He praises Michelangelo [199] but comments on the risible movement of the Madonna in the Cesi Chapel in Santa Maria della Pace, Rome [235].

Messer Troilo Mattioli, Also a Doctor (of Law)

Troilo Mattioli contributed to a group of poems celebrating the Magdalene of Gentile da Fabriano, to which Gilio also contributed.[7]

Troilo is chosen to discuss abuses [121—he effectively continues this until 140; Pulidoro says he has heard Troilo talking about abuses before, 121] and the representation of God [127–28]. He asks why in Passion scenes Christ is not represented as broken, wounded [133–37]. Troilo reports on having talked with artists; however, he strongly denounces the vanity of men [137]. He explains the importance of viewers being moved by sacred images [136]. He argues in favor of some license for historical painters: "Well, I think you are splitting hairs. Painting too needs its own decorum and freedom in many things" [172].

Messer Pulidoro Saraceni, Doctor of Medicine

Almost nothing appears to be known about Pulidoro, apart from his appearance in Gilio's *Dialogo*. He is mentioned as a doctor of medicine in Fabriano by Orazio Augenio in his *Epistolarum et consultationum medicinalium* of 1592.[8]

Pulidoro is asked to talk about the history of painting [98] and declares that knowing how to arrange colors is not enough [100]. Before Silvio Gilio begins properly, Pulidoro opens the discussion of histories and historical painting, arguing for the need for painters to have knowledge of arithmetic and geometry [115]. He attacks forced movements for figures in paintings [146]. He describes the mixed painter [198–222; 237–38]. He defines the difference between the fictional and the fabulous [215]. Mixed paintings should not be placed in churches [237]. He says he has seen the Cancelleria frescoes and has also read about them in Anton Francesco Doni's *Zucca* [212].[9]

Messer Silvio Gilio, Doctor of Law

Silvio Gilio contributed to a group of poems celebrating the Magdalene of Gentile da Fabriano, to which Giovanni Andrea Gilio also contributed.[10] Lodovico Jacobilli apparently recorded Silvio as having been appointed governor of Foligno, 22 February 1586, but the entry is a little ambiguous: "Silvio Gilio, o Giuliano da Fabriano Governatore da 22 Febraro 1586."[11]

Silvio is asked to describe the historical painter [114; 116–21]; he tries unsuccessfully to get out of it. He argues that the historical painter is a translator from words into images [132]. Silvio defends the representation of Christ in Michelangelo's *Conversion of Paul* [142–43]. He recommends drawing up rules [120; 131]. He introduces the discussion of the *Last Judgment* [156]. He seconds Francesco in praise of Michelangelo [157] and defends aspects of Michelangelo's *Last Judgment* [166]; for instance, he adduces Ezekiel as Michelangelo's source [166].

Messer Francesco Santi, *Letterato* and Merchant

Francesco is described as a well-mannered young person, both man of letters and merchant, and the master (*padrone*) of the paper mills (*valchiere*) belonging to Giovan Bernardino Santi, where the participants in Gilio's *Dialogo* meet. He had been in Rome [144: "I can't help laughing when I am in Rome and I walk through the Minerva"]. When the interlocutors sit down by the river bank, Francesco produces a copy of Giovanni Andrea Gilio's poem, written a few years earlier, which he gives to Silvio Gilio to read [89–90]. Francesco is the only interlocutor specifically identified as a *letterato,* which is interesting in view of the fact that the *Dialogo* was printed in conjunction with Gilio's first dialogue on the role of the *letterato* as courtier.[12]

In the *Dialogo,* Francesco is asked to describe the ways that characters within stories should be presented by historical painters [140–56]. He is critical of forced movements [125]. He laughs at the diving angel in the *Presepio* in Santa Maria sopra Minerva [144], and he condemns the angels with the instruments of the Passion in the *Last Judgment* [146–48]. However, he argues in favor of preserving the freedom of the brush [104; 204–5], and he defends and praises Michelangelo [129; 157]. He allows the historical painter a mixture of what is proper and improper [155–56]. He advocates graceful, natural movements [148–49].

How the Dialogue Structure Works

Each of the six interlocutors is given a role, which serves to mark out and draw attention to the principal themes addressed: M. Vincenso talks about the poetic painter, M. Silvio about the historical painter, M. Troilo about abuses in historical painting, M. Francesco about the ways characters within histories should be presented, M. Ruggiero about the *Last Judgment* (and about sacred painting in general, at the end), and M. Pulidoro about the mixed painter. Within each of these sections, the interchanges between the participants can function as a means of introducing exceptions and refinements, giving emphasis, and articulating and answering objections, so that possible differences in approach can be brought out and the correct path clarified; this dialogue structure can also function as a way of lightening the tone and varying the pace, especially through the introduction of digressions. However, the leading speaker within each of the sections essentially carries the day.

Notes

1. Page numbers (in brackets) correspond to this volume.
2. See Giuseppe Colucci, ed., *Antichità picene dell'abate Giuseppe Colucci patrizio camerinese,* vol. 17, *Delle antichità del Medio e dell'Infimo Evo,* vol. 2 (Fermo: Dai torchi dell'autore, 1792), 171.
3. Colucci, *Antichità picene,* 17:167. Unless otherwise indicated, all translations are by Michael Bury.
4. Ferdinando Ughelli, *Italia Sacra, sive de Episcopis Italiae, et insularum adjacentium, rebusque ab iis praeclare gestis . . .* (Venice: Sebastiano Coleti, 1720), 6 (col. 850).
5. Carlo Ossola, "La 'Topica Poetica' di G. A. Gilio da Fabriano," in *Retorica e poetica: Atti del III convegno Italo-Tedesco,* ed. Daniela Goldin and Gianfranco Folena (Padua: Liviana, 1979), 262n7.
6. Romualdo Sassi, "Sonetti di poeti fabrianesi in onore di Gentile da Fabriano," *Rassegna marchigiana* 2 (1923–24): 277.
7. Ossola, "La 'Topica Poetica,'" 262n7.
8. Orazio Augenio, *Epistolarum et consultationum medicinalium,* 2 vols. in 1 (Venice: Damianum Zenarium, 1592), 133v.
9. Anton Francesco Doni, *Foglie della Zucca* (Venice: Francesco Marcolini, 1552).
10. Ossola, "La 'Topica Poetica,'" 262n7.
11. Lodovico Jacobilli, *Discorso della Città di Foligno* (Foligno: Agostino Alterii, 1646), 55.
12. Giovanni Andrea Gilio, *Dialogo del letterato cortigiano,* ed. Paolo Cherchi (Ravenna: Longo Editore, 2002).

DIALOGUE ON THE ERRORS AND ABUSES OF PAINTERS (1564)*

GIOVANNI ANDREA GILIO

SECOND DIALOGUE OF GIOVANNI ANDREA GILIO from Fabriano [3][1] in which are discussed the errors and abuses of the painters with regard to histories; with many observations on the *Judgment* of Michelangelo and other figures both from the new as well as the old papal chapel.[2] With the statement of how sacred images should be painted.

To the most Illustrious and Reverend Monsignor, Cardinal Farnese.[3]

That painting has been honored and prized in every period, most illustrious Monsignor, and by almost every nation in the world, is witnessed by the works themselves and by the mentions that celebrated writers in different places have made of them. And now, because [painting] finds itself full of errors and abuses with regard to the truth of the subjects represented, it seemed to me that it needed to be corrected and purified in order to restore it to its proper form. Just as the great Michelangelo Buonarroti, Raphael of Urbino, and other excellent minds have restored its true character as an art, previously lost as a consequence of evil times and the ignorance of the painters.[4] It is certain that this most noble art was practiced for many years and centuries by noble and learned men who knew to give to all their figures, in every circumstance, the correct and

* Note to the reader: The page numbers in brackets given in the translation refer to the Italian text of Gilio's second dialogue, the *Dialogo nel quale si ragiona degli errori e degli abusi de' pittori circa l'istorie*, in *Trattati d'arte del Cinquecento: Fra manierismo e controriforma*, vol. 2, ed. Paola Barocchi (Bari: Laterza, 1961), 1–115. The brackets, which indicate the approximate start of a new page in the Barocchi edition, are placed where least disruptive to the flow of the text.

1. The *Due dialogi* (Two dialogues), of which this is the second, was printed by Antonio Gioioso at Camerino in 1564.
2. The old chapel is what we now call the Sistine (Sistina); the new is what we now call the Pauline Chapel (Paolina).
3. Cardinal Alessandro Farnese (1520–89).
4. Michelangelo Buonarroti (1475–1564) and Raffaello Sanzio (1483–1520).

appropriate decorum.[5] Nowadays, because it is practiced by many, mainly ignorant people, who do not know how to differentiate between figures in that way, and who are not alert to the need for it, I am resolved to give them some guidance to explain the care that needs to be taken over the painting of religious pictures [*pitture sacre*], secular histories [*istorie mondane*], and poetic fictions.[6] Because nearly everyone trusts in the saying of Horace that to painters and poets everything is permitted, I have written this dialogue in order to show them how far that license should be extended, so that those who know more than me will in the future have a field marked out in which they can run in any direction.[7] I am particularly astonished that this beautiful and excellent art does not have either a book or a set of rules [*regole*] laying out for painters the manner [*modo*] and method [*ordine*] they should adopt for every kind of figure they have to paint.[8] Therefore, because the majority proceed in a disorderly way, they commit an infinity of errors in their histories, as is clearly to be seen throughout the whole of Italy and especially in Rome.[9] For it seems to me that today, when modern painters have to produce a work, their first thought

---

5. Decorum [*decoro*]—as the principle by which a judgment is formed about whether a painted figure is appropriate to the person or type represented—is a key concept in this text. Among other features, the movements, gestures, expressions, physical characteristics, rank, and dress given to a figure are to be judged in terms of how they support or, if indecorous, undermine what the painted image ought to convey about the person in question. Dolce's term *convenevolezza* incorporated what Gilio means here by decorum. See Lodovico Dolce, *Dialogo della pittura intitolato l'Aretino* [Venice: G. Giolito de' Ferrari, 1557], in *Trattati d'arte del Cinquecento: Fra manierismo e controriforma,* vol. 1, ed. Paola Barocchi (Bari: Laterza, 1960), 164–66. The English translation is in Mark W. Roskill, ed. and trans., *Dolce's "Aretino" and Venetian Art Theory of the Cinquecento* (Toronto: University of Toronto Press in association with the Renaissance Society of America, 2000), 118–21. An important source for both Gilio and Dolce was Horace; see Rensselaer W. Lee, *"Ut pictura poesis": The Humanistic Theory of Painting* (New York: Norton, 1967), 34–35 and 38–39.
6. Barocchi notes this addition of the sacred to the traditional distinction between poetry and history; Barocchi, *Trattati,* 2:569, n3 to Gilio p. 3. In describing painters as ignorant [*ignoranti*], Gilio meant they were unable to read Latin. Dolce had remarked that painters would benefit from a knowledge of *lettere* (that is, Latin letters) and that they could not command their subject matter or create appropriate figures without in some way acquiring familiarity with the texts; see Dolce, *L'Aretino,* in Barocchi, *Trattati,* 1:170 (Roskill, *Dolce's "Aretino,"* 128–29).
7. Horace, *Ars Poetica,* in *Satires; Epistles; The Art of Poetry,* trans. H. Rushton Fairclough, Loeb Classical Library 194 (Cambridge, MA: Harvard University Press, 1926), 450–51 (lines 9–11). Konrad Braun (Conradus Brunus) had commented on Horatian license as a cause of errors; see his letter to Ioannes Cochlaeus, "de ratione Scribendi Methodum," in Braun, *De imaginibus,* in idem, *Opera Tria* (Mainz: Franz Behem, 1548), 110.
8. "modo e l'ordine"; the words recur later in the text with a similar meaning. See Gilio, *Dialogo . . . degli errori e degli abusi de' pittori,* in Barocchi, *Trattati,* 2:14; and Gilio, this volume, 100. See also note 42.
9. The examples of modern painting he chooses to discuss are almost all Roman.

is to twist the heads, arms, or legs of their figures so that they could be said to be strained [*sforzate*], and sometimes these movements [*sforzi*] are such that it would have been better to have done without them; **[4]** while they pay little or no attention to the subject of their intended painting.[10] But I published this work not to instruct but to open up discussion, not to reprove but to show what is involved, not to accuse but to advise caution; and I dedicate it to your most illustrious Lordship so that with that unerring judgment that makes you so admirable and deserving of honor and reverence by all men, you can judge and correct it. And when you happen to go into the Sistine Chapel you can consider whether the *Last Judgment* and the ceiling, as well as the other figures, observe historical truth.[11] And with this, may you accept my readiness to serve you, and may you be healthy and happy.

Your most illustrious and reverend Lordship's humble servant
GIOVANN'ANDREA GILIO.

---

10. Paolo Pino, *Dialogo di pittura* [Venice: Paolo Gherardo, 1548], in *Trattati d'arte del Cinquecento: Fra manierismo e controriforma,* vol. 1, ed. Paola Barocchi (Bari: Laterza, 1960), 115. Discussing invention [*invenzione*], Fabio, the painter in Pino's dialogue, recommends that "in all your works introduce at least one figure all strained, mysterious and difficult, so that those who understand what makes the art of painting perfect will judge you to be skillful" (in tutte l'opere vostre fateli intervenire almeno una figura tutta sforciata, misteriosa e difficile, acciò che per quella voi siate notato valente da chi intende la perfezion dell'arte). Unless otherwise indicated, all translations are by Michael Bury and Lucinda Byatt. There is no suggestion that this figure should be appropriate to the subject matter. Pino's idea contrasts with Dolce's, who advises that a graceful pose [*posar leggiadro*] might be more delightful than a strained movement [*movimento sforzato*], and that account needed to be taken of the different kinds of subject matter and what they involved; see Dolce, *L'Aretino,* in Barocchi, *Trattati,* 1:180 (Roskill, *Dolce's "Aretino,"* 146–47); and note 116. Dolce anticipated Gilio by expressing the need to adjust the poses of figures to the subject, but, by proposing an aesthetic reason for adopting graceful poses he invoked a criterion alien to the later writer. A similar conjunction of ideas can already be found in Leon Battista Alberti: "I have known many make serious mistakes in this respect. They represent movements that are too violent, and make visible simultaneously in one and the same figure both chest and buttocks, which is physically impossible and indecent to look at. But because they hear that those figures are most alive that throw their limbs about a great deal, they cast aside all dignity in painting and copy the movements of actors. . . . A painting should have pleasing and graceful movements that are suited to the subject of the action." Leon Battista Alberti, *On Painting and On Sculpture: The Latin Texts of "De pictura" and "De statua,"* ed. and trans. Cecil Grayson (London: Phaidon, 1972), 84–85 (book 2, §44). The Latin text of Alberti's *De pictura* had been published at Basel (Westheimer) in 1540, and an Italian translation, *La pittura di Leonbattista Alberti,* by Lodovico Domenichi at Venice (Giolito) in 1547.
11. The "other figures" were presumably those painted for Sixtus IV in the early 1480s. See Jorge María Mejía et al., *The Fifteenth-Century Frescoes in the Sistine Chapel* (Vatican City: Musei Vaticani, 2003).

SECOND DIALOGUE of GIOVANNI ANDREA GILIO of Fabriano concerning the errors of painters with regard to histories. [5]

To the most Reverend and Illustrious Monsignor Cardinal Farnese.
The snowy, rainy, cold winter of 1561 was over, having been the longest and the worst in living memory.[12] Because the sun was already nearing the end of Aries, the earth had regained its temperate mood and was sending forth the sweetest scents from beautiful flowers: not only from blooming plants but also from trees that in our country, having been held back by the length and severity of winter, were now covered, little by little, with new growth, partly flowers and partly leaves.[13] It was most pleasing to see the red, white, green, and other colors with which nature adorns the trees and plants in that season. All this seemed to invite the numbed hearts of men to rejoice, as if the gentle warm west wind brought sweet comfort to all those who had been kept indoors by the dense, wintry fogs; huddled around the warmth of the fire, with windows tightly shut, to escape the bitterness of the prolonged icy north wind that had kept much of Italy covered in deep snow for four months on end, and in Muscovy, Livonia, Lithuania, Poland, Germany, and other northern countries had brought more cold than ever, freezing lakes, rivers, and ponds in a way that no one could remember having happened before. In many areas of Italy great swamps were created by the excessive rains, bringing houses, vineyards, and huge trees down from the hills into the valleys below, engulfing them so that they were no longer recognizable as valleys, and drowning men and animals in the process. [6] Therefore, for those who had survived such a fate, it seemed that, having emerged from the darkest prison into bright light, they were revived by the new season whose clear, serene days, pleasant and beautiful, and accompanied by sweet birdsong, came to rejuvenate men's sluggish minds and to fill them with delight. For this reason, everyone sought to take relaxing walks in gardens or other pleasant places, both to give themselves exercise in such beautiful weather and also to restore their troubled minds among the lovely flowers and the sweet song of nightingales and other pleasant birds, which, filled with love, appeared as messengers of the lovely season that came, laughing and beautiful, to deck

12. Gilio set his dialogue in the spring of 1561. Dario Camuffo and Silvia Enzi identify 1561 (the year defined as from January) in northern Italy as having had a severe winter. Dario Camuffo and Silvia Enzi, "Reconstructing the Climate of Northern Italy from Archive Sources," in *Climate since A.D. 1500*, ed. Raymond S. Bradley and Philip D. Jones (London: Routledge, 1995), 150–51, table 7.1. Note also the calculation of the date of the event of the Last Judgment (Gilio, this volume, 161–62), which points to 1562 as the date of the composition of that part of the text; see also note 211.

13. The Sun is in Aries from 21 March to 20 April.

the bare countryside, shady valleys, and high mountains with flowers and turn them green.

Among the many people in our pleasant land who had gone out to amuse themselves was a group of six young men, for the most part doctors and scholars. They had ordered their servants to prepare an evening meal at M. Giovan Bernardino Santi's paper mills [*valchiere*] and, after lunching, they all went out to enjoy the day under the shady trees of his garden, contemplating the beautiful plants and the transparency of the clear, cool waters of the river Giano, which ran sweetly murmuring above and below his well-kept meadow, now all in flower.[14] These were the names of the members of this group: Messer Ruggiero Coradini, a canon and doctor; Messer Vincenso Peterlino, a doctor of law; Messer Troilo Mattioli, also a doctor; Messer Pulidoro Saraceni, doctor of medicine; Messer Silvio Gilio, doctor of law; and Messer Francesco Santi, a well-mannered young person, both man of letters [*letterato*] and merchant, the master of the mills.[15] After they had walked in the garden for quite some time, touching and smelling the white and red roses that were then starting to bloom, and other lovely and sweet-scented flowers, and after M. Pulidoro had discoursed on each with reference to Dioscorides and Mattioli, they reached the well-kept meadow and there they all paused, under the shade of the oaks and other trees beside the river, whose bank was covered with flowers and plants.[16] **[7]**

M. Francesco said: "Let us sit here on the bank for a while," and they did so, close to a small pool in whose bright, clear water some fish could be seen darting around. After they had enjoyed the scene for a while, M. Francesco added: "Watching the clear water has made me want to read out to you the poem that

---

14. *Valchiere* (*gualchiere*) were the mills where paper was made. See Francesco Sansovino, *Della origine et de' fatti delle famiglie illustri d'Italia* (Venice: Altobello Salicato, 1609), 195r: "And having come with the army to Fabriano, he stopped for the night among the valchiere where paper is made" (Et venuto con essercito a Fabriano, si fermò la notte fra le valchiere ove si fa la carta). The Giano, a tributary of the river Esino, rises on Monte Maggio and flows through Fabriano; it was on the banks of this stream that the paper mills were sited.
15. "Messer," an appellation of respect and standing, as in "Sir" or "Master," is abbreviated as M. throughout. For brief notes on the interlocutors, see "Dramatis Personae," this volume, 79–82. None of them were artists, nor is any claim made for their special knowledge of the art of painting. Vincenso Peterlino, Silvio Gilio, and Troilo Mattioli contributed to a collection of poems celebrating the Magdalene of Gentile da Fabriano (see fig. 34), which includes contributions from Giovanni Andrea Gilio himself; Carlo Ossola, "La 'Topica Poetica' di G. A. Gilio da Fabriano," in *Retorica e poetica: Atti del III Convegno Italo-Tedesco,* ed. Daniela Goldin and Gianfranco Folena (Padua: Liviana, 1979), 262n7.
16. Dioscorides, *De materia medica,* was the primary ancient source for botanical knowledge available during the Renaissance. Commentaries on Dioscorides were first published in 1554 by Pietro Andrea Mattioli (1501–77); see Mattioli, *Commentarii in libros sex Pedacii Dioscoridis Anazarbei De materia medica . . .* (Venice: V. Valgrisi, 1554). Unauthorized editions of Mattioli's text had appeared in the late 1540s.

M. Giovanni Andrea composed when the most Reverend Archbishop of Siena was here not many summers ago, as you know."[17]

M. Vincenso said: "Yes, please do just read it out, because I haven't heard it since," and this was echoed by the others. Then the courteous and polite young man, having taken out a copy of the poem, gave it to M. Silvio to read.[18] Holding it in his hand, the latter then started to read as follows:

A pleasant valley lies
Among the rugged, high Apennine peaks,
Where, from beneath a nearby rock,
The fair Giano rises, its water like
Pure liquid crystal flowing in a narrow course.
Its nymphs from the neighboring valleys often run
Among clear brooks, through shaded, winding ways, to join the limpid
stream,
Carrying tribute of cool, clear water
So that it may steadily grow.
Known by another more famous and beautiful name,
It flows full and foaming between wider banks

17. Francesco Bandini Piccolomini (1505–88) was archbishop of Siena from 1529 until his death in 1588. In 1556 he was made governor of Rome. In 1559 he became governor of Viterbo and vice-legate of the Patrimonio; see Christoph Weber, ed., *Legati e governatori dello Stato pontificio 1550–1809* (Rome: Ufficio Centrale per i Beni archivistici, 1994), 359 and 429. In 1556 Piccolomini had been nominated by Paul IV to join a special reform commission. See Giuseppe Alberigo, "Bandini Piccolomini, Francesco," *Dizionario Biografico degli Italiani* [*DBI*], 5 (1963), http://www.treccani.it/biografie/; and Ludwig von Pastor, *The History of the Popes from the Close of the Middle Ages: Drawn from the Secret Archives of the Vatican and Other Original Sources,* vol. 14, *Marcellus II (1555); Paul IV (1555–1559),* ed. Ralph Francis Kerr (London: Kegan Paul, Trench, Trubner, 1924), 186. He had apparently been in voluntary exile at Fabriano in 1552, when he was recalled to Siena on the orders of Julius III; see Giovanni Antonio Pecci, *Memorie Storico-Critiche della Città di Siena* (Siena: Pazzini Carli, 1755–60); facs. reprint, ed. Mario Pavolini and Ennio Innocenti (Siena: Cantagalli, 1988), 4:13. It may have been then that Gilio wrote this poem. In the first of the *Due dialogi,* Gilio mentions Piccolomini as someone who would outdo Maecenas as a patron of men of letters, if fortune allowed it; *Dialogo de le parti morali appertenenti a' letterati cortigiani,* in Giovanni Andrea Gilio, *Due dialogi. Nel primo de' quali si ragiona de le parti morali e civili appertenenti a' letterati cortigiani, et ad ogni gentil'huomo, e l'utile che i prencipi cavano dai letterati. Nel secondo si ragiona degli errori de' pittori circa l'historie* (Camerino: Antonio Gioioso, 1564; facs. reprint, Florence: S.P.E.S., 1986), 8r–v. The reprint is accompanied by a brief introduction by Paola Barocchi.

18. The *canzone* (song) has no title here; however, in Giuseppe Colucci, it is reprinted with the title "De' Gigli." Giuseppe Colucci, *Antichità picene dell'abate Giuseppe Colucci patrizio camerinese,* vol. 17, *Delle antichita del Medio e dell Infimo Evo,* vol. 2 (Fermo: Dai torchi dell'autore, 1792), 21. Colucci also describes the valley of the Giano, and notes the gardens, meadows, and woods.

And bequeaths that name to the city,[19] so near to the waters
That it becomes one with it.
The glorious Tiber
saw its banks embellished with rich spoils
And trophies; for which it is singled out.
Slender young trees and leaves
Are the splendor of the banks I praise, **[8]**
Where love so sweetly invites me
To gaze upon the infinite loveliness
Of banks, delightsome meadows, and fresh flowers
In verdant May and joyous April;
This gentle, charming season,
When valleys and woods, so leafy and beautiful at this time,
Often ring with sweet choruses of birdsong.
The earth, sweetly in love,
Opens its generous bosom to the eastern rays.
White and crimson roses,
Nodding flowers and pale violets
Color the knolls and pretty hilltops.
Thus nature exceeds all other
Marvels of human making.
The pleasant groves of choice maple, elm, and poplar
Enclose a flower-strewn meadow;
[And] when the day is stirred by a gentle breeze,
They dance together,
And when the day is warmest
The delightful sweet scent of the flowers and plants,
Stolen by the cool airs, is wafted all around.
At times I sense the air is filled
With love's sighs from that beautiful bosom.
Green and sunny slopes,
In full bloom, fair and lovely,
Are full of sweetness everywhere.

---

19. The name Fabriano was said to have originated as "Fabbro sul Giano" (*fabri ianus*) since, according to legend, the city was founded by a smith—that is, a *fabbro*. See the sixteenth-century account by the Dominican Giovanni Domenico Scevolini, "Dell'istorie di Fabriano," in Giuseppe Colucci, *Antichità picene dell'abate Giuseppe Colucci patrizio camerinese*, vol. 17, *Delle antichita del Medio e dell Infimo Evo* (Fermo: Dai torchi dell'autore, 1792), 9. Scevolini copied the whole of Gilio's poem into his manuscript; see Colucci, *Antichità picene*, 17:21. The waters of the Giano, used for industrial purposes in the town, lose the clarity and purity that characterized them upstream.

The soul seems to find fulfillment,
And seems to temper and suppress all less worthy thought.
Desire, overcome by such loveliness,
Gazes on the divine and blessed beauty of
That sweet face, on which Love
So marvelously painted crimson and white flowers.
And although everything else may succumb to
Cold mist or extreme heat,
Both of these always retain their natural color.
On such a sublime subject I gaze and meditate,
Even if consumed and dissolved by flames. **[9]**
Flowing slowly, gently,
From pool to pool, the river murmurs on,
Its current, now lazy and slack, now growing strong.
Its color changes to white
As it crashes, foaming, against
Hard rocks, delighting in fullness,
While held fast between banks on either side.
Where it pools, the water is so clear
That crystal by comparison would fail the test;
When the north wind strikes, snow or ice less cold appear.
Flowers are reflected in it,
As are the branches, the grasses rooted on its bank.
By the pool Amintha and Daphne, Galatea and Flora sing of their loves.
There human effort produces a thing worthy of great praise
By means of which fame is preserved for eternity.[20]
This alone teaches us how with sweet deception
The toll of time and death can be evaded; because
Memory is a poor guardian of fame's inner virtue
When passed down from father to son over such long periods.
Lucretia would not be so pure,
Nor Cleopatra covetous,
Nor the other women renowned for their beauty.
As for me, what more would I do,
If I could not preserve the reputation for beauty and purity
Of her for whom my thoughts alternate between turmoil and repose?
Oh song, if in sweet verse you could say all
I wish about the gentle valley,
Perhaps it would be first among all others.

20. This is a reference to the making of paper, used to preserve memory through writing.

Having finished reading the poem, which they all praised for its accurate depiction of the beautiful valley, the banks, meadows, woods, and the whole scene, M. Troilo said: "Gentlemen, do you hear the wonderful music of the nightingales here by the river? It seems really shameful that we should let them get the better of us." **[10]**

"You are right," replied M. Ruggiero. "It would be a good idea for us, too, to follow their example and make music until the heat of the day has passed, and then we can enjoy ourselves on the meadow that the prior of the Augustinians has spoiled by planting it with trees."[21]

"Let's start," said M. Francesco. "Here are the books."

This said, they were each handed a book and, after having sung several madrigals and having played a good piece of music on the viols, they started to discuss the loveliness of the gardens of Naples and how the garden of the Count of Mattalona surpasses all others there.[22] Then they talked about the gardens of the king of France, and those in Genoa, Florence, Siena, Lucca, Ferrara, and Mantua; and then about spring, summer, autumn, and winter, and what pleasures can be found in each: some praising one, some another.[23]

Having talked for a while about these, M. Vincenso said: "Look, gentlemen, what a beautiful sight it is to see such a variety of flowers on the trees and plants that cover this meadow and these gentle slopes. What painter could ever draw them so well from nature that they appear like the real thing?"

"Oh!" said M. Pulidoro. "Have there not been artists who have painted grapes that looked so natural that the birds came to eat them, thinking they were real?"[24]

"Certainly," added M. Vincenso, "that was the work of the ancient painters; but I think today neither the Flemings, who hold the palm for painting landscapes, nor the Italians would be able to achieve what was done then."

---

21. The Augustinian monastery in Fabriano was adjacent to the church of Santa Maria Nova, and Gilio himself describes it as being "larger than the one in Rome"; see Giovanni Andrea Gilio, *Discorso sopre le Città, l'Urbe, Colonia, Municipio, etc.*, in Gilio, *Due dialogi* (Camerino: Antonio Gioioso, 1564; facs. reprint, Florence: S.P.E.S., 1986), 140v.
22. Presumably a garden belonging to the branch of the Carafa family, members of which were counts of Mattalona (Maddaloni). Diomede (d. 1561), fourth count of Maddaloni, was granted the title of duke in 1558, by Charles V; see Francesco Dandolo and Gaetano Sabatini, *Lo stato feudale dei Carafa di Maddaloni* (Naples: Giannini, 2009), 48. Was Gilio's knowledge slightly out-of-date, or is this a sign that he had started writing by 1558?
23. The intention behind these remarks may have been to suggest the cosmopolitan experience and outlook of the group of interlocutors.
24. Pliny the Elder, *Natural History*, trans. H. Rackman, W. H. S. Jones, and D. E. Eichholz, 10 vols. Loeb Classical Library 330, 352–53, 370–71, 392–94, 418–19 (Cambridge, MA: Harvard University Press, 1938–63) (henceforth Pliny, *NH*), 9:308–11 (book 35, §65–66), in his account of the Greek painter Zeuxis.

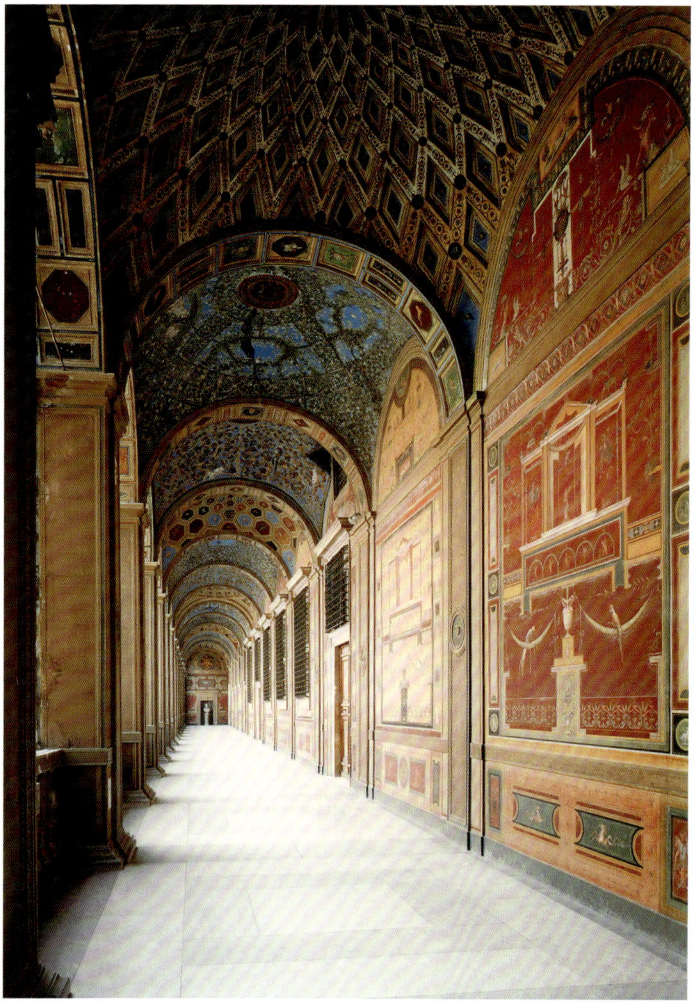

"I agree," said M. Silvio, "because if we look at the sort of flowers, fruits, plants, birds, and animals that can be found in the loggias of the papal palace [figs. 1–3] and of the Chigi, and in other palaces around Rome, although they are beautiful and alluring, they do not reveal the natural color or the allure [*vaghezza*] of the ones M. Pulidoro refers to."[25]

M. Pulidoro replied: "I will not deny that in our time painting has not reached the level of perfection that it had in the time of Apelles, Zeuxis,

25. The first- and second-floor *logge* in the Vatican palace were painted circa 1518–19 by Raphael and his pupils. Among these pupils, as a specialist in animals, fruit, and flowers, was Giovanni da Udine (1487–1564) (see figs. 1–3). Circa 1517–19, Giovanni also worked for Raphael on the loggia of Psyche in the villa of Agostino Chigi (now known as the Farnesina); see Nicole Dacos and Caterina Furlan, *Giovanni da Udine 1487–1561* (Udine: Casamassima, 1987), 24–30, 61–93, 101–6.

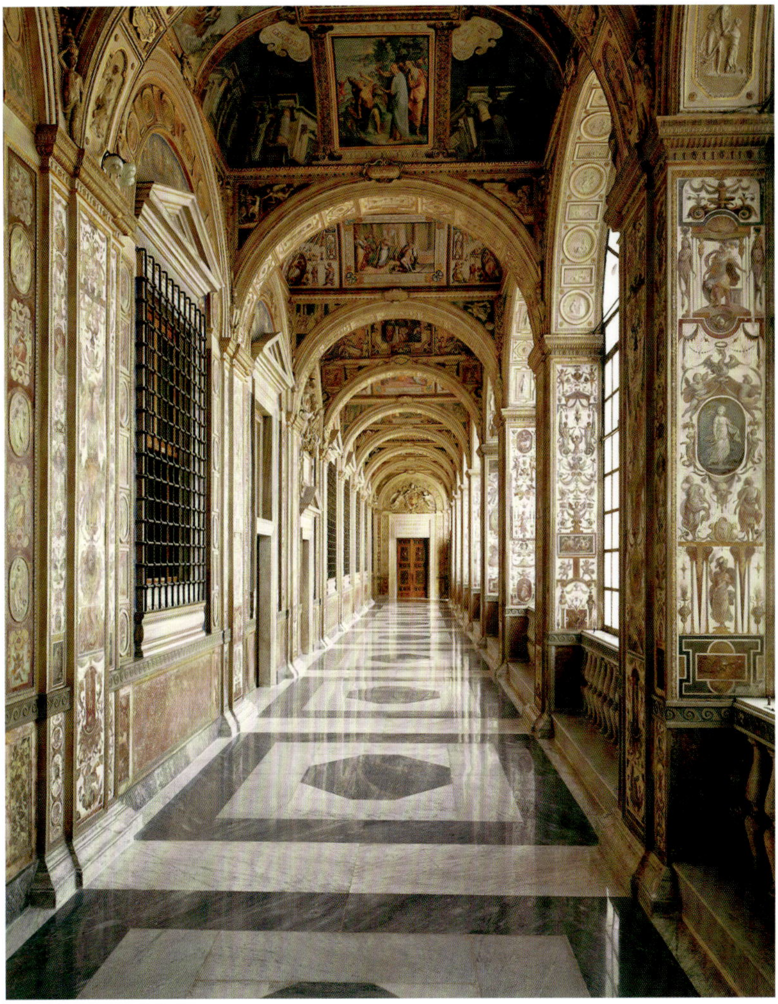

Protogenes, and those other famous men; **[11]** nevertheless, in the last three hundred years, or even less, it has reached a more perfect state than it had since it disappeared in the great ruin of Italy."

"What caused that?" said M. Troilo.

M. Pulidoro replied: "As a consequence of the barbarian invasions that ruined poor Italy and stripped it of material goods, men, honor, and courage, everything went wrong, with the loss of all civilized behavior."

M. Ruggiero added: "I should like to know how it happened that painting, being such an admirable art, praised by high and low alike, is today in the hands of poor and ignorant men. There are very few painters of our time who do not make mistakes when painting histories [*istorie*]."

M. Silvio replied to these words: "The sole reason that painting has fallen into the hands of poor and ignorant men is, I believe, because a nobleman

Fig. 1.
Raphael (Italian, 1483–1520) and workshop.
Loggia, first floor of the Apostolic Palace, completed 1519. Vatican City, Vatican Apostolic Palace.

Fig. 2.
Raphael (Italian, 1483–1520) and workshop.
Private loggia of Leo X, second floor of the Apostolic Palace, 1519. Vatican City, Vatican Apostolic Palace.

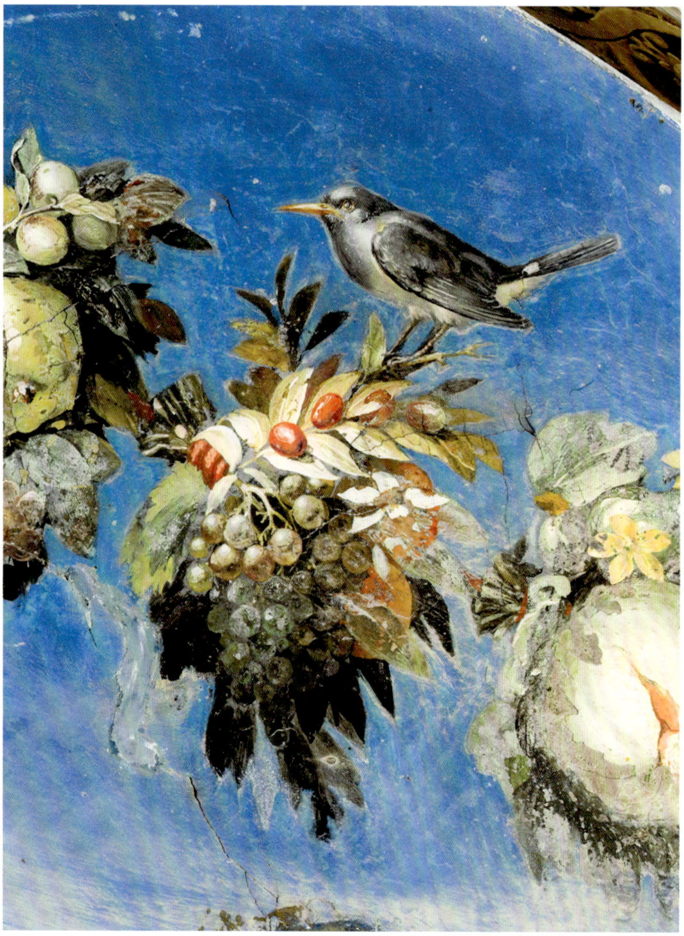

Fig. 3.
Giovanni da Udine (Italian, 1487–1564).
Detail of festoon, vault 6 (Story of Jacob) of second-floor loggia (private loggia of Leo X), 1519. Vatican City, Vatican Apostolic Palace.

would be ashamed to practice the art for monetary gain. I think that noblemen are to be found who know how to paint well, but they are held back by the groundless fear of suffering shame if they were caught with a palette, at work on a painting or sculpture. So that those who can paint do not practice it and those who cannot, do not care to learn. There could be another reason as well."

M. Francesco said: "What is that?"

M. Silvio replied: "Because a nobleman does not wish to grind up pigments, wear an apron all day, or dirty his hands with oil; and further he fears that he will be accused of disgracing himself doing it to earn money; and it does not occur to him that this art is so noble that it ennobles and exalts whoever practices it."[26]

26. Barocchi comments on Gilio's sensitivity to social class, revealed by this passage (*Trattati,* 2:572, n2 to Gilio p. 11). It is important evidence that a social stigma was attached less to the work of painting itself than to the practice of painting for monetary gain.

"That should not be so," said M. Vincenso, "because Alexander the Great (if we are to believe Pliny) went to watch Apelles's apprentices as they ground up pigments."[27]

M. Pulidoro added: "When the art was in the hands of nobles, there was no shame in this; but now that those who practice it seem to have changed, the standing of its supporters has diminished too. It cannot be denied that it was in the hands of noblemen in classical times, given that the people of Sicyon passed a decree, which was accepted by the whole of Greece; **[12]** and this was that only noble youths could learn painting, and that it should be placed in the first rank of liberal disciplines. Moreover, in order to ennoble it further, it was forbidden to slaves.[28] Thus the most noble Echione and Therimachus practiced it at that time. They were followed by Timagoras, Parrhasius, Polygnotus, and, most famous of all, Apelles, and many others whose fame will last forever."[29]

M. Francesco said: "If I remember well, I believe I read that in Rome painting was considerably elevated in status by the noble family of the Fabii; as a result, they were called Painters."[30]

"If we wish to consider noble artists, we will find," said M. Ruggiero, "that the emperors Hadrian, Severus Alexander, and Valentinian ennobled painting;[31] and Demetrius, who is also known as the conqueror of cities, devoted himself to geometry and to machines.[32] It is recorded that many great men in different

---

27. Pliny's account of Alexander in the studio of Apelles; see Pliny, *NH,* 9:322–25 (book 35, §85–86).
28. Pliny, *NH,* 9:316–19 (book 35, §77). Gilio interprets Pliny as saying that painting ranked high among the liberal disciplines.
29. Echione (Aetion in modern readings) and Therimachus are from Pliny, *NH,* 9:318–19 (book 35, §78); Timagoras and Polygnotus from 9:304–5 (book 35, §58); Parrhasius from 9:310–11 (book 35, §67–68); and Apelles from 9:318–33 (book 35, §79–97).
30. Pliny, *NH,* 9:274–75 (book 35, §19).
31. Dio Cassius describes Hadrian as a painter; see Dio Cassius, *Roman History,* vol. 8, *Books 61–70,* trans. Earnest Cary and Herbert B. Foster, Loeb Classical Library 176 (Cambridge, MA: Harvard University Press, 1925), 428–29 (book 69, 3.2). See Dolce, *L'Aretino,* in Barocchi, *Trattati,* 1:160 (Roskill, *Dolce's "Aretino,"* 256), for Hadrian and Severus Alexander as painters. On Valentinian, see Ammianus Marcellinus, who records him as an "elegant painter and modeller"; Ammianus Marcellinus, *History,* vol. 3, *Books 27–31; Excerpta Valesiana,* trans. J. C. Rolfe, Loeb Classical Library 331 (Cambridge, MA: Harvard University Press, 1939), 370–71 (book 30, §9, §4). On Severus Alexander's excellence in painting, see Aelius Lampridius, *Severus Alexander,* in *Historia Augusta: Volume II,* trans. David Magie, Loeb Classical Library 140 (Cambridge, MA: Harvard University Press, 1924), 230–31 (§27).
32. On King Demetrius of Macedonia, known as Poliorcetes (stormer of cities) and his interest in machines, see Plutarch, *Demetrius,* in idem, *Lives,* vol. 9, *Demetrius and Antony; Pyrrhus and Caius Marius,* trans. Bernadotte Perrin, Loeb Classical Library 101 (Cambridge, MA: Harvard University Press, 1920), 46–49 (§20–21); and Diodorus Siculus, *Library of History,* vol. 10, *Books 19.66–20,* trans. Russel M. Geer, Loeb Classical Library 390 (Cambridge, MA: Harvard University Press, 1954), 380–87 (book 20, §91–92).

periods undertook painting and also sculpture. But as time went on, as it gradually fell out of noble hands, it came under the sway of the ignorant; but I don't think this happened for any other reason than that noblemen, held back by that fear that you described earlier, M. Francesco, would not go out to paint temples, palaces, and other public and private places."

Once M. Ruggiero had finished talking, they all fell silent. Then M. Vincenso took up the subject again, saying: "I would like it very much, M. Pulidoro, if you could tell me (given that we have started to talk about painting) who its inventor was."

M. Pulidoro replied: "We cannot know for certain who was the inventor of such an admirable art, given that Pliny tells us that there was already a terrible argument between the Greeks and the Egyptians over this, since the latter claimed to have invented it six thousand years before the Greeks had even heard of it. The Greeks rebutted this by saying that the Sicyonians were the inventors long before them. Others believed that the Corinthians were the inventors. But all agreed that it had its origin in a man's shadow and the first rough outline that was drawn around it. The Egyptian Philocles was the first to use lines to distinguish the parts of the body. **[13]** Others give credit for this to Cleanthes of Corinth. The first to practice painting without color were Aridices of Corinth and Telephanes of Sicyon. A single color was then added and for a considerable time that is how painting was done. The first to add colors was Cleofante of Corinth, who came to Rome at the time of Tarquinius Priscus. This is all that Pliny tells us."[33]

M. Silvio said: "I would give credit for the invention to the Egyptians rather than to the Greeks."

"Why?" asked M. Pulidoro.

"Because," M. Silvio added, "if we consider ancient times, we find that, while God's people were in Egypt, painting must have been very well known in that country."

"For what reason?" said M. Vincenso. "The reason is this," replied M. Silvio. "Since God wanted to turn his people away from idolatry, he expressly forbade them to paint images of any object whatsoever; if it were not the case that they knew about painting, it would not have been necessary to forbid it."[34]

---

33. All the information in this paragraph comes from Pliny, *NH*, 9:270–73 (book 35, §15–16). Gilio's reading of the last painter's name as "Cleofante," not Ecphantus as in modern readings, matches Pino's reading. See Pino, *Dialogo*, in Barocchi, *Trattati*, 1:123; and idem, *Dialogo*, in Barocchi, *Trattati*, 1:419, n3 for Pino p. 123.

34. Exodus 20:4. Unless otherwise noted, direct quotations from the Bible are from the Douay-Rheims translation undertaken at the English College of Douay-Rheims and printed in two parts: New Testament (1582) and Old Testament (1609–10). On the religious and linguistic context of the Douay-Rheims Bible, see Brett Foster, "Gregory Martin's 'Holy Latinate

M. Ruggiero added: "I agree with M. Silvio, in that painting came before sculpture. We read that God caused the image of the cherubim to be carved on the Ark of the Covenant, which makes me believe that sculpture too was well known.[35] Moreover, on this point, I would add the example (which happened long before) of Jacob escaping with Leah and Rachel, his wives, when Rachel stole the idols of her father's gods.[36] If sculpture was therefore so well known in those early centuries under natural law, in the second age of the world, we can argue that painting must have been discovered much earlier than that. I say this because Pliny states that Cleofante of Corinth was the first to discover colors, and he lived at the time of Tarquinius Priscus. Also he came to Rome at that time, which was many years after Romulus. At the time of Romulus, Hezekiah reigned in Judaea; he was the fourth or fifth king after David.[37] And many years before David, there had been Moses, and before Moses, Abraham and the other patriarchs, so, by calculating the time, these are the grounds on which I give credit to the Egyptians for the invention of painting." **[14]**

"However it may have happened," said M. Pulidoro, "painting quickly attained a great reputation, because there was a succession of famous painters, up to Phidias and his brother Panaenus, who painted Minerva's shield at Elis so beautifully. Then Bularchus, who was a highly skilled artist alive at the time of Romulus, sold a panel of the war of the Magnetes for its weight in gold to Candaules, King of Lydia.[38] Igiemone was the first painter to distinguish men from women; Eumarus of Athens [was the first] to paint men's faces in different manners, that is, from the front, in profile, looking up, down, this way or that, ahead or behind; he was also the first to show the veins, joints, and muscles of the human body, and he discovered the way of making folds in garments.[39] Panaenus painted most beautifully the battle between the Greeks and the Persians at Marathon, portraying Alcibiades and the other famous Greek captains from life.[40] Not long after came Timagoras, Polygnotus, Parrhasius, Zeuxis, Apelles, and the other famous painters, who were all free men and noble, educated, and resourceful, and they did not make mistakes (as most of

Jerusalem': Roman English, Romanist Values, and the Rheims New Testament (1582)," *Prose Studies: History, Theory, Criticism* 28 (2006): 130–49.

35. Exodus 25:18–20: "Thou shalt make also two cherubims of beaten gold, on the two sides of the oracle."
36. Genesis 31:19 and 31:32–35.
37. 2 Kings (Fourth Book of Kings) 18; also referred to as "Ezechias."
38. Pliny, *NH*, 9:300–303 (book 35, §54–55).
39. This is a slightly confused account based on Pliny, *NH*, 9:302–3 (book 35, §56). The name Hygiaenon used in modern editions is given by Gilio as Igiemone; see Barocchi, *Trattati*, 2:572, n2 to Gilio p. 14.
40. Pliny, *NH*, 9:302–5 (book 35, §57), but Gilio mistakenly introduces Alcibiades, who was not one of the leading figures at Marathon.

ours do today) when they painted histories, because they had rules of proportion, line, and perspective; indeed, Eupompus of Sicyon said that no one could be a good painter unless he was also good at geometry, arithmetic, and poetry.[41] So all these men strove to acquire the skills appropriate to their art, in order to become perfect artists."

M. Troilo said: "You have spoken well and, given the very powerful reasons you have adduced, I cannot imagine how an ignorant person could be a good artist, because he knows only what he has to do but does not know in what way nor by what method he has to do it.[42] How could anyone who does not know what poetry is, or what fables are, be a good poetic painter? For Simonides said that painting was silent poetry and poetry was spoken painting."[43]

"And I," added M. Francesco, "would further say that he needs to know the histories, so that when he has to paint them he knows what is required.[44] **[15]** So it happens that paintings made in our time are for the most part poorly conceived, for they lack all four of the above-stated qualities. It is not surprising that the works are imperfect when the artists are ignorant."[45]

"How is it possible," responded M. Silvio, "for a blind person to travel along a steep and rocky path without tripping up?"

M. Pulidoro resumed the conversation and said: "It appears to many that they have reached the highest level of perfection when they have learned to arrange and manage colors; and they do not realize that they are behaving like the writer who knows how to form letters but does not know how to assemble syllables nor organize words."

M. Vincenso said: "You speak well about this. From that ignorance is born not knowing how to distinguish the true [*vero*] from the fictional [*finto*] and the fabulous [*favoloso*], the poetic [*poetico*] from the historical [*istorico*];[46] nor

41. Pliny, *NH,* 9:316–17 (book 35, §75–76). Gilio makes a mistake—it is Eupompus's pupil Pamphilus whom Pliny said had been thoroughly trained in every branch of learning (*omnibus litteris eruditus*), especially arithmetic and geometry; Pamphilus is quoted as asserting their necessity if perfection was to be achieved in painting.
42. "non sa in che modo né con qual ordine." See also note 8.
43. Plutarch, "Were the Athenians More Famous in War or in Wisdom?," in *Moralia: Volume IV,* trans. Frank Cole Babbitt, Loeb Classical Library 305 (Cambridge, MA: Harvard University Press, 1936), 500–501 (§3).
44. Compare the similar advice in Dolce, *L'Aretino,* in Barocchi, *Trattati,* 1:170 (Roskill, *Dolce's "Aretino,"* 128–29).
45. The four essential qualities mentioned by M. Francesco as necessary for good painting—arithmetic, geometry, poetry, and history—all depend on theoretical knowledge rather than practical experience.
46. Gilio's source for the distinction between the true, the fictional, and the fabulous may well have been Josse Bade's commentary on Horace's *Ars Poetica;* see Josse Q. Bade, ed., *De arte poetica libellus* (Paris: Jean Petit and Denis Roce, 1503), 4v. Glossing the word *materia* in line 38 of Horace, Bade writes: "The matter is threefold: either altogether true, something which actually occurred, as in histories; or not true, but truth-like,

how to distinguish the times, manners, ages, dress, and other qualities appropriate to the figures that they represent.[47] Because it should be understood that the painter is sometimes a pure historian [*puro istorico*], sometimes a pure poet [*puro poeta*], and sometimes a mixture of the two [*a le volte è misto*].[48] When he is a pure poet I think that it is legitimate for him to paint everything that his own imagination [*capriccio*] dictates, with those actions and movements, however, that are appropriate to the figures he is representing.[49] We have an

something which could have occurred, such as the plots in comedies; or neither true nor truth-like, such as many poetic fables, for example, Virgil's ships changing to nymphs, and many of the metamorphoses in Ovid." Cited and translated by Ann Moss, "Horace in the Sixteenth Century: Commentators into Critics," in *The Cambridge History of Literary Criticism*, vol. 3, *The Renaissance*, ed. Glyn P. Norton (Cambridge: Cambridge University Press, 1999), 68–69. See Bury, this volume, 34n52. See also Paul White, *Jodocus Badius Ascensius: Commentary, Commerce, and Print in the Renaissance* (Oxford: Oxford University Press, 2013). Bade gives his source for this threefold division as the *Rhetorica ad Herennium*, then ascribed to Cicero; see Bernard Weinberg, *A History of Literary Criticism in the Italian Renaissance* (Chicago: University of Chicago Press, 1961), 1:82. *Rhetorica ad Herennium* discusses the *narratio* or statement of the facts in a court case: "The kind of narrative based on the exposition of the facts presents three forms: legendary, historical and realistic [*fabula, historia, argumentum*]. The legendary tale [*fabula*] comprises events neither true nor probable [*neque veras necque veri similes continet res*] like those transmitted by tragedies. The historical narrative is an account of exploits actually performed [*gesta res*] but removed in time from the recollection of our age. Realistic narrative recounts imaginary events [*ficta res*] which yet could have occurred, like the plots of comedies." See [Cicero], *Rhetorica ad Herennium*, trans. Harry Caplan, Loeb Classical Library 403 (Cambridge, MA: Harvard University Press, 1954), 22–25 (1.8.13). This passage in Gilio's text was translated into German and commented on by Stefanie Rothlände. See Stefanie Rothlände, ed., and Doris Mueller-Ziem, trans., "Giovanni Andrea Gilio, *Degli errori de' pittori circa l'istorie* (1564)," in *Historienmalerei*, ed. Thomas W. Gaehtgens and Uwe Fleckner (Berlin: Reimer, 1996), 99–105.

47. The point made here about the figures refers to the issue of decorum; see note 5.
48. Dolce had divided subjects into fable [*favola*] and history [*istoria*]; see Dolce, *L'Aretino*, in Barocchi, *Trattati*, 1:164 (Roskill, *Dolce's "Aretino,"* 116–17). Pino (*Dialogo*, in Barocchi, *Trattati*, 1:115) had distinguished *poesie* from *istorie*, but neither of those earlier writers had lingered on the issue. Aristotle's *Poetics* lies behind the distinction between history and poetry; see Aristotle, *Poetics*, trans. Stephen Halliwell, in Aristotle, *Poetics;* Longinus: *On the Sublime;* Demetrius: *On Style*, trans. Stephen Halliwell, W. H. Fyfe, Doreen C. Innes, and W. Rhys Roberts, Loeb Classical Library 199 (Cambridge, MA: Harvard University Press, 1995), 58–63 (1451b). Gilio identifies a mixed mode as a separate genre and his model was evidently the epic as described by Aristotle, *Poetics*, 114–25 (1459a–1460a); see Charles Dempsey, "Mythic Inventions in Counter-Reformation Painting," in *Rome in the Renaissance: The City and the Myth; Papers of the Thirteenth Annual Conference of the Center of Medieval & Early Renaissance Studies*, ed. P. A. Ramsey (Binghamton: State University of New York at Binghamton, Center for Medieval & Early Renaissance Studies, 1982), 64–65. The mixing of truth, fiction, and fable is the subject of M. Pulidoro's discourse on the mixed painter later in the book; see especially Gilio, this volume, 214–16.
49. Even though their subjects may be fictional, painters must still observe decorum. The word *capriccio*, here translated as "own imagination," is defined by Baldinucci as meaning personal thought and invention (*proprio pensiero e invenzione*); see Filippo Baldinucci,

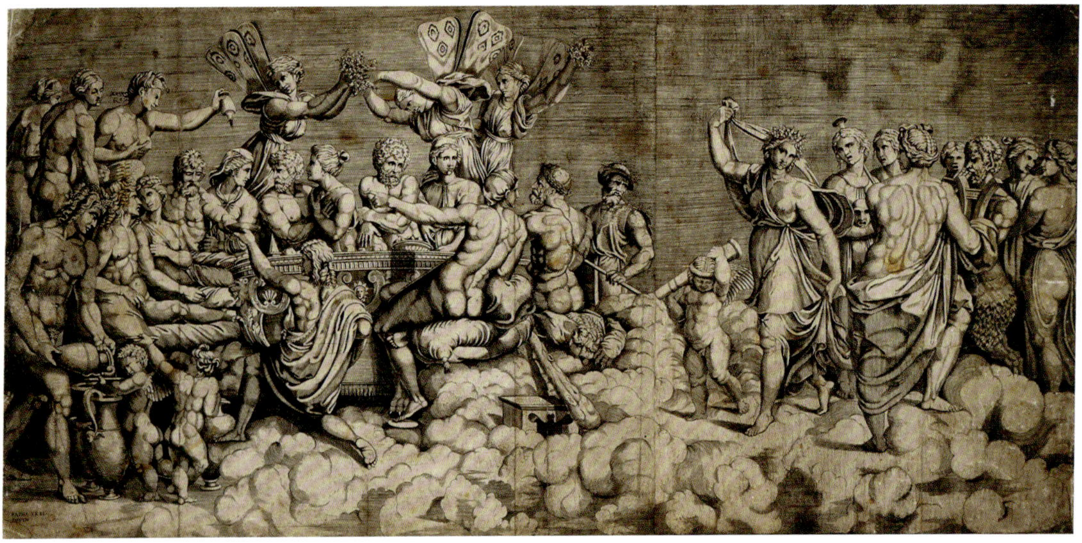

Fig. 4.
Anonymous, after Raphael (Italian, 1483–1520).
The Wedding Feast of Cupid and Psyche with the Olympian Gods, from the Villa Farnesina, engraving from two plates printed on two joined sheets, 33.9 × 71 cm.
London, British Museum.

Fig. 5.
Giorgio Vasari (Italian, 1511–74).
Paul III as Patron of Architecture, 1546, fresco.
Rome, Palazzo della Cancelleria, Sala dei Cento Giorni.

Fig. 6.
General view of the Sala dei Fasti Farnesiani in the Palazzo Farnese, Rome, with fresco by Francesco Salviati (Italian, 1510–63) showing Aeneas Ranuccio Farnese in the center.

example of this in the Chigi loggias where Raphael painted the Feast of the Gods with those actions and movements that he himself invented [fig. 4]. We can also describe in this way the loggias of the Pope, done by the pupils of Raphael of Urbino, and also the palace of Pope Julius's *vigna* and many other palaces in Rome.[50] Examples of the historical painter [*pittore istorico*] we have in the old and the new papal chapels where we see the Old and New Testaments and now the *Last Judgment* of Michelangelo; also many stories of saints that are to be found in Roman churches and other places.[51] Of mixed painters [*pittore misto*] we have the example of the hall in the Cancelleria and the one in the Palazzo Farnese in the Campo de' Fiori, the former done by Giorgio [Vasari] and the latter by Giacopo [*sic*] Salviati [figs. 5, 6].[52] In these three kinds of painting no

Vocabolario toscano dell'arte del disegno (Florence: Franchi, 1681), 28. For further discussion of the term, see note 68.

50. The Feast of the Gods was painted circa 1518 on the vault of the *loggia di Psiche* in the villa of Agostino Chigi, now known as the Farnesina (see fig. 4). The "palace of Pope Julius's *vigna*" refers to the Casino at the Villa Giulia in Rome, built by Giacomo Vignola for Pope Julius III. On the decoration of the Casino with mythological subject matter, under the direction of Prospero Fontana between 1553 and 1555, see Alessandro Nova, *The Artistic Patronage of Pope Julius III (1550–1555): Profane Imagery and Buildings for the De Monte Family in Rome* (New York: Garland, 1988), 136–204. Gilio's *Dialogo de le parti morali appertenenti a' letterati cortigiani* opens with one of the two interlocutors, Giovan Maria Gilio, visiting the Villa Giulia and examining the paintings, sculptures, fountains, and other beautiful things to be found there (1r–v); see Giovanni Andrea Gilio, *Dialogo del letterato cortigiano,* ed. Paolo Cherchi (Ravenna: Longo Editore, 2002). On the loggias of the pope and the Chigi loggias, see note 25.
51. The old papal chapel is the Sistine (Sistina), the new is the Pauline (Paolina).
52. In 1546, Vasari and assistants painted the Sala dei Cento Giorni in the Palazzo della Cancelleria with the acts of Paul III; see Julian Kliemann, *Gesta Dipinte: La grande*

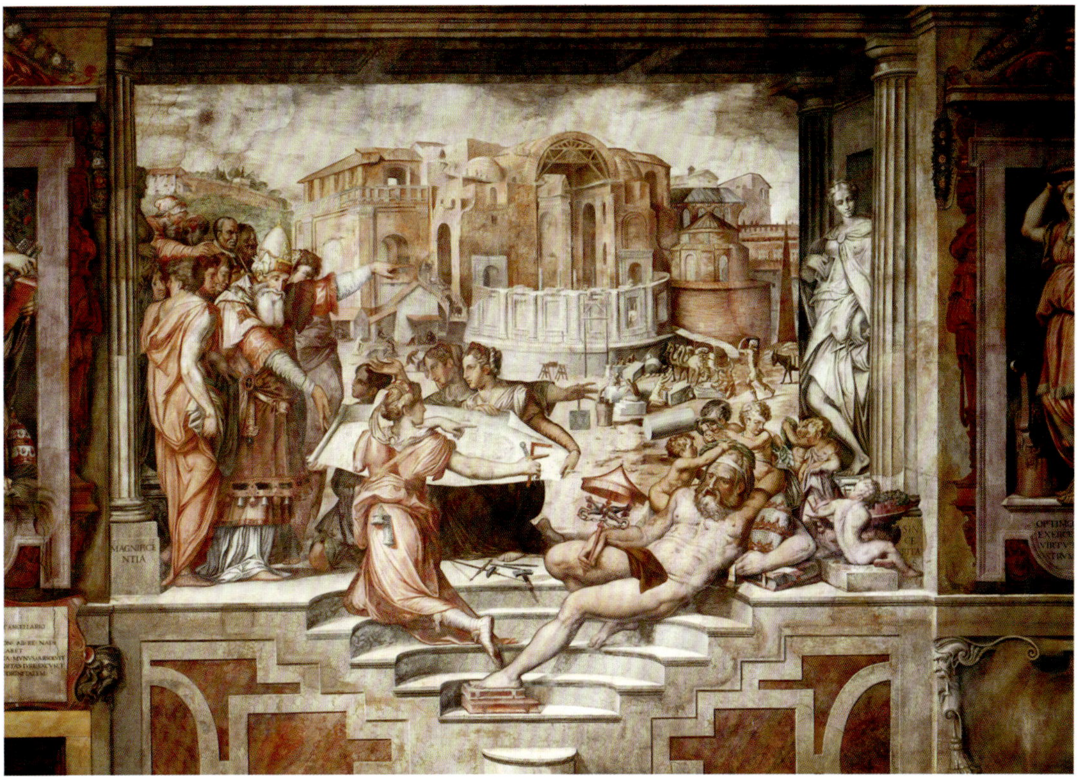
MAGNIFICE
NTIA

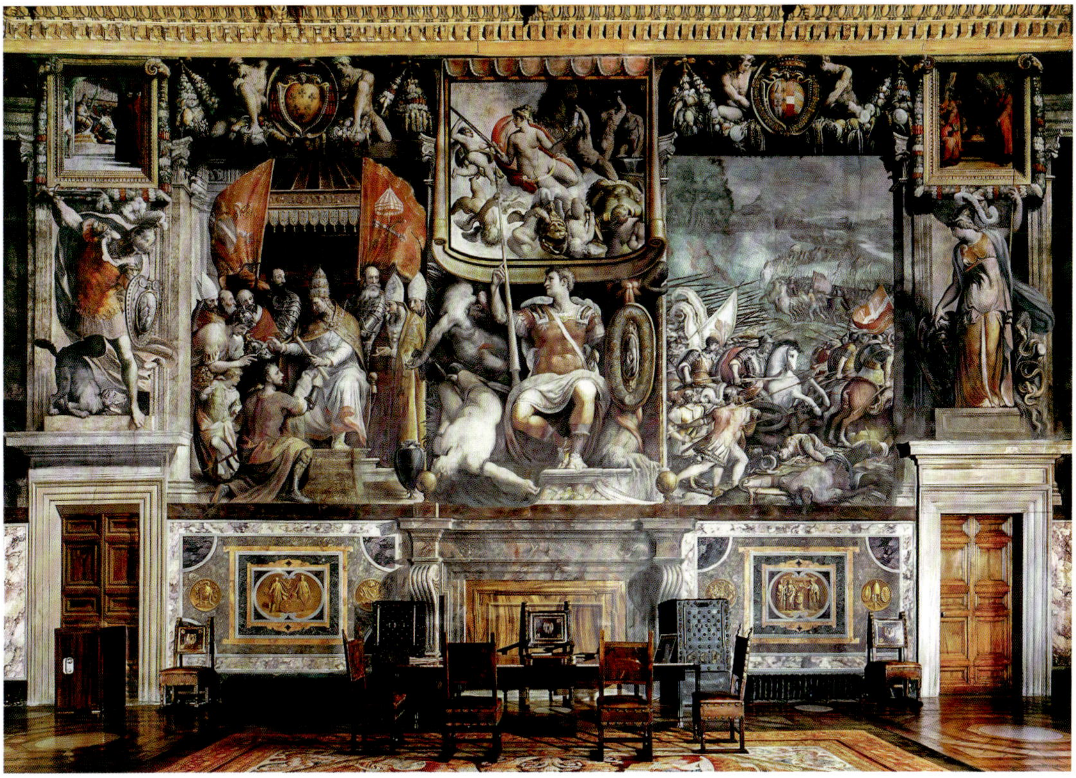

one observes what is proper to each, since the poetic painter [*pittore poetico*] will sometimes invent things that neither do nor can exist, justifying himself without further thought by reference to Horace's lines: **[16]** 'poets and painters were always granted equal power and liberty to invent whatever pleases them.'"

M. Francesco said: "If this were not the case, where would the freedom of the brush lie and where the glory and decorum [*decoro*] of poetry?"[53]

"Actually those things would be more securely based," replied M. Vincenso, "because when the art is regulated more, it is inevitable that the people who practice it will become more perfect. You will not deny that making up things that are neither true nor even lifelike [*verisimile*] is included under this precept."

"How not?" responded M. Francesco. "Do we not see that from the time of the ancients, because of the power of poetry, many things have been introduced that are neither true, nor lifelike?[54] I will give the example of the statues that are called terms, which appear to be men placed in tubs.[55] Further you will see an infinite number of monsters, some with the face of a man and the limbs of an animal, sometimes a horse, sometimes a dog, a half woman and half fish, others even more deformed than Horace's monster.[56] Some of these hold up columns, others support garlands and such like things, yet all are outside the natural order. Nevertheless, because of the power of poetry, they are allowed. Besides this, there are also all the fables, like people transformed into different animals of which Ovid and other poets have written at length: Lycaon turned into a wolf, Callisto into a bear, Actaeon into a stag, Cadmus into a snake, Daphne into a laurel, Philomela into a nightingale, Procne into a

decorazione nelle dimore italiane dal Quattrocento al Seicento (Milan: Silvana Editoriale, 1993), 37–51. Francesco (not Giacopo) Salviati decorated the Sala dei Fasti Farnesiani in the Palazzo Farnese, probably from circa 1552/3, with scenes of Farnese family history; Luisa Mortari, *Francesco Salviati* (Rome: Leonardo-De Luca, 1992), 122 (no. 36). On painters who mix poetry and history, see Gilio, this volume, 198–200.

53. Horace, *Ars Poetica,* 451 (lines 9–10). The translation follows Gilio's Italian, not Horace's Latin. The decorum of poetry and of painting is the capacity to find and express what is appropriate within the rules of the arts themselves. Michelangelo is later said to have restored the art of painting to its *decoro* (Gilio, this volume, 157). The need for painting to have its *decoro* is not contested, but it had to be regulated (Gilio, this volume, 172). Problems arise because the criteria of decorum—judgments about what is appropriate—come to be determined from within the art of painting itself, by the unregulated intellect of the painter equipped with all the requisite skills. This is essentially what Horace goes on to say in lines 11–13.
54. Aristotle, *Poetics,* 124–29 (1460b); see Donald Andrew Russell and Michael Winterbottom, eds., *Classical Literary Criticism* (Oxford: Oxford University Press, 1972), 84. Aristotle here makes the point that the excellence of Homer disguised absurdities that would have been intolerable in lesser hands.
55. A *term* is a pillar, capped by a head or head and torso, and used as a boundary marker. See also Gilio, this volume, 109–10.
56. On the monster described by Horace, see *Ars Poetica,* 450–51 (lines 1–5).

swallow, Atys into a pine, Rhodope and Haemus into mountains, Arethusa into a fountain, Ascalaphus into an owl, Nyctimene into a bat, ants into men, Battus into a stone; and Virgil even has the ships of Aeneas changed into sea nymphs, and so many other such things that it would take too long to tell of them all."[57]

M. Silvio said: "Truly poetic liberty is extensive, when one considers that the poets have not only changed people into animals and animals into people but, as M. Francesco has said, inanimate things into animate beings, as Virgil did with the ships of Aeneas and Ovid with the ants turned into men." **[17]**

M. Troilo said: "So do we not see things outside the natural order included under poetic license?"

"What things?" asked M. Vincenso.

M. Troilo added: "Painters have invented monsters that could not exist in nature in order to hold up columns and vaults. In place of columns we see in that city (since we have begun by giving Roman examples) sometimes the terms that you spoke of, sometimes half men and half snakes, sometimes simulated animals, sometimes dolphins, sometimes natural men, sometimes snakes, sometimes vines laden with grapes and leaves, sometimes ancient trophies, and other flights of imagination [*capricci*] done without observing rules or any law whatsoever; and all these are the ornament of painting."

M. Vincenso replied: "To everything you have said there is an easy reply. If we are discussing those fables that the ancients intended as fables, I admit that it is permissible to represent them while respecting both the beauty [*vaghezza*] and decorum [*decoro*] of the art. Because just as it was permissible for the poets to make them up and to write about them, so also it will be permissible for painters to paint them, following the path of the ancients who set the rules on these matters.[58] They also charmingly invented the practice of painting fauns and sylvan deities in ingenious and beautiful compositions, as Timanthes did when he painted on a small panel a Cyclops lying down with his legs bent. [Timanthes] wanted to show the size of that huge man, but, because the small

57. Ovid, *Metamorphoses,* vol. 1, *Books 1–8,* and vol. 2, *Books 9–15,* trans. Frank Justus Miller, rev. G. P. Goold, Loeb Classical Library 42, 43 (Cambridge, MA: Harvard University Press, 1916): Lycaon, 1:18–19 (1.230–39); Callisto, 1:92–95 (2.470–95); Actaeon, 1:136–39 (3.193–205); Cadmus, 1:218–21 (4.563–603); Daphne, 1:40–41 (1.543–53); Philomela, 1:334–35 (6.668); Procne, 1:334–35 (6.667–70); Atys (or Attis), 2:70–71 (10.103–5); Rhodope and Haemus, 1:294–95 (6.87–89); Arethusa, 1:278–83 (5.572–641); Ascalaphus, 1:274–77 (5.538–50); Nyctimene, 1:100–101 (2.589–95); ants into men, 1:384–89 (7.622–656); and Battus, 1:108–109 (2.688–707). The transformation of Aeneas's ships is from Virgil, *Aeneid, Books 7–12; Appendix Vergiliana,* trans. H. Rushton Fairclough, rev. G. P. Goold, Loeb Classical Library 64 (Cambridge, MA: Harvard University Press, 2001), 122–23 (9.114–22).

58. The authority of the ancients cuts through any doubts about the legitimacy of painting things that could not be found in nature.

size of the panel did not allow him to do it, he represented Satyrs measuring his big toe with a thyrsus."[59]

Interrupting his speech, M. Pulidoro said: "Truly the mind of man is great, and especially when he makes something that nature could not make itself, deploying his art in alluring and admirable inventions. In this regard I have heard that a panel, or perhaps a canvas, was brought to Francis, king of France, on which was painted an armed man who showed the whole of his back. The wise and ingenious artist, not being able to show his front too, as he wished, painted a mirror in the man's hand in which he displayed his face with the breast and everything else with such allure [*vaghezza*] that the generous king bought the figure for many hundreds of *scudi.* **[18]** Everyone thought that this was a beautiful and rare invention [*invenzione*]."[60]

And M. Vincenso continued his argument by saying: "Although such fictional [*finto*] and fabulous [*favoloso*] figures are pleasing, and given that the ancients even used those terms of which you speak and other fabulous fictions, nevertheless Vitruvius is not happy about it. He regrets that men, who ought to have been faithful imitators of nature, have tried so hard to legitimize things that nature cannot make and that cannot be either true or lifelike.[61] For which reason Horace, in order that overly inventive [*capricciosi*] men should not abuse the poetic license conceded them in the passage above, nor expend mental effort on vain and unnatural things, added to those lines quoted above:

> We too know that, and we often grant this license to others as well as demanding it for ourselves; not that tame animals may couple with wild ones, nor birds be put together with terrifying snakes, and tigers with lambs.[62]

This is because many monstrous things that are contrary to the correct rules have been introduced as a result of the ignorance of painters. And, if we think

59. Pliny, *NH,* 9:314–17 (book 35, §74), where it is the Cyclops's thumb, not his big toe, that the Satyrs measure.

60. Barocchi speculates about which painting Gilio had in mind (see Barocchi, *Trattati*, 2:575, n1 to Gilio p. 18)—perhaps the self-portrait of G. G. Savoldo, formerly identified as Gaston de Foix, in the Louvre. See Janet Cox-Rearick, *La collection de François Ier* (Paris: Éditions des Musées Nationaux, 1972), 41–42 (no. 51 F).

61. Vitruvius, *On Architecture,* vol. 2, *Books 6–10,* trans. Frank Granger, Loeb Classical Library 280 (Cambridge, MA: Harvard University Press, 1934), 2:104–9 (7.5.3–7).

62. Horace, *Ars Poetica,* 450–51 (lines 11–13); the translation follows Gilio's Italian, not Horace's Latin. Dolce too had quoted Horace's lines in order to define the absolute limits of the license conceded to painters. See Dolce, *L'Aretino*, in Barocchi, *Trattati,* 1:171 (Roskill, *Dolce's "Aretino,"* 130–31).

about Horace's precept carefully, we will find that he demands that in all things the order of nature must be preserved, and it is everything that can be categorized as well-regulated poetry that is conceded to the painter and the poet. We can think about this using the example of modern painters, because we do not have antique examples; and there is the example of the loggias in the Vatican done by such moderns. In the first, organized most beautifully, we see all sorts of grotesques painted and every kind of flower that could give verdant beauty to any loggia. Among these plants we see nothing repugnant to nature, as would be the case if jasmine produced roses, if orange trees produced plums, and other such things [see fig. 1].[63] Oh how one would laugh at someone who, as Horace says, painted dolphins in the woods and pigs in the sea, with fish in the skies and birds in the waves![64] **[19]** If we laugh at those things, why do we not feel like laughing at monsters that, as we have said, neither do nor can exist? But when everything is made to preserve its proper nature it will do honor to its maker, give happiness to its owner, and give pleasure to whoever looks at it. One sees also in the upper papal loggia many kinds of fish, birds, animals, fruit, and musical instruments, some done in one way, some in another, and their well-ordered variety makes the work seem elegant, charming, and beautiful [see figs. 2, 3].[65] What advantage would it be to the painter if, against Horace's precept, he were to paint doves giving birth to snakes, sheep to lions, or the other way round, lions to sheep and snakes to doves? Surely none, unless he wished to represent some prodigy of the kind that nature is accustomed to produce, either from playfulness or error; for one reads in Livy, Suetonius, and other ancient writers that this happened many times.[66] Or unless he wished to show the union of things that are naturally instinctively hostile, which Isaiah said would happen at the birth of the great Messiah, our Lord.[67] But if, beyond that, the painter wishes to picture such discordant things using the pretext of poetic license, what he makes will be governed more by subjective invention [*capriccio*] than by the laws of nature, of which art is the ape; and the artist will be more likely to attract laughter and shame than honor and praise."[68]

63. On the lower, first-floor loggia in the Vatican, referred to here, see note 25.
64. Horace, *Ars Poetica,* 452–53 (lines 29–30); Gilio elaborates on Horace's text.
65. On the second-floor loggia in the Vatican, referred to here, see note 25.
66. Livy, *History of Rome,* vol. 1, *Books 1–2,* and vol. 2, *Books 3–4,* trans. B. O. Foster, Loeb Classical Library 114, 133 (Cambridge, MA: Harvard University Press, 1919, 1922); and Suetonius, *Suetonius: Volume I* and *Suetonius: Volume II,* trans. J. C. Rolfe, Loeb Classical Library 31, 38 (Cambridge, MA: Harvard University Press, 1914).
67. Isaiah 11: 6–8.
68. Further to note 49, in this particular case, where it is set against the law of nature, *capriccio* has a negative significance, as Barocchi points out; see Barocchi, *Trattati,* 2:576, n3 to Gilio p. 19. Elsewhere, as seen in Gilio, this volume, 101–2, 120, it had a positive value. See Roland

M. Troilo said: "So in what would poetic liberty consist?"

M. Vincenso replied: "In many, many things. If somebody wanted to paint a forest, it could be made up of trees of different kinds: tall, short, bushy, dry, thin, thick, or however it seemed best. If somebody wanted to paint a landscape, it could be represented with mountains, hills, valleys, meadows, fields, rivers, ponds, springs, banks, fish, animals, birds of every kind; with cities, fortified towns, villas, palaces; and with men, some moving, some still, some sleeping, some awake, some walking, some drinking, and other suchlike things. However, one must be careful not to introduce features that are inappropriate to the place, as it would be if one were to paint Muscovy, Sarmatia, Gothia, Greenland, and other very cold northern countries and show them full of orange trees, citrons, lemons, and olives, with vines laden with large ripe grapes, laurels, olives, and other such things that only grow in warm or temperate countries. **[20]** It would be inappropriate too if one were to paint the sterile deserts of Arabia and Ethiopia full of the most pleasant gardens, of limpid springs, of clear and fresh streams, with beautiful birds flying around, or full of ornate and beautiful palaces, around which there were flowering green meadows, pleasant groves of laurels, myrtles, and other lovely trees; or indeed to introduce there the most noble cities, with seaports full of large, beautiful ships, peopled by tall, white-skinned men and women, while in northern parts one were to paint small, black, and uncouth men and women, with parrots or other birds that come from India in the trees.[69] How would you judge a painter who did such things?"

M. Francesco said: "Poorly, because all these things are contrary to the nature of the place."

M. Vincenso continued: "So the wise painter must know how to arrange things appropriate to person, time, and place. For it would not be good to give the pope the costume of a Turk, nor to the Turk the costume of the pope. As for the time, one should not represent Aeneas's arrival in Italy as taking place at the time of Emperor Justinian, nor the battles of the Carthaginians as happening in the presence of Pilate.[70] As for place, in churches one should not represent Vulcan using a steel net to catch Mars and Venus in bed, nor Jupiter in the form of a swan sleeping with Leda, nor the fall of the Giants, nor the battle of the Centaurs and the Lapiths, nor any other stories that are not pertinent, like

Kanz, "Der Capriccio-Begriff bei Vasari und Gilio in der Kontroverse um Michelangelos *Jüngstes Gericht*," in *Künste und Natur in Diskursen der frühen Neuzeit*, ed. Hartmut Laufhütte (Wiesbaden: Harrasowitz, 2000), 1:497–513.

69. Dolce makes a similar point; see *L'Aretino*, in Barocchi, *Trattati*, 1:167 (Roskill, *Dolce's "Aretino,"* 122–23). He uses particular narrative inventions to exemplify the need for painters to observe appropriateness to place.

70. On appropriateness in costume and time, see Dolce, *L'Aretino*, in Barocchi, *Trattati*, 1:165 (Roskill, *Dolce's "Aretino,"* 118–19).

the rape of the Sabines, the capture of the Capitol by the Gauls, the ruins of Carthage, or the life of Mohammed, Ali, and their other relatives.[71] Nor should anything be added repugnant to the subject, given the need to avoid what Horace said about the shipwreck survivor, that the artist had wanted to paint a cypress in that scene of shipwreck; and the same would be true if one wished to paint Saints Peter and Paul to embellish a scene of the defeat of Hannibal, and other similar examples, of which one might cite any number.[72] As for the terms you were speaking of earlier, I say that the ancients made them in that way for good reason, because the term represented two things: **[21]** first, dominion, which is something conceptual; and second, possession, a physical thing. The term affirms and displays this, substituting for the real live owner who could not stand there in person all the time, and at the same time representing the conceptual basis of true dominion, always firmly fixed in place, showing anyone who passed by the presence of the boundary dividing one field from another. It was cleverly conceived in this way in order to show that it had to be set in the ground. Indeed, according to Dionysius, to ensure that everyone would be content with what he owned, Numa passed a law stipulating that at the boundaries between fields, stone markers be placed which he had first consecrated; and further he ordered that every year, on the same day, homage should be paid to Jupiter Terminalis, to whom, or in whose name, the stones had been dedicated. [Numa] did this so that, if anyone removed these markers, it would be lawful for the person who noticed the misdeed to kill him for sacrilege, and by this means each landowner, secure in possession of his own fields, would not try to occupy those of his neighbor by fraud. It is said that this was why Jupiter Terminalis was worshipped in this form, but I believe that it was not Numa but his successors who portrayed him thus.[73] From being used in that way, these terms have been improperly transferred to become the supports for vaults and houses. This also applies to the monsters that are simulated on the friezes of cornices. As for the vines, the ivies, and the antique trophies that are painted or even sculpted on columns, I say that they are permissible as attractive fictions, because ivy is found climbing up walls and columns, as vines are too. For it is not these that do the work of supporting; they are only there as ornament and sometimes birds are painted on them as if they were eating the

71. On appropriateness to the location in which the picture is placed, see Dolce, *L'Aretino,* in Barocchi, *Trattati,* 1:188–89 (Roskill, *Dolce's "Aretino,"* 162–63).

72. Horace, *Ars Poetica,* 450–53 (lines 19–21). Dolce had discussed the need to consider appropriateness when deciding which figures to include in the representation of a subject. See Barocchi, *Trattati,* 1:168–69 (Roskill, *Dolce's "Aretino,"* 124–27).

73. Dionysius of Halicarnassus, *Roman Antiquities,* vol. 1, *Books 1–2,* trans. Earnest Cary, Loeb Classical Library 319 (Cambridge, MA: Harvard University Press, 1937), 530–35 (book 2, §74).

grapes and the ivy berries, and boys clamber up to catch them. And with this, one has to consider the difference between the fictional [*finto*] and the fabulous [*favoloso*]: fictional things can all fall under poetic license, but the fabulous only in the limited way described earlier.[74] The monstrous, if it is not a question of those prodigies and monsters of nature that I have already talked about, is not permissible at all.[75] Dolphins and men holding up columns and houses are seen by many people as ornament, but not by me, because, although it is something fictional, if one considers the literal effect of the fiction, one will find that it has no place.[76] **[22]** And the reason is that the fictional is that which plays the part of, or is able, naturally and really, to stand in for the truth [*vero*], otherwise it would not be fictional but fabulous [*favoloso*]. Nobody would be prepared to say that dolphins and men can hold up columns and vaults, and because this cannot exist in reality, it must not be used as a fiction."

M. Silvio said: "The opposite of what you have said can be seen in the obelisk at St. Peter's, which is supported by four lions or actually by four sphinxes [fig. 7].[77] This cannot fall within the rule you have stated."

M. Vincenso replied: "If those are sphinxes, it would not be surprising that fabulous beings supported that great structure: because one fabulous thing may well have a place alongside another. If they are lions, I would repeat Vitruvius's words, that men have been too presumptuous in accusing nature of imperfection or in wishing to contradict it.[78] At present this is accepted with the excuse that what we have inherited from the ancients is law. So the artist has to make every effort to imitate them, because in imitating those who are masters of this

74. That is, when following the fables of the ancient writers; see Gilio, this volume, 105.

75. See Gilio, this volume, 107.

76. The argument is close to Vitruvius, *On Architecture,* 2:104–7 (7.5.3–4). This is the domain of the fabulous (*favoloso*); see Gilio, this volume, 215.

77. The Vatican obelisk stood to the south of the basilica. Magister Gregorius, in his *Marvels of Rome,* describes it as the pyramid of Julius Caesar, but adds: "This pyramid is called by the pilgrims Saint Peter's needle, and with great effort they crawl under it where it is supported by four lions" (Hanc autem piramidem peregrini "Acum beati Petri" appellant. Sub quo magno labore reptant ubi super IIII eneos leones saxum fundatur). See Magister Gregorius, *Narracio de mirabilibus urbis Rome,* ed. R. B. C. Huygens (Leiden: E. J. Brill, 1970), 29. See also Magister Gregorius, *The Marvels of Rome,* ed. and trans. John Osborne (Toronto: Pontifical Institute of Mediaeval Studies, 1987), 11, 35, 91.

For a discussion of the persistent, but apparently false, belief that it was supported by lions, see Brian A. Curran et al., *Obelisk: A History* (Cambridge, MA: MIT Press, 2009), 64–66. Sixtus V provided bronze lions as supports when the monument was reinstalled in front of the basilica, but in the original arrangement the obelisk seems to have sat on bronze astragals; Rodolfo Lanciani calls them "dadi" or "gnoccoli." Lanciani, *Storia degli scavi di Roma e notizie intorno le collezioni romane di antichità,* vol. 4, *Dalla elezione di Pio V alla morte di Clemente VIII (7 gennaio 1566–3 marzo 1605),* ed. Paolo Liverani (Rome: Quasar, 1992), 163–64.

78. Vitruvius, *On Architecture,* 2:102–9 (7.5).

Fig. 7.
Anonymous.
The Vatican obelisk set against a background of Santa Maria della Febbre, 1540s, engraving, 49.7 × 30.5 cm. London, British Museum.

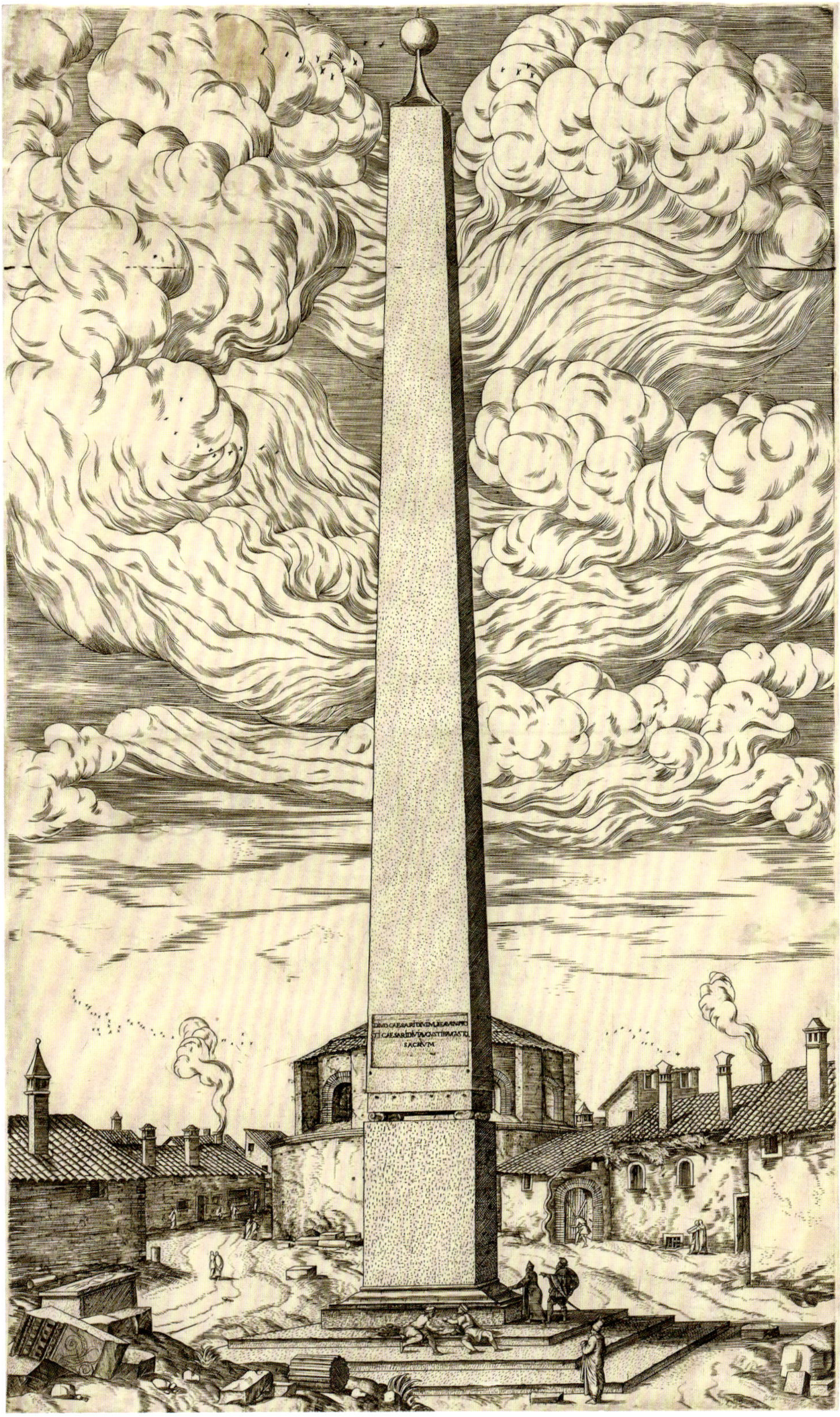

art we will say that he cannot err. There is no lack of opportunity for exercising freedom of the brush among poetical and fictional subjects, as we said earlier about landscapes, of which Ludius, a painter at the time of Augustus, was the inventor.[79] To start with [Ludius] painted the sea with boats, and, in the country, [he painted] those who ploughed the fields, walked, sat, stood, and slept. He also painted towns, palaces, villas, and the amenities of the countryside, as the Flemings so attractively do now. It is here that the painter's license is to be found, when he wants to paint day, night, a clear sky or one filled with clouds, the sun or moon, stars, the sea, rivers, lakes, springs, people fishing or swimming in the water, or doing one thing or another. Apelles was the first to paint the rain, the tempests, lightning, thunder, hail, and snow.[80] Piraeicus was the first to make up scenes in towns with artisans of every kind, shops full of goods, and other similar things.[81] This poetic license can even be extended to children's games, as can be beautifully seen in the tapestries woven with gold in the pope's public audience chamber, in the palace of Pope Julius's *vigna,* and in Palazzo Chigi in Trastevere [figs. 8, 9].[82] **[23]** Clever minds will not be short of beautiful and elegant fictions; what matters is knowing how to use them well. The law for poetry is truly very liberal, but there are rules. And anyone wanting to make a work should first take Horace's words into consideration, namely to identify and gauge his own strengths. Then he should shoulder the right weight for his stature, so as not to weaken in midstride. Those who do this will complete the task, and their works will be appropriately decorous.[83] In this way, the work shall be as the poet himself described:

Fig. 8.
Taddeo Zuccaro (Italian, 1529–66).
Scene with nymphs: preparations for the festival with narrow frieze of children's games visible beneath, 1553–55, fresco. Rome, Villa Giulia.

Fig. 9.
Master of the Die (Italian or German, active from 1530s), after Raphael (Italian, 1483–1520) and workshop, published by Antoine Lafréry (French, 1512–77, active in Italy).
Three putti before a large garland: the putto in the middle rides an ostrich, the one at the right pulls a feather from the ostrich's tail, and the one below holds the ostrich's leg, engraving from a series of four, 21 × 28 cm. London, British Museum.

79. Pliny, *NH,* 9:346–47 (book 35, §116); in modern editions, the name has been read as Studius or alternatively as Tadius. In the chapter in which Vitruvius denounces the monstrosities introduced into the wall decoration of his time, he had cited with approval the painting of realistic landscapes; Vitruvius, *On Architecture,* 2:102–3 (7.5.2).
80. Pliny, *NH,* 9:330–33 (book 35, §96).
81. Pliny, *NH,* 9:342–45 (book 35, §112).
82. Tapestries with swags and putti playing games, designed by Raphael and his workshop, decorated the lower walls of the Sala di Costantino in the Vatican on festive occasions. See Konrad Oberhuber and Achim Gnann, *Roma e lo stile classico di Raffaello (1515–1527),* exh. cat. (Milan: Electa, 1999), 238–39; and Giorgio Vasari, "Vita di Giovanni da Udine pittore," in Vasari, *Le vite de' più eccellenti pittori, scultori, e architettori: Nelle redazioni del 1550 e 1568,* vol. 5, ed. Rosanna Bettarini and Paola Barocchi (Florence: S.P.E.S., 1984), 451.

The Casino at the Villa Giulia (see note 50) has images of children playing in the painted vault of the semicircular loggia and also friezes with children's games decorating the vault of the main ground-floor room to the south (now the library) (see fig. 8); see Cristina Acidini Luchinat, *Taddeo e Federico Zuccari: Fratelli pittori del Cinquecento* (Milan: Jandi Sapi Editori, 1998), 1:32. The Palazzo Chigi in Trastevere is now known as the Farnesina. Which frescoes are being referred to remains uncertain; perhaps the soffits of the lunettes in the *loggia di Psiche,* or Sodoma's *Wedding of Alexander and Roxana* in the first-floor apartment?
83. Horace, *Ars Poetica,* 452–53 (lines 38–41).

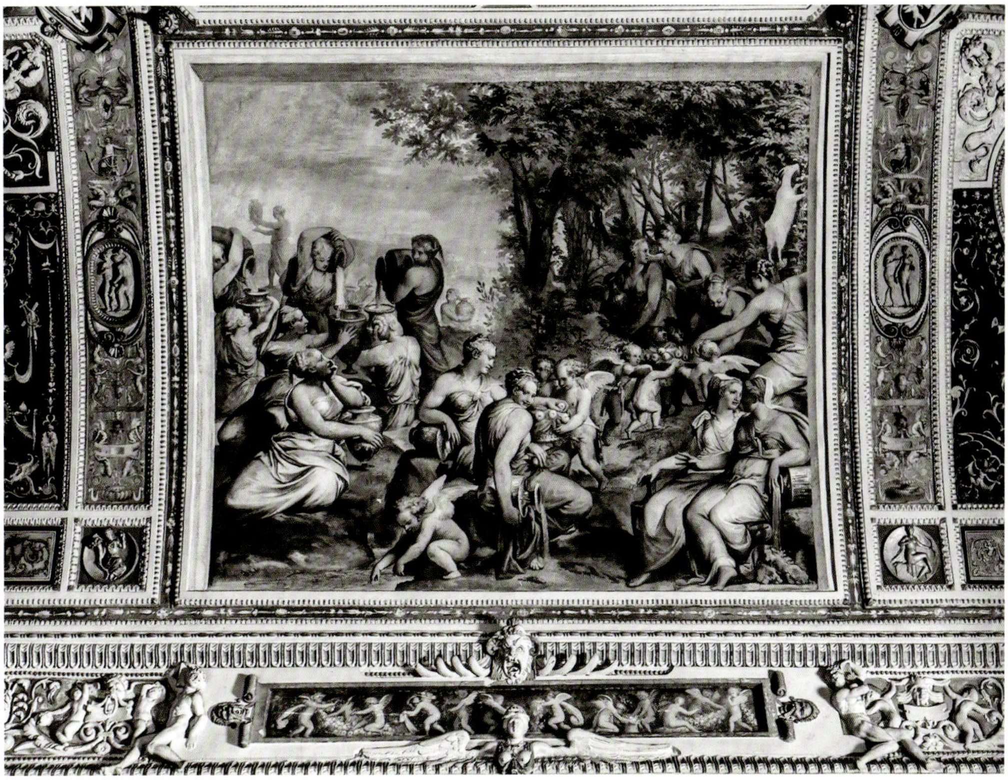

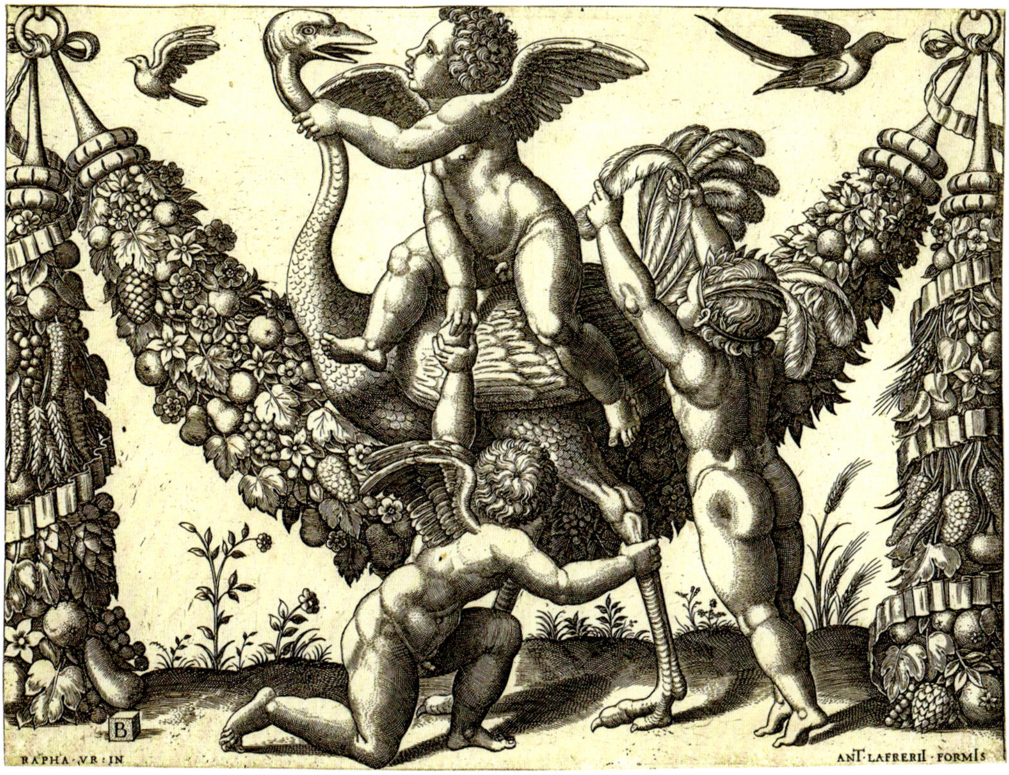
B
RAPHA · VR : IN
ANT · LAFRERII · FORMIS

> The poem will be like a beautiful painting, which delights and pleases you the more if you stand near it, while another likes to be seen from further away. One loves the dark, another light. And as the one does not fear the judgment of the good perceptive critic when it pleased him [seen] only once, the other will please [seen] ten times over.[84]

In truth, a beautiful, proportioned and well-understood figure attracts the eye so much, and pleases so much, that the viewers cannot tear themselves away. The more they look, the more it pleases them. This is also the effect of a beautiful poem, a beautiful comedy, or a beautiful history [*istoria*]: the more one reads, the more one sees, the more one hears, the greater the desire to read it, see it, and hear it. And, in the same way that the poet must respect the rules [*regole*] of poetry, so must the painter respect those of painting."[85]

"You have all spoken well about the different aspects of the poetic painter," said M. Francesco. "So it seems to me that as M. Vincenso has spoken of the qualities of the poetic painter, M. Silvio should describe those of the historical painter."

M. Silvio replied: "You place on me a burden unsuited to my powers, and M. Francesco could set it out and explain it much better, because he delights in histories and other such elegant things. **[24]** My profession is to go round the palaces pleading cases, drawing up summonses, and proffering articles and laws, not studying Pliny and those others who have written on the subject."

They all laughed at these words, and M. Francesco said: "M. Silvio is a shrewd person, one who knows that it is not good form to sing one's own praises, and he wishes us to praise him, taking into consideration that we know he delights in laws and articles but also in histories. So please don't torment us further, this burden falls on you. Take it on with the good grace [*garbo*] that you show in the other things that you do, and begin the exposition of the qualities necessary for a historical painter."

All the others said so too. Then [M. Silvio] said: "Since it pleases you that I should teach this lesson, I can't and don't want to refuse, because I would

84. Horace, *Ars Poetica,* 480–81 (lines 361–65); the translation follows Gilio's Italian, not Horace's Latin.

85. Summing up, M. Vincenso reminds us of the importance for the argument of Dolce's ideas: the scope for freedom of invention is wide, but there are rules and there is a need for painters and writers to observe those rules, in particular rules of decorum (*decoro*, or, in Dolce, *convenevolezza*) and, for Dolce, disposition (*ordine*); see Dolce, *L'Aretino,* in Barocchi, *Trattati,* 1:165 (Roskill, *Dolce's "Aretino,"* 118–19). Dolce specifies that even license is subject to limits; Dolce, *L'Aretino,* in Barocchi, *Trattati,* 1:171 (Roskill, *Dolce's "Aretino,"* 130–31). Behind Dolce lies Horace; see note 62. The great difference between Dolce and Gilio is that while Dolce was writing about painters and painting in general, in our text this discussion concerns the poetic painter alone.

consider it a failing; and even though I speak clumsily, I will do it willingly, simply to obey those who are in a position to command me."

"Don't make any more excuses," added M. Vincenso, "because I also work in your profession, and when I spoke earlier I did it to satisfy you. The present duty falls to you so don't waste any more time with excuses, just start when you're ready."

"So now," said M. Pulidoro, "let us discuss the historical painter a little, which requires many more details than the others. History needs much more attention than poetry because, while the latter is loose and broad, the former is fixed within limits that nobody is entitled to overstep.[86] And I think that Eupompus spoke well when he said that arithmetic and geometry are necessary to the painter, because if he lacks knowledge of them, I don't think he truly deserves the name of painter at all. Without them he will not know how to judge foreshortenings correctly, according to the rules, nor perspective, nor what the painting requires when seen up close, or when seen from a distance.[87] He who does not know these two subjects but who wishes to calculate the contours of the body by eye will often be deceived unless he has had great practice and long experience. **[25]** So one often sees figures deformed and misshapen, without any proportion whatsoever; some that have arms, legs, or other

86. Barocchi, *Trattati,* 2:577–78, n1 to Gilio p. 24, suggests that Gilio's preoccupation with content and moral values led him to take from poetry its traditional higher status and give the leading position to history. She refers to the contrast drawn by Aristotle, *Poetics,* 58–63 (1451b): while poetry revealed profound and general truths, which brought it close to philosophy, history could only tell of particulars. Gilio was not the only one to contest this order of values; see Anthony Grafton, "The Identities of History in Early Modern Europe," in *Historia: Empiricism and Erudition in Early Modern Europe,* ed. Gianna Pomata and Nancy G. Siraisi (Cambridge, MA: MIT Press, 2005), 53–54. What was commonly highlighted was the pedagogical function of history "as a source of moral principles exemplified in action, which could teach the intelligent reader prudence, and its literary nature as a genre that could not only inform, but move, its readers" (Grafton, "Identities of History," 54). Grafton sees fifteenth- and sixteenth-century writings on history as part of a massive early modern effort "to capture and use a world of particulars" (51). Cicero had taken a position very close to the one adopted here by M. Pulidoro; Cicero, *On the Orator* [*De Oratore*]: *Books 1–2,* trans. E. W. Sutton and H. Rackham, Loeb Classical Library 348 (Cambridge, MA: Harvard University Press, 1942), 242–45 (2.15.62). M. Ruggiero will quote later from this passage in Cicero; see Gilio, this volume, 196.

87. What are said to be Eupompus's precepts, emphasizing the importance of the painter being trained in arithmetic and geometry, along with other branches of learning, are cited above. See Gilio, this volume, 100; and Pliny, *NH,* 9:316–17 (book 35, §75–76). Barocchi (*Trattati,* 2:578, n1 to Gilio p. 25) interprets Gilio as opposing "the license of the Michelangelesque idea of the judgment of the eye ('giudizio dell'occhio')," but it is not evident that by the early 1560s Michelangelo was associated with such a view, for the texts asserting it are late; see David Summers, *Michelangelo and the Language of Art* (Princeton, NJ: Princeton University Press, 1981), 370–72. The distinction between paintings that need to be seen from up close and from far off is a response to Horace, *Ars Poetica,* 480–81 (lines 361–62), which M. Vincenso had cited a little earlier.

members longer than they should, with the result that it makes one laugh to see them. Foreshortenings that ought to produce an effect up close, produce it from a distance, and those that ought to produce it from a distance only produce it up close; and sometimes they produce no effect at all, or, more commonly, of a kind different from the one intended. And because this rule is observed by few, we see that mistakes are only avoided by a few. I wanted to say this in order to introduce you to the subject."[88]

M. Silvio said: "It is because of this, Gentlemen, that modern painters, whether they are painting histories, fables, or mixed subjects, commit an infinite number of mistakes, and very few paintings are to be found that have the proper correspondence (*debita proporzione*) with their subjects. With respect to histories, few are faithful and straightforward expositors of the truth of the subject matter; and it ought to be different, for the writer and the painter—I am speaking of historical writers and painters—are weighed on the same pair of scales. That great and learned man, Pope Gregory, said that painting is nothing other than history for the illiterate; for just as one person learns about what happened by reading a history, an illiterate person would do so by looking at a painting.[89] Therefore, as they are both essentially equal, we will make the same judgment about each of them: the painter with his brush is no less obliged to portray the plain and simple truth than is the historian with his pen."

M. Troilo said: "You should not judge a history to be untruthful if variations are introduced in the nonessential things [*accidenti*] that are apt to occur."[90]

---

88. Opening the discussion of the historical painter by insisting on the need for knowledge of arithmetic and geometry, M. Pulidoro asserts the importance for the painter of objective knowledge as opposed to reliance on the subjective judgment of the eye. One of the interlocutors in Pino's *Dialogo di pittura* (in Barocchi, *Trattati,* 1:106) had asserted that it was more praiseworthy for a painter to depend on measurement [*misura*] than to trust in his own judgment [*giudicio*]. What is clear is that Gilio is determined to demonstrate how the painter must base his work on objective principles, in order to ensure that the figures in his paintings will be natural-looking and dignified.
89. Gregory the Great's letter to Serenus: "For the worship of a picture is one thing but learning what should be worshipped through the story in a picture is another. For what writing provides for readers, this a picture provides for uneducated people looking at it, for in it the ignorant see what they should follow and the illiterate read the same from it. Thus a picture serves as a text, especially for pagans." See Gregory the Great, *The Letters of Gregory the Great,* trans. John R. C. Martyn (Toronto: Pontifical Institute of Mediaeval Studies, 2004), 3:744–46. For the original Latin, see Pope Gregory, *S. Gregorii Magni opera: Registrum epistolarum; Libri VIII–XIV,* ed. Dag Ludwig Norberg (Turnhout: Brepols, 1982), 874.
90. "Nonessential" translates the Italian word *accidenti,* which is here employed in contrast to "substance" [*sostanza*]. Gilio was making use of a very familiar Aristotelian distinction between the essential and the nonessential properties of an object. Howard Robinson, "Substance," in *The Stanford Encyclopedia of Philosophy*, ed. Edward N. Zalta (Stanford: Stanford University, spring 2014), http://plato.stanford.edu/archives/spr2014/entries/substance.

"That is true," replied M. Silvio, "but at the same time there are some nonessential things that are so closely connected with the substance [*sostanza*] of the history [*istoria*] that if they were altered, either by being more emphasized than they ought to be, or more concealed, the subject matter would be distorted. As would be the case for example if, wishing to show the defeat at Cannae, it were shown in a ship, in a city, or on the top of a mountain: who would be able to resist laughing at such a ridiculous artist?[91] **[26]** How would anyone who read such a history, written by someone in that way and set in those places, judge the writer or, indeed, how would he judge a painter who represented our Lord crucified on a cross of gold or silver, or on a cross so small or slight that it would not support a young child, let alone a man, or so long and large that it looked out of proportion, or if he made the shaft of roses, lilies, and violets, or if our Lord were dressed in royal garments embellished with gemstones and gold?"

"They would be judged the worst," said M. Pulidoro. "Nothing good could be said. But there are nonessential things that do not alter the sense of a history, as for example if one made the number of Pharisees who seized Christ greater or smaller than there actually were; the lights that they carried, the kinds of arms, the houses of Pilate, of Caiaphas, of Anna, of Herod more beautiful and more ornate than they actually were; the hill of Calvary higher or lower, Jerusalem bigger or smaller, and other such things."

Speaking again, M. Silvio said: "Rather, these additions will be an ornament to the painting. It will be the task of the good painter to know how to distinguish between the nonessential things that need to be avoided and those that should be used, those that may dishonor the subject and those that may enhance it. But before everything else he must find out about the subject of the history that he intends to paint; and then about the time, the place, the persons; and he must not mix things up in an ignorant manner, but give to each what is proper to it in an ordered way, so that decorum is observed in everything.[92] Horace showed this beautifully, saying:

> Sad words are always appropriate to a mournful face, and bitter, haughty and threatening language suits the face of anger; for one who is playful, sweet and frivolous speech is right and for the stern, ornate and weighty [speech].[93]

---

91. Cannae, a settlement in Apulia, was the site of the terrible Roman defeat at the hands of Hannibal's army in 216 BC.
92. Compare Dolce's similar remarks on the need for the painter to have knowledge of poetry and history in order to properly represent subjects and to design figures appropriate to them. See Dolce, *L'Aretino,* in Barocchi, *Trattati,* 1:170 (Roskill, *Dolce's "Aretino,"* 128–29). See also note 6.
93. Horace, *Ars Poetica,* 458–59 (lines 105–7); the translation follows Gilio's Italian, not Horace's Latin.

Although these are precepts intended for poets introducing various characters into their comedies or tragedies or other poems, nevertheless, if rightly considered, they fit painters too; **[27]** because with their colors [painters] can represent all the natural effects in faces, gestures, and every other human action that poets can represent with their pens. And on this point, the same poet added, a few lines further on:

> It is of great significance whether the master or the slave is speaking; whether a man weighed down by years or a talkative, unreliable boy in the bloom of youth; whether a powerful matron or a solicitous nurse; whether a roving merchant or a farmer with rich and fertile fields; or whether he is someone brought up in Colchis or Argos, Assyria or Thebes.[94]

To the painter it will perhaps seem difficult to use his colors to express joy, melancholy, languor, audacity, shyness, laughter, tears, and other passions of the soul in his figures. But if he thinks about the matter correctly, taking into account the power of the art of painting, he will find that this can be done both pleasingly and easily. Indeed, Cicero gives as an example the great artist Timanthes. Having painted Agamemnon's daughter Iphigenia about to be sacrificed before the altar, with such a grieving and tearful face that it seemed to move the onlookers to deep sorrow, and having painted the tearful expressions of the bystanders and the sorrow of her uncle, he despaired of showing yet more pain and melancholy on her father's face, although his grief ought to be greater than all the others. Therefore, Timanthes showed him covering his face, almost as if to demonstrate how, as a result of a father's pity for his daughter's feelings and inner grief, he could not look her in the face or even witness this tragic situation.[95] This was demonstrated even more clearly by the same poet [Horace] when he wrote:

> At the beginning nature shapes within us the disposition with which we meet every change of fortune: it helps us to enjoy, it arouses us to anger, or when sorrowful, it makes us cast our eyes filled with sadness down to the ground; the internal movements of the mind are then to be seen externally and are revealed by the tongue. But if what is said does not correspond to those inner states, then one will hear the Romans, both knights and others, laugh.[96] **[28]**

94. Horace, *Ars Poetica,* 458–61 (lines 114–18); the translation follows Gilio's Italian, not Horace's Latin.
95. Cicero, *Orator,* in idem, *Brutus; Orator,* trans. G. L. Hendrickson and H. M. Hubbell, Loeb Classical Library 342 (Cambridge, MA: Harvard University Press, 1939), 360–61 (22.74).
96. Horace, *Ars Poetica,* 458–59 (lines 108–13); the translation follows Gilio's Italian, not Horace's Latin.

That painters can represent such gestures so that anyone, however ignorant, can recognize them, is shown by the figures created by the ancients and by many modern painters. As for example one reads of Aristides the Theban (albeit his works are somewhat crude) who, in painting the ruin of his native country, represented a young child suckling and the mother, who had been wounded in the breast, appearing to fear that her child would drink her blood rather than her milk; her action was so piteous and full of grief that Alexander the Great sent it as something quite extraordinary to Pella, the place he came from, to ensure the memory of such a worthy work. That same painter painted a sick person with such naturalness that while prostrated, [the sick man] appeared to show on his face the severity of his pains and the torments of his sickness.[97] But why do I go on borrowing examples from the ancients when there are so many by Michelangelo and Raphael in Rome? Raphael, in the *Transfiguration*, which is now to be seen in San Pietro in Montorio, painted an old man who brings his possessed son to the Apostles [fig. 10]. [The old man] appears hardly able to walk and shows in his face the great suffering he is going through on account of his son's illness. And the son himself, with his strained movement [*atto sforzato*], swollen throat, and distorted hands, as is characteristic of those afflicted in this way, appears to refuse to approach the Apostles.[98] What can one say about Michelangelo's bearded Saint Paul? Does he not appear to show ecstasy, terror, stupor and to be out of his mind following the great event that has happened to him?[99] And in order not to go on recounting every example, it is enough to finish by saying that the excellent painter will easily know how to express the appropriate gestures suitable to every passion and every occasion. But any painter who represents those gestures clumsily will be mediocre, and it will be appropriate to apply to him Horace's description of those who cannot convey well the emotions of the characters they introduce into their fables: **[29]**

> Then, Telephus and Peleus, if you speak in an inappropriate way about what was inflicted upon you, I shall be forced either to burst out laughing or to fall asleep.[100]

Everything I have said belongs so much to the substance of a history that the artist who does not take notice will produce works more worthy of derision than of admiration. The alert and prudent painter must first of all seek to master

---

97. Pliny, *NH*, 9:332–35 (book 35, §98–100).
98. Raphael's altarpiece of the Transfiguration (see fig. 10); see Jürg Meyer zur Capellen, *Raphael: A Critical Catalogue of His Paintings*, vol. 2 (Landshut: Arcos-Veri, 2005), 195 (no. 66).
99. Michelangelo's *Conversion of Paul* in the Pauline Chapel in the Vatican. See fig. 14.
100. Horace, *Ars Poetica*, 458–59 (lines 103–5); the translation follows Gilio's Italian, not Horace's Latin.

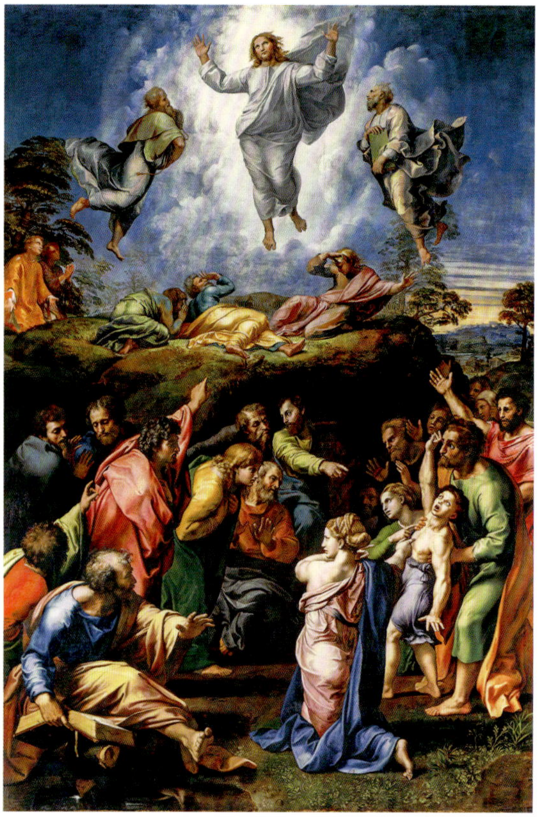

the subject of the history. Then he must compose it in the way it should be, and in doing that he should imitate the architect who, before beginning the structure he intends to build, makes a wooden model of it or draws a plan of it on paper. So he must make sketches, cartoons, 'modelli,' and he must not trust his mind because it is unreliable: a fine imaginative idea [*capriccio*] will sometimes occur to him and if it is not put down on paper it will be forgotten. I do not place the painter in any better position than the writer, who, according to Horace, should not publish his work without having made many corrections and changed it ten times.[101] Petrarch clearly showed that he did this when he wrote:

> So many of them I tear up, and [again] prepare and write them.[102]

Fig. 10.
Raphael (Italian, 1483–1520).
Transfiguration, 1516–20,
oil on panel, 405 × 278 cm.
Vatican City, Musei Vaticani,
Pinacoteca.

101. Horace, *Ars Poetica,* 474–75 (lines 289–94); see also Gilio, this volume, 149–50.

102. "Tante ne squarcio, n'apparecchio e vergo": Francesco Petrarch, *Trionfo d'Amore,* in *Canzoniere, Trionfi, Rime Varie,* ed. Carlo Muscetta and Daniele Ponchiroli (Turin: Einaudi, 1958), 484 (part 3, line 117).

I do not believe that anyone has such a refined and elevated intellect that he can write a perfect poem immediately on putting pen to paper. Rather, once a poem has been written, it must be thought about and polished, exchanging the literal for the metaphorical in the use of words, ornamenting it with figures, purging it of mistakes, and improving the concept. I will say this of the painter who has made his sketch: he will not wander into error if he goes about gradually adjusting and correcting it; if he thinks about character, the subject matter that he is painting, the clothes that are necessary, the appropriate movements; and if he makes the beginning agree with the middle and the middle with the end.[103] For poor understanding of the subject results in infinite errors, and in my view the worst thing is to abandon truth in response to some subjective idea [*capriccio*] that abuses it. This has become dominant to such an extent these days that few are seen doing the opposite." **[30]**

M. Pulidoro said: "Since I hear you mention abuses, I would very much like M. Troilo to talk a little about them. I have on occasion heard him discuss them in a way that pleased me a lot, and in the meantime M. Silvio can take a short rest and think up further elegant ideas to add to what he has already said."

"Thank you," replied M. Silvio, smiling, "and I know that what M. Troilo says will be more learned and better argued than anything I have done."

"I do not make any such claim," said M. Troilo. "You say this so that we praise you and show our approval of the fine discourse that you have made up to this point. However, if you think I should contribute my share, I am happy to do so."

"Come on," said M. Francesco, "don't waste more time making excuses. Do continue, or rather do start because, given that there are so many abuses, it will take some time to describe them all."

M. Troilo said: "Indeed, you have to believe that today the abuses of the painters are infinite in number. But I don't propose to speak about all of them because it would be too great a task. I will tell you, however, about many that have been little noticed but which are of greater importance than some realize. So among other abuses there are those concerning the two thieves who were crucified with our Lord, who are painted as if crucified in a different way

103. Dolce too recommends drawing (see Dolce, *L'Aretino,* in Barocchi, *Trattati,* 1:170–71 [Roskill, *Dolce's "Aretino,"* 128–29]), but in significantly different terms. While Dolce had the artist try out in sketches the various *fantasie* that the story provokes in his mind, Gilio stresses the opportunity offered by a sketch for the painter to improve his understanding of the subject, to make corrections, and to move toward the most appropriate representation of the theme. Gilio is closer to Alberti, *On Painting and On Sculpture,* 102–5 (book 3, §61). The point about coherence in the composition of the whole story carries an echo of Horace, *Ars Poetica,* 462–63 (line 152); it was a point that underlies Dolce's idea of disposition (*ordine*) in invention; see Dolce, *L'Aretino,* in Barocchi, *Trattati,* 1:166 (Roskill, *Dolce's "Aretino,"* 120–21).

from our Lord: not fixed with nails as they actually were, but tied with ropes. The extent to which this is a mistake is witnessed by church history, in which one reads that Helena, having dug up the three crosses from under the ground, would not have had the least sign by which to identify which was our Lord's and which those of the thieves, if the miracle of the moribund woman healed by the true Cross had not presented the clearest proof."[104]

M. Francesco interrupted, saying: "You've reminded me by what you've said of something that I have until now regarded as uncertain. However, digressing a little, do explain it to me."

"What is it?" said M. Vincenso.

"In Jerusalem," continued M. Francesco, "how can the distance between one cross and another be known?" **[31]**

"That," said M. Troilo, "cannot really be known, I think."

"How is that?" responded M. Ruggiero. "Have I not heard our Reverend Father brother Antonio recount that on Calvary, in the precise place where the crosses stood, Helena built a church in which either she or someone else then built three small chapels, not far from one another?[105] An observant Franciscan friar in Osimo, a city in the March of Ancona, showed the measurements to the archbishop of Siena, who was returning from Loreto, and, according to those measurements, the chapels were so close that it was impossible for the crosses to have stood in a row, but instead those of the thieves would have had to be lower, or turned sideways."[106]

"I can prove that this distance cannot be known, on the following grounds. After the fall of Jerusalem, the pagans built the temple of Venus on Mount Calvary, and this too was then destroyed by order of Constantine the Great. Among the ruins, the pagans then set the statue of Venus, which was smashed when Helena arrived in Jerusalem, and when she wished to find the Cross she found the whole place full of briars and thorns, and so overgrown that it was impossible to say where the crosses had been, or even where they might have been, at the time of the Passion. All three crosses were then found in the same ditch, with the three nails and the *Titulus Crucis,* all of which gave no clue as to which had been Christ's, or which the thieves', if the miracle had not indicated

104. The belief that Christ and the thieves had been crucified in exactly the same way had been held by the church fathers Ambrose and Augustine. Gilio's proof depends upon the well-known story of the discovery of the true Cross by Saint Helena, in Rufinus of Aquileia's *Historia Ecclesiastica,* in *The Church History of Rufinus of Aquileia: Books 10 and 11,* trans. Philip R. Amidon (Oxford: Oxford University Press, 1997), 16–17 (book 10, §7–8). See also Jacobus de Voragine, *The Golden Legend: Readings on the Saints,* trans. William Granger Ryan (Princeton, NJ: Princeton University Press, 1993), 282.

105. It has not been possible to identify "brother Antonio."

106. The archbishop of Siena, Francesco Bandini Piccolomini, had been mentioned earlier as having visited Fabriano; see note 17.

them, as I said.[107] Therefore, if the place or the distance were not revealed by God, I cannot imagine how it would be possible to guess it among those ruins, given that the memory of the place and the crosses has been lost for so many centuries."

M. Vincenso said: "Those are very good arguments, and we must believe that the great God—given that there is nothing to contradict [the idea]—revealed it himself, so that such a great mystery should not remain hidden."

"Now, do continue," said M. Francesco. Returning to the subject, M. Troilo said: "The other abuse I note is that of making Saint Peter a decrepit old man at the time of our Lord's Passion. **[32]** This, it seems to me, could not be the case because from the time of the Passion until the last year of the reign of Nero, when Peter was crucified, there were 37 years. Also they always make Saint John the Evangelist a beardless youth, when at the time of the Passion he was 31 years old."

M. Pulidoro said: "I think that painters have drawn on what Saint Mark says in his account of the Passion about the capture of our Lord and the flight of the Apostles when he writes: 'And a certain young man followed him, having a linen cloth cast about his naked body; and they laid hold on him.'[108] Most [commentators] believe this to be John, which cannot be, because John also followed Jesus and made it possible for Peter to enter Caiaphas's house.[109] Rather, [this young man] was the son of the innkeeper in whose house the Savior had eaten the paschal meal with the Apostles."

"So, therefore," said M. Troilo, "being 30 or 31 years old, Saint John must have been a bearded man and not a youngster of 17 years or more; and when he died in Ephesus, he was over 99 years old.[110] Again they paint Saint Joseph as a decrepit old man; it does not seem to me likely that God would have entrusted his son's mother to someone decrepit, unable to endure all the hardships necessary to take his son into Egypt and then bring him back again to Judaea. And in any case, if we want to believe Origen, the glorious Virgin was married to conceal this great sacrament from the Devil and also to escape the infamy of adultery; but it would have fallen out worse if she had been married to a decrepit, useless old man rather than to a mature or even young man, which would have been more appropriate given that he had to serve rather than be served.[111]

107. The account of the finding of the Cross (*inventio Crucis*) largely follows Rufinus of Aquileia's account; see note 104. The *Titulus Crucis* is the superscription INRI that was placed above Christ on the Cross.

108. Mark 14:51.

109. John 18:15–16.

110. Voragine, *The Golden Legend*, 55.

111. The reference to Origen is to a group of homilies on the infancy narrative of Matthew, wrongly attributed to the Alexandrian theologian Origen: "Homilia XVII. In Vigilia Nativitatis Domini. (Ex Origene)," in Venerabilis Bedae, *Opera Omnia*, vol. 6, and Paul

"Shall we not call it an abuse to paint Saint John the Baptist clad in sable pelts that only barely cover his buttocks, when he should wear camel and wear it long, according to Jewish custom?[112] Painters for the most part also represent Mary of Cleophas, Mary of Alpheus, and the other Marys, at the time of the Passion of our Lord, as young women aged 17 or 20 years old, not knowing that at that time one had four sons and the other two, and all were apostles of our Lord.[113] Also one finds some painters representing the Magdalene at the foot of the Cross all neat, perfumed, loaded with jewelry and golden chains, wearing clothes of velvet and puffed up with vanity, for they don't realize that she was no longer a sinner but a fervent disciple. **[33]** They also paint Saint Francis as ruddy, stout, and well dressed, with neatly combed, perfumed, and curled mustaches, and wearing a cowl of the finest cloth, all pleated, with a silk cord, so that he looks more like a general or a provincial of the order than the model of penitence that he was; they fail to consider that he only ever wore a single coarse, rough tunic. The same could be said of Saint Dominic, Saint Benedict, Saint Bernard, and Saint Romuald. Should we not call it an abuse to paint Saint Jerome with a red hat, like the one worn by cardinals today? Because, although he was a cardinal, he did not wear such garments, given that Pope Innocent IV,

Winfrid [Paulus Winfridus Diaconus], *Opera Historica, sive opera eius omnium pars prima*, Patrologia Latina, series secunda 95, ed. Jacques-Paul Migne (Paris: Migne, 1851), 1162–65; see Roland Gauthier, "Saint Joseph d'après deux series d'homélies latines du Vie siècle sur S. Matthieu," in "Saint Joseph durant les quinze premiers siècles de l'Église," special issue, *Cahiers de Joséphologie* 19 (1971): 168–69. Gilio repeats the arguments of the Pseudo-Origen. There was a tradition of denouncing images of Joseph that made him too old. For example, Bernardino da Feltre deplored his being shown as an old man (*vecchiarello*); see Da Feltre, *Sermoni di Beato Bernardino Tomitano da Feltre: Nella redazione di fra Bernardino Bulgarino da Brescia M. O.*, vol. 1, ed. Carlo Varischi da Milano (Milan: Cassa di Risparmio delle Provincie Lombarde e Banca Del Monte, 1964), 393, 398, and 400. Jean Gerson, in his sermon "In Festo Nativitatis B. Mariae Virginis," criticizes representations of Saint Joseph as an old man and dismisses the evidence of the *de infantia Salvatoris*. He cites Isaiah 62:5 and uses the arguments deployed in Gilio's text; that is to say, the need for Joseph to help the Virgin on the Flight into Egypt and the need to hide from the Devil the mystery of the incarnation. However, Gerson does not mention the marriage as a way of escaping the infamy of adultery, which the Pseudo-Origen does. See Jean Gerson, "In Festo Nativitatis B. Mariae Virginis," in *Oeuvres complètes*, vol. 5, *L'oeuvre oratoire*, ed. Palémon Glorieux (Paris: Desclée, 1963), 344–62, esp. 352–53.

112. This point is taken up again later; see Gilio, this volume, 233.

113. Gilio seems to have slightly confused the names of the Marys. A legend of the eleventh century, *Trinubium Annae* (The three husbands of Anna), or *De tribus Mariis et tribus maritis* (On the three Marys and their three husbands), supposed that the Virgin's mother, Anna, had three husbands, so that the Virgin (the daughter of Joachim) had a half sister Mary, whose father was Cleophas and who married Alpheus and had four sons by him (James Minor, Joseph Justus, Simon, and Jude), as well as another half sister, also called Mary, whose father was Salome and who married Zebedee and had two sons by him (James Major and John the Evangelist). See "Catalogus codicum hagiographicorium bibliothecae civitatis Carnotensis," *Analecta Bollandiana* 8 (1889): 197.

who lived 700 years later, introduced the red robes and hats for cardinals; before then no hats were worn, nor were any such robes![114] Yet it seems that the art of painting loses prestige if it does not show the ostentation and conceit of the world, whereas it should show the opposite, to provide a model for people to imitate.[115] For those glorious saints chose wildernesses and hermitages for no other reason than to escape vainglory and the lusts of the flesh. They wanted to teach the flesh to obey the spirit, the senses to obey reason; they ate to live, they did not live to eat."

M. Francesco replied: "All this follows from the ignorance of painters who, if they were educated men, would not make mistakes when things were so clear and obvious. And if they had taken the trouble, when making the models, sketches, and cartoons you spoke of before, to inform themselves properly about everything, this would not happen. It appears to them, when they have created a saint, that they have done everything required if they have expended all their ingenuity and care on twisting his legs or arms or neck, forcing him into a strained pose that is both inappropriate and ugly; and then, without further thought, they set to work with the brush.[116] Oh, what a loathsome way of doing things! '*Quis ferat haec?*' said Persius."[117]

M. Troilo continued: "There is another thing that seems to me to have introduced abuse, because it is against divine law. That is, that while God commanded Moses that the children of Israel should not portray his image in any form, given that he is spirit (and as spirit he cannot be known, let alone painted),

---

114. On cardinals' hats, see Carol M. Richardson, *Reclaiming Rome: Cardinals in the Fifteenth Century* (Leiden: E. J. Brill, 2009), 130–34.
115. Giuseppe Scavizzi, *The Controversy on Images from Calvin to Baronius* (New York: Peter Lang, 1992), 98, suggests that this line of criticism was initiated by Erasmus.
116. On the value of preparatory drawings in providing the opportunity for painters to improve their understanding of the subject matter, see Gilio, this volume, 120–121; and see note 103. The condemnation of painters who do not work in that way but who are satisfied to concentrate on the design of a figure in an ingeniously twisted pose, both inappropriate and ugly ("e farlo sforzato, di sforzo sconvenevole e brutto"), echoes Gilio's letter of dedication to Alessandro Farnese; see Gilio, *Dialogo . . . degli errori e degli abusi de' pittori,* in Barocchi, *Trattati,* 2:3–4; and Gilio, this volume, 85–87. Dolce had written of the need for painters to avoid always creating figures in movement and, rather, to vary them and to match their poses to the subject matter: "But such movements should not be uninterrupted and present in all the figures, because men are not always in motion, or so violent that they look deranged. It is necessary rather to moderate these movements, to vary them and even to omit them according to the variety and circumstance of the subjects. And a graceful pose is often more pleasing than a strained [*sforzato*] . . . one [that is out of place]." See Dolce, *L'Aretino,* in Barocchi, *Trattati,* 1:180 (Roskill, *Dolce's "Aretino,"* 146–47 [translation modified]). See also notes 10 and 183.
117. Aulus Persius Flaccus, *Satires,* in *Juvenal and Persius,* ed. and trans. Susanna Morton Braund, Loeb Classical Library 91 (Cambridge, MA: Harvard University Press, 2004), 48–49. Satire 1, line 2, has "quis leget haec?"—namely, "who will read that?"; Gilio alters it to say, "who could bear that?"

painters do represent him in various ways; [34] and they were not to portray the image of anything there might be on the earth, in the heavens, or in the sea. And now painters represent God as an old man, with a white beard. Do you believe that this commandment also extends to us?"[118]

"As for painting God's image," said M. Pulidoro, "there is no way of showing that he is spirit; because what form or semblance would we give to something when we do not know what or how it is? As for other images of the heavens, the sea, and the earth, the prohibition on portraying them was imposed on that people [of Israel] because they were too obstinately inclined to evil and idolatry; for being surrounded by pagans and being moved by their example, the easiest thing would be that they too, through weakness of the flesh, would become idolaters. But given that we do not have that inclination and are not subject to that danger nor that zealotry, the Holy Church does not prohibit us from such things, because we will not adore images as God, as they would have done."[119]

M. Ruggiero said: "Why then is God the Father painted as an old man, if we do not know what form he has?"

M. Pulidoro replied: "Because he cannot be painted as spirit, given that we do not know what form, color, or being he might have (and it was this that made many commit idolatry), he is therefore painted as an old man, and the Church tolerates this in order to show that many mysteries attributed by the pagans to the gods were carried out by our own true, great God: like the creation of the world, the expulsion of the rebel angels, the wise government of the world, and many other similar things. He is painted as an old man in order to demonstrate the supreme knowledge that he possesses, because he existed before all things and before the world; also because the prophet Daniel saw him in that form, served by thousands of angels, and so too John the Evangelist saw him in his revelations."[120]

---

118. Exodus 20:4; and Deuteronomy 4:15–18.

119. The argument that the prohibition of Exodus 20:4 was intended for Jews—who, unlike Christians, ran the danger of falling into idolatry—had been put forward by many writers, including Ambrogio Catarino (Lancellotto Politi), *Disputatio . . . de cultu et adoratione imaginum* [Rome, 1551], in *Enarrationes* (Rome: A. Blado, 1552), cols. 121–28 (one of a series of short tracts, continuously paginated, beginning with the *Disputatio pro veritate Immaculatae Conceptionis beatissimae Virginis* [Rome, 1551] and often found bound in with Catarino's *Enarrationes*).

120. Daniel 7:9–10; and Revelation (Apocalypse of Saint John), especially chapter 1:12–15. Braun (*De imaginibus,* 20) uses both these examples when arguing that God as invisible spirit made use of "images" when he presented himself to men in human form. In his treatise *Trattato de la emulatione che il demonio ha fatto a Dio* (On the Devil's emulation of God), Gilio insists that God as pure spirit could never be seen; see Giovanni Andrea Gilio, *Trattato de la emulatione che il demonio ha fatto a Dio* (Venice: Francesco de' Franceschi, 1563), 76v–77r. In book three of his *Trattato,* Gilio interprets as allegory the corporeal forms frequently used for the representation of God; see especially 86v–87r.

"I think," added M. Troilo, "that the Church tolerated and tolerates this not only for our instruction but also to allow the ignorant, who cannot read, to see those figures and to understand that our great God created everything, as M. Pulidoro said earlier, and not Jupiter, as the poets asserted.[121] **[35]** But there is one thing, I think, in which the painters are wrong."

"What is that?" asked M. Pulidoro.

"You know that the works of the Trinity that are internal, are divided between them," remarked M. Troilo, "for example divine generation, in which the Father generates, the Son is generated, and the Holy Spirit proceeds from both of them; all their other works are common to all three persons. The creation of the world, the governing of it with such wisdom as passes our understanding, these are not among the works divided but belong to all three persons. Given that this is the case, in the Creation of the world painted in the [Sistine] Chapel, Michelangelo would have been more correct to represent all three persons, rather than only one, for that alone denotes the unity of the essence, not the person of God. The reason is clear: the work is common to all three and not to one person, and the persons are three, not one."[122]

M. Silvio replied: "The Scriptures say: 'God created the heaven and the earth and all things,' as we read in Genesis, and throughout the Scriptures you will always find 'I am God, God created, God said, God sent.'[123] This seems to refer to the Father alone, rather than to the others, given that there can be no discord or envy between the divine persons. Nevertheless it seems that in saying God, one may also refer to all three of the persons implied by this name."

M. Troilo said: "The name God cannot be said to be the appropriate one to use for a single person, but it is for all three. The name refers to the essence rather than to the persons, because when we mean the Father, we say Father; when we mean the Son, we say Son; and when we mean the Holy Ghost, we say

---

121. The ignorant viewers of painting are those who cannot read Latin. Gilio had written of ignorant painters in his prefatory letter to Alessandro Farnese; see note 6. The *Index of Prohibited Books,* issued by Paul IV in 1559, forbade publishing, reading, or possessing vernacular translations of the Bible without the written permission of the Roman Inquisition. See John W. O'Malley, *Trent: What Happened at the Council* (Cambridge, MA: Belknap, 2013), 160.

122. The theological elaboration of the differentiation between "opera Trinitatis ad intra" (that is, the internal relations between the three persons), when they are distinct, and the "opera Trinitatis ad extra" (that is, the external acts, such as the creation of the world), when the three persons are inseparably one, is often traced back to Augustine. See Augustine, *De Trinitate libri XV,* in *S. Aurelii Augustini tomus octavus,* Patrologia Latina, series prima 42, ed. Jacques-Paul Migne (Paris: Migne, 1845), col. 824 (book 1.4.7). Gilio covers the same ground in his 1563 *Trattato de la emulatione che il demonio ha fatto a Dio,* 59r–62r, explicitly attributing the ideas to Augustine.

123. The supposed quotation is an elaboration of Genesis 1:1.

Holy Ghost.[124] When we use the name God alone, we mean all three persons; in saying God, we never refer to a single person, but to all three. Therefore your argument does not convince me; but you have to accept mine because the creation of the world is an external work, proper to all three persons, and all three should have been painted, not just one. **[36]** And my argument is not gainsaid by Abraham who, seeing three, adored one. Indeed, it works in my favor. As a proof that the creation belonged to all three, one reads that in creating man, God said: 'Let us make man to our image and likeness'; and when God wanted to confound the language of men, he said: 'Let us go down,' speaking jointly.[125] Yet sometimes, the reference is to one only, as when the Bible says: 'I repent of having made man and of having created Saul king.'[126] This is done for no other reason than to demonstrate the distinction between the persons on one hand and the unity of the essence on the other. In some places I remember having seen this mystery [of the creation] represented with the three divine persons and not with only one. I approve of this more and get more pleasure from it, because one alone suggests the pagan more than the Christian, since Ovid depicts Jupiter creating the world in that way. Therefore, to distinguish ourselves from paganism, it would be best to paint three, not one."

M. Vincenso replied: "I think it is heretical to paint the Trinity with three heads on a single torso, as you see in many places, and particularly in our convent of San Luca;[127] because although the essence is one, the persons are distinct. As well as being heretical, I think it is monstrous too.[128] In short, I maintain that the external works (as you call them) should be attributed to three rather than to one!"

M. Troilo started again: "Another thing I am thinking about is what the painters before Michelangelo were accustomed to doing when they painted prophets, sibyls, and other figures to whom some divine revelation was given: they represented a ray or rather a glory of light around that person, denoting

---

124. Augustine argues that the Trinity's inseparable activity "ad extra" entailed its inseparable being (*essentia*); see Mary T. Clark, "De Trinitate," in *The Cambridge Companion to Augustine,* ed. Eleanore Stump and Norman Kretzmann (Cambridge: Cambridge University Press, 2001), 95–96.

125. Genesis 1:26 for the creation of Adam and 11:7 for the Tower of Babel.

126. Two separate biblical passages have been elided: "It repented him that he had made man on the earth," Genesis 6:6; and "It repenteth me that I have made Saul king," 1 Samuel 15:11.

127. The convent of San Luca, close to the center of Fabriano, houses a community of Benedictine nuns.

128. Antoninus, in his *Summa theologica moralis* of 1446/1459, had condemned such a representation as against the faith and also specified that such an image "is monstrous in the nature of things" (monstrum est in rerum natura); see Creighton Gilbert, "The Archbishop on the Painters of Florence," *Art Bulletin* 41 (1959): 76, 81.

mental enlightenment, the elimination of ignorance, and the clarity of the true light. Now, instead of employing that ray or glory of light, modern painters represent little angels or *spiritelli* who speak into their ears, or bring them a book, or do something else inappropriate for the Holy Ghost, who is responsible for that revelation and enlightenment. For one never reads of the Holy Ghost appearing in the form of an angel or '*spiritello*,' but rather in the form of a dove, or of tongues of fire, or of a cloud. **[37]** And although that glory of light is not right either in the case of the manifestation of which I speak, it is nevertheless appropriate for showing the light of grace that someone receives."

M. Silvio replied: "I do not think this is an error, because one reads that God, talking to Moses and to his people in the desert, spoke to him by means of an angel; and he did the same to Samuel, David, Isaiah, Jeremiah, Daniel, and the other prophets. Besides which, he has always revealed his secrets by means of angels and for this reason Paul said that all angels are ministers of God.[129] There are plenty of examples of such angels in the New Testament too: the one who revealed to the glorious Virgin that she was chosen for the incarnation of the eternal Word; to Zacharias, father of the great Precursor, that he would bear a holy and providential son;[130] to the Marys and to the Apostles the news of the Resurrection of the Son of God; and to many others, too many to name.[131] Given all these examples it does not seem to me an error, but rather something entirely blameless and perfectly appropriate to these sacred mysteries, to represent an angel speaking into someone's ear or bringing a book and it seems to me that this is more suitable than creating the glory of light you spoke of earlier" [fig. 11].[132]

M. Francesco interjected: "Your opinion, M. Silvio, could be right if the *spiritelli* were meant to represent angels involved in one of the mysteries you referred to; but Michelangelo's intention was to represent a *spiritello* or something like it, not an angel.[133] So I am more of the opinion of M. Troilo than of

---

129. Hebrews 1:14: "Are they not all ministering spirits . . . ?"
130. Luke 1:28 for the Annunciation and Luke 1:11 for Zacharias. The precursor is John the Baptist.
131. Matthew 28:2–7; John 20:12–13.
132. Aquinas, *Summa theologica,* II.2.q.CLXXII, art. II, had concluded that prophetic revelation was conveyed by angels. The English translation is from Thomas Aquinas, *Summa theologiae,* vol. 45, *Prophecy and Other Charisms (2a2ae. 171–78),* ed. and trans. Roland Potter (London: Blackfriars in conjunction with Eyre & Spottiswoode, 1975), 35.
133. For the "spiritello," see Charles Dempsey, *Inventing the Renaissance Putto* (Chapel Hill: University of North Carolina Press, 2001), esp. 3–61. These figures were described by Vasari as "putti": Giorgio Vasari, "Vita di Michelagnolo Buonarruoti," in Vasari, *Le vite de' più eccellenti pittori, scultori, e architettori: Nelle redazioni del 1550 e 1568,* vol. 6, ed. Rosanna Bettarini and Paola Barocchi (Florence: S.P.E.S., 1987), 43–45. They are sometimes referred

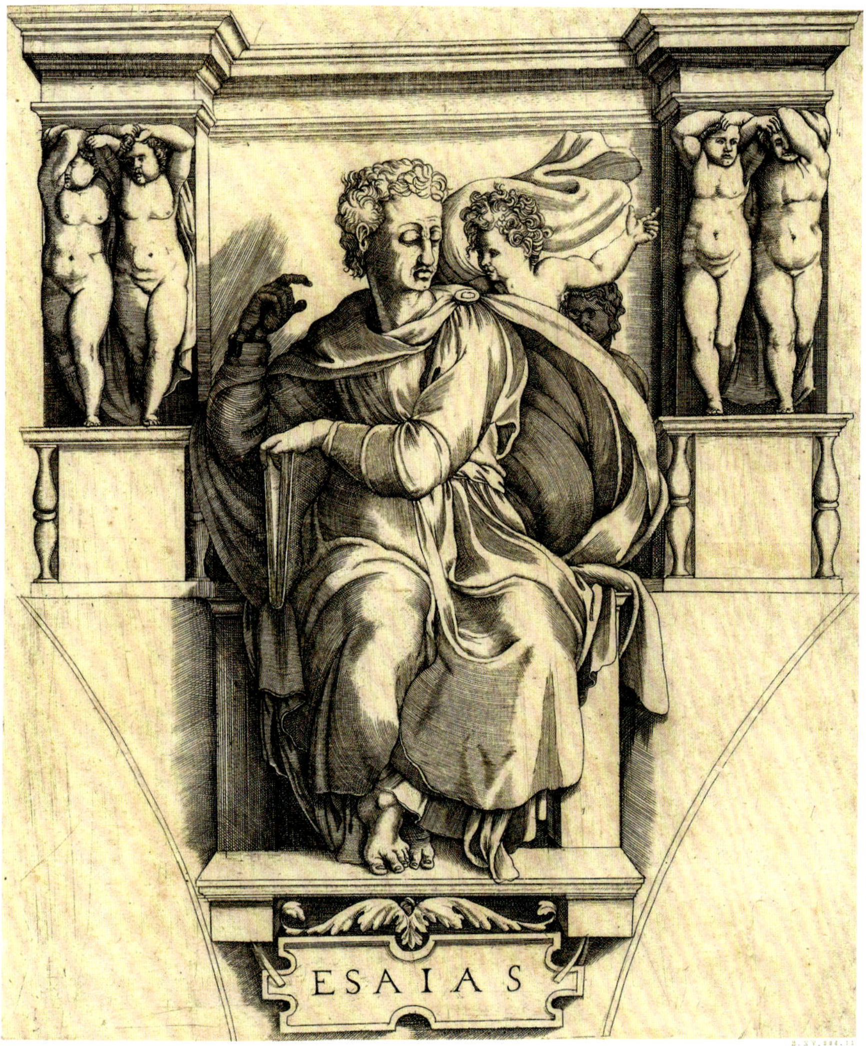

yours, because it seems to me one cannot in any way attribute that form to the Holy Ghost."

M. Troilo continued: "You know that in the Scriptures we find many mysteries performed by the Father, others by the Son, and others by the Holy Ghost,

Fig. 11.
Attributed to Enea Vico (Italian, 1523–67), after Michelangelo Buonarroti (Italian, 1475–1564).
The prophet Isaiah, from the Sistine Chapel ceiling, engraving, 34.8 × 29.5 cm. London, British Museum.

to in the modern literature as "genii"—see, for example, Charles de Tolnay, *The Sistine Chapel* (Princeton, NJ: Princeton University Press, 1945), 164–65; and John W. O'Malley, "The Theology behind Michelangelo's Ceiling," in *The Sistine Chapel: The Art, the History, and the Restoration,* ed. Carlo Pietrangeli (New York: Harmony, 1986), 114. Emile Mâle identifies them as angels: Mâle, *L'art religieux de la fin du moyen âge en France: Étude sur l'iconographie du moyen âge et sur ses sources d'inspiration* (Paris: Hérissey, 1922), 264n3; see also Edgar Wind, *The Religious Symbolism of Michelangelo: The Sistine Chapel,* ed. Elizabeth Sears (Oxford: Oxford University Press, 2000), 145–47.

accepting that all three divine persons were concordant in all of them. The voice that is heard when the Son was baptized in the river Jordan is attributed to the Father, [as is the voice heard] at the Transfiguration on Mount Tabor, when he says: *Hic est Filius meus*, etc.;[134] to the Son is attributed the act of becoming flesh and the fulfillment of all the mysteries of our redemption; **[38]** while to the Holy Ghost [is attributed] the appearance as a dove at the Baptism, as a white cloud at the Transfiguration, and as tongues of fire at Pentecost. Therefore, in the mysteries appropriate to the Father, only the person of the Father must be painted; in those pertinent to the Son, only the person of the Son; in those pertinent to the Holy Ghost, only the Holy Ghost![135] As for mysteries revealed by an angel, I say that it is legitimate to represent them with an angel if that is how they are described in the Bible. Apart from that, I do not accept their legitimacy, since Peter says that the prophets were inspired to speak by the Holy Ghost and not by angels, whose work was different.[136] Therefore, because they spoke and revealed divine secrets through the revelation of the Holy Ghost, I heartily approve the use of that glory of light, as more fitting than an angel for the representation of the Holy Ghost. Yet, whatever the case, all these streams rise from the same source: what is said here, is said in order to avoid confusion about persons and mysteries and to give to each subject its proper and appropriate decorum [*decoro*]."[137]

"You have spoken well," said M. Silvio, "because it is order that gives beauty and grace to all things. And although it is true that one praises God in different ways, that does not mean that one can confuse times, mysteries, or persons with the excuse that one does everything for the glory of God, nor does it mean that everything is permissible to the painter. I would find it more praiseworthy if abuses were made to wither away and the art of painting were brought back to the purity it had earlier. Rules [*regole*] and specifications should be drawn up by someone who has the knowledge, so that it would not be permissible for everyone to follow their own personal conceptions [*capriccio*] but only to do what they ought. That would be something new, beautiful, pleasant, and useful for

134. Matthew 17:5, Mark 9:6, Luke 9:35: "This is my [most] beloved son."

135. Augustine, *De Trinitate,* col. 824 (book 1.4.7).

136. 2 Peter 1:19–21.

137. Clarity is an overriding consideration, in terms of both textual and visual identification. Light may not be entirely correct as a way of representing the Holy Ghost, but it avoids the confusion introduced by using angels or *spiritelli.* Here there may be an echo of Quintilian, *The Orator's Education,* vol. 3, *Books 6–8,* ed. and trans. Donald A. Russell, Loeb Classical Library 126 (Cambridge, MA: Harvard University Press, 2002), 326–29 (VIII.2.1). The common practice (*commune uso*) of painters representing angels with wings so as to allow them to be identified easily is invoked in Gilio, this volume, 193, 233. On decorum, see note 5.

the ignorant, for they would not make mistakes.[138] Many other things could be said about the subject matter of histories, which the prudent painter can think about for himself; being careful, however, above everything else to treat such subject matter simply and clearly, because to mix it with the poetic and the fictional [*finto*] is nothing other than to disfigure truth and beauty and to produce something false and monstrous. So Horace says: 'He lies who mixes the false and the true.'[139] **[39]** For it is the case that the historical painter is nothing other than a translator who translates history from one language into another; that is, from the language of the pen into that of the brush, from writing into painting.[140] And if one does not translate faithfully, blame follows and one becomes worthy of derision—or of sleep, as Horace said.[141] I think that the artist who accommodates his art to the truth of the subject matter is cleverer than the one who distorts the plain subject for the sake of the alluring beauties [*vaghezza*] of the art of painting.[142] For many do this with the idea of being judged more per-

138. The desire to return to the purity of earlier painting [*purità primiera*] is a point picked up again below, in relation to the artists who came before Michelangelo; see Gilio, this volume, 160. In his dedication to Alessandro Farnese, Gilio had expressed amazement that there was no book or set of rules to inform painters how they should make every kind of figure; see Gilio, this volume, 86. Toward the end of the *Dialogo,* M. Ruggiero speculates that such rules had been published in earlier times but that the books containing them had subsequently been lost; see Gilio, this volume, 230.
139. Horace, *Ars Poetica,* 462–63 (line 151). Actually Horace writes approvingly of the clever blending of fact and fiction; his word *mentior,* used of a poetic fiction, carries the sense of "to invent"; but here *mentior* is translated into Italian as *mentire*—that is, "to lie." For a less rigorous position, see Gilio, this volume, 155–56, where M. Francesco approves of a judicious mixture of fact and fiction in histories.
140. The Gregorian notion of images as the bible of the illiterate—seeing text and image as equivalent, with no recognition of the real differences between them—seems to be dominant here; see note 89. Gilio interweaves this theological idea with the Horatian idea of "ut pictura poesis." See Barocchi, *Trattati,* 2:584, n1 to Gilio p. 39.
141. These words from Horace (*Ars Poetica,* 458–59 [line 105]) had been quoted earlier, in their context; see Gilio, this volume, 119.
142. Scavizzi (*Controversy on Images,* 98) argues that the "beauty" of art is a theme of scholastic origin that had been taken up by, for example, the Catholic theologian Hieronymus Emser. The theme laid out by Emser in the discussion of abuses, in his defense of images against Karlstadt's iconoclasm, is that a simple image (*schlechte bild*) was preferred in the past because 1) it could save the great sums now spent on images and the money given to the poor; and 2) "the more artfully images are made the more their viewers are lost in contemplation of the art and manner in which the figures have been worked. We should turn this contemplation from the images to the saints which they represent." Hieronymus Emser, *Das man der heyligen bilder in den kirchen nit abthon, noch unehren soll* [Dresden, 1522], in *A Reformation Debate: Karlstadt, Emser, and Eck on Sacred Images; Three Treatises in Translation*, ed. and trans. Bryan D. Mangrum and Giuseppe Scavizzi (Toronto: Centre for Renaissance and Reformation Studies, 1991), 86. Hall quotes the passage from Emser, translating the German phrase Emser had used—*schlechte bild*—to mean a "bad image" rather than a "simple image"; Marcia B. Hall, *The Sacred Image in the Age of Art: Titian, Tintoretto,*

fect and brilliant, and they think that by such means they will add to the charm, grace, and excellence of their works; to such men Horace's lines are fitting:

> Many have often begun grand and weighty works; and so that they may seem more elegant, behave like the tailor who, to make his work a fine one, adds to one piece of cloth others of different colors. They invent Diana's altar, or her grove, or clear murmuring streams winding among delightful and extensive, fertile fields, although this was not the place for such things."[143]

M. Troilo added: "I have identified another abuse with respect to the person of our Savior, which it would seem no one knows how to correct, and it is this: [painters] do not know, or do not wish to know, how to express his disfigurement at the time of the Passion, when he was beaten, when Pilate showed him to the people saying 'Ecce homo,' when in such pain he remained nailed to the Cross, so that Isaiah said of him that he no longer had the form of a man.[144] It would move people to repentance much more if he were seen bloody and deformed, rather than beautiful and delicate."[145]

M. Pulidoro said: "I think that they do it in order to display the power of the art of painting, for that has always been what those practicing it have wanted to do. For they can then represent all the muscles and all the limbs of [Christ's] beautifully constructed body, for no finer has I think ever been seen.[146] **[40]** It

---

Barocci, El Greco, Caravaggio (New Haven, CT: Yale University Press, 2011), 21. What Emser seems to imply is a plain or unadorned image. The word *vaghezza* is used here by Gilio to describe the kind of beauty that belongs to painting itself: an attractive and alluring beauty that painters may deliberately cultivate at the expense of the truth of the subject matter. Compare Gilio's later use of the same word, where the *vaghezza* of the art of painting is said to appeal only to the few; Gilio, this volume, 186. For an extended discussion of the word *vaghezza,* see Stuart Lingo, *Federico Barocci: Allure and Devotion in Late Renaissance Painting* (New Haven, CT: Yale University Press, 2008), esp. 143–48.

143. Horace, *Ars Poetica,* 450–51 (lines 14–19); the translation follows Gilio's Italian, not Horace's Latin.

144. Isaiah 52:14 and 53:2–3.

145. Moving the emotions of the audience was a fundamental aim of ancient rhetoric (Cicero, *Orator,* 356–57 [21.69]). Gilio here brings that tradition together with the theological tradition, which Scavizzi calls *excitatio,* the arousing or exciting of emotion; see Scavizzi, *Controversy on Images,* 96–97. The reference to Gregory of Nyssa below confirms the theological component.

146. On the beauty of Christ, see the letter of Publius Lentulus: "He is the most beautiful among the children of men," in Ernst von Dobschütz, *Christusbilder: Untersuchungen zur christlichen Legende,* vol. 2 (supplements) (Leipzig: J. C. Hinrichs, 1899), 308**–329**. In the later 1520s, Giovio, in his life of Raphael, wrote of Raphael being sometimes excessive in bringing out muscles in order to display "the power of art above nature" (vim artis supra naturam);

is for this reason that Fra Sebastiano's flogged Christ in San Pietro in Montorio has been so much praised" [fig. 12].[147]

M. Troilo replied: "A painter would show the power of the art much better if he represented Christ afflicted, bloody, covered with spittle, flayed, wounded, deformed, livid, and ugly, to such an extent that he did not have the appearance of a man. This would be brilliance, this would be the power and potency of the art, this would be decorum and the perfection of the artist.[148] Because what transpires from Fra Sebastiano's flogged figure is that the scourgings and beatings were done as a joke, with whips made of some soft material, and not with thick knotted ropes or even worse things. And from such frivolous representations no one will ever learn to understand the harshness of the suffering, the taunts, the distress, the wounds, and the other great miseries.[149] The painter who knows how to differentiate between mysteries and between times can represent both kinds of effect. If he wants to show the delicacy of Christ's body, its beauty, its grace, its muscles, as you said before, we have the mysteries of the Nativity, the Circumcision, the Adoration of the Magi to represent

---

see Paolo Giovio, *Scritti d'arte: lessico ed ecfrasi,* ed. Sonia Maffei (Pisa: Scuola Normale Superiore, 1999), 260.

147. Sebastiano del Piombo was assisted by Michelangelo in the design; see Michael Hirst, *Sebastiano del Piombo* (Oxford: Clarendon, 1981), 49–65.

148. The argument about the opportunities for painters, if they did not idealize such subjects, is very similar to what Giovanni Paolo Lomazzo writes in his unpublished *Il libro dei sogni* (ca. 1563). There, "Leonardo da Vinci" remarks on how many representations of the Last Supper are the reverse of what they should be, for they fail to show weather-beaten, unkempt apostles in a humble setting; see Lomazzo, *Il libro dei sogni,* in *Scritti sulle arti,* ed. Roberto Paolo Ciardi (Florence: Marchi and Bertolli, 1973–74), 1:101. Ciardi noticed the similarities to Gilio's views. There is no evidence of contact between Gilio and Lomazzo; however, Lomazzo was in Rome at some point after August 1561 and before January 1564. See Lomazzo, *Il libro dei sogni,* 1:viii.n9; and Roberto P. Ciardi, "Lomazzo, Giovanni Paolo," *DBI,* 65 (2005). Gilio and Lomazzo may have been independently responding to discussions provoked by Michelangelo's *Last Judgment.* Lomazzo's "Leonardo" goes on to argue that the expectations of patrons and viewers are the cause of inappropriate idealization, and he makes reference to the controversies around the *Last Judgment;* see note 181.

149. Barocchi cites Ambrogio Catarino (Politi), who, in discussing the value of images in reminding us of what we owe to God, exemplifies his case by referring to the image of Christ beaten and crowned with thorns. See Catarino, *De certa Gloria,* in *Opuscula* (Lyon: M. Bonhomme, 1542), 69: "Hinc adorare compellimur, . . . considerantes minime convenire membrum delicatum sub capite spinoso et flagellato." Barocchi, *Trattati,* 2:584–85, n1 to Gilio p. 40. Gilio was probably here drawing on the literature of meditation on the Passion of Christ. Compare, for example, the way that the fourteenth-century *Meditations on the Life of Christ,* once attributed to Saint Bonaventura, turns the scene of the Flagellation into a meditation; Pseudo-Bonaventura, *Meditations on the Life of Christ,* trans. and ed. Isa Ragusa and Rosalie B. Green (Princeton, NJ: Princeton University Press, 1961). In the discussion of memory images in [Cicero], *Rhetorica ad Herennium,* 220–21 (3.22.37), exceptional beauty and singular ugliness are recommended as especially memorable.

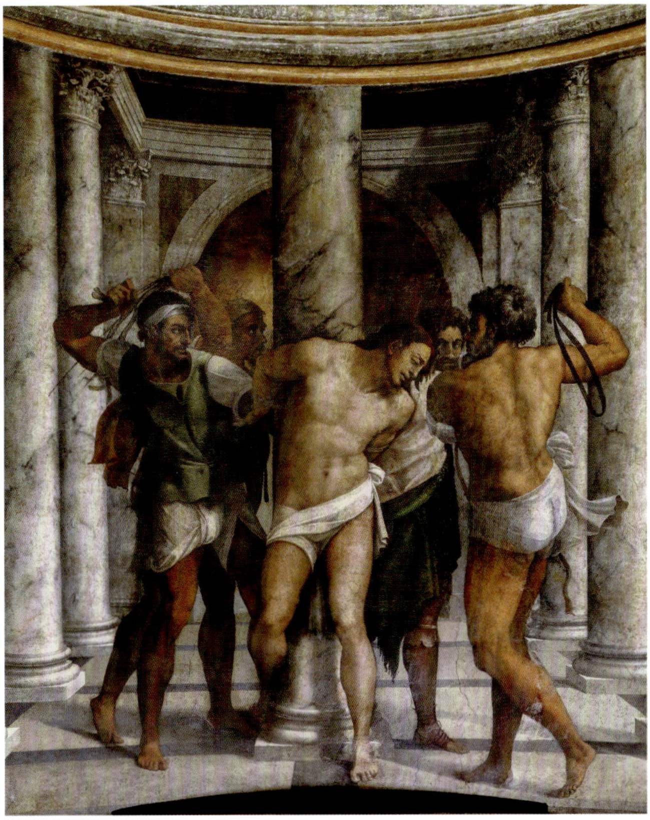

him as a suckling babe, beautiful and sweet. Then we have the Baptism in the Jordan as an opportunity to show him naked, where anatomy and all the secrets of the art can be displayed. There can be shown the perfection of intellect, the potency and power of beauty, the decorum of modesty, and the marvelousness of the holy. In the Flagellation, the Ecce Homo, the Crucifixion, the Deposition, and the Entombment there is the opportunity to show him bloody, ugly, deformed, afflicted, emaciated, and dead. For showing him as glorious, divine, and in authority, we have the Transfiguration, the Resurrection, the Ascension, and finally his coming to judge the living and the dead on the day of judgment. These are the distinctions that the prudent painter must make."[150]

M. Francesco responded: "Can he not show the power of the art in all these?"

150. Dolce had criticized Michelangelo's failure to achieve diversity of types, always producing muscular figures in strong movement. Dolce, *L'Aretino,* in Barocchi, *Trattati,* 1:193 (Roskill, *Dolce's "Aretino,"* 170–71). On the different images of Christ, depending on his age and actions, see Braun, *De imaginibus,* 32–33.

Fig. 12.
Sebastiano del Piombo (Italian, ca. 1485–1547).
Flagellation of Christ, 1516–24, mural painting in oil. Rome, San Pietro in Montorio, Cappella Borgherini.

M. Troilo replied: "Such a painter would be like the one who wanted to paint cypresses, which led Horace to comment that cypresses were not appropriate in every scene.[151] **[41]** If someone wants to show beauty where ugliness is required, or the opposite, he will be behaving like the one who wanted cypresses. Mysteries and times are distinguished only by giving to each what properly belongs to it. These are the distinctions that a prudent painter must make. If the great scholar Gregory of Nyssa was moved to tears by the figure of Isaac placed ready for sacrifice on the altar, how much more would spectators be moved to remorse seeing the image and form of our Savior nailed to the Cross in a torment of pain, stricken, bloody, deformed; as the Prophet says: "The sorrows of hell compassed me about."[152] These are the qualities to show to Christians in order to make them grieve and repent and dwell with amazement in contemplation of the degradation, abasement, and humility of the eternal Word, which the heavens could not contain, come to save us; and how, moved by great charity, he chose to die a shameful death for those who had attacked him so much. Many times have I discussed this with painters and they with one voice have retorted: 'Painting will not tolerate this, it would be against the decorum of the art [*decoro dell'arte*].'[153] Oh the vanity of men, trivializing what is true, right, and of the greatest importance, in order to make room for fictions that are worth nothing at all. If art is the ape of nature, why should it not imitate it in this respect? If it can represent the aberrations and tricks of

---

151. Horace, *Ars Poetica,* 450–53 (lines 19–21).

152. Psalms 17:5. Scavizzi, *Controversy on Images,* 97, notes how this example of Gregory of Nyssa weeping at the sight of the Sacrifice of Isaac had been used earlier in the theological literature on images—for example, in Braun, *De imaginibus,* 129. It exemplifies one of the primary functions of Christian images: to arouse sympathetic emotion (the theme of *excitatio*); see note 145.

153. Earlier, the "decoro della poesia" had been invoked, where it was linked to the freedom of invention; Gilio, this volume, 104. Beauty's fundamental importance for painting had been asserted, for example, by Alberti: "But . . . [the painter] should be attentive not only to the likeness of things but also and especially to beauty, for in painting, beauty is as pleasing as it is necessary. The early painter Demetrius failed to obtain the highest praise because he was more devoted to representing the likeness of things than to beauty. Therefore excellent parts should all be selected from the most beautiful bodies, and every effort should be made to perceive, understand and express beauty"; see Alberti, *On Painting and On Sculpture,* 98–99 (book 3, §55). Vasari, in the preface to part 3 of the *Lives,* had defined design [*disegno*] as "the imitation of what is most beautiful in nature when [designing] all the figures." See Giorgio Vasari, "Proemio della terza parte," in Vasari, *Le vite de' più eccellenti pittori, scultori, e architettori: Nelle redazioni del 1550 e 1568,* vol. 4, ed. Rosanna Bettarini and Paola Barocchi (Florence: S.P.E.S., 1976), 4. Alberti had also explicitly aligned the dignity of painting with the dignity of what was represented. See Alberti, *On Painting and On Sculpture,* 84–85 (book 2, §44).

nature in creating the lame, the deformed, or the blind, why should the painter not show this mystery as it ought to be? On that account I see the fault lying more with the vanity of painters than with the rules of painting. I see Saint Stephen stoned without stones; Blaise intact and handsome with his torture instrument, without a trace of blood;[154] James the Apostle without clubs to his head; Sebastian without arrows; [and I see] Lawrence on the gridiron neither burnt nor scorched, but white; [all this] for no other reason than because the art of painting will not tolerate [anything else], and in order that muscles and veins can be shown. Oh what pointless vanity, what infinite error, to give greater value to that which serves no purpose than to that which gives the figures their essential nature and perfection and which alone deserves to be seen and contemplated; all on the pretext that painting does not require it!"

M. Silvio added: "If the ancient paintings were found, many more secrets of the art would be seen than are known today; **[42]** but from their statues, we can draw clear proof of the skill of the ancient painters and sculptors. Each of you can have seen this in many sculptures in Rome and especially the Belvedere Laocoon [fig. 13]. [Laocoon], along with his sons, seems to express the pain, suffering, and torment he experienced in being strangled by snakes.[155] Certainly it would be something new and admirable to see a Christ on the Cross dramatically altered in appearance by wounds, spittings, taunts, and blood; Saint Blaise lacerated and gouged with carding combs; Sebastian so full of arrows as to resemble a porcupine; Lawrence burnt, scorched, and split open on the gridiron, torn and deformed. It would not be so difficult to show such essential aspects, if one thinks that Apelles tried to represent the most difficult things, never attempted by anyone else, like dazzling light, thunderclaps, lightning, snow, hail, rain, and other such things.[156]

"Myron represented the Demos of the Athenians as changeable, hot-tempered, fickle, unjust; but, on the other hand, as easily moved, benign,

154. The word used in the text is *eculeo* (Latin: *equuleus* or *eculeus*), which seems to have been used to mean "rack," but it was also used as a generic term for instruments of torture. See "martyres cum equuleis" in Sicard of Cremona, *Mitrale, sive De officiis ecclesiasticis summa,* in *Sicardus Cremonensis Episcopus, Petrus Sarnensis, Anonymi saeculi XII,* vol. 1, Patrologia Latina, series secunda 213 (Paris: Migne, 1855), col. 42; also Guillaume Durandus [Gulielmus Durandus], *Rationale divinorum officiorum,* ed. Anselme Davril and Timothy M. Thibodeau (Turnhout: Brepols, 1995), 1.3.14.

155. Sonia Maffei, "La fama di Laocoonte nei testi del Cinquecento," in *Laocoonte, fama e stile,* ed. Salvatore Settis (Rome: Donzelli Editore, 1999), 191–93.

156. Pliny, *NH,* 9:332–33 (book 35, §96): "[Apelles] even painted things that cannot be represented in pictures—thunder, lightning and thunderbolts."

merciful, glorious, humble, ferocious, and cowardly.[157] Apollodorus painted Ajax struck by lightning, in a most beautiful way: he appeared to be all on fire inside, with the burning heat trying to burst out in many places.[158] Protogenes of Caunus accidentally represented the spittle that forms in a dog's mouth when it pants; and another painter the steam exhaled from a horse's nostrils when it sniffs and snorts.[159] Others still have alluringly portrayed the most difficult things, rarely attempted by anyone else. How much greater praise, glory, and greatness would painters acquire if they knew how to represent well those essential things you described earlier; in which, apart from seeing what is true, one could contemplate the cruelty of tyrants, the patience of martyrs, and the power of divine grace that sweetened their torments and enabled them to withstand every terrible torture."

M. Vincenso said: "I would not like the painter to follow what is said in the *Infantia Salvatoris,*[160] nor in the book called the *Transito della Madonna,* which was condemned by Saint Jerome in a letter to Paola,[161] nor in the book called the *Acts of Clement,* which is rejected from among the sacred canonical texts, as mentioned by Voragine in the life of Clement from his *Golden Legend.*[162] **[43]**

157. Gilio means Parrhasius, not Myron; see Pliny, *NH,* 9:312–13 (book 35, §69). Pliny characterizes Parrhasius's painted personification of the Athenian "Demos" in exactly this way.
158. Pliny, *NH,* 9:306–7 (book 35, §60). Pliny does not mention the effect of the lightning; that part of Gilio's description comes from Virgil's account of the death of Ajax. See Virgil, *Aeneid, Books 1–6,* in Virgil, *Eclogues; Georgics; Aeneid, Books 1–6,* trans. H. Rushton Fairclough, rev. G. P. Goold, Loeb Classical Library 63 (Cambridge, MA: Harvard University Press, 1999), 264–65 (1.44–45).
159. On Protogenes, see Pliny, *NH,* 9:336–39 (book 35, §102–3); the other painter is Nealces (Pliny, *NH,* 9:339 [book 35, §104]).
160. This is the *Liber de Infantia,* or the *Historia de Nativitate Mariae et de Infantia Salvatoris,* now called the Gospel of Pseudo-Matthew, which was already being printed in the fifteenth century. See James K. Elliott, ed. and trans., *The Apocryphal New Testament: A Collection of Apocryphal Christian Literature in an English Translation* (Oxford: Oxford University Press, 1993), 84–99; and Bart D. Ehrman and Zlatko Plese, *The Apocryphal Gospels* (Oxford: Oxford University Press, 2011), 73–113.
161. "Appendix: The Assumption of the Virgin, 3. Latin, A. *The Narrative of Pseudo-Melito,*" in Elliott, *The Apocryphal New Testament,* 708–16. A printed Venetian edition is described by Victor Masséna (Prince d'Essling), *Les livres à figures vénitiens de la fin du XVe siècle et du commencement du XVIe* (Florence: Olschki, 1909), 2/2:638 (no. 2559).
162. The reference to the *Acts* is confusing. Jacobus de Voragine, in his *Legenda Aurea,* refers to having taken material from three sources for his life of Saint Clement: first, "ex eis gestis que communiter habentur" (this is what strictly could be called the *Acts*); second, from what he calls the Itinerary (*Itinerarium*) of Clement; and third, from a report by Leo, bishop of Ostia. The second is the so-called *Clementine Recognitions* (*Recognitiones*), a text that claims to describe Peter's travels in the East; Jacobus warns that it should be regarded as apocryphal (Voragine, *The Golden Legend,* 714). See Anthony Hilhorst, "The Chapter on Clement in Jacobus de Voragine's *Golden Legend,*" in *The Pseudo-Clementines,* ed. Jan N. Bremmer (Leuven: Peeters, 2010), 285–306, esp. 291 and 305. The so-called Gelasian decree ("Decretum Gelasianum") had declared the *Clementine Recognitions* apocryphal, along

Fig. 13.
Attributed to Nicolas Beatrizet (French, active in Italy, fl. ca. 1540–ca. 1565).
The sculptural group of the Laocoon set within a niche, engraving, 44.4 × 29.2 cm. London, British Museum.

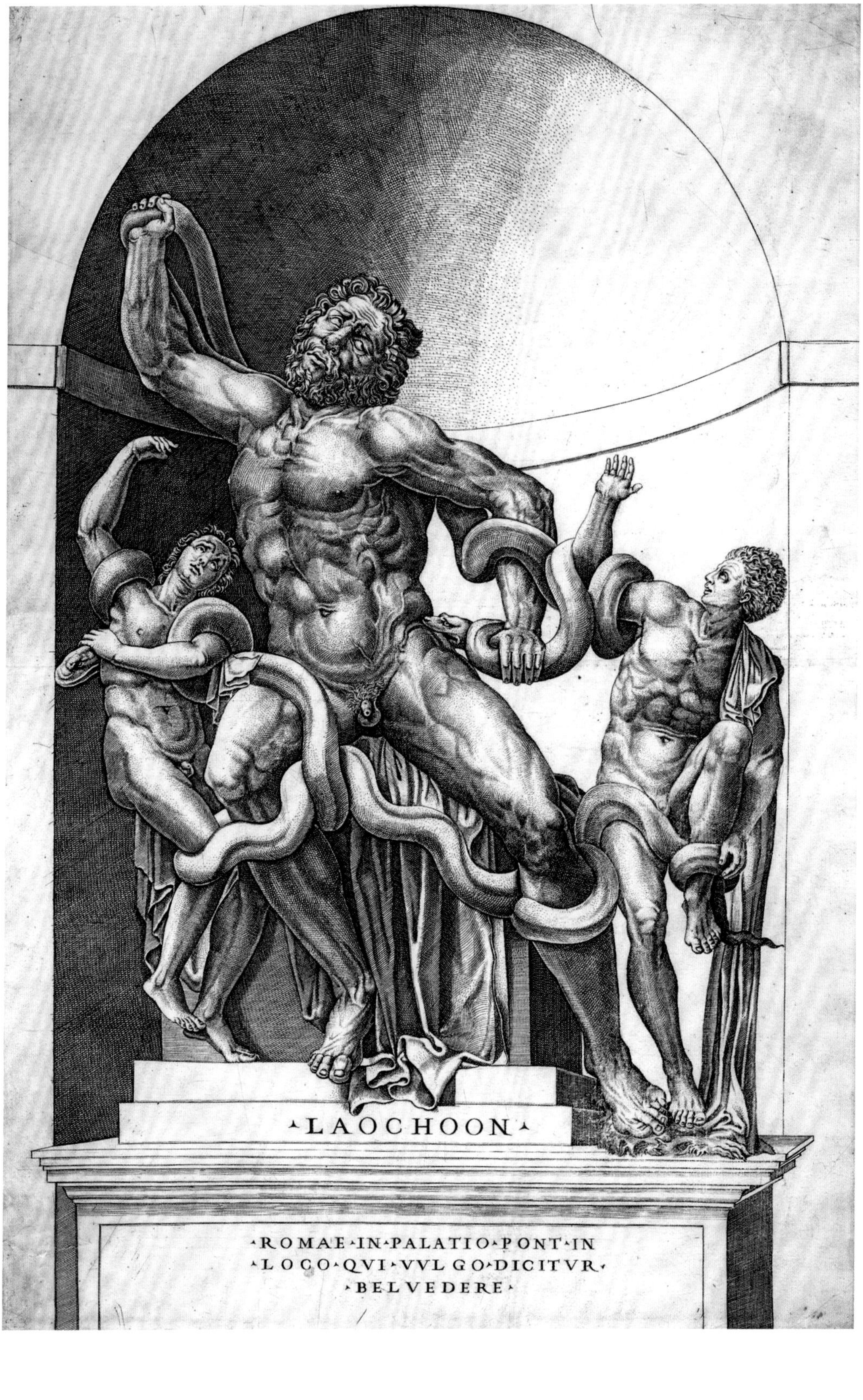
LAOCHOON
ROMAE IN PALATIO PONT IN
LOCO QVI VVLGO DICITVR
BELVEDERE

Nor would I like him to follow Pietro de' Natali in his *Catalogus,* nor the life of Saint Peter about the things concerning Simon Magus in the abovementioned lives of saints, nor the *Miracles of the Madonna* that have been printed, because they are false, full of fables, and apocryphal; nor indeed any apocryphal book, but only [books by] good writers.[163] Does not the [painter] consider an abuse the dragon of Saint George or that of Saint Margaret, and the Tarasque of Saint Martha; or the Virgin letting drop her belt for Saint Thomas when she ascended into heaven, because he was not present at her funeral?[164] Nor would I like [the painter] to follow the opinion of the crowd in composing his histories, but rather, if he does not wish to make mistakes, the opinion of learned and wise men, of authoritative and approved writers. Because by reading good books to learn the truth about the subject matter, he will be able to know what are abuses and what are not."

M. Silvio said: "Now that M. Troilo has so learnedly pointed out the abuses in such a way that anyone, however stupid he might be, can easily recognize them by himself, it falls to M. Francesco to expound for us those points that the painter must take into account in relation to the people he intends to include in his works."

with many other texts, including the "Liber de infantia Salvatoris" (Infancy of Christ) and the "Liber qui appellatur Transitus, id est Assumptio sanctae Mariae" (Death and Assumption of the Virgin). See *S. Gelasius I Papa / S. Avitus / S. Faustinus . . . ,* Patrologia Latina, series prima 59, ed. Jacques-Paul Migne (Paris: Migne, 1847), col. 162; also Wilhelm Schneemelcher and Robert McLachlan Wilson, eds., *New Testament Apocrypha,* vol. 1, *Gospels and Related Writings* (Cambridge: James Clarke, 1991), 38–40.

163. Petrus de Natalibus (Pietro de' Natali, ca. 1330–ca. 1382; see E. Paoli, "Natali, Pietro de," *DBI,* 77 [2012]), *Catalogus sanctorum et gestorum eorum* (Lyon: E. Gueynard, 1519; compiled 1369–72). Alison K. Frazier, *Possible Lives: Authors and Saints in Renaissance Italy* (New York: Columbia University Press, 2005), 452, lists the early editions. An edition had been printed as recently as 1543 by Giunti at Venice. Johannes Vasaeus had raised doubts about the reliability of the text in the list of the books that he used in the compilation *Chronici rerum memorabilium Hispaniae: Tomus prior* (Salamanca: Ioannes Iunta, 1552), 8v–9r. The story of Peter and Simon Magus is told in detail in the life of Peter in the *Legenda Aurea,* where Voragine named Clement as a source; in the life of Clement, Voragine warns that the source was apocryphal (*The Golden Legend,* 714). The *Miracoli de la Madonna* is known in many printed editions from the fifteenth century onward. On the Venetian editions, beginning in 1491, see Masséna, *Les livres à figures vénitiens* (1908), 1/2:70–77.

164. The legend of George had been classified as apocryphal in the Gelasian decree (see note 162 and *S. Gelasius I Papa,* col. 164), and it was described as apocryphal in Voragine, *The Golden Legend,* 238. The story of Saint Margaret, swallowed by and then bursting out of the dragon, had also been described as apocryphal in Voragine, *The Golden Legend,* 369. Dolce, in his discussion of errors in pictorial invention, had criticized Titian for his carelessness when he painted Saint Margaret astride the dragon; see Dolce, *L'Aretino,* in Barocchi, *Trattati,* 1:170 (Roskill, *Dolce's "Aretino,"* 126–27). Representations of Saint Thomas receiving the girdle from the Virgin assumed into heaven had been judged apocryphal by earlier writers, including Saint Antoninus, archbishop of Florence, in his *Summa Theologica* of 1446/1459; see Gilbert, "The Archbishop," 76 and 81–82.

M. Francesco replied: "You may think that I will be carrying my lance like a good jouster, but you are quite wrong. Yet, whatever happens, I will try to make my lazy, unschooled beast run and strike home, although do not laugh if you see my lance go wide of the mark; for he who does as much as he is capable of is not obliged to do more."

"Come now," said M. Pulidoro and the others, "we know how fit you are to appear fully armed in any grand tournament; so spur on your horse, because the trumpet has already sounded the signal to start."

"Since that is how things are," said M. Francesco, "let us see what needs to be considered with respect to the people the painter intends to include. The first thing is to take care to attribute to them the elements, both essential and accidental, that are appropriate, in order to preserve decorum in everything: in age, sex, rank, place of origin, manners, dress, gestures, and everything else proper to men. As Horace said: **[44]**

> you must note the behavior of people of different ages and give them what is appropriate to their years, active or mature, and to their characters.[165]

For some kinds of dress, gestures, and behavior are suitable for people of rank, and other ones are suitable for the lower classes; some for old people, others for the young; some for a pope, others for an emperor, king, or other ruler, and yet others for private men. To rulers must be given dignified, venerable, and stern actions, unless one is depicting an extremely effeminate Sardanapalus surrounded by women,[166] or Gaius Caligula passing triumphantly between Naples and Pozzuoli over a bridge of boats,[167] or Nero with his lyre and stage dress in the theater,[168] or Elagabalus among women, himself dressed as a woman and engaged in insane acts that I don't intend to describe because I don't want to sully my tongue or my voice with such monstrosities.[169]

---

165. Horace, *Ars Poetica*, 462–63 (lines 156–57); the translation follows Gilio's Italian, not Horace's Latin. This whole section engages with the central concept of figural decorum; see note 5.
166. Diodorus Siculus, *Library of History*, vol. 1, *Books 1–2.34*, trans. C. H. Oldfather, Loeb Classical Library 279 (Cambridge: Harvard University Press, 1933), 424–29 (2.2.23).
167. Suetonius, *Lives of the Caesars: Gaius Caligula*, in idem, *Suetonius: Volume I*, trans. J. C. Rolfe, Loeb Classical Library 31 (Cambridge, MA: Harvard University Press, 1914), 1:444–45 (4.19).
168. Suetonius, *Lives of the Caesars: Nero*, in idem, *Suetonius: Volume II*, trans. J. C. Rolfe, Loeb Classical Library 38 (Cambridge, MA: Harvard University Press, 1914), 2:108–15 (6.20–21).
169. Elagabalus was emperor from AD 218 to 222; see Dio Cassius, *Roman History*, vol. 9, *Books 71–80*, trans. Earnest Cary and Herbert B. Foster, Loeb Classical Library 177 (Cambridge, MA: Harvard University Press, 1927), 462–65 (80.13).

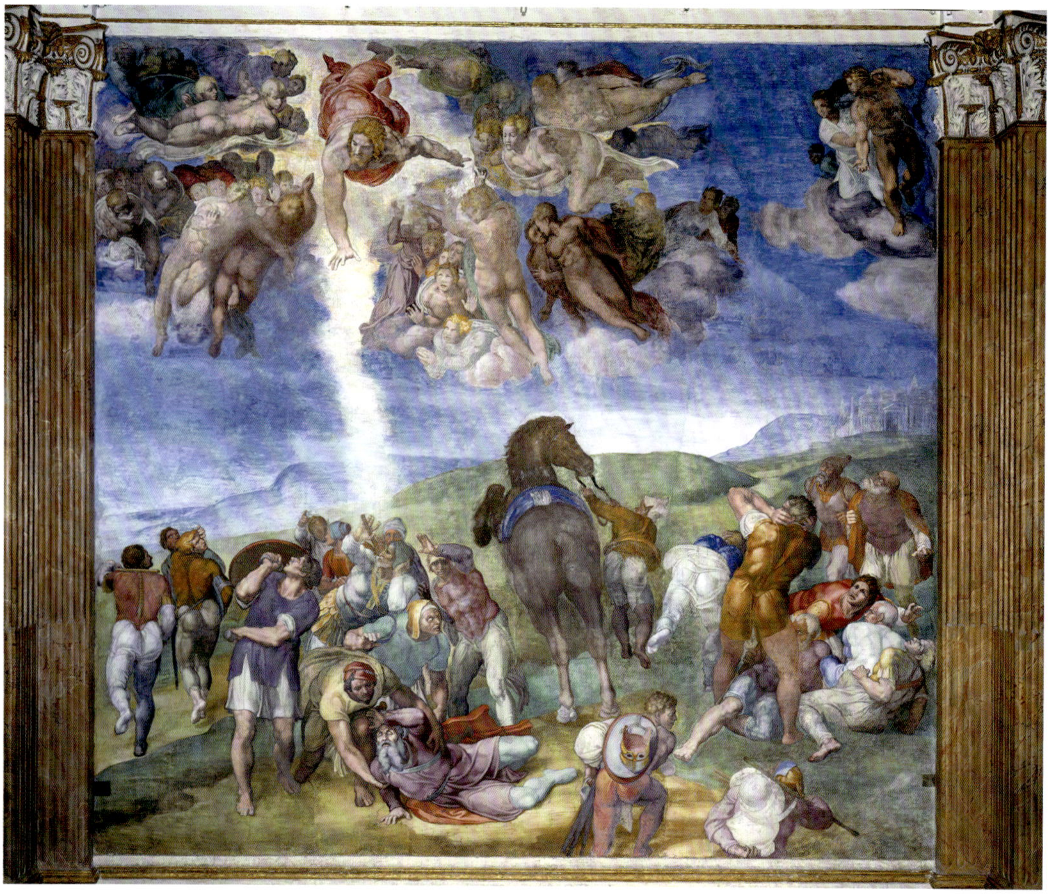

"So it seems to me that Michelangelo seriously failed in the Christ who appears to Saint Paul at his conversion, who without any dignity [*gravità*] or decorum [*decoro*] at all, appears to fall from the heavens in an action that lacks reverence; for this apparition ought to have been handled with the gravity [*gravità*] and majesty that belongs to the King of Heaven and Earth and to a Son of God [figs. 14, 15]. It reduces the devotion of the spectators and produces a certain harshness in their hearts. This should not be the case."[170]

M. Silvio said: "We must realize that although our Lord clearly performs an action that, at first glance, appears ungainly and violent to us, weighted down

170. Michelangelo's *Conversion of Paul* in the Pauline Chapel in the Vatican. The language is reminiscent of Ambrogio Catarino (Politi), *Disputatio*, col. 144: "On the other hand there are compositions made with such artifice that sometimes unsuitable actions do not preserve decorum in the figures; they have no dignity and they utterly fail to excite devotion" (Alias autem econtrario tanta arte compositas, ut quibusdam importunis gestibus interim personarum decorem non servent, nihil gravitatis habentes, nihil devotionis excitantes). On Catarino's influence on Gilio, see Bury, this volume, 8, 24–25.

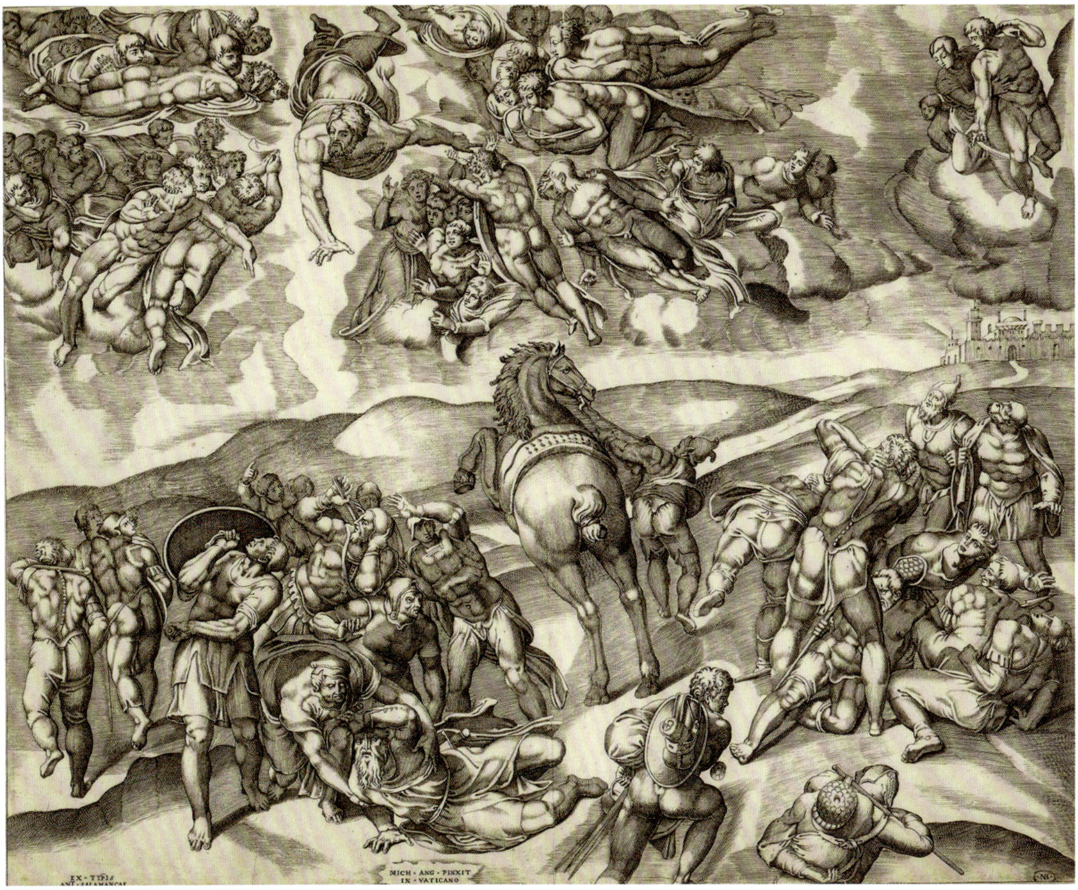

Fig. 14.
Michelangelo Buonarroti (Italian, 1475–1564).
Conversion of Paul, 1542–45, fresco, 625 × 661 cm. Vatican City, Vatican Apostolic Palace, Pauline Chapel.

Fig. 15.
Nicolas Beatrizet (French, active in Italy, fl. ca. 1540–ca. 1565), after Michelangelo Buonarroti (Italian, 1475–1564), published by Antonio Salamanca (Milanese, ca. 1478–1562).
Conversion of Paul, engraving, 42.5 × 53.3 cm. London, British Museum.

[by our bodies], he suffers no hardship, no violence, nor disaster; indeed, I praise it for showing the power of [divine] grace, which at times can be violent, as it was in the case of this great persecutor [of Christians], who had to be transformed into the 'chosen vessel.'[171] It also demonstrates the agility of [Christ's] glorious body."

M. Francesco continued to speak, saying: "I certainly think that our Lord's glorious body in itself suffers no violence or hardship; but it does suffer in terms of dignity and majesty. Tell me, by your faith, what suits such majesty best, according to you, and what gives it greater dignity, glory, and greatness: **[45]** solemn movements, which are venerable and proper to such majesty; or nimble, impetuous ones; or movements that make him appear cast down from the heavens, unable to stop his headlong fall? If actions should correspond to the status of the person, as I believe they should, I would always judge solemn, venerable,

171. The naming of Paul as Christ's "vas electionis" is from Acts 9:15.

saintly, and devout actions more fitting for him than ungainly, unpleasant, impetuous ones, with no reverence whatsoever, even though his body is agile and nimble. Even if from Christ's point of view these are not matters of consideration, they must be from ours, because we perceive devotion or scandal depending on how the figures are represented."

M. Vincenso said: "Certainly, in representations of our Lord, majesty and gravity are required so that those who are ignorant may learn the truth and show him the reverence he is due."[172]

M. Francesco added: "I can't help laughing when I am in Rome and I walk through the Minerva and see, in the chapel of the Presepio, an angel acting like a dove when, folding its wings as they sometimes do, it seems to plunge headfirst downward, or as if released from a sack, it falls out of the sky [fig. 16]. With its wings trailing, its awkward and poorly understood action [*atto*] makes it look more like a large bat than an angel. If the painter had understood the true nature of angels, he would not have shown it in an action that is so unsuitable to it and so lacking in decorum.[173] In my opinion Michelangelo's bearded Saint

172. The argument from secular principles of decorum, whereby the way a person is represented should be appropriate to their status and character (e.g., Dolce, *L'Aretino,* in Barocchi, *Trattati,* 1:165 [Roskill, *Dolce's "Aretino,"* 118–19]) turns into a matter of ensuring that the representation shows proper respect and elicits the required devotion. A similar argument is adopted to deal with the nudes in the *Last Judgment;* see Gilio, this volume, 183–84.

173. In the seventeenth century, the first chapel on the right on entering Santa Maria sopra Minerva (the Caffarelli Chapel) was known as the *cappella del Presepe,* and this may or may not have been the case earlier; see Filippo Titi, *Studio di pittura, scoltura, et architettura, nelle chiese di Roma (1674–1763),* ed. Bruno Contardi and Serena Romano (Florence: Centro Di, 1987), 88. However, there is no trace of an angel represented in the manner described. What was once the third chapel on the right (now, with the opening of the Baptistery chapel, the fourth on the right), the Gabrielli Chapel, has a fresco of the *Adoration of the Shepherds* (*Presepio*) on the left lateral wall; Walther Buchowiecki, *Handbuch der Kirchen Roms: Der römische Sakralbau in Geschichte und Kunst von der altchristlichen Zeit bis zur Gegenwart* (Vienna: Hollinek, 1970), 2:704–5. This was painted by Battista Franco in 1550, as noted in Fabrizio Biferali, *Battista Franco "pittore viniziano" nella cultura artistica e nella vita religiosa del Cinquecento* (Pisa: Edizioni della Normale, 2007), 149–58; and Rita Parma Baudille, "L'ultimo lavoro romano di Battista Franco: La cappella Gabrielli in Santa Maria sopra Minerva," *Arte/Documento* 6 (1992): 183–96. The painting contains a diving angel that could be the one criticized here by M. Francesco. Battista Franco was a painter who, according to Vasari, had decided to study and imitate Michelangelo alone: Giorgio Vasari, "Vita di Battista Franco," in Vasari, *Le vite de' più eccellenti pittori, scultori, e architettori: Nelle redazioni del 1550 e 1568,* vol. 5, ed. Rosanna Bettarini and Paola Barocchi (Florence: S.P.E.S., 1984), 459. Barocchi thinks that the reference might be to Filippino Lippi's *Annunciation* in the Carafa Chapel (Barocchi, *Trattati,* 2:589, n2 to Gilio p. 45), noting that Possevino had thought Gilio meant an angel of the Annunciation, which would fit with the subject of Lippi's Carafa altarpiece; Antonio Possevino, *Bibliotheca selecta,* vol. 2 (Rome: Domenico Basa, 1593), 317.

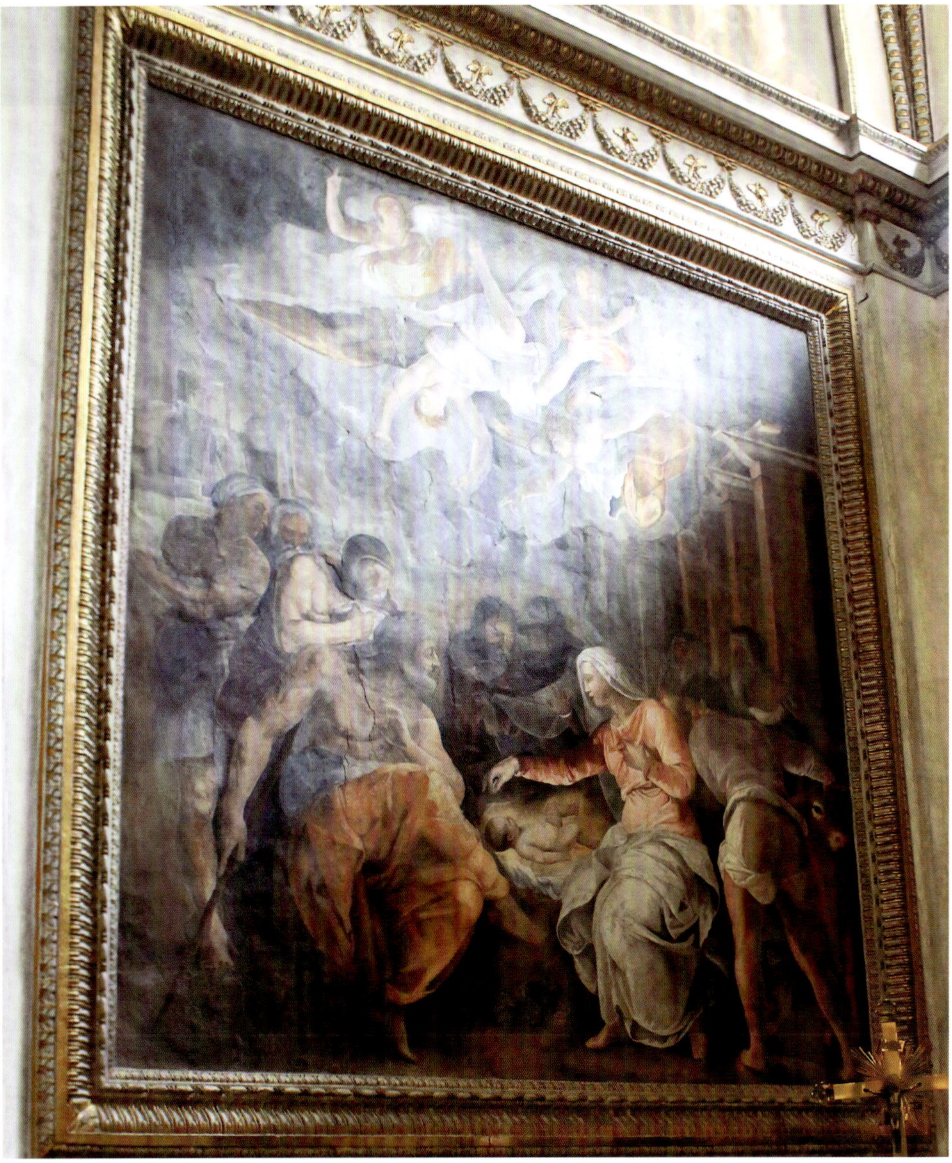

Paul in the new chapel is also a mistake, for Paul was 18 or 20 years old, while Michelangelo has made him look 60 [see fig. 14]. It seems to me that a small error committed by Michelangelo is much more significant than a large error made by anyone else, for he is the prince of all painters and none of the others has such high standing, nor is held in such high regard as he is; in the past he set, and he still sets, the standard for all painters, both those living now and

Fig. 16.
Battista Franco (Italian, before 1510–1551).
Adoration of the Shepherds, ca. 1550, fresco. Rome, Santa Maria sopra Minerva, Cappella Gabrielli.

those to come.[174] Many other characteristics can be taken into account in the [representation] of people, like not making someone young look old, or, if old, young, as is popularly said of the first Magus [among those] who went to offer gold, myrrh, and frankincense to our Lord: being young, and not wishing to let an older man make his offering first, he miraculously became old, and the older man became young.[175] **[46]** And there are other similar characteristics that the prudent painter may learn about and observe for himself."

M. Pulidoro added: "There is another thing that amazes me."

"What is that?" asked M. Troilo.

M. Pulidoro continued: "It is the movements that many painters have their figures make. One sees such awkward, wretched things of this kind, so exaggerated and quite outside the natural order. I am left amazed because this is something that painters should think about very carefully indeed."

"You are right," added M. Francesco, "because they are so much part of any figure that, however beautiful [the figure] may be, if it fails in those respects, it loses prestige and also appeal [*vaghezza*]. Movements must always be in harmony with subject matter, person, place, status, time, and anything else that may pertain to the figures being painted. This is why I do not praise the movements made by the angels in Michelangelo's *Last Judgment,* I mean those who bear the weight of the Cross, the column, and the other sacred mysteries, since they look more like acrobats or jugglers than angels.[176] Yet an angel would be able to hold up the entire terrestrial globe without effort, and certainly a cross or a column, or anything of that kind."

---

174. The *Conversion of Paul* by Michelangelo in the Pauline Chapel in the Vatican, painted circa 1542–45. Using the example of Donatello's wooden crucifix, Dolce had identified what is implicit here, that complete mastery of the skills of their art could coexist with a painter's or a sculptor's failure to respect figural decorum: "Donatello was . . . told that he had put a peasant onto the Cross—even though in modern times no equal of Donatello's in the art of sculpture may be found." Dolce, *L'Aretino,* in Barocchi, *Trattati,* 1:165 (Roskill, *Dolce's "Aretino,"* 118–19).

175. A text of uncertain date—the *Excerptiones patrum, Collectanea,* in *Venerabilis Bedae,* Patrologia Latina, series secunda 94, ed. Jacques-Paul Migne (Paris: Migne, 1850), col. 541, once believed to have been the work of the Venerable Bede—distinguishes the three Magi by age: old, young, and intermediate. The popular belief described here emerged in liturgical dramas of the early fifteenth century; see Richard C. Trexler, *The Journey of the Magi: Meanings in History of a Christian Story* (Princeton, NJ: Princeton University Press, 1997), 95–102.

176. Gilio's words are *mattacini* (acrobats) and *giocolieri* (jugglers). Lomazzo, in his manuscript *Libro dei sogni,* probably composed circa 1563 (1:lxxxi–ii), reported that some people compared Michelangelo's figures to rough laboring types and actors (*fachini* and *istrioni*); Lomazzo, *Il libro dei sogni,* 1:101. Very strong movements evidently conveyed an idea of low social status. Already in the fifteenth century, Alberti (*On Painting and On Sculpture,* 84–85 [book 2, §44]) had criticized figures shown with strong twisting movements, writing that they looked like actors (*istrioni*). See also note 10.

M. Silvio said: "That was done only to show the dignity and power of the art, and beyond that, out of reverence for those sacred instruments; for although certainly a single angel could carry them effortlessly, without trouble, this would not have given them the appropriate majesty. So I think he represented that crowd of angels to make the instruments more revered, solemn, and devout."

M. Francesco added: "I think they would have acquired more in glory and greatness if they had been designed with the reverence appropriate to angels, not to the art of painting; for smoke should not be extracted from light, but rather the glory of light should be extracted from the smoke.[177] For that reason, those movements fit neither the persons nor the subject matter, nor the place, given that the nature of the angel is such that no task whatsoever can burden it.[178] **[47]** This can be seen in the revolutions of the celestial orbs, each orb being moved effortlessly by its own individual angel. Moreover, I think those sacred mysteries will not appear in the heavens as the material things they once were but rather as shining, flashing fire, like the cross that appeared to Emperor Constantine in the southern or the eastern sky, whichever it was, because I have found references to both.[179] And when they have to be shown as they once were, then the column should not be made so huge that an angel could not easily hold it, given that an angel holds up the solar orb, which according to astronomers is many times larger than the earthly globe. Indeed, the form of that column can be seen any day in Rome, at either Santa Prassede or Santa Pudenziana, whichever it is.[180] Therefore it was not necessary to make so many groups of angels, with all their entanglings, dancing about and making movements more suited to acrobats or jugglers than to the heavenly spirits that angels are. I will say the same of the Cross, which should not be so inappropriately scaled as to require such numbers of dancers to hold it nor so many acrobats to perform their tricks on it: some along its length, some its breadth, some across it, some beside it, some on its back, some above, and some below. For it was carried by our Savior on his shoulders, when he was weak and failing from loss of blood, and so humiliated by injuries and insults that he no longer had the appearance

177. Horace, *Ars Poetica,* 462–63 (line 143): "Not smoke after flame does he plan to give, but after smoke the light."

178. On the representation of angels, see Braun, *De imaginibus,* 36.

179. The Cross shining brighter than the sun would appear at the Last Judgment, according to Braun, *De imaginibus,* 33, citing Chrysostom, Homily on 24 Matthew. See Saint John Chrysostom, *The Homilies of Saint John Chrysostom on the Gospel of Saint Matthew* (London: Aeterna, 2015), line 77.

180. The Column of the Flagellation is preserved in the basilica of Santa Prassede; it is baluster-like and quite small. See Bruno Maria Apollonj Ghetti, *Santa Prassede* (Rome: Marietti, 1961), 75–76.

of a man. Even Simon of Cyrene carried it; so much the more could one angel carry it."

M. Silvio said: "As for the multitude of angels, I think that they give glory and grandeur to those sacred instruments, which will appear on that day glorified, sowing confusion among sinners and exalting the majesty of the Savior and the glory of the blessed."

"You argue very well," said M. Francesco. "But not with regard to the dancers, who provoke laughter rather than encourage devotion. For even if celestial spirits were there in millions, they would not be enough to reveal the magnificence of those instruments.[181] And what do you think of the movements of Saint Blaise and Saint Bartholomew, as well as of Saint Andrew who, stripped naked and in a strained pose, has lifted the cross onto his shoulders?[182] And the same is true of many others, so that focusing on these, one can easily get the measure of the rest. **[48]**

"Therefore the prudent painter must take care not to have his figures make any unseemly movement that does not fit the person, the subject, or the place, age, and time. I remember I once saw a Saint John the Baptist making a gesture with his little finger as he held the cross, which even if one were to examine a thousand men, would not be found to be used by a single one of them; and the saint was painted like that because the person who painted him gestured in this way himself. Universal models [*regole*] should not be extracted from such individual peculiarities, but from things that nature brings about attractively and nobly in a perfect man, animal, bird, or whatever else. Nor would I want a painter to behave like the one who, in order to show a little muscle in a saint's knee or at the top of his foot, twisted the leg in a way that nature could only have achieved by using a winch, not by the natural order of things. The intelligence, expertise, and excellence of the artist is known when, wishing to give a movement to a figure, he does it using the precept outlined above, so that it does not seem violent, but fitting, attractive, and natural."[183]

---

181. The derision aimed at the *Last Judgment* is also reported by Lomazzo, *Il libro dei sogni,* 1:101–2: "It is said that he had the idea of depicting on that wall a crowd or rabble of rough laboring types and actors who would go jumping around up there" (Dicesi che egli aveva pensato di fare in quella facciata una gabbia overo ciurma de fachini e de istrioni che andassero saltellando di là su). The context is a dialogue between "Leonardo da Vinci" and "Phidias," in which Lomazzo draws attention to expectations among contemporary audiences of religious narrative painting that they will witness nobility and splendor. See also note 148; and Bury, this volume, 18–19.
182. From the description of the pose, Saint Andrew is understood to be the standing figure with a cross toward the right edge of the fresco, often identified as Dismas, the good thief.
183. The discussion turns from requiring movements to be appropriate to each person to advice that unusual, idiosyncratic, strained, and unpleasing movements should be avoided. Moderate movements derived from the study of what is usual in nature, not violent

M. Vincenso said: "What kind of movement will it be, if it is to be attractive, peaceful, and natural?"

M. Francesco replied: "That is the way I describe movements [*sforzi*] made by a man or animal when they perform an action [*atto*] of their own volition, and not as a result of force or violence imposed on them from outside. So the painter must pay attention to what nature can do attractively: if he is making a galloping horse, he must take note of the most suitable and noble action that nature gives to a beautiful horse when it runs. I will also say the same about men, whether naked or clothed, standing or walking, or doing whatever they want to: the painter must always be ready with whatever pleasing movement nature can deploy for the action in question, so that the movement seems autonomous and not violently imposed by others. Unless one were to paint someone being tortured, since this makes a man do things that he cannot do by himself; but I will not talk about this now. Because nature, in various parts of the body, can exhibit hidden features, as when someone turns, twists, stretches, contracts his limbs, bends down, or straightens up, **[49]** these should not be taken as a norm [*regola*] in every action or movement. For a movement someone makes when bending down is not appropriate when sitting down, or that made in sitting down when standing up again. Sometimes a movement is needed in one action that does not suit another. This is where the painter must take great care, learning to discriminate between actions, giving to each what is proper to it, and not confusing them in a clumsy way. That means not having movements where they should not be, and avoiding ones that nature can only perform in an awkward way. It must always be borne in mind that art imitates nature, not nature art, and account should always be taken of the status of the person, the character of the subject, the place, and the time, so that every action required is represented with the appropriate movement. However, as was said earlier, it would be best if the painter were to make his cartoons, sketches, or models several days beforehand, so that he can revise and think about them a hundred times over, not as a father but as a judge: he can add, subtract, alter, and correct the matter as he wishes;[184] he can ask questions, inform himself, read and fully absorb the whole subject matter and all the particularity of both its essential nature and details. He must not work blindly, hurriedly setting to work and deploying the brush. Because, as Horace says, a poet cannot be good unless his poem contains many crossings-out, having been altered ten or even twenty times; and I will say the same of the painter, if he does not do the

movements devoid of beauty and grace, had been recommended by Alberti, *On Painting and On Sculpture,* 82–85 (book 2, §43–44). For related ideas in Dolce's *L'Aretino,* see note 116.

184. On the importance of drawing, see also Gilio, this volume, 120–21.

equivalent.[185] It happens that in their figures of whatever shape or size, the new anatomists of frenzy attribute to men, weapons, and horses alike such awkward movements, flexions, and actions that nature weeps and the art laughs at seeing so many blunders, barbarisms, and errors being made all the time."[186]

M. Pulidoro said: "I think painting is no less dishonored by ignorant painters than poetry by ignorant poets."

"I believe," M. Francesco replied, "there are many more ignorant poets than painters."

M. Vincenso added: "Poets have an extra advantage."

"What is that?" asked M. Troilo.

"If poetry were lost and the fountain of Pegasus dried up in the great heat, it would be restored by having recourse to Fra Baldassarre Olimpo of Sassoferrato, and therefore I think Sassoferrato is as indebted to him as Florence is to Dante and Arezzo to Petrarch."[187] **[50]**

"I am not sure about a lot of the things you say," added M. Pulidoro. "Once when Il Deserto and some other academicians were joking with a bookseller in Siena, the latter said to them: 'Attend as much as you like to your Dantes and Petrarchs, but for me Olimpo is good business, because I don't sell more than ten Petrarchs or five Dantes in a year, but I sell over a thousand of Baldassarre Olimpo's works.'"[188]

185. Horace, *Ars Poetica,* 474–75 (lines 289–94); see Gilio, this volume, 120. Horace's lines follow a passage in which excess and violence of language have been described as a consequence of liberty (lines 282–83).

186. "I nuovi notomisti del furioso" is the phrase in Gilio's text, translated here as "the new anatomists of frenzy."

187. The fountain of Pegasus was Hippocrene. The Franciscan Caio Baldassarre Olimpo Alessandri da Sassoferrato, born circa 1486, recorded until 1533, wrote both sacred and profane poetry. He chose popular subject matter, including amorous and obscene verse (R. Avesani, "Alessandri, Caio Baldassare Olimpo da Sassoferrato," *DBI,* 2 [1960]), and his language was judged impure because of his use of dialect forms. See Barocchi, *Trattati,* 2:591, n1 to Gilio p. 50.

188. In his *Topica poetica,* Gilio mentions his acquaintance with Il Deserto, a member of the Sienese Accademia degli Intronati. Gilio, *Topica poetica* (Venice: Oratio de' Gobbi, 1580; facs. reprint, Munich: W. Fink, 1970), 12r. This academician can be identified as Antonio Barozzi, from Genoa; see Jane E. Everson et al., *The Italian Academies 1525–1700: A Themed Collection Database,* London, British Library, 2009–; http://www.bl.uk/catalogues/ItalianAcademies/Default.aspx. According to Marcello Marcucci, the founders of the Intronati were six Sienese noblemen: Lo Scaltrito (Archbishop Francesco Bandini Piccolomini); L'Arsiccio (Antonio Vignali); L'Importuno (Francesco Sozzi); Il Sodo (Marco Antonio Piccolomini); Il Moscone (Giovan Francesco Franceschi); and Il Cirloso (Alessandro Marzi). Marcello Marcucci, "Accademia Senese degli Intronati," in Marcello Marcucci and Natalina Crevani, *Accademie e istituzioni culturali in Toscana,* ed. Francesco Adorno, Accademia toscana di scienze e lettere "La Colombaria," Serie Studi 92 (Florence: Leo S. Olschki, 1988), 454. Founded in 1525, and then suspended during the Republic, the Intronati resumed activities in 1559 but was closed down by Cosimo I in

They all laughed and M. Francesco returned to the argument, saying: "I don't see any less confusion in the costumes than in the movements; many [painters], thinking to give their works greater appeal [*vaghezza*], have so confused the clothing that you can no longer distinguish the Greek from the Latin, the Turkish from the French, or the Spanish from the Arab; whereas the opposite should be the case, so that one nation may easily be distinguished from another. Because if one paints an army made up of different nationalities, and they all wear Roman military garb, it will be impossible to tell one from the other; and, although a figure may not speak, the clothes nevertheless reveal his identity.[189] And if it happens that one cannot obtain clear information about the dress of those one might wish to paint, as would be the case with a Scythian, or a native of China or of the Moluccas, about whom we know little, then one must have recourse to writers or, if they make no mention of dress, to neighboring peoples. Otherwise, painters should heed Horace's advice: 'You either follow what is generally accepted or invent things that are most suitable for it.'[190]

"This was not respected by Giorgio [Vasari] in the Saint Paul he painted in the chapel of Pope Julius at San Pietro in Montorio, which shows [Paul] in Roman military dress; because, although Jerusalem was full of Roman soldiers and he was a Roman citizen, it does not follow that he was a soldier or wore military clothing only suitable for soldiers [fig. 17].[191] Michelangelo did not do this with his Paul in the new chapel, although he was wrong to make him old, seeing that he was actually young [see fig. 14] **[51]**.[192] If we are willing to believe the histories, we will find that Hannibal's soldiers, while fighting the Romans in Italy, wore their own dress and carried their own weapons, while the Arabs for the most part fought naked or without armor. The Turks and other barbarous nations used Turkish dress and weapons, or those dictated by the custom of their own countries. I don't know where this abuse started among the modern painters, namely giving Roman military dress indiscriminately to every nation, even when depicting Turks, Arabs, Moors, and other foreigners; to my mind this is a bad practice."

1568 (Marcucci, "Accademia," 457). On Francesco Bandini Piccolomini, who had resided at Fabriano in 1552, see note 17.

189. In contrast to Dolce, *L'Aretino*, in Barocchi, *Trattati*, 1:165 (Roskill, *Dolce's "Aretino,"* 118–19), who treats the subject as a straightforward matter of decorum (*convenevolezza*), M. Francesco emphasizes the way that giving figures the correct dress leads to narrative clarity.

190. Horace, *Ars Poetica*, 460–66 (line 119).

191. Vasari's altarpiece of the *Conversion of Paul* for the Del Monte Chapel in San Pietro in Montorio was commissioned by Pope Julius III and probably painted in 1551; Paola Barocchi, *Vasari pittore* (Florence: Barbèra, 1964), 133.

192. The *Conversion of Paul* in the Pauline Chapel. On the age of Paul, see Gilio, this volume, 145.

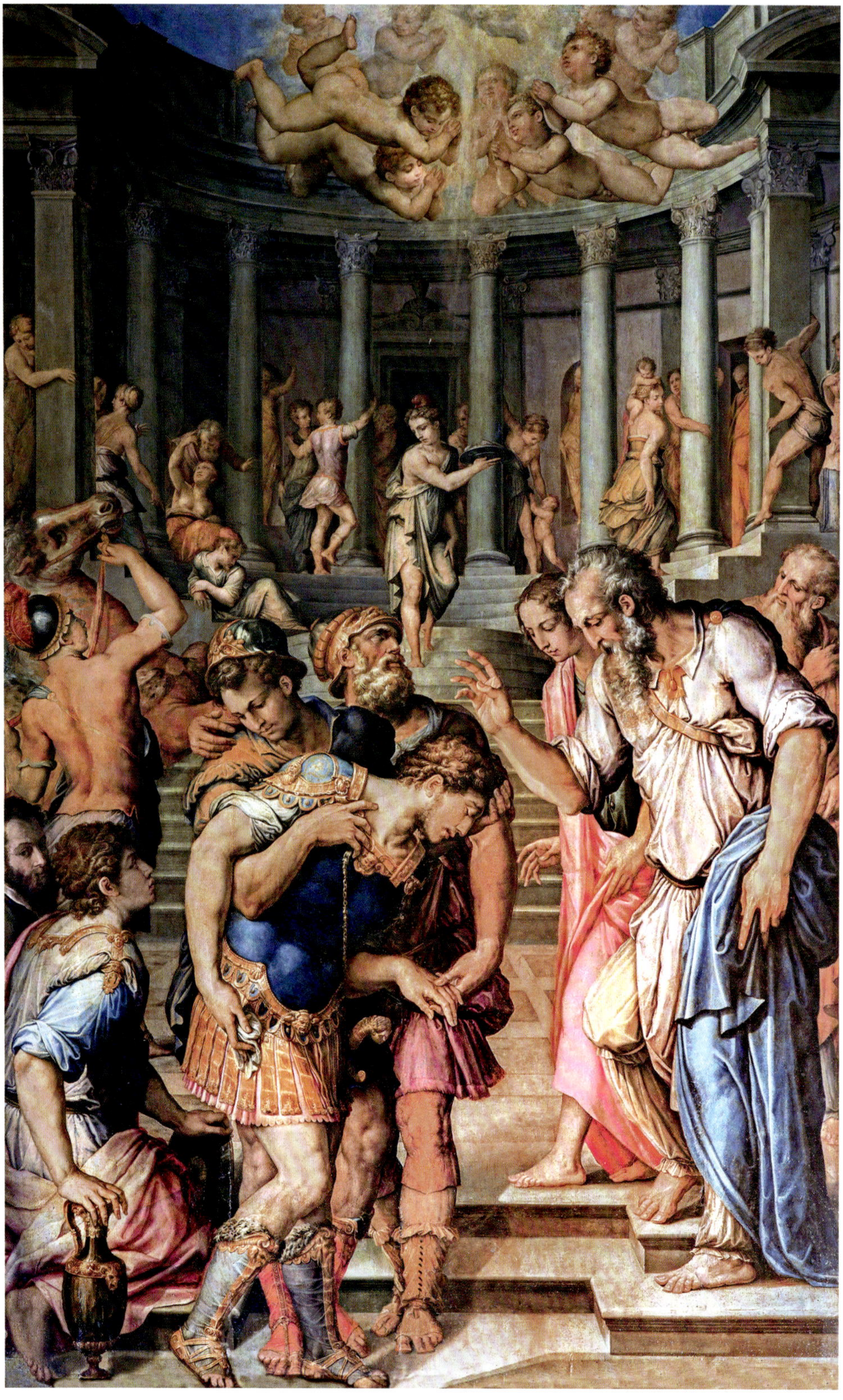

M. Silvio said: "I think that this form of dress was common to Greeks and Romans, if what is shown by the statue of Pyrrhus, now displayed in M. Luca de' Massimi's house, is accurate; for he is wearing Roman military garb [fig. 18].[193] The same can also be said of others."

M. Francesco replied: "It could well be that the Romans, wishing to honor those famous Greeks in their city, dressed their statues in military costume. But what we need to know is whether the Greeks honored their own countrymen and also Romans by showing them in Greek dress. I would like it more if foreign nations were shown in their own costume. If a painter wanted to paint the wars of our time, he should paint the ornaments, clothes, and arms that soldiers use today so that we are remembered by posterity, as the Romans and those who followed them are by us. For if the Romans and those later peoples had only been concerned about preserving the memory of Greek dress and weapons, there would be no knowledge of Roman dress and weapons; and if the painters of two hundred or more years ago had set out only to preserve the memory of Roman dress, there would be no knowledge of the dress of their own times, whether of soldiers or of citizens and women. This can be seen in many places, of which I am heartily glad, providing insight into differences between periods and into the inconstancy of men's minds. And if the painters of earlier times had taken care to show the dress of popes and cardinals, before the latter started to wear the red hat under Pope Innocent IV, we would now know how they dressed when those consecrated heads and backs were not yet decorated with crimson (for according to some they used to wear dark blue, as evidenced by certain figures in San Martino ai Monti).[194] **[52]** This applies to the popes too, who, from Paul II onward, wore papal miters embellished with gold and gems, according to Platina.[195] So it would be good if painters gave

193. It is now thought to represent Mars; see Phyllis Pray Bober and Ruth Rubinstein, *Renaissance Artists and Antique Sculpture: A Handbook of Sources* (London: Harvey Miller, 1986), 66 (no. 24). Ulisse Aldrovandi recorded it in the house of Angelo de' Massimi; see Aldrovandi, *Delle statue antiche* (Venice, 1556), in Lucio Mauro, *Le antichità della città di Roma* (Venice: Giordano Ziletti, 1556), 168–69. An engraving by Jacob Bos of this statue, then believed to represent King Pyrrhus of Molossar, was published by Antonio Salamanca in 1562; see Christopher L. C. E. Witcombe, *Print Publishing in Sixteenth-Century Rome: Growth and Expansion, Rivalry and Murder* (London: Harvey Miller, 2008), 162–64.

194. Innocent IV reigned from 1243 to 1254. The paintings in Santi Silvestro e Martino ai Monti, referred to here, are no longer extant. The thirteenth-century murals, now lost, that decorated the apse of the Oratorio di San Silvestro in the attached monastery and that were recorded in seventeenth-century watercolors were apparently not discovered until major works of reconstruction were undertaken in the seventeenth century; see Maria Andaloro, *La pittura medievale a Roma 312–1431: Atlante percorsi visivi*, vol. 1, *Suburbio, Vaticano, Rione Monti* (Viterbo: Università della Tuscia, 2006), 255.

195. Paul II reigned from 1464 to 1471. On Paul II's love of display, see Richardson, *Reclaiming Rome,* 136–37. On the context of Platina in the sixteenth century, see Stefan Bauer, *The*

Fig. 17.
Giorgio Vasari (Italian, 1511–74).
Conversion of Paul, ca. 1551, oil on panel. Rome, San Pietro in Montorio, Del Monte Chapel.

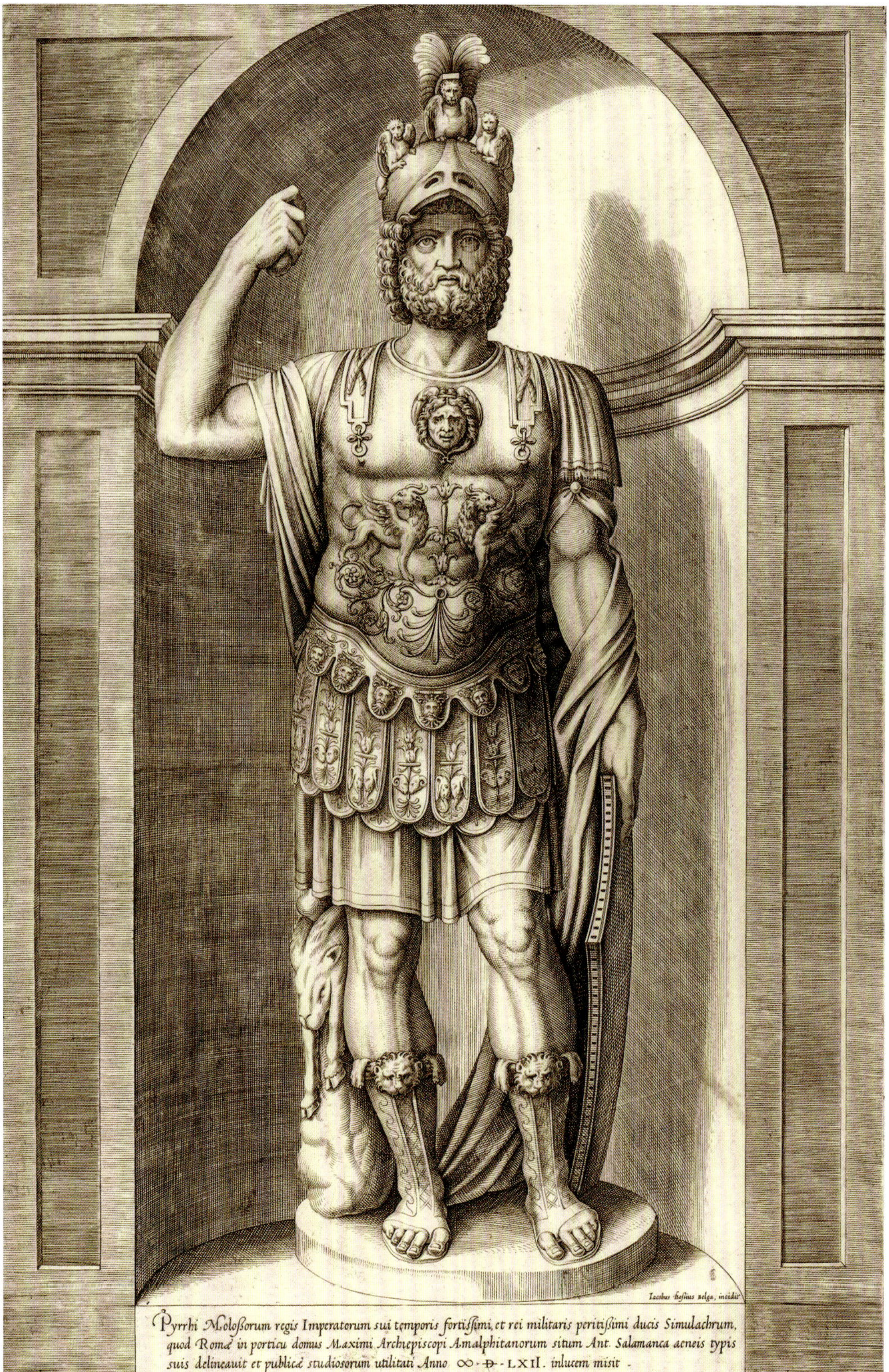
Iacobus Bossius Belga, incidit
Pyrrhi Molossorum regis Imperatorum sui temporis fortissimi, et rei militaris peritissimi ducis Simulachrum, quod Romæ in porticu domus Maximi Archiepiscopi Amalphitanorum situm Ant. Salamanca aeneis typis suis delineauit et publicæ studiosorum utilitati Anno ∞·Ↄ·LXII. inlucem misit.

modern dress to their modern figures, unless they are representing ancient Romans or Greeks, in other words those wars waged by the Romans against the Carthaginians, Gauls, or others. In the latter case it is more appropriate to show the soldiers in ancient military dress, because it would be no less an error to give them modern dress than to give modern soldiers ancient dress.[196] Another mistake I also notice among painters is that when they paint women they use garments to accentuate the relief of their breasts, buttocks, and thighs so that it actually looks as if the garments are glued on or, as is sometimes the case, as if a high wind were blowing and their garments, flattened against their bodies, bring out the relief; although not all parts at the same time.[197] I have observed many times that, even if a woman is dressed in the thinnest conceivable cloth or other material—unless it be very fine gauze or gossamer, neither of which are in use for clothes—it is not possible for such marked relief to be created.[198] They sometimes represent veils or hair in the same way, so that it seems that there is always a wind lifting them up and making them flutter. In certain places in his *Last Judgment* Michelangelo has done this, not realizing that on that day all winds and tempests will have ceased, and heaven and earth will have lost their powers [fig. 19].[199] For this reason, I would recommend that everything be done with great care, so that it appears that the artist is imitating nature, not following subjective conceptions [*capriccio*]. I shall not say that such things should be so strictly regulated that it is not permitted, from time to time, to do the contrary, provided that those things are what nature can do in an attractive way and provided that they can actually occur. License should always be used sparingly, because anyone wanting to extend it further than he ought will show himself to be lacking in awareness and care. An artist who

Censorship and Fortuna of Platina's "Lives of the Popes" in the Sixteenth Century (Turnhout: Brepols, 2006). Bartolomeo Platina, in his life of Paul, writes of Paul outdoing his predecessors in the splendor of his tiara, adorned with very expensive precious stones; see Onofrio Panvinio's edition of Bartolomeo Platina, *Historia de vitis pontificum Romanorum* (Venice: Michele Tramezzino, 1562), 256v–257r. As Schlosser points out, Gilio's interest in historical truth connects with contemporary developments in archaeological and historical research; see Julius von Schlosser, *La letteratura artistica: Manuale delle fonti della storia dell'arte moderna,* trans. Filippo Rossi, ed. Otto Kurz (Florence: Nuova Italia, 1964), 428. Onofrio Panvinio was a leading figure in these developments. Panvinio, after his return to Rome following the death of Paul IV in 1559, devoted himself to the study of Christian cult buildings (Stefan Bauer, "Panvinio, Onofrio," *DBI,* 81 [2014]).

196. Dolce, *L'Aretino,* in Barocchi, *Trattati,* 1:165 (Roskill, *Dolce's "Aretino,"* 118–19).

197. A reference to Alberti, *On Painting and On Sculpture,* 86–87 (book 2, §45), where wind-blown garments were recommended, but with the proviso that movements of clothing not be represented as against the direction of the wind.

198. Dolce, *L'Aretino,* in Barocchi, *Trattati,* 1:182 (Roskill, *Dolce's "Aretino,"* 150–51), wanted clothes to show the body underneath but not to appear stuck to the body ("ma non si, che taglino o che il drappo paia attaccato alle carni").

199. Revelation 7:1 and 21:1.

Fig. 18.
Jacob Bos (Netherlandish, active 1549–82), published by Antonio Salamanca (Milanese, ca. 1478–1562).
Pyrrhus (Mars), 1562, engraving, 36.3 × 30.4 cm. London, British Museum.

knows his subject well may therefore make a charming mixture of what is and isn't exactly correct, whenever he wants, and for this he will always receive honorable praise.[200] **[53]** Yet no one should let himself be carried away by the false belief that painters can do anything, as if there were neither reasons nor rules to constrain them within due and appropriate limits; and this belief has misled many into doing things that, rightly considered, lacked decorum and due proportion.

And if painters had, from time to time, thought about preserving the memory of the way things were done, it would be seen how much the world has changed in everything, not only from kingdom to kingdom and province to province, but from city to city and nation to nation, apart from the Turks and other barbarians who have always dressed in the same way. The extent of this change among the Romans is demonstrated by medals, statues, and other depictions, because as the Empire declined, so did fortune, virtue, strength, and all other good things, not just dress, arms, and customs. For, living in Constantinople, the emperors gradually abandoned Roman customs, clothing, and weapons and adopted Greek ones. The whole effort of fortune, after the decline of the Empire, was concentrated on Justinian, who through the skill and good luck of Belisarius and Narses achieved a glorious victory over the Vandals and the Goths, expelling the former from Africa and the latter from Italy; and let this suffice."[201]

M. Silvio said: "Now it remains to plow the greatest and deepest ocean that there is, in order to complete our discussion of the historical painter."

"What is that?" responded M. Francesco.

M. Silvio replied: "The discussion of the *Last Judgment* that Michelangelo painted in the Sistine Chapel, in which he has shown what the art [of painting] is capable of [see fig. 19]. He has done this in such a way that it amazes not only those who see it but everyone in the world who hears about it."

M. Troilo said: "We should have some representation of it in front of us in order to discuss it properly."

---

200. Here M. Francesco articulates a less rigorous position than the one put forward by M. Silvio earlier, allowing some blending of fiction into a historical painting; see Gilio, this volume, 131–33. There is an allusion to Horace, *Ars Poetica,* 462–63 (lines 151–52); compare also Dolce, *L'Aretino,* in Barocchi, *Trattati,* 1:171 (Roskill, *Dolce's "Aretino,"* 130–31). Elsewhere such license was permitted only to poetic and mixed painters, not to historical ones; see Gilio, this volume, 100–104, 199–200.

201. M. Francesco is asserting that one of the values of historical accuracy is a moral one: to demonstrate the mutability of earthly life. That the inconstancy of men's minds was revealed by changes in fashions of dress was a point that he had made a little earlier; see Gilio, this volume, 151, 153.

"That is well said," replied M. Francesco. "I will straight away have a print of it brought, which I have hung up on the wall of the room below the dovecote" [fig. 20].[202]

[54] And having said this he ordered a servant to bring it to him; he immediately went and brought it to M. Francesco, who, as soon as he received it, opened it because it was folded, saying: "Here my lords is the composition of the brilliant Michelangelo; the place where I think all modern painters learn what and how great the art of painting is. For in it he has achieved such excellence that he deserves to have statues erected to him in every country and even in every city, in order that those who come after may hold him in the same veneration as we hold Apelles, Zeuxis, and the other famous painters, and in sculpture Praxiteles, Phidias, and those others whose fame in the world will never die. For truly he deserves eternal praise for having restored the art to its decorum [*decoro*], and for having elevated it and rendered it illustrious, thus equaling the ancients and surpassing the moderns."

M. Silvio said: "You have put it well, but however much one says, it deserves more. And because the subject is an ecclesiastical and theological one, the person to talk about it is M. Ruggiero. He is a canon and a doctor who has carefully studied Holy Scripture."

M. Vincenso replied: "That's well said, so M. Ruggiero, without making any excuses, perform your part and inquire into whether Michelangelo has in this case followed the opinion of the holy doctors and observed the truth of the history."

M. Ruggiero replied: "You have placed too great a burden on me, yet I will obey your instructions. If we consider its purity as history, I think we will find there more personal invention [*capricci*] than truth. For Michelangelo has preferred to satisfy the art [of painting] in order to demonstrate what and how great it is, rather than the truth of the subject matter. He has behaved like a person in love who, to please his beloved, has regarded everything as permissible.[203] And I think the reason for this is that finding himself with such a large

202. By 1562, several prints of the *Last Judgment* were available. From the description it may be supposed that the one referred to here was of some size: Giulio Bonasone's engraving measured 58 × 44.2 cm (see fig. 20), but Gilio may have been thinking of the very large, ten-plate engraving by Giorgio Ghisi that measured 122 × 107 cm (see fig. 21); or the ten-plate engraving by Nicolas Beatrizet (see fig. 22). See Alida Moltedo, ed., *La Sistina Riprodotta*, exh. cat. (Rome: Fratelli Palombi, 1991), 57 (no. 10), 68 (no. 17); and Michael Bury, "Niccolò della Casa's *Last Judgement* Dissected," *Print Quarterly* 27, no. 1 (2010): 3–10.

203. Following M. Francesco's praise of Michelangelo for having restored the art of painting to its true decorum, M. Ruggiero demonstrates all that has been sacrificed by Michelangelo's exclusive focus on the qualities of the art itself. Earlier M. Troilo criticized painters for

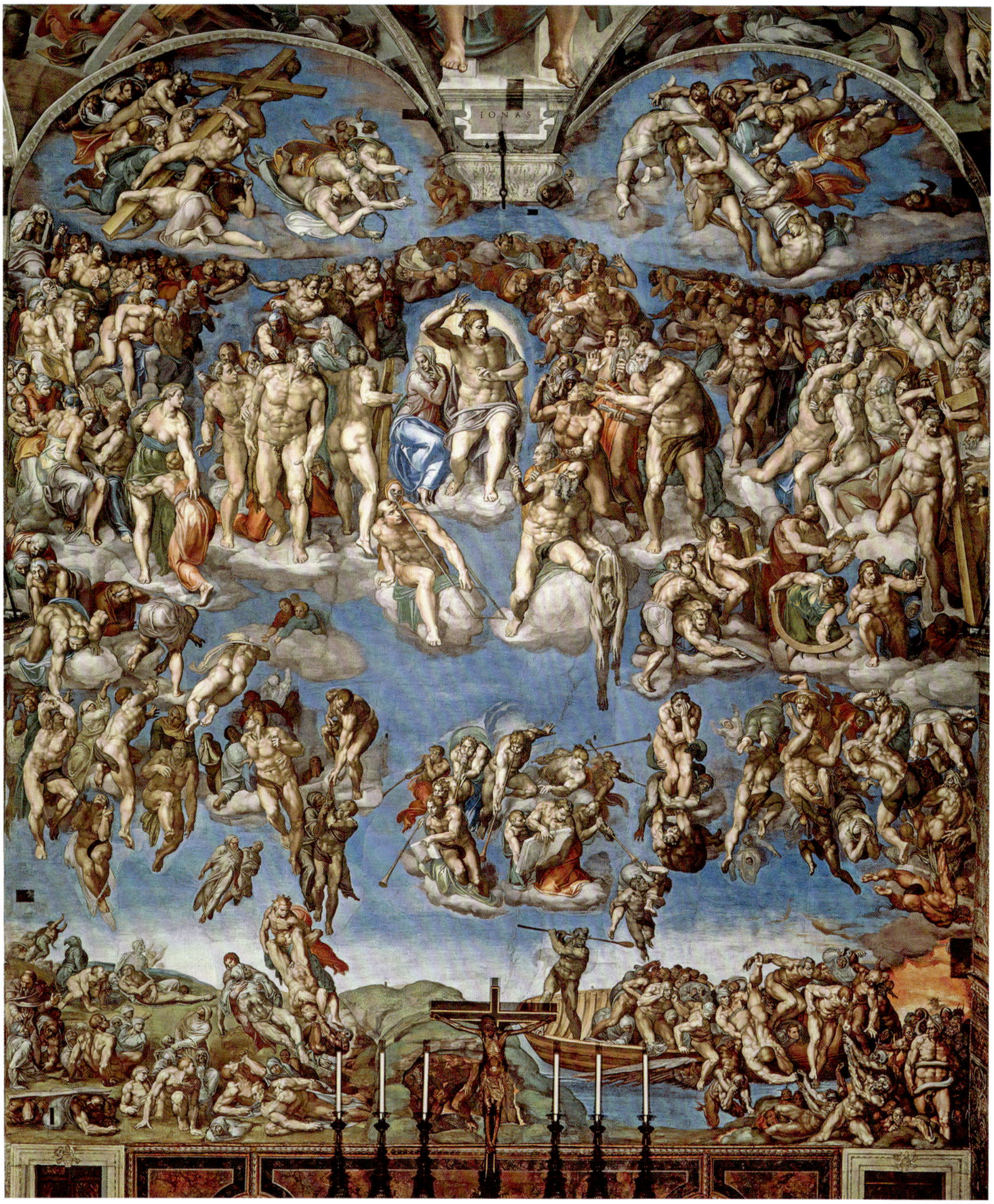
IONAS

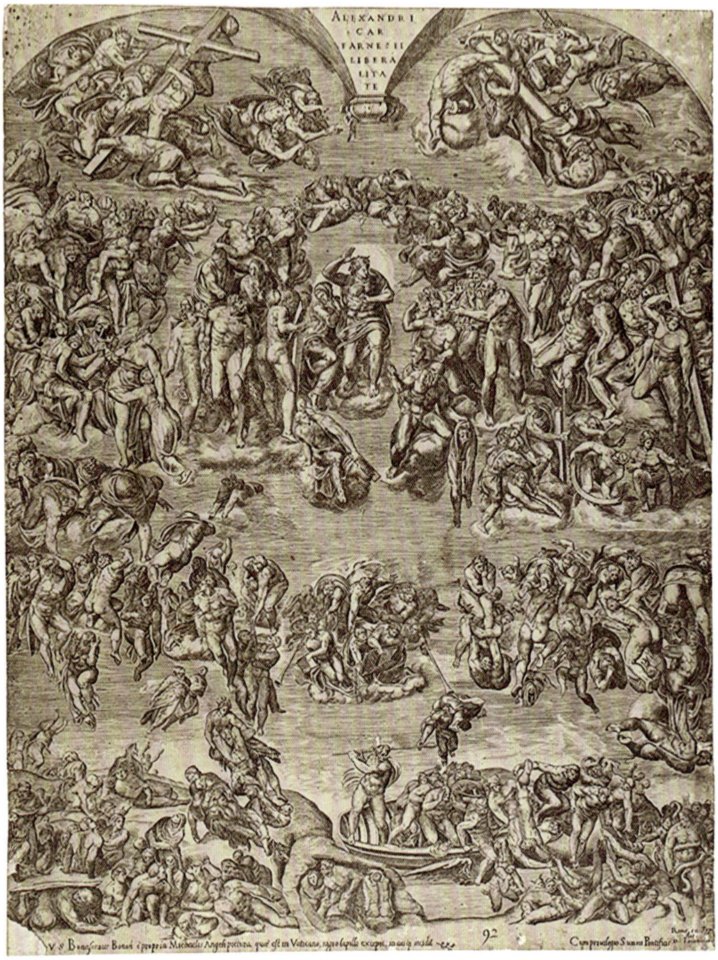

space and so many figures with which to show every possible movement and pose that the human body can gracefully adopt, he did not wish to lose the opportunity of leaving to posterity a record of his extraordinary mind.[204] **[55]**

avoiding the representation of the tortured Christ, deriding their defense that to do so would be an offense against the *decoro dell'arte* (see Gilio, this volume, 136–37). Here M. Ruggiero may be alluding to Michelangelo's own self-criticism in "Giunto è già 'l corso della vita mia," the famous sonnet in which he sees himself as having reached the end of his life, where "affectionate fantasy" is described as having made the art (of painting and sculpture) into his "idol and sovereign." The sonnet was circulating by 1554; see James M. Saslow, *The Poetry of Michelangelo: An Annotated Translation* (New Haven, CT: Yale University Press, 1991), 476–77.

204. Ascanio Condivi, *The Life of Michelangelo,* trans. Alice Sedgwick Wohl and ed. Hellmut Wohl (University Park: Pennsylvania State University Press, 1999), 83: "In this work Michelangelo expressed all that the art of painting can do with the human figure, leaving out no attitude or gesture whatsoever." Condivi, *Vita di Michelangelo Buonarroti,* ed. Giovanni Nencioni (Florence: S.P.E.S., 1998), 49: "non lasciando in dietro atto o motto alcuno."

Fig. 19.
Michelangelo Buonarroti (Italian, 1475–1564).
Last Judgment, 1535–41, fresco, 140 × 120 cm. Vatican City, Vatican Apostolic Palace, Sistine Chapel.

Fig. 20.
Giulio Bonasone (Bolognese, active 1531–after 1576), after Michelangelo Buonarroti (Italian, 1475–1564).
Last Judgment, engraving, later 1540s, 58 × 44.2 cm. New York, Metropolitan Museum of Art, Joseph Pulitzer Bequest, 1917.

And it is a wonderful thing that no single figure in this portrayal does the same as another, and none resembles another. In order to achieve this he set aside devotion, reverence, historical truth, and the honor due to such a very important and great mystery, which no one should think about, let alone see, without experiencing the greatest terror."

M. Pulidoro replied: "I don't think there is a painter, even the most stupid, who does not know that Michelangelo wished to satisfy the art [of painting] rather than the historical truth. What he has failed to do came not from ignorance but from the desire to show posterity the excellence of his mind [*ingegno*] and the excellence of the artistic skill [*arte*] that he possesses."[205]

M. Silvio said: "So now, in terms we can understand, start pointing out to us in turn the places where he has satisfied the art rather than the truth, telling us about the order of events, which I have never fully understood."

M. Ruggiero replied: "I am happy to do it; but be on your guard to recognize the different elements—the true, the fictional, and the fabulous—that are to be seen there. I say then that the historical painter is in all respects like a writer: whatever the one describes with his pen, the other must describe with his brush. However, both must faithfully and fully display the truth, not allowing into their works anything concealed, contaminated, or imperfect.[206] And it appears to me that the artists who came before Michelangelo paid more attention to truth and devotion than to ostentation."

---

205. Barocchi interprets M. Ruggiero and M. Pulidoro as accusing Michelangelo of "excessive formalism"; Barocchi, *Trattati,* 2:592, n1 to Gilio p. 55. But Gilio is not working with a form/content polarity. Michelangelo is instead being accused of failing to represent the historical truth established by the theologians and of failing to edify his audience because he was pursuing a personal, subjective vision of the Last Judgment that would advertise his "ingegno" and his mastery of the art of painting; see Dempsey, "Mythic Inventions," 65–66. M. Ruggiero is explicit in claiming that Michelangelo's failure to satisfy historical truth was not the result of ignorance, and he makes the same point again below; see Gilio, this volume, 172–73.

Although Aretino put it in different words, his letter criticizing the *Last Judgment* carries an essentially similar charge. He claims that Michelangelo had chosen to display no less impiety of irreligion than perfection in painting ("non meno impietà d'inreligione che perfettione di pittura") and that our souls have greater need of the feeling of devotion than of the pleasure brought by lively drawing ("le anime nostre han più bisogno de lo affetto de la divotione che del piacere che porta seco la vivacità del disegno"). Originally written in November 1545 and addressed to Michelangelo, the letter had been published in 1550 and readdressed to Alessandro Corvino, with some verbal differences. See Pietro Aretino, *Il quarto libro de le lettere* (Venice: Bartolomeo Cesano, 1550), 83r–84v; and Giovanni Poggi, Paola Barocchi, and Renzo Ristori, eds., *Il Carteggio di Michelangelo,* vol. 4, *1533–1552* (Florence: Sansoni, 1979), 215–19.

206. On the different types of subject, see note 46; on the historical painter being like a writer of history, see Gilio, this volume, 132–33.

"The people of that time," said M. Silvio, "were coarser, and since they were neither intellectually alert nor inventive, they relied on the past; they could only produce clumsy work. Look how their intellectual capacity is revealed by the fact that, not knowing how to superimpose Christ's feet on the Cross, they did it in the Greek manner, with four nails, like the one in the entrance of our church of San Venanzio![207] Nor on occasion, out of a certain affectation of dignity [*prosopopeia*], did they worry much about inventing things that deserve laughter rather than wonder: as I have heard is the case in the church of the Dominican friars at Rimini, which has an angel of the Annunciation with a palm's length of white beard.[208] **[56]** I think the painter who painted that must have been one of those pigheaded ones, since he only did it that way in order to make the glorious Virgin appear more chaste [*onesto*], as if she might have acted improperly or had lascivious thoughts when she spoke to the angel. There are still others to be seen, you know, that are no less ridiculous."

M. Ruggiero went on to say: "If those painters erred in minor ways, these err in major ones, and it would be best to make a regulated mixture [*regolata mescolanza*] of the two to produce a mean that compensates for the defects of each, so that the works have a proper correspondence [*debite proporzioni*] with the type of subject."[209]

---

207. Gilio was a canon of the church of San Venanzio at Fabriano. M. Silvio's characterization of the early painters is very much in line with Vasari's comments in the "Proemio delle vite" (Preface to his lives): "they undertook their work not according to the rules of [painting and sculpture] which they did not have, but according to the quality of their minds [*ingegni*]. And thus their hands gave birth to those badly painted figures and those awkwardnesses which are still seen today in old houses"; see Vasari, *Le vite de' più eccellenti architetti, pittori, et scultori Italiani . . . nell'edizione per i tipi di Lorenzo Torrentino, Firenze 1550*, ed. Luciano Bellosi and Aldo Rossi (Turin: Einaudi, 1986), 98.
208. Zeri suggests that in the Romagna there had been an iconography of the Annunciation of the Death of the Virgin figuring a bearded angel, and that Gilio had mistaken the precise subject of the painting at Rimini; see Federico Zeri, "L'Angelo con la barba: L'Annunziazione del transito della Vergine (e un errore di Giovanni Andrea Gilio)," in *Hommage à Michel Laclotte: Études sur la peinture du Moyen Âge et de la Renaissance*, ed. Pierre Rosenberg, Cécile Scailliérez, and Dominique Thiébaut (Milan: Electa, 1994), 304–10. The word translated here as "affectation of dignity"—*prosopopeia*—has a technical meaning in rhetoric as a form of personification, but that is not the sense here. The point made with the Fabriano example was the early painters' lack of technical inventiveness, while the Rimini example was to illustrate their lack of imagination or understanding of character, which could lead to an absurdly inappropriate treatment of figures. That is to say, they revealed deficiencies in both *arte* and *ingegno.*
209. Zeri interprets "those painters" to mean the ones who came before Michelangelo and "these" as the moderns; Federico Zeri, *Pittura e Controriforma: L'arte senza tempo di Scipione da Gaeta* (Turin: Einaudi, 1957), 31. M. Ruggiero asserts that the intention to observe truth and convey devotion is more important than *ingegno* and mastery of the art of painting, but both are necessary.

"Let us come back to our subject," said M. Troilo. "Start by telling the story [*istoria*] of the judgment."

M. Ruggiero continued, saying: "The first thing you should note is that we can know neither the hour, nor the day, nor the time of the judgment, except through conjecture. Our Lord did not want to reveal anything about this to his disciples because it is reserved to God the Father, so that neither angels nor men can have knowledge of it."[210]

"Whatever do you mean?" responded M. Vincenso. "The seven days that passed during the creation of the world and Daniel's seven weeks signify nothing other than the seven thousand years of the earth's duration, of which, as many agree, six thousand five hundred and sixty-one years have passed."[211]

M. Ruggiero said: "The opinions of these doctors are probable, not necessary. It is enough for me that no one can know [the time of judgment] with certainty, except by divine revelation. It will come when no one expects it. The Savior said that it will come as a thief in the night.[212] The world will be just as we see it now and as it was at the time of Noah. People will be eating, drinking, playing, they will be marrying and doing what they do now, the Lord wanting to indicate that men will be taken by surprise.[213] But first will appear the son of perdition (as Paul says), the Antichrist, whose reign shall last for three and a half years, according to John in the Apocalypse.[214] Once this horrible monster has been killed by the thunderbolts of heaven, no one knows how much time will pass before the last day. **[57]** As soon as men's sins are heaped up high, then the signs predicted by the Evangelists will come: there will be wars, famines, plagues, and earthquakes; the sun and moon will be obscured, the stars will fall, and the powers of the heavens will be thrown into confusion, with other signs."[215]

---

210. Matthew 24:36: "But of that day and hour no one knoweth, not the angels of heaven, but the Father alone"; also Acts 1:7.
211. Here Gilio simplifies Daniel's complex prophecy (Daniel 9:24–7), isolating the seven weeks of verse 25. The following calculation of the date of the Last Judgment depends on the idea that the creation occurred five thousand years before the birth of Christ. This is slightly surprising given that the authoritative *Chronicon* of Saint Jerome, following Eusebius, dated the creation to 5199 BC. M. Vincenso's further observation that 6,561 years have already passed suggests that this part of the text was composed in 1562; see note 12.
212. 2 Peter 3:10; 1 Thessalonians 5:2. The decree on preaching of the Fifth Lateran Council had forbidden preachers from predicting any fixed time for the coming of the Antichrist and the Last Judgment; see Nelson Minnich, "Prophecy and the Fifth Lateran Council 1512–1517," in *Prophetic Rome in the High Renaissance Period,* ed. Marjorie Reeves (Oxford: Clarendon, 1992), 63, 85–87.
213. Matthew 24:36–44.
214. Revelation 13:4–5; 2 Thessalonians 2:3–4; John 17:12.
215. Matthew 24:6–8; Luke 21:9–11; Revelation 6:12–13.

M. Silvio said: "Tell me something, M. Ruggiero: do you believe that these signs must actually occur in reality, or, rather, should they be interpreted allegorically?"

M. Ruggiero answered: "Some will really occur, I believe, and some not. The wars, famines, earthquakes, plagues, and other ills, such as the eclipse of the sun and the moon, will I think actually occur; but the stars will not fall, since in reality that could not happen: this should be interpreted allegorically, namely that in this time the prelates of the church and other great men may have to lose their faith and abandon heavenly matters for the sake of worldly things. And when I say that this could not happen in fact, this is because even the smallest star is fixed in the sky and cannot fall. Moreover, the size of the stars is such that, in the eighth sphere, the astronomers say that there is no star so small that it is not larger than the whole earth. So, if it did fall, the world would be completely overwhelmed."

"How is that?" replied M. Troilo. "We see hundreds of stars falling in the summer."

M. Pulidoro laughed at this answer and said: "M. Troilo, you shouldn't believe that what you have seen falling are actually stars."

"What are they then?" replied M. Troilo.

M. Pulidoro said: "They are vapors that rise up from the earth, which move upward so very quickly that they ignite and, as they fall, they make those flashes or brilliant lights you describe. Nor should you believe, as some do, that those vapors fly into the sky and that as soon as they reach the element of fire they ignite. This is not true and cannot be so, since they cannot pass through the second region of the air or rise any higher than the clouds. That this is the case can be seen from the fact that they ignite and fall just a short way above us; and moreover I share the opinion of many that fire in its element has no action whatsoever. **[58]** On the subject of the stars we have used Aristotle's *Meteorology*.[216] Now, M. Ruggiero, do continue."

M. Ruggiero resumed the discussion: "Once the aforesaid signs have passed, and men nevertheless persevere in their evil ways, at a moment no one will be expecting it, the glorious symbols of our redemption will appear in the midst of the heavens, not bent over or sideways, as Michelangelo has made them and as you see them here, nor in ugly, material form as they were at the time of the Passion, but resplendent, shining, glorious, and in majesty. They will be supported with great magnificence by thousands of angels, with none of those movements, dances, and tricks performed by tangled groups of them, in the

216. Aristotle, *Meteorologica*, trans. H. D. P. Lee, Loeb Classical Library 397 (Cambridge, MA: Harvard University Press, 1952), esp. 8–27 (book 1, ch. 3) and 68–71 (book 1, ch. 9); on shooting stars, see *Meterologica*, 28–34 (book 1, ch. 4).

way you can see that Michelangelo has done.[217] That they have to be so resplendent and bright is the opinion of the learned scholar Origen and of Basil, and it is likely that this will be the case, as a way of humiliating unbelieving tyrants and persecutors of the Cross. And we can put what happens here down to a personal conception of Michelangelo's [*capriccio*], satisfying more what the art of painting fancies [*capriccio*] than the truth. Afterward our Lord will come in majesty, power, and glory, surrounded by all the angels of heaven. Then, as John says, all the tribes of the earth shall bewail themselves, and the world, filled with horror and fear, will see the Son of Man in glory among the heavenly clouds.[218] But it is not known at what time this coming will take place. Some have said that it will be at dawn, as when he was resurrected; others have said [it will be] at the time he ascended into heaven, when the angels told the Apostles: '[He] shall so come, as you have seen him going into heaven.'[219] Others say that it will be at midday, when he rendered up his spirit to God on the Cross, and that it will also be on the same day of Friday: and this is the opinion that I find most convincing.[220] Afterward he will send his angels with their trumpets to gather the elect from all four corners of the world."

M. Vincenso said: "Michelangelo respected this: here is a group of seven angels, who sound their trumpets and summon the people to judgment, as John says" [see fig. 19].[221]

M. Ruggiero said: "As for the seven angels, which are described by Saint John in that passage, this mystery should be understood not as the day of judgment but as the tribulations suffered by the Church from [the] moment [of the angels' appearance] until the day of judgment. **[59]** As proof that this is true, the apostle says that each sounded his trumpet in turn, announcing the future tribulation at the appropriate moment.[222] Afterward, they remain grouped together in one place; and the Gospel says that they shall be sent to the four corners of the world to gather the elect."[223]

M. Silvio said: "Take note, M. Ruggiero: the words of the Gospel do not say that 'He will send his angels to the four corners of the earth,' but that they shall gather together the elect from the four corners of the earth."

"This does not matter," said M. Ruggiero. "When the Lord says 'from the four winds, from the farthest parts of the heavens to the utmost bounds of

217. Compare Gilio, this volume, 146–48.

218. Revelation 1:7.

219. Acts 1:10–11.

220. The Italian reads "medesimo dì di Venere"; that is, *venerdì* – Friday.

221. Revelation 8:2; M. Vincenso echoes Condivi, *Vita di Michelangelo*, 49.

222. Revelation 8:2–13 and 9:1–19.

223. Matthew 24:31; Mark 13:27.

them,' I think he did not wish to infer anything other than that from the four corners of the world, namely from the whole world, the mortal remains of all the dead will be gathered. The good angels [will gather] those of the elect and the demons those of the damned and they will carry them to the valley of Josaphat, where rigorous hearings will take place."[224]

M. Francesco said: "How will it be possible for such a small place to hold so many people?"

M. Ruggiero answered: "This shall be a marvelous sign of divine power, because nothing is impossible for him. Some say that all the elect will remain in the air and the damned on the ground."

M. Pulidoro said: "Even if the elect remain in the air, how will such a narrow valley hold thousands of millions of men once they have risen from the dead? Because an army of one hundred thousand would occupy more than ten miles of land, so what will such numbers, the thousands of millions, do?"

M. Ruggiero replied: "I've already told you that this will be a sign of God's infinite power. And others have said (which I find quite convincing) that our Lord will remain in the air above the said valley, and the people will be spread around; not that the valley will hold all of them, but they will also occupy the nearby country and all the space they need, and all shall see the Lord in judgment in the air above the valley, as Matthew says."[225] **[60]**

M. Vincenso said: "I have frequently heard preachers say that souls do not take up space; therefore, if this were so, it would not be very difficult for them all to stay in that valley."

M. Ruggiero replied: "It is true that the theologians assert that souls do not occupy space; but on that day they will not just be souls, but souls and bodies, and although the bodies will be glorified, they must nonetheless take up some room. But please, let us leave these subtleties and return to the story. On that day, our Lord in majesty surrounded by angels will shine a thousand times more brightly than the sun. Once the mortal remains of the dead have been gathered together with the living in the valley, Archangel Michael (as some have said), or in truth our Lord, shall call the dead with a loud voice (in the same way that he once called Lazarus) and they will rise from the dead. Then the great mystery of the Resurrection shall take place 'in a moment, in the twinkling of an eye,' in a moment indivisible, as Paul said.[226] And here I note another personal invention [*capriccio*] of Michelangelo's, where he has paid more attention to his brush than to the truth; and this is that in the act of rising from the dead those

224. Joel 3:2, 3:12.
225. Matthew 24:30.
226. 1 Corinthians 15:52.

involved do different things for different purposes, as you can see. Some are already fully clothed with flesh, some only in part, some just beginning to be covered, some are naked, others dressed in pieces of cloth or the shrouds with which they were buried; one, as if embarrassed, tries to free himself from them, one gives signs of not really being awake, one shows doubt as to where divine justice wants him to go; one emerges from a cave, another just sits, a further one kneels; some do one thing, some another.[227] This is all wrong: they seem to represent a crowd of slugabeds rather than men raised from the dead."

M. Silvio said: "But it seems to me that this is one of the most appealing and beautiful mysteries to be found in the whole of this history, because it shows clearly that each person must come forth at the time of the Resurrection, wherever they are buried. I would say the same about what they are draped in, for we have the testimony of Scripture, which tells us that when Lazarus was raised from the dead, he was bound in winding bands, with a napkin over his face after the manner of the Jews.[228] **[61]** Furthermore, how many people have been buried in sacks, sheets, veils, and other cloths according to the customs of different places? And this was, I think, done deliberately [by Michelangelo], in order to show the variety of the dead and the differences in customs between peoples, for which reason I consider it well done. As for those rising from the dead—those who are skeletons, those half-covered in flesh, and those completely fleshed—this should not be regarded as his own personal conception [*capriccio*], for we have the prophecy of Ezekiel that clearly describes the effects of the Resurrection as Michelangelo has shown it.[229] And because the artist altered things a little, he should not be judged unfaithful, for Horace says: 'Do not try to translate your work word for word, as, in such a case, a faithful interpreter would.'[230] As for the man who lifts himself up and surveys the heavens, I don't think that this is intended to mean anything other than that having been resurrected he doesn't know whether he deserves pity or justice; he behaves thus because he is in doubt."

M. Ruggiero said: "The events will not happen as you think, nor as Michelangelo has shown them. As for the clothes, all will be resurrected naked, and as the clearest and quickest proof of this I will adduce the Resurrection of our Lord. He was buried with the cloths of which the Gospel speaks, but he rose

227. This echoes Condivi, *Vita di Michelangelo,* 49–50.

228. John 11:44.

229. Ezekiel 37:1–10; Condivi, in describing the *Last Judgment,* had cited Ezekiel as Michelangelo's source. See Condivi, *Vita di Michelangelo,* 49, with English translation in Condivi, *The Life of Michelangelo,* 84.

230. Horace, *Ars Poetica,* 460–61 (lines 133–34); the translation follows Gilio's Italian, not Horace's Latin.

naked and those cloths remained behind in the tomb.[231] And this was in order to show us that naked we came out of our mother's womb, naked we return to dust, and naked we will be resurrected, as Job said.[232] As for the prophecy of Ezekiel, I would reply that to the Prophet was shown only the mystery and not the actual way it would happen. Paul tells us that it will be in an instant, in the twinkling of an eye, in a moment indivisible and imperceptible, so there will be no time at all for the dead to come out of underground places, kneel down, crouch, prop themselves up, rub their eyes as if they had been asleep, arrange their features, call others to awake, and such like vanities. It will happen so fast that the putting on of the flesh will not be observable, as I will show you in an example. **[62]** If you cast a drop of water onto very dry, fine powder, you will see it becomes covered in powder so quickly that what you are aware of is the outcome, not the process. The same will be true of our resurrection: the soul, at the sound of the trumpet and the voice of the Lord, will take on flesh with such speed that it will not be seen happening but only as finished fact. As for Horace's lines that you mention, I say that the poet means that you should pay attention to the sense rather than to the words. Jerome, too, said this in the letter he wrote concerning the best kind of interpretation. The learned Isidore also said the same thing, since words were created to express concepts, and not the other way round.[233] But whoever corrupts the subject matter by making alterations deserves to be censured. For while the altering of unimportant nonessential elements [*accidenti*] is of no significance, to infect the substance is an inexcusable error.[234] And Horace did not mean to say that the translator should pay attention to the intention of the author rather than to his words, because imitation is one thing, translation something else.[235] And to return to the subject of the

231. Luke 24:12; John 20:5–8.
232. Job 1:21.
233. Jerome, *Liber de optimo genere interpretandi (Epistula 57),* ed. G. J. M. Bartelink (Leiden: E. J. Brill, 1980); and Jerome, "Letter LVII to Pammachius on the Best Method of Translating," in Philip Schaff and Henry Wace, eds., *A Select Library of Nicene and Post-Nicene Fathers of the Christian Church,* 2nd ser., vol. 6, *The Principal Works of Jerome,* trans. William H. Freemantle (New York: Christian Literature Company, 1893), esp. §5–6, where Jerome himself cites Horace. The reference to Isidore is probably to Isidore of Seville's *Etymologie;* see Isidore, *The Etymologies of Isidore of Seville,* ed. and trans. Stephen A. Barney, W. J. Lewis, J. A. Beach, and Oliver Berghof (Cambridge: Cambridge University Press, 2006).
234. See Gilio, this volume, 116–17.
235. The translator should not be slavish, but it is not imitation (*imitare*) that he should aim to achieve either; imitation was understood as a process of adaptation. Vincenzo Danti was to define the difference between copying (*ritrarre*) and imitating (*imitare*) through the analogy of the difference between history and poetry; Danti, *Trattato delle perfette proporzioni* [Florence: Eredi di Lorenzo Torrentino, 1567], in *Trattati d'arte del Cinquecento: Fra manierismo e controriforma,* vol. 1, ed. Paola Barocchi (Bari: Laterza, 1960), 252–53.

resurrection, I say that it will happen very quickly and there will not be some resurrected first and others afterward, some early, others late, but all together at exactly the same moment in time."

M. Francesco said: "Well, I don't agree. The apostle told the Thessalonians that the dead in Christ will rise first.[236] By saying first [*primi*], Paul presupposes a second, and hence an ordered succession that cannot happen without a distinction of time, as there is an order of rank. I would also like to point out another authoritative source, again in the Gospel: our Savior says that the angels will separate the good from the wicked; this separation could not be carried out without lapse of time, nor could the placing of some on the right and others on the left.[237] Michelangelo has therefore done well and your opinion is wrong."

M. Ruggiero replied: "You are mistaken, M. Francesco, because the words of the apostle in this passage do not presuppose any priority of time, only of rank. In the same way that we say that 'the first [*primi*] after the pope are the cardinals': this does not mean that the cardinals always follow the pope, but that the first rank after the pontifical is that of the cardinalate. **[63]** If the apostle had wished to denote time, he would have used the adverb *prius,* which the Latins use for time."

M. Vincenso said: "The word first [*primi*] also denotes priority of time. As we say 'so-and-so was the first to enter Rome, the said captains were the first to launch the assault,' and other similar things."

M. Ruggiero replied: "Given that it may be true what you have said, nevertheless in this passage it does not mean sequence but only rank, because the blessed will be noblest and the damned the most contemptible. In order to indicate the status of the blessed, Paul said that the dead in Christ shall rise first. As for the separation of the damned from the blessed, I say this will happen in an imperceptibly brief moment, like the resurrection. So the angels and the demons, who are also called angels in the Scripture, will make their choice in an instant: the good angels will choose the elect, the demons the damned; the elect will be taken up into the air, the damned will remain on the ground."

M. Troilo said: "I would very much like to know one thing: whether we will reassume the very same body as the one we leave, or whether we will have a newly created one (because, if we think about it carefully, grain produces grain, but not the same grain that was sown);[238] and, given that our body turns to dust, whether that same dust will be remade into flesh or not."

---

236. 1 Thessalonians 4:15: "For the Lord himself shall come down from heaven with commandment, and with the voice of an archangel, and with the trumpet of God: and the dead who are in Christ, shall rise first."

237. Matthew 13:49 and 25:31–33.

238. 1 Corinthians 15:35–38.

M. Ruggiero replied: "We will definitely reassume the same body that we leave when we die; this is something human weakness finds difficult to comprehend, since it seems impossible that something that nature has formed over such a long time, using so many means, could be put together in an instant. But if we consider our origin [and] the natural causes that underlie it, and if we bear in mind God's power, it doesn't seem to us impossible that he could bring this about. Our first birth, on Earth, is natural, and the second will be miraculous. Job announced this, saying: 'I will again be wrapped in my skin,' and note that he said 'my,' namely 'the same skin that I have now, no other.'[239] And in the example you gave, from Paul, about the grain, I say that grain is sown bare and it is born clothed, complete with stalks, but our body shall be of a different nature, even if it has the same flesh. **[64]** In this it will be different from grain, because that is reborn as the same species, with the same nature, although its adornments are different, not the same grain as was sown but another. Our flesh will be the same flesh, but with a different nature and with different adornments, because our first body was sown on the earth and was born there, but our resurrected body will have left behind earthiness, material weight, and corruptibility, and will arise spiritual, agile, nimble, and glorious. First we are born as the sons of Adam, as earthly man; afterward we will rise up as sons of Christ, as heavenly man. And just as in the world we have borne the image of earthly man, so in heaven will we bear the image of heavenly man, as Paul said."[240]

M. Pulidoro said: "How will this be achieved, it being the case that so many thousands of men have been burned and their ashes cast into the winds and the rivers? So many too have been eaten by wild beasts, birds, and fish, and by men, like the Anthropophagi, the Laestrygonians, and the Cannibals;[241] one reads in various places how, in Jerusalem, mothers ate their own children, and this also happened in Rome at the time of the Goths.[242] Seeing that as a result of being eaten, the flesh of one has been converted into that of another, if it is to be as you have described, then substance will have to be extracted from one

239. Job 19:26: "And I shall be clothed again with my skin, and in my flesh I will see my God."

240. 1 Corinthians 15:49: "Therefore as we have borne the image of the earthly, let us bear also the image of the heavenly."

241. On the Anthropophagi, see Herodotus, *The Persian Wars,* vol. 2, *Books 3–4,* trans. A. D. Godley, Loeb Classical Library 118 (Cambridge, MA: Harvard University Press, 1921), 218–19 (4.18); and on the Laestrygonians, see Homer, *Odyssey,* vol. 1, *Books 1–12,* trans. A. T. Murray, rev. George E. Dimock, Loeb Classical Library 104 (Cambridge, MA: Harvard University Press, 1919), 364–67 (10.81–133).

242. On Jerusalem, see Josephus, *The Jewish War,* vol. 3, *Books 5–7,* trans. Henry St. J. Thackeray, Loeb Classical Library 210 (Cambridge, MA: Harvard University Press, 1928), 236–39 (6.201–13). There was cannibalism reported at the time of Alaric's siege of Rome, AD 410; see Saint Jerome's letter to Principia in *Jerome,* ed. and trans. Stefan Rebenich (London: Routledge, 2002), 128.

and given to another. How that can be I don't know. Moreover, it would not be proper to remove substance from wild beasts, birds, and fish, converting it into human substance, because that would be monstrous."

M. Ruggiero replied: "If we insist on thinking about our makeup according to the order of nature, then what I have said could not happen, and neither could the resurrection of the dead. According to your principles as a philosopher, you rightly think that these things contradict one another, and so, to an even greater extent, they contradict the resurrection, because your principles do not allow a return to life from a state of nonbeing. But if through our faith as Christians, we consider how it will be, we will have no doubts whatsoever, because for God nothing is impossible, given that he created everything from nothing. **[65]** When he wished to create a woman, he took a rib from Adam's side, and from that simple, hard bone, without diminishing, damaging, or deforming Adam himself, he made a woman. He also, in the period of the new law, multiplied the bread and fishes in the Apostles' hands, so that many thousands of people could be fed, and enough was left over to feed as many again. Do you doubt that he who made the woman without diminishing the substance of the man, and multiplied the loaves and fishes in the hands of the Apostles, could not extract substance from wild beasts, birds, and fishes, and convert it into human substance, or [take it] from one man to give to another? And if he did not want to extract [substance] from those that I have said, do you doubt that he could not increase it as much as he wished, in whatever way he wished, and in whomsoever he wished? For he multiplied [the number] of loaves and fishes in the hands of the Apostles, and he increased the meal in the widow's barrel at the time of Elijah, and the oil in the widow's jar at the time of Elisha.[243] You believe surely that God has the power to remove substance from men, from wild beasts, birds, and fish, and can convert it into man's true substance in a moment, even an instant. And that he can do it without diminishing the substance of men, beasts, birds, or fish, and without making something monstrous in the way you said. And that this be true even if those bodies have been reduced to ashes and thrown to the winds or into rivers, to the east, west, south, and north, or if they have disintegrated in fire, water, air, and earth: because on that day each element shall give up its dead, as John said."[244]

243. The creation of Eve is at Genesis 2:21–22. The miracle of the loaves and fishes is at Matthew 14:16–21, Mark 8:5–9, Luke 9:12–17, and John 6:9–13. Elijah and the widow's barrel of meal is at 1 Kings (Third Book of Kings) 17:12–16; and Elisha and the widow's pot of oil is at 2 Kings (Fourth Book of Kings) 4:2–7.

244. Revelation 20:13. For this whole argument about the reconstitution of bodies at the Last Judgment, see Augustine, *De civitate Dei: Libri XXII,* in *S. Augustini Tomus Septimus,* Patrologia Latina, series prima 41, ed. Jacques-Paul Migne (Paris: Migne, 1845), 22.20.

M. Pulidoro replied: "I grant that it may be as you say, because for God nothing is impossible; and you have argued well that we must believe it through faith, since the opinion of philosophers is useless and erroneous in these matters. God has laid down one rule for material things and another for spiritual things, and Aristotle's opinions concern the former and not the latter, which is the sphere of faith where the rules of nature fail." **[66]**

M. Silvio said: "Do you believe, M. Ruggiero, that men will rise from the dead as men, and women as women, or shall they all be male, or all female?"

M. Ruggiero replied: "Augustine and other theologians state that males will rise up as male, and females as female, so that each of the sexes will adorn heaven, as they did the earth, while the male and female damned shall do the same for hell."[245]

M. Francesco added: "Do you believe that some will be resurrected older and some younger than the others, some larger and some smaller, as they were while living in the world, or will everyone be the same?"

M. Ruggiero replied: "Again, Augustine is of the opinion that all will be resurrected as aged thirty-three and as having the same individual stature that they had or would have had when alive. That was the age when our Savior died, which Paul has called the age of the perfect man.[246] As for stature, I've already said and I'll say again that even small children, even those with a soul who died in their mother's body, will grow in stature to the size they would have been if they had died at the age of thirty-three. On the other hand, those who died old and decrepit will cast off their years until they appear to be the same age as our Redeemer was when he died, since he was the first to provide us with a model [*regola*] and to show us how people will be resurrected. And since he rose again to everlasting life, we too shall rise to everlasting life. Nor shall there be any deformity among the blessed: no one maimed, lame, withered, crippled, or blind, or carrying any other defects that make the body ugly.[247] Instead, these deformities shall remain among the damned, and indeed will be magnified in order to make their condemnation and its penalties more severe. According to some, this will be the difference between the blessed and the damned: that the latter will not lack the defects that make the body loathsome and ugly, while with the blessed, only those parts that make a body beautiful, charming, and attractive, fit for the state of glory, will remain. In the case of martyrs, the scars of their wounds shall gleam and shine as a great sign of their faith and constancy and of the cruelty of tyrants."[248]

245. Augustine, *De civitate Dei,* 22.17.

246. Augustine, *De civitate Dei,* 22.15–16. Paul's letter to the Ephesians 4:13.

247. Augustine, *De civitate Dei,* 22.15–16, 22:19.

248. Augustine, *De civitate Dei,* 22.19; Braun, *De imaginibus,* 105.

M. Silvio said: "How then can one represent the action of the resurrection of those who have been buried in underground places, whether tombs or something similar, if they are not to be shown emerging from them?" **[67]**

M. Ruggiero replied: "I told you a short time ago that the angels will collect the mortal remains of all the dead, including those buried in caves, underground places, and tombs, and those who were burned and thrown to the winds or into rivers or in any other place, and they will carry them to the valley of Josaphat, where the great mystery of the resurrection will take place.[249] This is what our Lord meant when he spoke of the angels who will gather the elect from the four winds and from the four principal corners of the world. So no one will be allowed, of their own volition, to leave the place where they were buried; because, if this were to be the case, those who were devoured by wild beasts, by birds, and by fish would have to come out from the mouth of the wild beast or fish, or the beak of the bird. How indecorous and monstrous that would be, I leave you to judge for yourselves. As for the clothes they were wrapped in for the grave: if the earth has consumed them, then [the clothes] cannot be recovered for the bodies; if not, then they will remain in the grave, as our Lord's did, because the resurrection will be of the body, not of clothes. You may say: 'Well, this is how Lazarus rose from the dead.' To which I will answer that Lazarus had his grave clothes only very shortly before and also that he was not brought back to life to face judgment at the final resurrection, but to return to the world and so to die once more."[250]

M. Troilo said: "Well, I think you are splitting hairs. Painting too needs its own decorum [*decoro*] and freedom in many things."

M. Ruggiero replied: "It shall have both, when art gives way to nature and imitates it, as it must, in everything; and when fiction gives way to truth, and shadow to light. And any painter who behaves differently seems to me like the tailor who makes a pair of trousers for a man who has one leg shorter or fatter than the other, and makes both legs the same and, if the customer complains, he replies: **[68]** 'I know how to make trousers, not legs.' As if the legs should be designed to fit trousers, rather than trousers the legs. Another personal invention [*capriccio*] that I should mention is [Michelangelo] having painted men who do not look wide awake and do not seem to know yet where divine justice orders them to go. However, in no way can this be what happens, if that was his pretext for making them like that. Because those who have died, whether shortly before or much earlier, must know what God's decision is, since they know the place where their souls have been. If this was in paradise or in

249. Joel 3:2, 3:12.

250. John 11:44.

purgatory, then they are certain of being saved; if it was hell, then they know they are damned. Also, the resurrection, as I told you earlier, will happen so fast that they will not have a chance to think about what they will do, let alone do it. Therefore, I regard this as fable [*favola*]."[251]

M. Francesco said: "It could be that this was only done to warn us, to show us the different fates of men, since strange things happen at times in the course of life. It may have been done so that everyone may more readily think about these things."

M. Ruggiero replied: "It is one thing to die, but quite another to rise again from the dead. What you say does not form part of the mystery of the resurrection, for the reasons I have told you. This is why the artist must always do his utmost, in every way he can, to show the truth, so that anything he has left out can be excused on the grounds that it could not be represented, not that he did not wish to show it or did not understand it. I certainly believe that Michelangelo, as was asserted earlier and is indeed public knowledge, did not err through ignorance but rather because he wished to embellish his brush and satisfy the art [of painting] rather than the truth. I am certain that he would have gained more approval and been more admired if he had painted this mystery as history demanded, rather than as he has shown it.[252] I note another example of personal invention [*capriccio*] too among those flying to meet Christ: some are about to set off, others have almost reached their desired goal, as if to do this were in our power. And among the angels, some pull the resurrected up in one way, others in a different way. All this is mere fable and has no substance."

M. Troilo said: "On the contrary, I approve of this as one of the fine inventions in that history, and it seems to me that it also conforms to Paul's account of how we shall rise into the air to meet our Lord. **[69]** If this is correct, and these persons are doing that, why do you criticize him so?"[253]

M. Ruggiero replied: "Four things will happen in an instant: the resurrection of the dead, the separation of the good and the evil, the snatching up of the saved, and the transformation of the bodies.[254] And I told you, if you remember, that when the Lord comes to judge the world, it will be filled with living people, just as now and as it was in the time of Noah.[255] Those who died in grace

251. On the issue of the decorum of the art of painting, see note 53. On fable, see Gilio, this volume, 105–6. The *favoloso* is something neither true nor lifelike; see also Gilio, this volume, 100–101, 174, 214–15.
252. See Gilio, this volume, 160.
253. 1 Thessalonians 4:15–16.
254. The interpretation follows Augustine, *De civitate Dei,* 20.20.
255. See Gilio, this volume, 162.

will rise up at the call of the archangel; together with the resurrected elect, the living who are predestined to glory will be snatched up into the air, and in that instant they will die and rise again, so that in a trice these mortals will become immortal. This is the transformation of which Paul spoke.[256] Notice the apostle's words. He says, 'we shall be snatched up together.'[257] The word together does not mean first one and then another, nor someone in France, someone in Lombardy, and someone in India, but it means 'all together'; and the term snatched up does not sound as though one could go by oneself, of one's own volition, but rather that one will be transported by someone else. Note also the force of the term snatched up, which indicates the violence and speed of the action."

M. Francesco added: "Therefore, there will be men alive at that time?"

M. Ruggiero replied: "Just like now. The elect will be snatched up into the air by the good angels, and the damned taken by demons to the valley of Josaphat. It would be impossible if the living were to come from all around the world at that moment to hear the horrible and fearful sentence on the damned, and the sweet, delightful, and long-awaited one on the elect, who will proceed in glory into heaven while the damned go in anguish into hell."

"Tell me," said M. Francesco, "the damned who are still alive when carried away by the demons, will they die while they are being taken to the valley, or afterward?"

M. Ruggiero replied: "They too shall be raised from the dead when snatched up, so that they are ready to suffer the eternal punishments. The other personal invention [*capriccio*] I notice is that the angels perform those actions of hauling up the blessed, some with cords [*cordoni*], others with rosaries, and some by the arms, as you can see here, as if entry to heaven required violence. **[70]** This was perhaps to show that demons hold the blessed back and do not let them reach the desired end of beatitude, or rather, weighted down by the body as they were in the world, they need help from those who pull them up by force.[258] To what extent all this is fable, I will not waste any effort in telling you."

---

256. 1 Corinthians 15:51–52.

257. 1 Thessalonians 4:16 (Vulgate). Douay-Rheims translates the Latin verb *rapire* as "taken up," but in English this lacks the violence and speed that M. Ruggiero alludes to at the end of this paragraph. For this reason, "snatched up" has been used to convey Gilio's definition of the action.

258. The significance of the rosary as indicating prayer is clearly stated in the next paragraph, and the person hauled up by that means is a central component of the fresco. As Dempsey points out ("Mythic Inventions," 69), it completely contradicts the peculiar modern idea that sometimes surfaces in the literature: that Michelangelo was putting forward an argument that salvation was through faith alone (*sola fide*) in the painting. However, the representation was not approved of by M. Ruggiero. The reference to ropes or cords [*cordoni*] may be to the figure immediately to the right of the one grasping the rosary. He appears to

M. Pulidoro replied: "I would not criticize Michelangelo for this. His having shown those actions for bringing up the blessed was meant to indicate the different ways in which we can be saved: the rosary means that prayer has been the reason for that person's salvation, for others it has been piety [*religione*], and so on for others. So I approve and praise [what he has done]."

M. Ruggiero replied: "All those who are saved will achieve their salvation by these means, because without prayer and other good works it is impossible for anyone to be saved, so it was not necessary to introduce them in order to show those consequences. For that reason I do not praise him. There is in my opinion another area where there is something equally derisory, and this is that angels fight against the damned who are attempting to climb up to the region of the blessed; they deal out great blows in order to force them back down [see fig. 19]. On the other side devils appear to be struggling to prevent the flight of the blessed up into the heavens, and for that reason we see a great fight between angels and devils; to gain possession of one man, devils have seized his hair to pull him down into the abyss while angels have hold of his feet to pull him up to heaven, as though the fate of this man depended on who wins him by force. Tell me if you [don't] think this is ridiculous, I leave it to your judgment."

M. Vincenso said: "I think it was done to show how evil spirits are always tempting us and battling with us, and how we are defended by angels."

M. Ruggiero said: "Even if that were true, this is not the place to show these things. For on that day Lucifer's realm will be fully prepared and it will only remain for him to be condemned to the eternal flames with the rest of his followers. **[71]** As a result, all temptation will cease and there will be no need to come to blows, because the mere presence of an angel and any of the blessed will be enough to make their adversaries flee. In addition, the evil spirits will know who is damned and who is saved, and knowing that, they will not be tempted to think of winning them in a fight. Apart from not being capable of doing it, they would not have the courage. Therefore, Horace was right when he said:

> In ancient times it was wisdom to separate private from public and profane things from sacred.[259]

Although this precept was intended for poets, it is also appropriate for painters, who have to separate the true from the false and not confuse the two. Because

be pulled up by means of bands around his torso, which are attached to a cord held by the angel; it seems likely that Gilio interpreted this as a reference to scourges (*cordoni di penitenza*) for self-flagellation as a devotional practice.

259. Horace, *Ars Poetica*, 482–83 (lines 396–97); the translation follows Gilio's Italian, not Horace's Latin.

if we try to think correctly about the fact of those rosaries and cords [*funi*] that I mentioned a little earlier, we will discover that it reveals a certain contempt for religion, rather than reverence, for these [things] are not the main causes of our salvation, the Lord is.[260] Therefore they should not be invested with what is not appropriate to them; they provoke laughter rather than penitence, and instead of dignifying prayers and pious practices, they bring them into contempt. Therefore, I do not approve of them. Another personal invention [*capriccio*] I notice too in this history is the mixing of the blessed and the damned in the air, in a confused way, on the right- and left-hand sides, which is contrary to the text of the Gospel."[261]

M. Silvio said: "I would say that in this passage right and left do not refer to any material place or arrangement, as we usually understand them, but that right refers to beatitude and left to damnation. And as for the saints, I think that without distinction of place or position, they will set the Savior in their midst so as to render more glory and greatness to his Majesty."

M. Ruggiero replied: "It would be worse, in my opinion, because the damned would stand in the place of the blessed and the blessed in the place of the damned, creating confusion with such a sorry mixing. **[72]** Moreover, whenever possible the literal meaning must always be preserved. In this passage, taking the right as the right and the left as the left neither offends the letter nor misrepresents the meaning, and by accepting this interpretation, the order of the story is preserved. For our Lord, as man, will have both right and left sides.[262] Although Michelangelo has observed this in part, he should not have placed the damned in the air like the blessed, because, as was said earlier, this will not happen."[263]

M. Silvio replied: "What do you say about the two open books, which are with the group of seven angels sounding trumpets?" [see fig. 19].

M. Ruggiero said: "I think the truth is that there will be no books."[264]

"How can that be?" replied M. Silvio. "Haven't you read the Revelations of Saint John in which it is written that the books will be opened?[265] Does not the Church sing of the bringing out of written books, in which we will see all of our deeds recorded?"[266]

260. The Italian word for *cords* used in this sentence is *funi,* in contrast to *cordoni* used earlier; the two words are here understood as synonymous. See also note 258.

261. Matthew 25:32–34.

262. That Christ will be as a man at the Judgment, see Augustine, *De civitate Dei,* 20.6.

263. See Gilio, this volume, 174–75; and Barocchi, *Trattati,* 2:597, n1 to Gilio p. 72, citing Braun, *De imaginibus,* on the literal translation of the words of scripture from the letter to Cochlaeus that prefaces the volume: "Verba scripturarum et patrum ita imitor, ut nusquam ab ipsis, nisi quantum tractatus ratio exigit, discedam."

264. Augustine, *De civitate Dei,* 20.14.

265. Revelation 20:12.

266. A reference to verse five of the hymn *Dies Irae,* used as the sequence for the Requiem Mass.

M. Ruggiero said: "It is true that one reads what you say, but in reality the only books that will be produced will be the books of conscience. And so you don't think I'm expressing an idiosyncratic view, I want to prove it by quoting Paul's letter to the Romans in which he said, 'their conscience bearing witness to them, and their thoughts between themselves accusing, or also defending one another, in the day when God shall judge the secrets of men.'[267] I will also add, on this point, a saying from the book of Wisdom: 'For inquisition shall be made into the thoughts of the ungodly,' meaning that on that day our consciences will be unable to conceal, either in words or in thoughts, any sin committed.[268] For this reason it was said that books will be opened. But if they truly do have to appear, I don't believe that they are properly placed so low down, in a position where they can be neither seen nor read, given that the people are placed high up, as you can see.

"Another personal invention [*capriccio*] that I notice too is that Christ has no beard, the rightness or wrongness of which even shoemakers are able to judge [fig. 21].[269] For during the forty hours that Christ lay dead in the tomb he suffered no loss, given that his body underwent no corruption, as the Prophet said.[270] **[73]** But if he were to have lost all his hair, it would have affected his head as well as his beard, because in this I don't think that one would be more exempt than the other. But he could not have lost either since such very holy flesh cannot be destroyed."[271]

M. Francesco said: "I think that Michelangelo truly did this on a whim [*capriccio*], since I can think of no other way of defending him; because if Christ were to have lost his beard, he would have been without it at the time of the Resurrection, just as much as at the time of the judgment. Seriously contradicting himself, in the *Conversion of Paul,* which occurred at the time of the Resurrection, Michelangelo paints him with a thick, red beard, but in the *Last Judgment,* beardless" [see fig. 14; cf. fig. 19].[272]

M. Ruggiero said: "It is almost as if he had lost it by some accident between the day of the Resurrection and the day of the Last Judgment. I find it astonishing that Michelangelo did not wish to correct this, since I've heard that many people pointed it out to him. In this he could have imitated the great Apelles,

---

267. Romans 2:15–16.
268. *Liber Sapientiae* (Book of Wisdom) 1:9.
269. An allusion to the story of the shoemaker who criticized a painting by Apelles, eliciting from the painter the subsequently proverbial "cobbler stick to your last"; Pliny, *NH,* 9:322–25 (book 35, §85). The point is made explicit below; see note 273.
270. Psalm 15:10; Acts 13:37.
271. The letter describing Jesus, supposedly written by Publius Lentulus, has him with a beard; see the letter in Dobschütz, *Christusbilder,* 2:308**–329**.
272. The *Conversion* painted by Michelangelo in the Pauline Chapel in the Vatican.

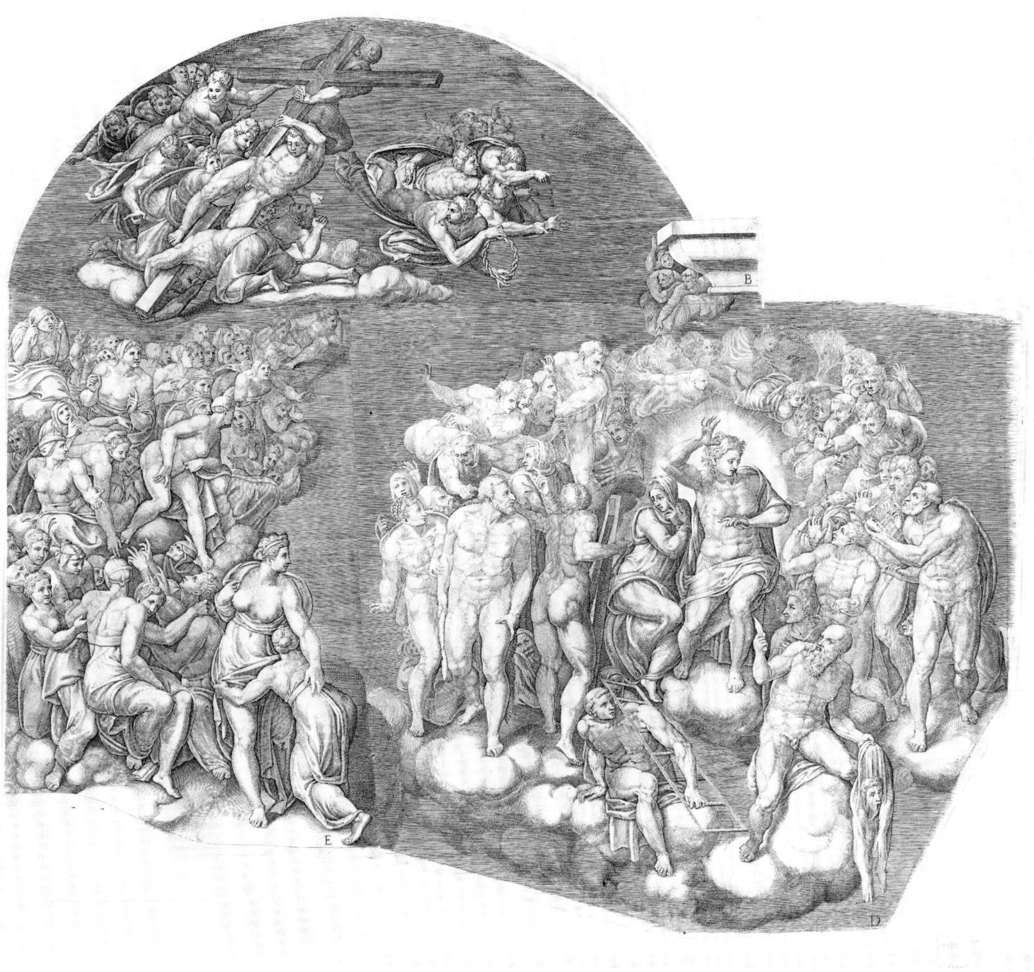

who put his works on public display to discover errors. If they were brought to his attention by those whose profession gave them the requisite knowledge, he would then correct them; like the error concerning a shoe, noticed by a shoemaker.[273] I have often wondered why Michelangelo painted Christ standing, when Scripture says that he will be seated on the throne of his Majesty" [see fig. 21].[274]

Fig. 21.
Giorgio Ghisi (Italian, ca. 1520–82), after Michelangelo Buonarroti (Italian, 1475–1564).
Last Judgment, ca. 1545, engraving set of ten plates, detail of the top left section incorporating three of the plates, irregularly shaped sheet, approx. 64.8 × 71.4 cm. New York, Metropolitan Museum of Art. The Elisha Whittelsey Collection, The Elisha Whittelsey Fund, 1959.

273. Criticism of Michelangelo for painting Christ without a beard had already been reported by Nino Sernini in his letter to Ercole Gonzaga, 19 November 1541, following the unveiling of the fresco; see Ludwig von Pastor, *The History of the Popes from the Close of the Middle Ages: Drawn from the Secret Archives of the Vatican and Other Original Sources*, vol. 12, *Paul III (1524–1549)*, ed. Ralph Francis Kerr (London: Kegan Paul, Trench, Trubner, 1923), 659. Barocchi, *Trattati*, 2:598, n2 to Gilio p. 73, cites other examples, including Dolce, *L'Aretino*, in Barocchi, *Trattati*, 1:190 (Roskill, *Dolce's "Aretino,"* 166–67). On Apelles and the shoemaker, see note 269.

274. Matthew 19:28 and 25:31.

M. Vincenso said: "I think that this was done for two reasons. One is that the throne and the sitting down do not mean in this case a material throne of the kind we use, nor a real act of sitting down. Rather, the former means the souls of the just, it being written: 'The soul of the just is the throne of Wisdom';[275] and by the sitting-down is meant the authority to judge, the truth of which is witnessed by the Psalm where we read: 'Thou that sittest upon the cherubims,' and in another place: 'Said the Lord to my Lord: Sit thou at my right hand.'[276] If we try to take these words literally it would produce an absurdity, for God would become a material being, which he is not. The other reason is the terrifying awfulness of the sentence on the damned, which would not have been delivered sitting down. **[74]** I note a hidden meaning in Christ's action: his raised right arm signifies the terribleness of the curse with which he drives away the damned; his left arm, bent in the manner of one who wishes to make an embrace, signifies his love toward the blessed and his wish to gather them together, to embrace them, and to give them the heavenly kingdom."

M. Ruggiero replied: "Anyone who wanted to interpret the words of the Gospel in a mystical and allegorical way could accept your view. But first one must take the literal meaning, when this can properly be done, and only then the other meanings; whenever possible the literal meaning should be preserved. That our Savior has the authority to make this judgment I think no Christian can doubt. As for his sitting down, as he is truly man as well as God, I think that he really will sit down, and the theologians think likewise.[277] As for what the Psalms say, we cannot interpret literally their references to sitting, because we must avoid the iniquity of the thought, as you have pointed out so well.[278] Therefore a different interpretation must be given, not a literal one, because that

275. "Anima justi sedes sapientiae," quoted by Augustine, Gregory, and Bernard, has no precise source in the Bible; see Augustine, *St. Augustine on the Psalms,* ed. and trans. Scholastica Hebgin and Felicitas Corrigan (Westminster, MD: Newman, 1960–61), 2:377.

276. Psalm 79:2 and 109:1. See Durandus, *Rationale divinorum officiorum,* 1.3.7, where the meaning "reigning over the angels" is asserted; and Acts 2:34.

277. M. Vincenso's interpretation of Christ's gestures follows Condivi, *Vita di Michelangelo,* 50. On literal versus metaphorical interpretation, see Gilio, this volume, 176; and note 263 for Braun's letter to Cochlaeus. Augustine had proposed criteria for distinguishing between literal and metaphorical meanings; see Augustine, *De doctrina Christiana,* ed. and trans. R. P. H. Green (Oxford: Clarendon, 1995), 146–47 (book 3, §33). According to Augustine, the figurative should be preferred when a literal interpretation contradicted "good morals" or the "true faith."

278. In his 1563 *Trattato de la emulatione che il demonio ha fatto a Dio,* 110r–v, Gilio, discussing the idea of God (as opposed to Christ) as seated, writes: "God is said to sit, not in a bodily sense like a man, but in authority, because he has government and dominion over all creatures, and thus David said: The Lord has reigned over the peoples, God sits on the throne of his holiness" (Dicesi sedere Iddio non corporalmente, come fa l'uomo, ma per potenza, havendo egli il governo, e dominio di tutte le creature, onde diceva Davide, Il Signore ha regnato sopra le genti, Iddio siede sopra la sede santa sua). The reference to David is to

cannot fit the case. So we would say that being seated above the cherubim, whose name means 'wealth or fullness of knowledge,'[279] signifies only that our Savior, having risen from the dead and ascended into heaven, received as a man from his Father all the treasures of divine knowledge and wisdom, which he, as the Word, had always had. As for being seated on the right hand, by this is meant the supreme level of beatitude, which our Savior attained once he had ascended into heaven, because God, as spirit, has neither right nor left, nor a body to be seated. But the sitting down in judgment should be understood as actual fact, since nothing absurd or inappropriate arises as a consequence. The Apostles will also be seated, through the promise made to them by the Savior.[280] As for increasing the terror of the damned, I say that this cannot fail to happen, for even if he is sitting down, his face shall have two effects at one and the same time. To the sinners he will show a face so terrible and fearsome that they will be unable to look at it, but, as John writes, 'they say to the mountains and the rocks: **[75]** Fall upon us, and hide us from the face of him that sitteth upon the throne and from the wrath of the Lamb: For the great day of their wrath is come, and who shall be able to stand?'[281] The elect by contrast will see him as so pious, so beautiful, so gentle, so benign, so meek, so shining, so divine that, even if they wanted to, they could not and indeed would not know how to take their eyes away, since that vision will bring them beatitude.[282] For this reason I do not approve of the fact that some of the blessed look up and some down, some this way and some that, some at their companion and some elsewhere, so that they seem rather to be at a market or fair than at the day of judgment. As if anything could be more powerful, better attract attention, or be more delightful than the glorious, divine face of the King of Glory in majesty, power, and glory, to make them look elsewhere and concentrate on something more pleasurable and joyous than the face of the Son of God; that face in which the divine essence will be seen to shine in a way that will make it a thousand times more splendid than the sun.[283] But

---

Psalm 46:9 (Vulgate). Here Gilio is very closely following Braun, *De imaginibus,* 26. See also Michele Di Monte, "Gilio, Giovanni Andrea," *DBI,* 54 (2000).

279. Gilio is drawing on the traditional Augustinian interpretation of cherubim as representing *plenitudo scientiae* ("a fullness of knowledge").

280. Matthew 19:28.

281. Revelation 6:16–17.

282. This is the Beatific Vision (*visio beatifica*): the perfect happiness of the just who are granted direct knowledge of God. Thomas Aquinas, in particular, had developed this theology; he cites 1 Corinthians 13:12 in *Summa contra Gentiles (Liber de veritate catholicae fidei contra errores infidelium),* 3.51 (5–6). The English translation is in Thomas Aquinas, *Summa contra Gentiles: Book 3, Providence, Part 2,* trans. Vernon J. Bourke (Notre Dame, IN: University of Notre Dame Press, 1975), 175–77. For Augustine's comments, see *De civitate Dei,* 22.29.

283. Dolce had made the point that it was quite wrong for Michelangelo to have shown the blessed embracing, for they should have been rapt in contemplation of the divine; see Dolce, *L'Aretino,* in Barocchi, *Trattati,* 1:190 (Roskill, *Dolce's "Aretino,"* 166–67).

this line of reasoning will be dismissed with the same reply: that the brush, the eye, and poetry too, demand their share; for it would be neither beautiful nor attractive [*vago*] if everyone, as though stupefied and mad, were to behave identically in staring at him."

M. Silvio said: "I don't think that this calls for much discussion, because, apart from the fact that it would be very stupid if everyone gazed in the same way, it would also show a certain ignorance in the artist if all the people in such a crowd were to perform exactly the same action [*gesto*].[284] For example, not all the many people attending a sermon look at the preacher's face, although they may be listening diligently. It must be supposed that their hearts are filled with that perfect happiness the beatitude you mention will bring, even if they do not look at Christ's face."

M. Ruggiero laughed at this and said: "Indeed, what a most beautiful and praiseworthy action [*gesto*] that would be for explaining to those of us looking at the painting [*istoria*] how great the effects of beatitude will be. Earlier it was discussed how man reveals his interior affections through exterior signs;[285] one who is suffering mental anguish shows it in the manner described by Petrarch: 'one sees from outside how I burn within.'[286] **[76]** If sorrowing reveals sadness and rejoicing happiness, and these are carnal passions, shall beatitude be of lesser standing and less potent than the passions? In response to your remark about the preacher, I say that the object of hearing is the voice and this does not necessarily involve the eye, although the body's movements and the effort of delivering [a sermon] do render the sound more complete to the ear.[287] So I will say that beatitude will not just be the object of the eye but of all the senses,

284. A case where tension is seen to arise between what the art of painting might require and what the subject requires. In that sense, it is comparable to the question of how to represent the suffering of Christ and the martyrs, where the issue was beauty; see Gilio, this volume, 133–35. Here the question is about the representation of feeling and emotion by means of physical movement and gesture, and the key issue related to this is variety. The importance of variety of movement and gesture for the success of any painting had been strongly asserted by Alberti, *On Painting and On Sculpture,* 84–85 (book 2, §40 and book 2, §43); and also by Dolce, *L'Aretino,* in Barocchi, *Trattati,* 1:179–80 (Roskill, *Dolce's "Aretino,"* 144–47). For an exposition of the tradition that Gilio was setting himself against, see Alexander Nagel, *The Controversy of Renaissance Art* (Chicago: University of Chicago Press, 2011), 233.

285. See Gilio, this volume, 118–19.

286. The English translation is from Francesco Petrarch, *The Canzoniere; or, Rerum vulgarium fragmenta,* trans. and ed. Mark Musa (Bloomington: Indiana University Press, 1996), 56–57 (poem 35, line 8); see also Francesco Petrarch, *Canzoniere, Trionfi, Rime Varie e una scelta di versi Latini,* ed. Carlo Muscetta and Daniele Ponchiroli (Turin: Einaudi, 1958), 50.

287. The importance for the orator of movement and gesture was a commonplace; see, for example, Quintilian, *The Orator's Education,* vol. 5, *Books 11–12,* ed. and trans. Donald A. Russell, Loeb Classical Library 494 (Cambridge, MA: Harvard University Press, 2002), 118–21 (11.3.65–68).

for according to Boethius, it contains all the perfections.[288] Do you deny that it will steal the hearts and minds of men and send them into ecstasy? If you don't believe me, then believe Paul who says this.[289] If beatitude fills me with such sweetness and joy, and disengages us so much from what is outside ourselves that we cannot feel, see, or imagine anything else (in this regard we could read Dante's verse), what would you say? Listen to Dante's words, here:

> O imagination, which so steals us at times from outward things that we pay no heed though a thousand trumpets sound about us.[290]

Or in another place:

> And therefore when a thing is heard or seen that keeps the soul strongly bent on it, the time passes and one is not aware.[291]

If a man's words have the power to keep the attention of many, who gaze at him and listen to him speaking, do you deny that the presence of our Lord would not have more power and efficacy? Here is Virgil's testimony: 'All were hushed and held their gaze bent upon him.'[292] I don't want to say any more about whether it is well done or not, because you know it already. Michelangelo should have had not the blessed but the damned perform those actions [*gesti*], since out of fear they will not be able to look at our Lord's face." **[77]**

M. Francesco said: "I agree with you, M. Ruggiero; but tell me something else: when our Savior does actually have to sit, what will his seat consist of?"

M. Ruggiero replied: "There are many opinions, expressed by many different people: some say that it will be formed of cherubim, others of seraphim or other angels, or that it will consist of a shining cloud, like the one that carried him to heaven on the day of his ascension; or something else fully appropriate to the glory of such majesty."[293]

M. Troilo said: "If my memory serves me, you said before that we will be naked when resurrected.[294] If that will be the case, why has Michelangelo shown so many people dressed and women with their hair so elegantly arranged?"

---

288. Boethius, *Consolation of Philosophy,* in Boethius, *Theological Tractates; The Consolation of Philosophy,* trans. H. F. Stewart, E. K. Rand, and S. J. Tester, Loeb Classical Library 74 (Cambridge, MA: Harvard University Press, 1973), 274–87 (3.10).
289. The reference to Paul might be to 2 Corinthians 3:16–18.
290. Dante Alighieri, *The Divine Comedy: 2. Purgatorio,* trans. John D. Sinclair (New York: Oxford University Press, 1939), 220–21 (canto 17.13–15).
291. Dante, *Divine Comedy: 2. Purgatorio,* 56–57 (canto 4.7–9).
292. Virgil, *Aeneid, Books 1–6,* 316–17 (2.1).
293. On the cherubim, see Psalm 79:2 (Vulgate). On the cloud, see Acts 1:9.
294. Gilio, this volume, 166–67.

M. Ruggiero replied: "He is using the license that you speak about, which covers up, redeems, exonerates, and glosses over all the defects of the painters.[295] It is used to bestow legitimacy on their mixing of the false with the true, the sacred with the profane; just what Horace said was not conceded by 'men, nor gods, nor booksellers' shelves.'[296]

"But I will say that certain fictions have been invented for the purpose of maintaining decency, and they are praiseworthy and should not be omitted. Their purpose is to hide the shameful parts of the holy figures in a graceful way; and this Michelangelo has done with Christ, the Virgin, and with many other figures. But he has also made many, both men and women, entirely naked, which, I think, rather than being a source of pleasure, leaves the majority of spectators scandalized."[297]

M. Troilo said: "If they are all to be resurrected naked and you approve of paying attention to the accuracy of even the smallest detail, do you seriously blame this representation of what will actually happen? And anyway it does not seem to me a matter worthy of great concern, given that we are dealing with figures painted on the wall and not with real people, who could generate the kind of scandal you speak of."[298]

M. Ruggiero replied: "It is true that all will be resurrected naked and that at that time no one will experience shame, just as it was in the period before our ancestors first sinned; **[78]** for all will be celestial beings and man will have reacquired the innocence that was lost with Adam. Now we no longer possess [that innocence], and because of our corrupted nature we always give in to our worst side and make our decisions accordingly, twisting our judgment to suit

295. M. Troilo had earlier spoken about license; see Gilio, this volume, 105.

296. Horace, *Ars Poetica,* 480–81 (lines 372–73); the translation follows Gilio's Italian, not Horace's Latin. The English translation stresses Gilio's more literal translation of Horace's *columnae* as *colonne* in Italian. What is not conceded by Horace is that poets could be mediocre. Gilio (this volume, 132) had mistranslated Horace, *Ars Poetica,* 462–63 (line 151), wrongly making him disapprove of mixing fact and fiction. However, Horace had noted approvingly an ancient practice of separating the sacred from the profane; see lines 396–97, cited by Gilio, this volume, 175.

297. The naked figures in the *Last Judgment* had provoked hostile comment even before the unveiling, if credence is given to Vasari's story about Biagio da Cesena; see Vasari, "Vita di Michelagnolo Buonarruoti," 6:69–70. Sernini, in his letter to Ercole Gonzaga dated 19 November 1541, had reported criticism of this feature immediately after the unveiling (Pastor, *History of the Popes,* 12:659), and the figures form an important element in Aretino's notorious letter criticizing Michelangelo's *Last Judgment* (see note 205), as well as in Dolce's *L'Aretino.*

298. Aristotle, *De Anima,* in Aristotle, *On the Soul; Parva Naturalia; On Breath,* trans. W. S. Hett, Loeb Classical Library 288 (Cambridge, MA: Harvard University Press, 1957), 154–57 (3.3 [427b]). The defense that painted nudes will not scandalize people of healthy mind had been deployed in Dolce's *L'Aretino;* see Dolce, *L'Aretino,* in Barocchi, *Trattati,* 1:189 (Roskill, *Dolce's "Aretino,"* 162–63).

our own convenience. Therefore, I suggest that if we see the private parts of little children we are not scandalized; having regard for their innocence and purity, they being without knowledge of evil and sin, natural instinct does not enable us to fall.[299] But if we see the private parts of grown men and women, it brings shame and scandal, especially when the people and the contexts are such that these things ought not to be in evidence at all. In the case of saints, apart from making one blush, indescribable remorse would be provoked in the mind, seeing that a saint would not only have avoided displaying his private parts to others but would not even have looked at them himself. So if we venerate the saints for a sanctity that abhors this behavior, why should the painter, against the laws of sanctity, decency, and decorum, try to force them so inappropriately to behave in the opposite way?[300] In these cases, therefore, I praise fictions and those who use them to cover up the shameful parts of their figures and especially their holy figures. In this they imitate Apelles: when painting the portrait of King Antigonos, who was blind in one eye, [Apelles] portrayed him in profile so that he only displayed his good side, hiding the imperfect one.[301] And it is not valid to say 'they are painted men' because paintings too edify and scandalize. So I would regard it as a matter of prudence for the painter to remove all opportunities for laughter, mockery, and scandal."

M. Vincenso said: "I think Michelangelo wanted to imitate the ancients, who, for the most part, made their figures naked in order better to show the excellence of the art in the portrayal of muscles, veins, and other parts of the body."[302]

M. Ruggiero replied: "The ancients did not have the pure, chaste, and holy religion that we do. And to appreciate the truth of this, think of how the cult of Jupiter was founded on rapes, adulteries, and incest; **[79]** that of Priapus on the monstrous nature of his member; that of Venus on carnal lasciviousness; that

299. Barocchi cites Braun, *De imaginibus,* 51; see Barocchi, *Trattati,* 2:601, n1 to Gilio p. 78. Braun, following Augustine (*De civitate Dei,* 14.17), discusses nakedness and its problems after the fall.

300. The abuse introduced by painters who represented saints in such a way that they aroused evil thoughts and desires is discussed by Hieronymus Emser in his reply to Karlstadt of 1522 (in Emser, *Das man der heyligen bilder,* 86). Emser contrasts old pictures where the limbs of saints were decently covered.

301. Pliny, *NH,* 9:326–29 (book 35, §90). The desirability of fiction is here primarily motivated by a need to defend devotional efficacy, but M. Ruggiero aligns it with secular notions of dignity and decorum, as M. Francesco had done, for example, when criticizing Michelangelo's Christ in the *Conversion of Paul;* Gilio, this volume, 142–44.

302. In 1506, Raffaello Maffei had characterized the use of the naked figure by the ancient Greeks "as much on account of displaying artistry as of procuring sensual desire" (tam ob artis ostentationem quam ob libidinem reperta); see Kathleen W. Christian, *Empire without End: Antiquities Collections in Renaissance Rome, c. 1350–1527* (New Haven, CT: Yale University Press, 2010), 199, 245n81.

of Cybele on the tearing-off of the virile members of her Corybantes.[303] And I could say the same of the other gods. The Romans (as Pliny writes) took from the Greeks the custom of making statues and paintings of naked figures;[304] as [for example] we read about Apelles, who produced that beautiful figure of the naked Venus coming out of the sea, which was kept for a long time in the palace of Augustus.[305] Phidias too made a beautiful statue of Venus, which was not safe from certain very lascivious young men, resulting in it being stained by their lust.[306] The painters who came before Michelangelo never made the figure of the glorious Virgin naked, nor, except in martyrdoms, that of any other saint, and even then they covered the shameful parts; and did so too for the figure of our Lord, while a youth, at the Baptism, at the Flagellation, at the Crucifixion, and at the Resurrection. And this was because of modesty [*onestà*], which must be given priority with sacred figures.[307] To demonstrate the purity, chasteness, and reverend nature of religion, the historian must use his pen and his words to instill chasteness through the ears of his reader, and painters must use their brushes and colors to instill chasteness through the eyes of their viewers; and from this arises decorum in the painting, praise for the artist, and devoutness among the people. It is not enough to say: 'I am not scandalized, because they are paintings,' since scandals are caused even by paintings. And the Lord's words shall come to pass for those who give no heed to scandal: woe to him through whom [scandals] come.[308] We should imitate, in this case, Noah's sons Shem and Japhet, who walked backward in order to cover, and not see, their father's virile parts as he lay sleeping; and not Noah's other son Ham, who derided his father and was therefore cursed forever.[309] And Seneca was right when he repeated Aristotle's view that 'we should never be more modest and sober than when we are discussing or dealing with matters of the gods. If we enter a temple we should stand devoutly in awe. **[80]** If we go to offer sacrifices, we must lower

303. The priests of Cybele practiced self-castration. See Ovid, *Fasti,* trans. James G. Frazer, Loeb Classical Library 253 (Cambridge, MA: Harvard University Press, 1931), 206–7 (4.243–44).
304. Pliny, *NH,* 9:140–41 (book 34, §18).
305. Pliny, *NH,* 9:328–29 (book 35, §91).
306. Not Phidias, but Praxiteles, whose Cnidian Aphrodite is described by Pliny, *NH,* 2:590–91 (book 7, §127) and 10:16–17 (book 36, §21).
307. On Michelangelo's failings and the need to have regard for modesty (*honestà*) when representing holy figures and religious subjects, see Dolce, *L'Aretino,* in Barocchi, *Trattati,* 1:188–90 (Roskill, *Dolce's "Aretino,"* 162–65).
308. Luke 17:1.
309. Genesis 9:22–23. Nicolas of Lyra interprets Ham's telling his brothers that he had seen their father naked as inciting them to mock him ("ut incitaret eos ad derisionem patris"); see his *Postillae* on Genesis 9 in Nicolas of Lyra, *Postillae perpetuae in universam S. Scripturam* (Rome: Sweynheym and Pannartz, 1471–72). On the context for the commentaries and analysis, see the essays in *Nicholas of Lyra: The Senses of Scripture,* ed. Philip D. W. Krey and Lesley Smith (Leiden: E. J. Brill, 2000).

our eyes and draw our clothes around us.'[310] Macrobius wrote that philosophers abhor discussing obscene fables when talking about sacred matters: like Saturn, who ripped off his father's genitals and cast them into the sea, with the naked Venus emerging from the froth; or like Vulcan, who trapped Venus and Mars in his net as they were committing adultery; and other similar instances.[311] Therefore, if the idolatrous pagans abhorred filth and indecency in words, thoughts, and deeds, should we take pleasure in contemplating naked, indecent, and scandalous sacred figures when celebrating the divine offices and offering the most holy sacrifice of the Mass? Certainly we should not do so. Let the painter who delights in painting the saints naked always remember that he will be subtracting from much of the reverence he owes them. So let him be satisfied with modesty and appropriate decorum, rather than with the attractions [*vaghezza*] of the art of painting, which will only please a few. I do not think those shameful parts, small as they are, conceal such secrets of nature, or such art, that the artist risks being regarded as ignorant or clumsy if he does not represent them. If nothing is at stake, why then take so much trouble to place them in front of the eyes of viewers? They have no other motive, I believe, than to provoke laughter in a thousand indecent and idle conversations among foolish young men."

M. Silvio said: "I admit that it would have been much better to have clothed them than to have them naked, and in this case fiction is to be preferred to truth, for reasons of our edification, for the devotion of the people and the peace of the ignorant who do not know how to distinguish the true from the false and are unable to give to persons, places, and times what is appropriate to them."[312]

---

310. Seneca, *Naturales Quaestiones,* 7.30.1: "Egregie Aristoteles ait numquam nos verecundiores esse debere quam cum de diis agitur. Si intramus templa compositi, si ad sacrificium accessuri vultum submittimus, togam adducimus, si in omne argumentum modestiae fingimur"; Seneca, *Natural Questions,* vol. 2, *Books 4–7,* trans. Thomas H. Corcoran, Loeb Classical Library 457 (Cambridge, MA: Harvard University Press, 1972), 290–91. The translation follows Gilio's Italian, not Seneca's Latin.

311. Macrobius, *Commentarii in somnium Scipionis,* book 1, chapter 2, where a distinction is made between two kinds of fable: those that merely gratify the ear and those that encourage the reader to good works (§7). The latter are divided into two types: one in which "the setting and the plot are fictitious, as in the fables of Aesop. . . . The second rests on a solid foundation of truth, which is treated in a fictitious style." This is called "narratio fabulosa," and examples are the stories of Hesiod, and so on (§9). "Narratio fabulosa" is further subdivided: the first where matters base and unworthy of the gods are presented (Macrobius here cites the story of Saturn castrating his father), and the second involving a decent and dignified conception of divinity presented beneath a modest veil of allegory. Only this last type of fable is appropriate to philosophical treatises (§10–11). This is part of a wider discussion of the legitimacy of the use of fable by Plato and by Cicero. Fable is never appropriate when dealing with the highest of all gods (§14). See Macrobius, *Commentary on the Dream of Scipio,* ed. and trans. William Harris Stahl (New York: Columbia University Press, 1952), 83–87.

312. M. Silvio's Italian reads: "Confesso che molto meglio sarieno state velate che nude, et in questo caso il fitto si proponga al vero, per nostra edificazione, per devozione de' popoli e pace degli ignoranti."

M. Pulidoro said: "Earlier the unsuitable movements of figures were discussed.[313] Now look at the unseemly self-exposure of the saints in front of Christ; see how inappropriate are the actions of Saint Bartholomew, Saint Lawrence, Saint Andrew, or Saint Simon for saints in the presence of the King of Glory [see fig. 21]. Does it not look as though they are watching bullfights from the front of a viewing stand, or indeed learning to act in a dumb show, since holding the cross behind him, as this saint does, seems so much effort?[314] **[81]** Do you believe that on that day Saint Peter will have to display his keys, Saint Bartholomew his skin, Saint Lawrence his gridiron, Saint Sebastian his arrows, Saint Blaise his combs, Saint Catherine her wheel, and the other saints the instruments of their martyrdoms [fig. 22]? And in order to make people laugh more he has made Saint Catherine bend over in front of Saint Blaise with a rather indecent action. He, standing above her with his combs, seems to threaten her to stay still, while she, turning toward him, seems to ask: 'What shall I do?' or something of the kind."[315]

M. Ruggiero said: "This is one of those things that ought not to be allowed, so that something done to inspire dread and fear does not become the occasion of laughter and idle tales among the crowd; and to prevent what should be a source of devotion from producing evil. Another personal invention [*capriccio*] I notice is that Saint Peter and many other saints whose bodies were decomposed into ashes have been privileged over our Savior, who, despite the fact that he came out of the tomb without losing a single hair (for he suffered no corruption), appears in the *Judgment* without a beard, while all those other saints are bearded.[316] And another [*capriccio*] is that on that day there will be no

313. See Gilio, this volume, 140–50.

314. The movement of the saint with a cross had been criticized earlier by M. Francesco (who identified him as Andrew); see note 182.

315. The figures of Saints Catherine and Blaise in the fresco were felt to be so problematic that they were cut out, and new plaster was laid for a repainting by Daniele da Volterra in 1564. Fabrizio Buranelli et al., *The Last Judgment: I, The Restoration* (New York: Rizzoli International, 1999), 132–37, 275–78, identify the censorship interventions of the sixteenth century. The idea that such figures might provoke derisive laughter was not a theoretical invention of Gilio's. It can be verified in the survival of a pasquinade; see Valerio Marucci, Antonio Marzo, and Angelo Romano, eds., *Pasquinate romane del Cinquecento* (Rome: Salerno, 1983), 1:498 (no. 462): "O you who criticize the Florentine, think about the painting a bit. You will see that every figure is entirely appropriate within the chapel of the divine Jesus. There is Saint Catherine, with bowed head, naked as nature made her, and other saints standing there soberly, showing their arses to don Paolino" (O voi che riprendete 'l fiorentino, / considerate un poco la pittura: / vedrete che sta ben ogni figura / nella capella di Gesu divino. // Sta santa Caterina a capo chino, / nuda si come fecce la natura, / ed altri santi stanno con misura / a mostrar i lor culi a don Paulino). Lomazzo, at more or less the same time as Gilio, independently reported similar reactions to the *Last Judgment;* see note 181.

316. See Gilio, this volume, 177–78.

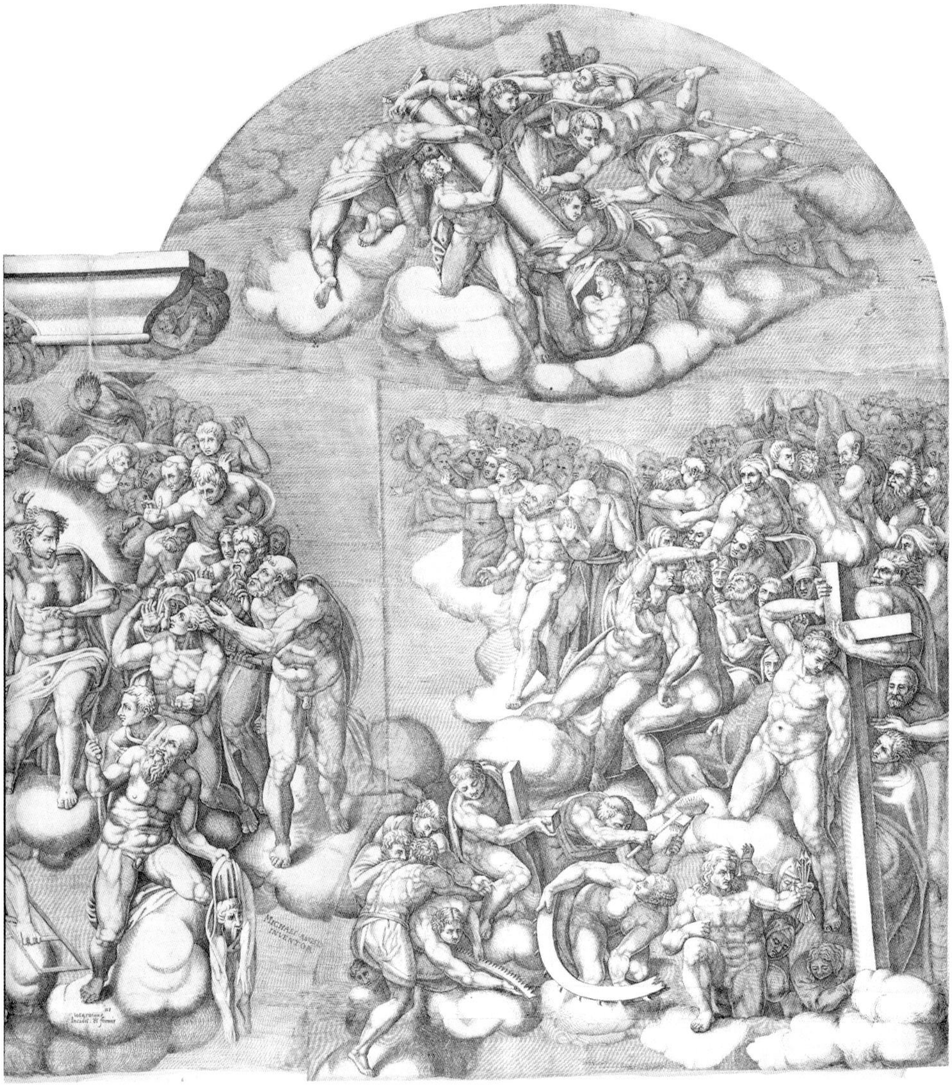

Fig. 22.
Nicolas Beatrizet (French, active in Italy, fl. ca. 1540–ca. 1565), after Michelangelo Buonarroti (Italian, 1475–1564), published by Antoine Lafréry (French, 1512–77, active in Italy).
Last Judgment, 1562, ensemble of three plates from original engraving set of ten plates, detail of top right, ca. 65 × 53 cm.
New York, Metropolitan Museum of Art. The Elisha Whittelsey Collection, The Elisha Whittelsey Fund, 1959.

old age, no childhood, no baldness or anything else that makes any part of the body ugly and deformed, as I told you earlier; yet here we see the decrepit, the bald, and children and people of all ages.[317] Sometimes I laugh to myself thinking of a published [representation of the] *Judgment,* from which the painter Piersimone took the design that he painted in the Crocefisso delle Carceri.[318] In this painting (as you know) we see Noah raising the ark high above his head; Abraham with his son Isaac as a young child carrying a small bundle of wood

317. See Gilio, this volume, 171.

318. A small oratory on the via del Colle Paganello in Fabriano, known as S. Liborio, was also called the Crocifisso delle Carceri; see Romualdo Sassi, *Le chiese di Fabriano* (Fabriano: Arti grafiche "Gentile," 1961), 33–34. The oratory was suppressed in 1784.

on his shoulder; Joshua dressed in armor, with a mace, sword, and helmet; the innocents who were slaughtered by Herod; and following other things of no consequence, our Lord sitting on a wheeled car, under which the Devil and Death are chained, with so many ridiculous and trifling fables and fictions that I am amazed even to think of it [figs. 23a–e].[319] And being an absurd person, [Piersimone] has added cauldrons filled with souls, and devils making a fire while others drag a peasant by his hair to plunge him in, and other vanities that ignorant people firmly believe will occur in that way. **[82]** And these people, who defile the paper they use, are absolutely convinced, as are many, many others, that they have fulfilled what is required of them and observed the rules. If, as I said at the beginning, painters were fully to inform themselves of the truth and subject of the story they are to represent, not just once but ten times over, and if they were to study, read, reread, ask questions, and act as the most faithful interpreter should do, in the manner that befits a good historian, then the works they make would be praiseworthy.[320] But groping their way blindly and foolishly forward, without further thought, makes them commit endless stupid mistakes and earns them the name of daubers who spoil walls and paper."

M. Francesco said: "Such daubings should be treated as they deserve and ignored; we would do them too much honor if we were to regard them as we would beautiful and lovely things. But we have left one thing unsettled."

"What is that?" asked M. Troilo.

M. Francesco continued: "The answer to the question of the instruments of martyrdom displayed by the saints in the *Judgment,* which you and M. Ruggiero disapproved of so much but which to me seem well done for the sole reason of making manifest the testimony of their faith.[321] Because, even if they are not going to be displayed on that day, I think there will be some clear sign to amplify the glory of these saints and to bring confusion to tyrants. And also to show the ignorant that on that day the Lord will not forget and never will forget his elect, ensuring that they receive the reward for their unwavering constancy and most perfect faith."

M. Ruggiero replied: "It will not happen that the martyrs display any instruments, either to prove their faith or to bring confusion to tyrants, because

319. The description of the Old Testament figures makes it likely that Piersimone's printed source was the famous multiblock woodcut of the *Triumph of Christ* after Titian. See David Rosand and Michelangelo Muraro, *Titian and the Venetian Woodcut: A Loan Exhibition,* exh. cat. (Washington, D.C.: The Foundation, 1976), 37, nos. 1, 2; and Michael Bury, "The 'Triumph of Christ,' after Titian," *The Burlington Magazine* 131, no. 1032 (1989): 188–97.

320. See Gilio, this volume, 119–21, 149.

321. Gilio, this volume, 187–88.

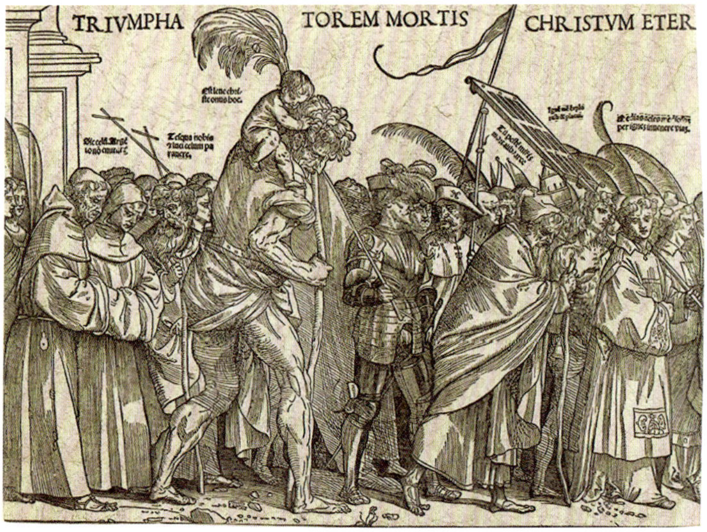

a.

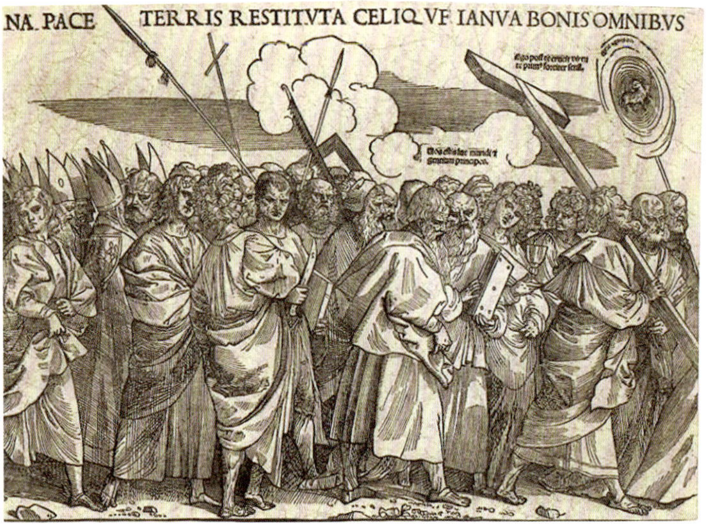

b.

Figs. 23a–e. Anonymous, after Titian (Venetian, ca. 1488–1576), published by Gregorio de' Gregoriis (Italian, active ca. 1480–1528).
Triumph of Christ, 1517, woodcut of five blocks on five sheets, each sheet: 38.2 × 53 cm. New York, New York Public Library.

testimony enough will be the torments and the punishments suffered in hell by their persecutors. And since the martyrs will appear alive, glorious, and grand before their eyes, the weight of remorse on the consciences of their persecutors will be enough for them to be recognized; and, as a consequence, the tormented will say: **[83]** 'Behold, those whom we once thought mad are numbered now among the children of God,' and other similar words that are written in the book of Wisdom.[322] But we can allow this as one of those fictions permitted for the sake of the ignorant, in order that their minds may take in whatever

322. M. Ruggiero is paraphrasing from *Liber Sapientiae* (Book of Wisdom) 5:4–5: "We fools esteemed their life madness, and their end without honour. Behold how they are numbered among the children of God and their lot is among the saints" (Nos insensati, vitam illorum

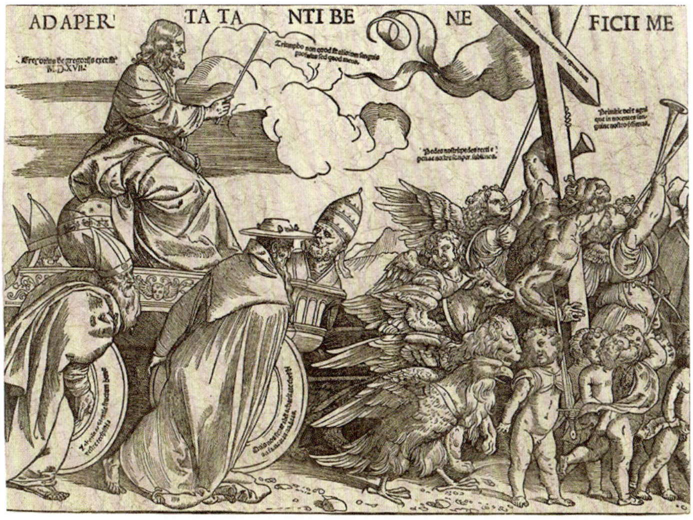

c.

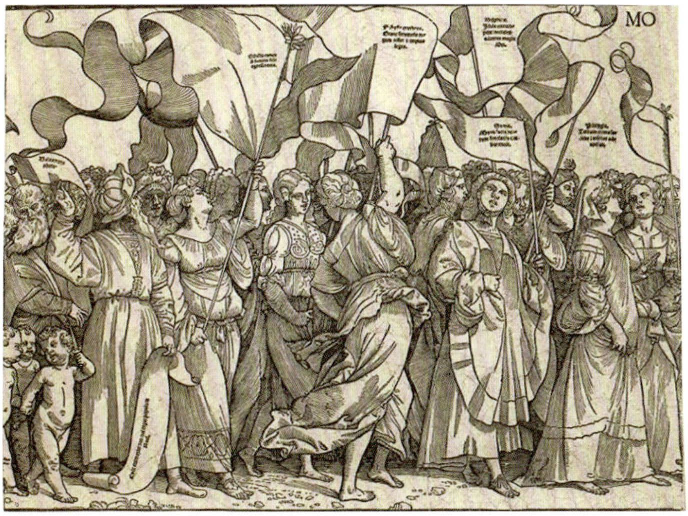

d.

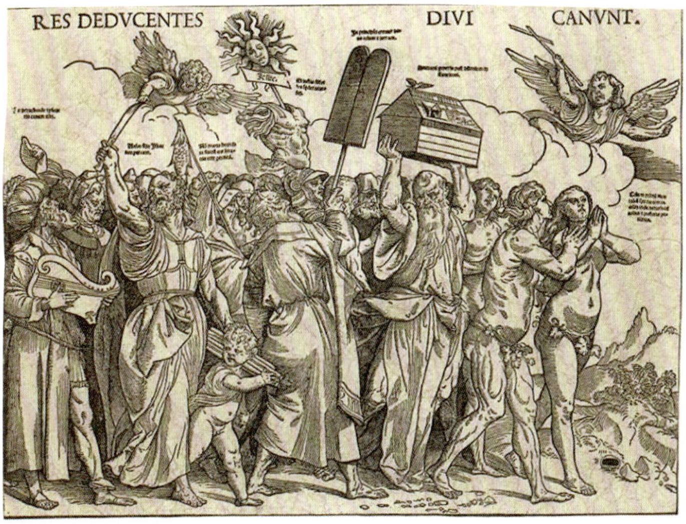

e.

little they can. Another personal invention [*capriccio*] I notice is that of having painted the glorious Virgin fearful and terrified, as if she does not have the courage to ask her angry son about the course of this great mystery, insecure in the face of God's anger; and, as a result, she withdraws herself as much as she can beneath her son" [see figs. 19, 21].[323]

M. Vincenso said: "I think he did that only to point out to us the title she has of Mother of Mercy, and he shows her fearful, as one who shrinks from such severity and the loss of so many. He is also showing that the nature of women is to be compassionate and meek: she turns aside in order not to witness such severe justice."

M. Ruggiero replied: "All this conjecture of yours is false, because on that day when this event happens, the title of which you speak will no longer exist. She then will know that the time for pity has passed and that the time for justice is come, and she will know who deserves reward, who punishment, both who are destined for glory and who for torment. She will also know that God is immutable; therefore she does not have the thought or the fear you mention. So it will not be necessary for her to pray for any of the damned; just as Augustine said that it is an insult to a martyr to pray for him, so it is an insult to pray for the damned.[324] On that day the glorious Virgin will bring her will into conformity with that of her son and will feel repugnance for the damned rather than pray for them. And I tell you further that she, along with the Apostles and other saints, will condemn the wicked to hell; and because of this I don't think she will feel the anguish or compassion you speak of. However, we can place this too among conceded fictions, solely to show the ignorant that she is the Mother of Mercy, and mother to all.[325] We have already spoken of the Cross, the lance,

aestimabamus insaniam, et finem illorum sine honore; Ecce quomodo computati sunt inter filios Dei, et inter sanctos sors illorum est).

323. Scipione Saurolo, in his letter to Carlo Borromeo, 6 September 1561, with its accompanying report, had commented on the diminished status of the Virgin in Michelangelo's representation; see Bartolomeo Nogara, "Per la storia della Cappella Sistina," *Monatshefte für Kunstwissenschaft* 3 (1910): 160–62. Barocchi points out that Gilio seems to be responding to the way Vasari and Condivi described the Virgin; Barocchi, *Trattati,* 2:604, n2 to Gilio p. 83. Condivi's words are followed quite closely: "but His mother, . . . slightly fearful in appearance and almost as if uncertain of the wrath and mystery of God, draws as close as she can beneath her Son" (timorosetta in sembiante e, quasi non bene assicurata dell'ira e secreto de Iddio, trarsi quanto più può sotto il Figliuolo; Condivi, *Vita di Michelangelo,* 50). The translation is from Condivi, *The Life of Michelangelo,* 87. On Vasari, see Vasari, *Le vite . . . 1550,* 907.

324. Augustine, *Sermons,* in *The Works of St. Augustine: A Translation for the 21st Century; Part 3: Sermons,* vol. 5, *On the New Testament (148–183),* ed. John E. Rotelle, trans. Edmund Hill (New York: New City, 1990–92), 121–22 (159.1).

325. The issue of how the Virgin should be represented at the Last Judgment had been raised by earlier writers, and to show her interceding for mercy for sinners had been condemned.

and other sacred instruments, so let us pass over them. Michelangelo has not wanted to keep to the common usage of painters who give wings to angels and make devils black, with tails and horns. **[84]** I do not approve of that because you cannot easily distinguish between them."[326]

M. Troilo said: "Finish telling the story of the Last Judgment. After the sentence, what happens then?"

M. Ruggiero replied: "Once the joyful sentence has been passed on the blessed, their glory will increase with the blessing of the Savior, and they will be carried up to heaven, all glorious and blessed, where our Lord shall deliver the kingdom to the Eternal Father, as Paul states.[327] And he shall place his elect, blessed by God, among the heavenly hierarchies, each according to his deserts. The Eternal Word shall be seated with the glorified humanity on the right of the Father, a position that, as the Word, he had always occupied, to bless the elect for eternity.[328] But think now of when he turns to the wicked, his face full of anger, frightful to behold, and when he curses them and chases them away, condemning them to the eternal flames, just think what crying, what shouts, what screams will come from the damned, hearing themselves cursed and condemned to eternal punishment. When I think of it and speak of it, I feel myself shudder with horror and fear."

M. Francesco said: "What do you say, M. Ruggiero, about all the embracing among the damned as they leave this world?"[329]

Josse Clicthove, *Sermones Judoci Clichtovei Neoportuen* . . . (Cologne: Quentel, 1535), 22v: "Nor then will the Virgin Mary bend her knees before the judge, displaying her breasts to plead for sinners, nor will the Blessed John the Baptist recline forward on his knees, in order to intercede for mankind, as painters depict the form of the judgment. . . . Then also there will be no more place for pity, as now, but only for justice" (Neque tunc beata virgo Maria flectet genua ante iudicem, ostendens illi ubera ad rogandum pro peccatoribus, neque B. Iohannes Baptista tunc etiam procumbet ad genua, ut intercedat pro hominibus, quemadmodum pictores depingunt formam iudicii. . . . Tunc etiam amplius misericordiae non erit locus sicut nunc, sed solummodo iustitiae). The danger of falling into the heresy of apocatastasis is perhaps being hinted at.

326. Aretino, in his letter criticizing Michelangelo's *Last Judgment,* had commented on the angels lacking any celestial ornament ("privi d'ogni celeste ornamento"); see the letter to Alessandro Corvino in Pietro Aretino, *Il quarto libro de le lettere* (Venice: Bartolomeo Cesano, 1550), 83v. See also Gilio, this volume, 231–32. Konrad Braun approved the representation of angels with wings; Braun, *De imaginibus,* 36.

327. 1 Thessalonians 4:16 and 1 Corinthians 15:24.

328. Matthew 26:64.

329. Falling forward out of the boat, one of the damned is pulled back by a companion. Could it be this suggestion of mutual aid that is being referred to here? Otherwise there are no embraces among the damned. But some of the blessed kiss and hug, and they had been criticized for it by Dolce, *L'Aretino,* in Barocchi, *Trattati,* 1:190 (Roskill, *Dolce's "Aretino,"* 166–67). See also Lomazzo, *Il libro dei sogni,* 1:102, reporting on what is being said about the painting: "It is also said about those kisses given up there, that they are not appropriate, inasmuch as they are things for marriages and for brothels" (Dicesi ancora che quei biasci

M. Ruggiero answered: "I think that the opposite will be true, because kissing is a sign of love and friendship and charity, which there cannot be among them, otherwise they would not be damned. Instead there will be discord, hate, enmity, envy: the son will curse the father and the father the son, and among them will be all the evil to make their sufferings even worse; and if they could fight and injure and kill one another, as they did in the world, they would do nothing else. Once the sentence is given, therefore, they will be dragged to hell by devils. These things being done, fire will come from heaven and consume all things. Then shall fail the power of the heavens, the earth, and all the elements; there will be no birds, fish, or animals of any sort. The earth will no longer produce trees or plants. Some have said that even the heavens, the sun, the moon, and the stars shall cease to move and that all things will remain in that state and in that position where God placed them when he created them. **[85]** Then, as John says, there will be a new heaven and a new earth.[330] The other thing I don't like is that in a matter of such importance Michelangelo has inserted the fable of Charon, who, with his winged boat, ferries the souls of the damned across the Stygian marshes, raising his oar to hit those who do not get aboard quickly enough, in order to make room for others [see fig. 19].[331] Do you not think that ignorant people will be firmly of the belief that down below, there are rivers, marshes, boats, judges reviewing cases, and the dog with three heads collecting tolls?"

M. Vincenso said: "I think that in doing this [Michelangelo] has wished to imitate Dante, who imagines him in hell in just that way, saying:

> The demon Charon, with eyes of burning coal, beckons to them and gathers them all in, smiting with the oar any that linger."[332]

M. Pulidoro asked: "Do you know why Charon is said to ferry the souls of the dead?" They all replied that they did not. M. Pulidoro added: "Well, I'll tell you right now. In his book of ancient myths, Diodorus Siculus writes that

---

che di là su si fanno, che non se gli convengono, imperò che elle sono cose da nozze e da bordello).

330. Revelation 21:1.

331. Scipione Saurolo, in his letter to Carlo Borromeo, 6 September 1561, with an accompanying report, had criticized the inclusion of the "fabulosam Acherontis Cimbam" (the fabled boat of Acheron) in the *Last Judgment;* see Nogara, "Per la storia della Cappella Sistina," 162. See also Dempsey, "Mythic Inventions," 65–66. Gilio does not register the fact that the Charon figure is driving the damned out of his boat, unlike Dante's Charon, who uses his oar to force the damned to embark.

332. Dante Alighieri, *The Divine Comedy: 1. Inferno,* trans. John D. Sinclair (New York: Oxford University Press, 1939), 52–53 (3.109–11).

in Egypt (if I remember well), there was a custom of disemboweling the dead and packing them with myrrh, incense, cinnamon, and other sweet-smelling things. After the Egyptians had preserved the body like this for many days, they told the dead man's friends and also forty judges that the body would pass the marshes on a certain day. The judges, sitting in a tribunal on the other side, waited for the body to cross over. It was ferried (as were all those who died in that country) by a boatman called Charon, who charged a certain price for the body. Once the boat arrived before the tribunal, the body was set before the judges and in their presence everyone was free to make accusations against the dead person. If the crimes were proved to be as charged, then the dead body was condemned to remain unburied. If not, it was absolved and buried with great honor; and if the accuser did not prove his accusations true, he was severely fined. This was the way in which the deceased were handed over to the gods of Hades.[333] **[86]** Orpheus, who was a very ancient poet, used this fact to imagine Charon ferrying the souls in hell, and for this reason too, I think, Minos and Rhadamanthys were invented as judges of the souls of the dead."[334]

M. Ruggiero replied: "Yes, truly that could be the reason. And Dante, imitating other poets, was able to imagine it thus. But neither Augustine, Jerome, Ambrose, Gregory, nor the other doctors have imagined it in that way, neither as doctors, theologians, nor historians. And no historian would have come up with such a fiction, because if he had, he would have acquired the name of poet and lost that of historian. A historian should imitate theologians rather than poets. And this is how Michelangelo should have behaved, because if in the secular field the poetic corrupts historical subjects, could we say that it enhances spiritual subjects in the case of sacred things of such importance? In this respect, the position of the pagan philosophers seems better than our own, for they, according to Macrobius, do not allow anything from fable to enter their discussions of the Supreme God; these are Macrobius's own words:

> We should not assume, however, that philosophers approve the use of fabulous narratives, even those of the proper sort, in all disputations. It is their custom to employ them when speaking about the Soul, or about spirits having dominion in the lower and upper air, or about gods in general. But when the discussion aspires to treat of the Highest and Supreme of all gods, called by the Greeks the Good (*tagathon*) and the First Cause (*proton aition*), or to treat of Mind or Intellect, which the Greeks call *nous,* born

333. Diodorus Siculus, *Library of History,* 1:308–15 (1.91–92).

334. Dante, *Divine Comedy: 1. Inferno,* 72–73 (5.4–12); and Virgil, *Aeneid, Books 1–6,* 562–63 (6.432–33), for Minos. On Rhadamanthys as judge, see Virgil, *Aeneid, Books 1–6,* 572–73 (6.566–69).

> from and originating in the Supreme God and embracing the original concepts of things, which are called Ideas (*ideai*), when, I repeat, philosophers speak about these, the Supreme God and Mind, they shun the use of fabulous narratives.[335]

Elsewhere, reporting Cicero's opinion, he said:

> philosophers should refrain from using fiction since no kind of fiction has a place with those who profess to tell the truth.[336]

When Cicero discusses history in his book *De Oratore,* he writes:

> For who does not know history's first law to be that an author must not dare to tell anything but the truth? And its second that he must make bold to tell the whole truth? That there must be no suggestion of partiality anywhere in his writings? Nor of malice?[337]

In this respect, Konrad Braun said:

> Thus the usage of sacred images is to be regulated so that people are offered holy not profane things, true histories, not the fables and dreams of inquisitive men.[338] **[87]**

So Michelangelo, when he had to paint such an important article of our faith, ought to have imitated the theologians and not the poets, because theology and poetry are direct opposites. Many other fabulous and false things are to be seen there that are not worth discussion. This is as much as I will draw attention to in this beautiful and holy story, which should be painted in a faithful, pure, simple, true, and chaste way; just as it should be faithful, pure, simple, true, chaste, and complete if written or preached about. It should be full of fear,

---

335. See note 311. Macrobius, *Commentary,* 85–86 (1.2.§13–14). For a discussion of the imperfect text of Macrobius printed by Gilio, see Barocchi, *Trattati,* 2:547; Barocchi corrected Gilio's Latin.

336. Macrobius, *Commentary,* 84 (1.2.§4). Macrobius is reporting what a critic of Plato's use of myth (Colotes) had said. Gilio mistakes the meaning and attributes Colotes's idea to Cicero.

337. Cicero, *On the Orator* [*De Oratore*], 242–45 (2.15.62).

338. Braun, *De imaginibus,* 144. Braun's treatise was dedicated to Alessandro Farnese. Chapter 22, 143–45 ("De abusibus imaginum") concerns the abuses; see Giuseppe Scavizzi, *Arte e architettura sacra: Cronache e documenti sulla controversia tra riformati e cattolici (1500–1550)* (Reggio Calabria: Casa Editrice del Libro, 1982), 222. In *Controversy on Images* (111n123), Scavizzi notes that both Gilio and Braun dedicated their books to Alessandro Farnese.

terror, and wonder so that the spectators gasp, tremble, and repent rather than laugh and make fun of it, treating it as a thing of little importance.[339] Because not everyone wants to learn how to paint, but everybody must learn to be a good Christian."[340]

M. Silvio said: "I have often heard the opposite said to preachers: that they should preach in a manner that is joyful and happy, full of sweetness."[341]

M. Ruggiero replied: "When someone, because of his virtuous life, is certain of his salvation, I would agree with you. But for those of us who are sinners, no, because being unwilling to abandon sin out of love, at least we might do it out of fear. And this [subject] seems to me an excellent way of terrifying ourselves."

"But who would believe," asked M. Vincenso, "that the resurrection of the dead might be introduced into a game of cards?"

"How you do mean, a game of cards?" responded M. Francesco.

M. Vincenso replied: "Take the tarot cards and you will see a painting of the angel sounding the trumpet and the resurrected dead leaving their tombs."[342]

"That is really bad," replied M. Francesco, "and worth discussing."

"Do you think it well done," added M. Vincenso, "that one of the guardians of men, venerated by the Church, a heavenly and angelic creature, a divine messenger of such importance, should have been introduced into a card game,

---

339. On laughter, see Gilio, this volume, 187–88.

340. As Barocchi points out, this is very similar to the point made by Aretino in his letter to Alessandro Corvino about the *Last Judgment,* published in 1550; Barocchi, *Trattati,* 2:605, n2 to Gilio p. 87. See note 205.

341. Barocchi draws attention to the traditional rhetorical idea of teaching by delighting (*delectando docere*); see Barocchi, *Trattati,* 2.605–6, n3 to Gilio p. 87. See also John W. O'Malley, "Content and Rhetorical Forms in Sixteenth-Century Treatises on Preaching," in *Renaissance Eloquence: Studies in the Theory and Practice of Renaissance Rhetoric,* ed. James J. Murphy (Berkeley: University of California Press, 1983), 238–52. The reference may be to the epideictic oratory of praise, wonder, and love; see Debora K. Shuger, *Sacred Rhetoric: The Christian Grand Style in the English Renaissance* (Princeton, NJ: Princeton University Press, 1988), 178–79.

342. The twenty-one picture cards specific to the tarot pack were called "triumphs" (*trionfi*); one of them showed the angel blowing the trumpet and the dead being resurrected (another, mentioned below, showed the Devil). See Michael Dummett, *The Game of Tarot: From Ferrara to Salt Lake City* (London: Gerald Duckworth, 1980), 390–91. Card games of all kinds were the target of censure, and, in the first dialogue of his *Due dialogi,* Gilio had advised his educated courtier to avoid them, except as an occasional pastime; see Gilio, *Due dialogi* (1564), 58v. But tarot seems to have attracted particular opprobrium, as may be seen from a mid-fifteenth-century Dominican sermon: "There is nothing in this world connected with gaming that is so hated by God as the game of triumphs" (Non est res in hoc mundo quod pertineat ad ludum tantum Deo odibilis sicut ludus triumphorum). The unknown Dominican describes the *trionfi* as twenty-one steps down to hell because they introduced into a card game things that deserved the highest respect, thereby subverting Christian values. Robert Steele, "A Notice of the *Ludus Triumphorum* and Some Early Italian Card Games," *Archaeologia* 57 (1900): 185–200.

among the curses, the false oaths, the cheating, and the villainies of gaming? **[88]** And no one gives a thought to it, and if it is thought about, no one says anything, and if anything is said, no one prohibits it or tries to comply. Should Demosthenes intervene to defend this, he would become a Gnaeus Sicinius."[343]

"You put the case well," said M. Francesco, "and in order to make it easier for men to be ruined in body and soul, the Devil has been added too, so that a desperate man with the card often in his hands can promise himself to the Devil or call on him for help. But it seems to me that we should also talk a little about the mixed painter and that the responsibility for doing so should fall on M. Pulidoro."[344]

"Quite right," they all said. "Now, M. Pulidoro, it's your turn and, as preachers do, you should now clear your throat a little by spitting, which we will allow on this occasion."

M. Pulidoro replied: "I think our discussion has been quite a lengthy one, and if we wish to add this subject as well, given that it involves many things, it may become overtaxing, so it would be a good idea if we had a brief rest."

M. Francesco said: "I believe we should go on, given that we have started to discuss it. There is still a long time to go before our evening meal. Look at the sun and how high it is. And I don't think that we could have a better pastime than this."

"I agree," said M. Troilo. "Now begin, M. Pulidoro, because I have never understood what a mixed painter is."

"Since you are all in agreement," M. Pulidoro said, "I will do as you wish. You should know that there are many elements that belong to the mixed painter, and it is because they are poorly understood that today we see so many errors and confusions in paintings. Many think that because they know how to handle colors, they can do everything properly, using the pretext of poetic license."

M. Vincenso said: "We can truly say that men perfect in any branch of knowledge [*scienza*] are today rare; and I am referring to painting as much as to all the others. Today we no longer find men of the caliber of Socrates, Plato, or Aristotle, Demosthenes, Cicero, or Virgil, or any of the other great philosophers, poets, or orators. We can also say that there are no longer men like Gregory, Augustine, Jerome, Ambrose, Chrysostom, Cyprian, and others. **[89]** They with their learning sustained the Church, defending it from the frequent

---

343. Demosthenes as the exemplary orator is contrasted with Gnaeus Sicinius, of whom Cicero writes: "a man of coarse but hilarious wit—the only oratorical quality that he possessed." Cicero, *Brutus*, in *Brutus; Orator*, trans. G. L. Hendrickson and H. M. Hubbell, Loeb Classical Library 342 (Cambridge, MA: Harvard University Press, 1939), 184–85 (§216).

344. After the very extended section devoted to the historical painter, the discussion moves on to the third and final type, the mixed painter; see Gilio, this volume, 101–2.

fierce attacks of heretics and unbelievers, rooting out the schismatics, defending religion, increasing faith, and doing other great works in Christ's name. These great scholars have enlightened everyone with holy, catholic, and perfect doctrine. It is therefore not surprising that painting has declined, when the same is the case with all the other branches of knowledge. So the world should be grateful to Michelangelo, because not only has he revived a branch of knowledge [*scienza*] that was almost lost but he has brought it to such perfection that we cannot envy the ancients. He has given it such luster with his knowledge that, if [painting] has not overtaken the quality for which men like Apelles, Timagoras, Zeuxis, Protogenes, Polignotes, and others are famous throughout the world, it has equaled it. Indeed, we can say that if [Michelangelo] had not existed, painting would have been almost lost to those who practice it.[345] But I will stop for now: begin, M. Pulidoro, to tell us about the qualities of the mixed painter."

M. Pulidoro began speaking again, saying: "We will call a mixed painter he who produces a pleasant mixture of the true and the fictional [*cose vere e finte*] and who sometimes adds fabulous things [*le favolose*] as well, in order to increase the allure [*vaghezza*] of the work. But when one wishes to work in this genre, one must make sure that the different elements agree with one another and that, whether the result of imitation or personal invention [*capriccio*], they appear to have originated from one individual, at a single moment in time.[346] They should be organized in such a way that the beginning is in agreement with the middle and the middle with the end, and in such a way that all the elements are connected together and are proportionately related to one another; so that any viewer will regard the fabulous and fictional parts as true and real. If this is

345. Barocchi notes that M. Vincenso's unqualified praise of Michelangelo is comparable to Giorgio Vasari's remarks in Vasari, "Proemio della terza parte," 4:10–11; see Barocchi, *Trattati,* 2:606, n1 to Gilio p. 89. But here, at the start of the discussion of the mixed painter, it is not Michelangelo's mastery of the art of painting but his knowledge and understanding of the whole potential of painting, of painting as a *scienza* (a branch of knowledge), that is being praised. In the genre of mixed painting, Michelangelo will be credited with reviving ideas and approaches to invention, many derived from literature and rhetoric, that were known to the ancients but had been lost since. For a definition of the difference between *arte* and *scienza,* see Benedetto Varchi, *Lezzione nella quale si disputa della maggioranza delle artie qual sia più nobile, la scultura o la pittura* [Florence: Lorenzo Torrentino, 1549], in *Trattati d'arte del Cinquecento: Fra manierismo e controriforma,* vol. 1, ed. Paola Barocchi (Bari: Laterza, 1960), 6–8.

346. Raffaello Borghini misinterpreted Gilio's mixed painter as one who made his own inventions and did not depend on either poetry or history. Raffaello Borghini, *Il Riposo* (Florence: Marescotti, 1584), 53–54; reprint with introduction and analytical index by Mario Rosci (Milan: Edizioni Labor, 1967). For an English translation, see Borghini, *Raffaello Borghini's "Il Riposo,"* ed. and trans. Lloyd H. Ellis (Toronto: University of Toronto Press, 2007), 58.

not done, the work will have neither beauty nor excellence.[347] And one can give examples from Homer and Virgil, who made such a sweet, lovely, and beautiful mixture in their poems that every time [the poems] are read they please more, and if the world were to last forever, they would forever please and be admired."[348]

M. Silvio said: "If I remember correctly, Virgil was criticized by Hyginus, as Gellius tells us."[349]

M. Pulidoro replied: "You are right: it was for using the figure that the Greeks call prolepsis, the anticipation of time or events; **[90]** that is, simply changing the order by saying later what should have been said earlier.[350] This happened when Palinurus spoke to Aeneas in hell, declaring:

Eripe me his, invicte, malis; aut tu mihi terram
Inice (namque potes) portusque require Velinos

which, in the vulgar tongue, can be translated as:

> Unconquered Aeneas, rescue me from such sufferings; cover my body with earth, and it will be easy for you, but seek the port of Velia.[351]

Hyginus said that it was not appropriate to name something that could not be known to or understood by someone. In this instance, Palinurus died while

347. Horace, *Ars Poetica,* 462–63 (151–52); also Bernardino Daniello da Lucca, *Della Poetica* (Venice: Nicolini da Sabio, 1536), 41–42 (cited by Barocchi, *Trattati,* 2:606, n2 to Gilio p. 89): "But my sons, be careful always to mix true things with false in such a way that there is no discrepancy between the beginning and the middle, and the middle and the end. I say mix the true with the false and the fictional because the poet is not required, like the historian, to describe things as they really were and actually happened, but rather as they ought to be" (Ma siate accorti figliuoli, di mescolar sempre con le vere le false cose in guisa che ne'l primo dal mezzo, ne il mezzo dal fine, si discordi. Dico mescolar le cose vere con le false et fitte perchè non è tenuto il poeta com' è l'Historico di descrivere le cose tali quali elle veramente state et avvenute sono ma ben quali esser devrebbono). Daniello also makes the point that everything must seem to be like the truth: "Ben è vero che egli dee sempre vedere ch'esse al vero somiglianti siano." See Daniello, *Della Poetica,* 43.

348. Adducing Homer and Virgil is a strong indication that Gilio had in mind the epic poet as his model for the mixed painter; see Gilio, this volume, 100–101. See also Dempsey, "Mythic Inventions," esp. 70.

349. Aulus Gellius, reporting Hyginus's lost commentary on Virgil; Gellius, *Attic Nights* [*Noctes Atticae*], vol. 2, *Books 6–13,* trans. J. C. Rolfe, Loeb Classical Library 200 (Cambridge, MA: Harvard University Press, 1927), 254–59 (10.16).

350. The Italian text has the word *Cataprolepsim.* Aulus Gellius cites Hyginus using the Greek *kata prolepsin,* meaning "by anticipation." It is to the rhetorical figure of prolepsis that reference is being made.

351. Virgil, *Aeneid, Books 1–6,* 558–59 (6.365–66); the translation follows Gilio's Italian, not Virgil's Latin.

Aeneas was sailing to Italy and before Rome was built. Velia was built during the reign of Servius Tullius, by Phocaeans who, exiled by Harpalus (the prefect of King Cyrus), left their city more than six hundred years after Aeneas arrived in Italy. And although Virgil gave these words to Palinurus as a spirit who could have foreseen the future, it was not appropriate to have Aeneas find the port of Velia, given that it did not even exist."

M. Vincenso said: "In the case of this passage, Alciati defends Virgil from Hyginus's accusations, saying that the poet is not talking about the city or port here, but about the fields and river after which the city was named; and indeed Virgil uses the names of other rivers and countries to represent cities that did not exist at the time, for example, when he writes: 'Camarina appears far off, and the fields of Gela, then steep Agragas and the rest that follows.'"[352]

M. Pulidoro replied: "I'll leave such matters to those who know more than I do, but Virgil was also attacked by the same Hyginus for these verses in Book VI:[353] **[91]**

Eruet ille Argos Agamemnoniasque Mycenas,
Ipsumque Aeaciden, genus armipotentis Achilli,
Ultus avos Troiae, tempia et temerata Minervae!;

which, translated, means:

> He will destroy Mycenae and Argos and he will conquer one who had his origin from the once famous Achilles, undefeated in arms. He will avenge his ancient Trojan ancestors and the desecrated temple of Minerva.[354]

And this only for having confused times and persons, namely that Pyrrhus, about whom Virgil is talking, came to Italy at the time of Curius and Fabricius, summoned by the city of Tarentum to wage war against the Romans.[355] The Greek war was fought many years later by L. Mummius.[356] So that middle verse was wrongly placed there because, having started to recount the Greek war, the poet should have continued, describing what came later without making

352. Virgil, *Aeneid, Books 1–6,* 418–19 (3.701 and 3.703, omitting 702); and Andrea Alciati, *Parergon Iuris Libri VII Posteriores* (Lyon: Sebastianus Gryphius, 1544), 5.21.41.
353. Aulus Gellius, *Attic Nights,* 2:254–59 (10.16).
354. Virgil, *Aeneid, Books 1–6,* 592–93 (6.838–40); the translation follows Gilio's Italian, not Virgil's Latin.
355. The references are to Manius Curius Dentatus and Gaius Fabricius Luscinus, Roman heroes of the war against Pyrrhus (third century BC).
356. Lucius Mummius Achaicus, consul in command against the Achaean Confederacy (second century BC).

reference to Pyrrhus, who came earlier. Because, although the Romans beat Pyrrhus and vanquished Greece, historical decorum demands that one follow the chronological order of events, not invert it. Therefore, Hyginus thought that Virgil, if alive, would have corrected the mistake. [Hyginus] then praises, as being appropriate, what [Virgil] said of Aeneas at the beginning of the work:

> Who once chased out by the will of the Fates, came to Italy, and to the Lavinian shores.[357]

Do you think, gentlemen, that if Hyginus had seen the boat that Michelangelo represented in Noah's Flood on the Sistine ceiling [fig. 24], he would have taken him to task as he did Virgil, because at that time no one knew about boats? If we wish to believe the Greek and Latin authors, we find that the first boat was the one that sailed to Colchis on the quest for the Golden Fleece, and as a memorial it was then placed in the heavens by the gods, complete with stars. The Holy Scriptures say that the descendants of Noah were the first to inhabit the islands.[358] **[92]** Pliny states that Danaus was the first to take an Egyptian ship to Greece, because before that rafts made of timbers tied together were used for sailing, what in Venetian is called a 'zattera.'[359] According to Plutarch, Theseus used a ship with thirty oars, and it was preserved in Athens for many years, the parts being restored as they perished.[360] Some others praise the Mysians and the Trojans because the first inventors of boats were in the Hellespont. The Erythraeans invented the bireme (or lightweight galley), Aminocles the trireme, Corinth the quadrireme, Nesichton of Salamis the quinquereme, Xenagoras of Syracuse the ship with six banks of oars, Mnesigiton the ship with ten banks of oars; Alexander the Great made ships with twelve banks of oars, Ptolemy Soter with fifteen, Antigonus with thirty, Ptolemy Philadelphus with forty, Ptolemy Philopator with fifty; Hippus of Tyre invented cargo ships, the Cyrenians invented the cutter, the Phoenicians the skiff, the Rhodians the yacht, the Cypriots the yawl. The Phoenicians were the first to use the stars, the Copaeans the oar, Icarus the sail, Daedalus the mast and yard, the Tuscans the anchor, Tiphys the tiller.[361] From time to time, others have added further things necessary to navigation. So you can think about whether a boat at the

357. Virgil, *Aeneid, Books 1–6*, 262–63 (1.2–3); and Aulus Gellius, *Attic Nights*, 254–59 (10.16).
358. Perhaps a reference to Genesis 10:5.
359. Pliny, *NH*, 2:644–45 (book 7, §206).
360. Plutarch, *Theseus*, 23, in *Plutarch, Lives*, vol. 1, *Theseus and Romulus; Lycurgus and Numa; Solon and Publicola*, trans. Bernadotte Perrin, Loeb Classical Library 46 (Cambridge, MA: Harvard University Press, 1914), 48–49 (§23).
361. Pliny, *NH*, 2:644–47 (book 7, §206–9).

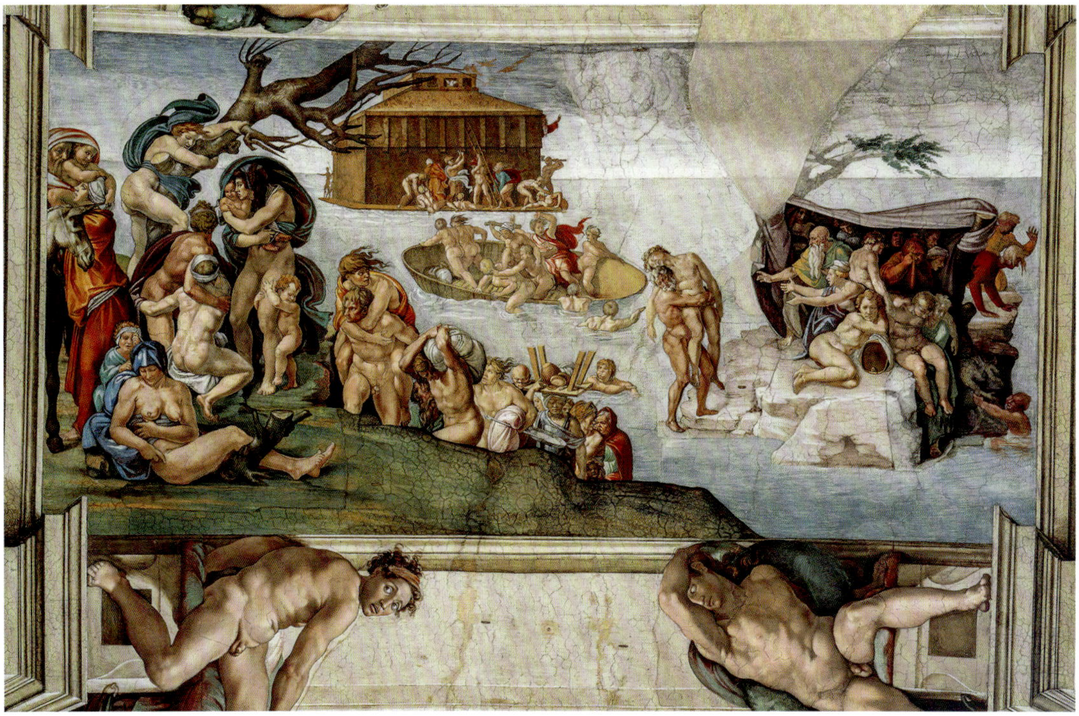

time [of Noah] would have been so ornate and beautiful, whether it would have existed at all: I think not."

M. Francesco said: "There are many arguments that can be used to defend this. The first is that if the descendants of Noah were the first to start living on islands, then we must believe that they had some wooden vessels suitable for sailing. What's more, if we are to believe Berosus the Chaldean, a most ancient author, Noah was the man whom the Latins call Saturn, who was driven away by his sons and came to Italy, to the place that is now Rome. Here ruled Janus, who welcomed him gladly; and, because [Saturn] taught farming and the use of fire, he was adored there as a god.[362] Therefore his descendants, in order to commemorate the man and the many benefits they had received from him, portrayed on bronze medals the ship in which he came. Ovid wrote:

> The reason for the ship is known to everyone, because with it he came to the Tiber. **[93]**

362. Berosus (Berossus) was the author of a history of Babylon that survives only in fragments. In the late fifteenth century, the Dominican monk Giovanni Nanni (Annius of Viterbo) claimed to have discovered a complete text; it is to the forged texts in Annius's *Antiquitates,* published at Rome in 1498, that Gilio is referring. See Ingrid Rowland, *The Culture of the High Renaissance* (Cambridge: Cambridge University Press, 1998), 53–59.

Fig. 24.
Michelangelo Buonarroti (Italian, 1475–1564).
The Flood, 1508–10, fresco, 280 × 570 cm. Vatican City, Vatican Apostolic Palace, Sistine Chapel.

A little further on, the poet then added:

> His descendants then drew the ship on copper as a commemoration of the arrival on the sacred Tiber of the scythe-bearing god, after he had circled the whole world.[363]

If we try to gather together all these authoritative sources, we may conclude that there were boats at that time and the sea was crossed. Another thing that also persuades me is that if Noah's ark was at sea for so many months, in violent storms and rain, eventually landing on the mountains of Armenia, then Noah's sons or grandsons may have taken it as a model and thus started sailing. Moreover, if it is true that Noah came to Italy, then he had to build a ship and it would have been a handsome one, as can be seen from those very ancient medals that have the two-faced Janus on one side and a beautiful, ornate ship on the other."[364]

M. Pulidoro replied: "This may well be true, but you will not tell me that the ship was so ornate and beautiful that today there are perhaps none like it. Because we have to believe that rafts, not ships, were used for sailing at that time, like those invented by King Erythrus on the Red Sea, as I said earlier; and if not rafts, then some hollowed-out log or chest, or tub, or other rough and awkward object.[365] And I would have been better pleased if Michelangelo had used his ingenuity to find a similarly awkward and barely seaworthy object, such as is not seen nor used today, to show the crudity of that time and the primitive nature of the people. Because beautiful, highly decorated ships are seen every day in the ports of large coastal cities, viewers get no sense of wonder or delight from seeing one, as they would have from something cruder."[366]

M. Francesco said: "Anyone wanting to introduce such subleties into this matter would undermine all freedom of the brush, which would be a bad

363. Ovid, *Fasti*, 18–19 (1.233–34 and 1.239–40). Barocchi notes that Gilio conflated the lines; see Barocchi, *Trattati*, 2:607, n1 to Gilio p. 9. The translations follow Gilio's Italian, not Ovid's Latin.

364. On bronze coins of the Roman republican period with Janus on the obverse and a ship on the reverse, see Michael H. Crawford, *Roman Republican Coinage* (Cambridge: Cambridge University Press, 1975), 2:718–19.

365. Pliny, *NH*, 2:644–45 (book 7, §206).

366. The importance of the wonderful (*maraviglia*) in the epic poem is from Aristotle, *Poetics*, 120–25 (1460a); see the translation of *Poetics* by Bernardo Segni, *Rettorica e poetica d'Aristotele* (Florence: Torrentino, 1549), 341. M. Pulidoro's concluding remarks make clear that the deployment of the rhetorical figure of anticipation (prolepsis) to produce *maraviglia* was the point of this whole discussion; to use prolepsis, with its anachronistic content, might be justified if it made people marvel. According to M. Pulidoro, Michelangelo's boat does not elicit that response.

thing. But given that it is as you say—that the earliest [boats] invented were awkward and ill-suited to purpose, and that greater pleasure would perhaps have been given by the thought of the readiness of those simple people to boldly set sail without any experience or skill, putting their lives at risk **[94]**—nonetheless, Michelangelo, like Virgil, has been able to anticipate the passage of time by showing us the future already in the present. In this respect, Horace's lines are apt:

> The strength and beauty of order, if I am not mistaken, is that while [the poet] says many things at a particular point, he keeps back many things that could have been said, to be used at a more suitable moment.[367]

For sometimes these anticipations make the work pleasing and entertaining, as Virgil showed beautifully when, in the first book, he described Aeneas's fortunes at sea and his arrival at Carthage; in the second the ruins of Troy and his departure; and in the third the sea journey he undertook to reach Italy; while he reserved for another place his description of what the ships in which he set out were made of."[368]

M. Pulidoro said: "The anticipation that Michelangelo introduced here was not what you think; for, if he had shown to those people a boat of the type we now have and as he has painted it, it would have been appropriate and would have given them the same sense of wonder that we would feel if it had been something not yet seen in our countries. And to us it would have brought wonder if he had made it crude and awkward and clumsy, at the thought, as I said earlier, of the primitive nature of those early people and how much progress the world has gradually made since. So anticipation, when introduced in a suitable way by a highly skilled artist, can give pleasure to spectators and beauty to the work, as long as it is kept in due proportion. What will we say of the reputation of those who paint the very ancient poet Orpheus playing the lyre in Roman military dress, given that he lived hundreds of years before Rome? But I do not approve of [anticipation] being used frequently, least of all by anyone who is not perfect and expert in the art. **[95]** Hyginus was right when he said that fictions about things of recent memory are pleasing, but things so far back are not.[369] It

367. Horace, *Ars Poetica,* 452–55 (lines 42–45); the translation follows Gilio's Italian, not Horace's Latin.
368. Virgil, *Aeneid, Books 7–12,* 118–21 (9.77–106) for the account of the wood used for the ships. On Horace's approval of beginning a story in the middle of things, see *Ars Poetica,* 462–63 (lines 148–49).
369. This may be a further reference to Aulus Gellius's citation of Hyginus, *Attic Nights,* 254–59 (10.16), slightly misunderstood; see Gilio, this volume, 200–201.

is also necessary to point out that the fictions should be about things that can properly exist.[370] We have an example of this in the horses of Praxiteles and Phidias that are to be seen on the Quirinal [fig. 25]. Although they do not have bridles, they act as they would have if they did have them. See how important it is to use fictions and anticipations well and appropriately, and, in ordinary stories, to arrange them attractively."[371]

M. Troilo said: "It seems to me that in some cases the use of such fictions can be pleasing, in certain others not. In a single story I do not approve of them being used so often that they become the norm [*regola*], nor that every insignificant dauber, wishing to be an Apelles, uses such things for every little figure he paints. In a lengthy story one can allow them, because occasional fictions usually give pleasure, but when they occur frequently they are annoying."

M. Pulidoro replied: "You are of my opinion. So I do not praise Michelangelo when in his picture of the crucifixion of Saint Peter he imitated Praxiteles by representing so many men on horses without bridles, when it would have been enough to make just one [figs. 26, 27]. Further than that, and more importantly, [I do not praise] his painting Saint Peter as crucified without nails, without ropes or anything else to show the atrociousness of the martyrdom. And it seems to me that so many fictions among so few figures are not attractive."[372]

M. Vincenso said: "One could reply that it is not necessary, because everybody knows that Saint Peter was crucified; and just as one cannot say that a man has been hanged without presuming it to have been a violent and cruel death, likewise one cannot say that Saint Peter was crucified and fail to understand the atrociousness of the martyrdom, implying the cross, the nails and the ropes, and everything else needed for such an execution. What Michelangelo has done in this case is for the sake of embellishing the story, both to introduce a new usage in a new way and to display an aspect of the type of mixed painting [*mistura*] that you spoke of, so that here one may experience that saint's suffering. If

370. See also Gilio, this volume, 110, 214–15. The distinction being made is between fiction that is lifelike (*verisimile*) and the fabulous.

371. The antique marble figures of the *Dioscuri* (*Horse Tamers*) on the Quirinal were believed to be works by Phidias and Praxiteles; see Bober and Rubinstein, *Renaissance Artists and Antique Sculpture,* 159 (no. 125).

372. Michelangelo's frescoes of the *Conversion of Paul* and *Crucifixion of Saint Peter,* in the Pauline Chapel in the Vatican, were painted circa 1542–50. The restoration, completed in 2009, confirmed that in the *Crucifixion,* Michelangelo did not originally paint nails for the hands and feet of Saint Peter; those seen now were added later. Saint Peter's loincloth was also shown to be an addition; see Maurizio De Luca, "Il Restauro della Cappella Paolina," in Maurizio De Luca et al., *La Cappella Paolina* (Vatican City: Musei Vaticani, 2013), 45. The early prints of Giovanni Battista de' Cavalieri and Michele Grechi show that there were never ropes and that the horses of the soldiers in the upper left of the *Crucifixion* did not have bridles. On the issue of showing the pain and suffering of martyrdom, see Gilio, this volume, 134–35.

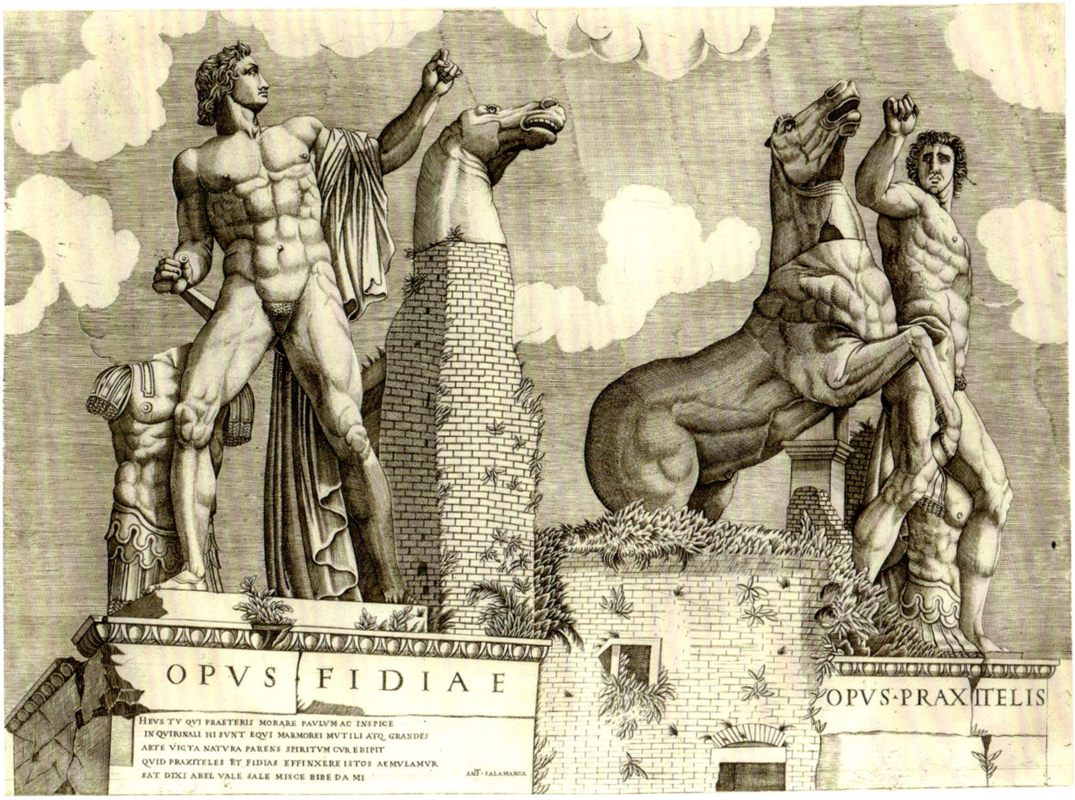

Fig. 25.
Anonymous, published by Antonio Salamanca (Milanese, ca. 1478–1562).
Horse Tamers (The Dioscuri), engraving, 37 × 50.5 cm. London, British Museum.

you look at him in the position that he is in, you will judge from his movement the anguish of a man turned upside down; **[96]** you can tell it from his eyes and from the curving of his chest, which make it appear that in his distress, he is suffering the agonies of death. Michelangelo assumes that the novelty of it will give more delight to the spectator and allure [*vaghezza*] to the work than if he had represented the atrociousness of nails, ropes, or chains."

M. Pulidoro replied: "If it were known to everyone that Saint Peter was crucified head downward I would to a certain extent concede the point; but because I take it for granted that the majority of people do not know it, I am of the opposite view. And if you were to say, 'He has done it only for learned men and for courtiers,' then he will have done the opposite of the apostle Paul. For you must know that Paul said: 'to the wise and to the unwise, I am debtor.'[373]

373. Romans 1:14. Compare the points about the importance of intelligibility in Dolce, *L'Aretino*, in Barocchi, *Trattati*, 1:191 (Roskill, *Dolce's "Aretino,"* 166–67). This passage raises a question about who did have access to the Pauline Chapel—it was certainly not open to everyone. See Margaret Kuntz, "Designed for Ceremony: The Cappella Paolina at the Vatican Palace," *Journal of the Society of Architectural Historians* 62, no. 2 (2003): 231–32, 242–43. See also Bury, this volume, 7.

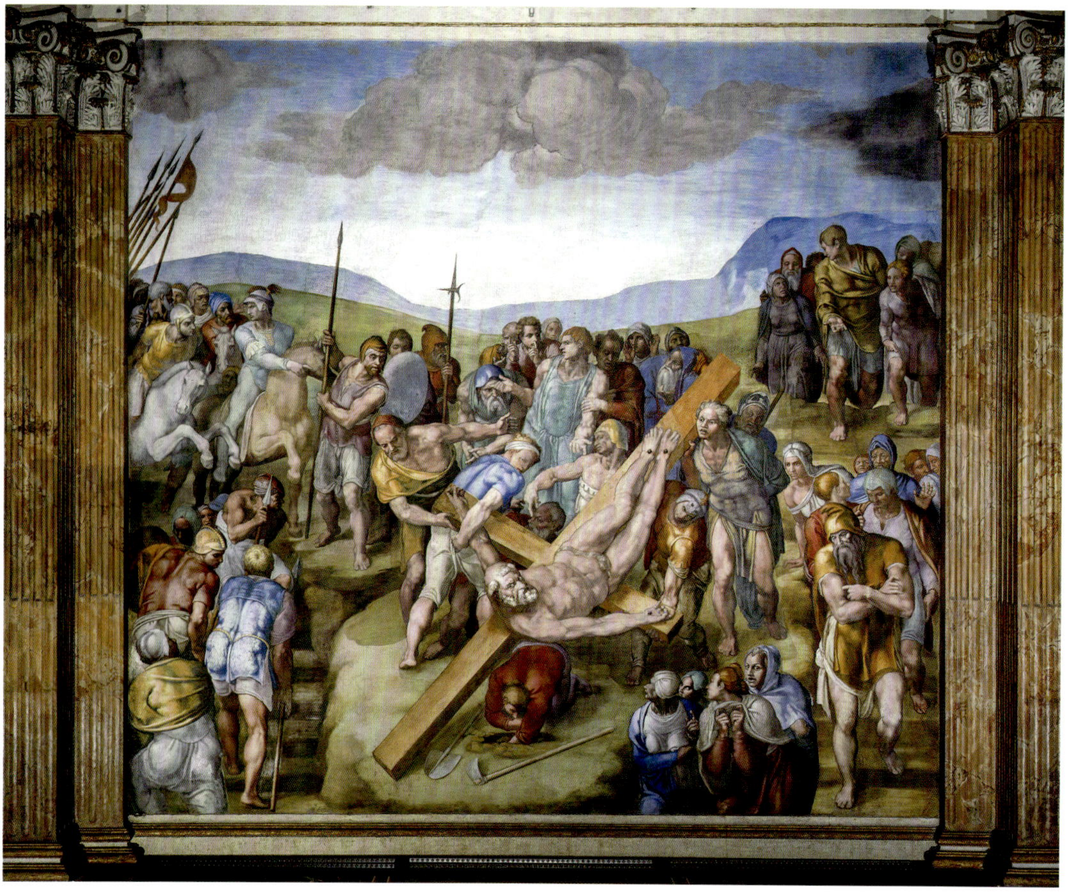

So it is in this case; one must proceed in such a way that everyone can learn to know the truth. There is another reason too: to show truthfully, without fiction, the cruelty of the tyrant who condemned him to this death, the patience of the martyr, and the power of divine grace that gave him such endurance during his martyrdom; and also for the sake of the devotion of people who consider such fictions to be amusing fables and who are stimulated to good works by true examples. Such a fiction might be acceptable in the case of a horse or in something else poetic, invented to add something alluring [*vaghezza*]. [However, it should be avoided] because it could give rise to an ignorant painter thoughtlessly painting a crucified Christ that way; and another might learn from him and then another and it could be taken as the rule and, what would be worse, as an object of laughter. These painters would defend themselves on the authority of Michelangelo, who, because of his preeminence, is believed not to make mistakes. How much of an error it is to see a person crucified without nails, you must judge. Someone else might want to paint him without a cross; and thus the true and important things would be reduced to fictions. Furthermore,

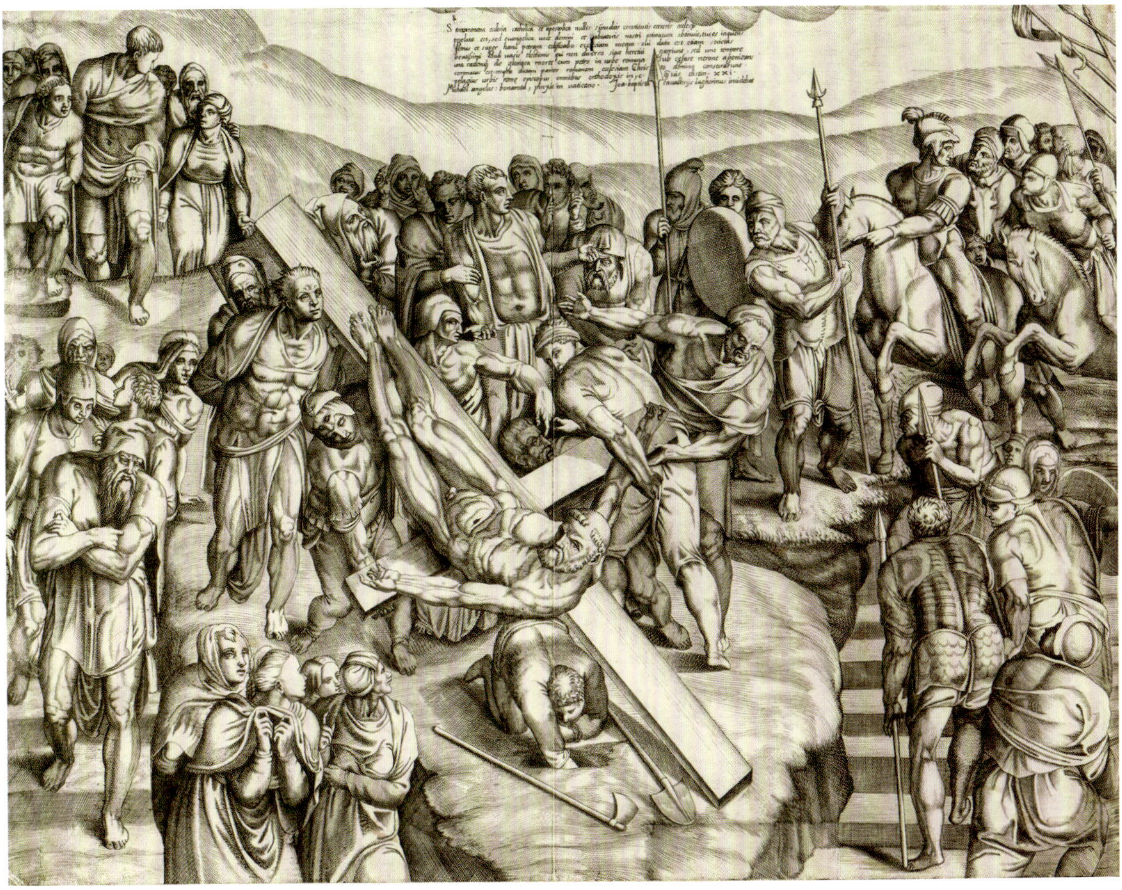

Fig. 26.
Michelangelo Buonarroti (Italian, 1475–1564).
Crucifixion of Saint Peter, 1545–50, fresco, 625 × 661 cm. Vatican City, Vatican Apostolic Palace, Pauline Chapel.

Fig. 27.
Giovanni Battista de' Cavalieri (Italian, ca. 1525–1601), after Michelangelo Buonarroti (Italian, 1475–1564).
Crucifixion of Saint Peter, engraving, 42.5 × 53.3 cm. London, British Museum.

they might move on to the fabulous and the monstrous, which would be much worse. So, when a person makes a work he should think it over, again and again, considering very carefully whether it is well or badly done, whether it will provoke scandal or contrition. But in sacred things I would not permit such fictions and I would exhort all painters not to introduce them. Not dissimilar, it seems to me, is the case of painting our Savior crucified on a tree with so many branches, with so many trunks, so many inscribed strips of paper and so many leafy twigs that it disgusts me to see them [fig. 28]. **[97]** It appears as though the Passion of our Savior has been reduced to fable rather than anything else, by all these fantasies and fictions.[374] Using this pretext, crosses are made so full of branches, leaves, balls, frills, and leafy twigs that they have lost the form of a cross. How much better it would be if all these things retained the simplicity of their true nature rather than being spoiled through these fictions, with the loss

374. On the iconography of the *Arbor Vitae* that is here being criticized, see Gertrud Schiller, *Iconography of Christian Art,* vol. 2, *The Passion of Christ* (London: Lund Humphries, 1972), 133–36.

of reputation and decorum. For there would be no lack of ways and means for those who seek out alternative methods to convey their thoughts."

M. Silvio said: "One could argue that those trunks, branches, and leaves you mention are only intended to show first the concordance of the New and Old Testaments and then the marvelous fruits that the wood of the Cross has produced through the Passion of our Savior: the greatest meanings reduced to a small image.[375] As for those crosses with balls and leaves, like those of the bell towers of the Santo at Padua, I think that they are intended to mean that the holy Cross will always be in flower, embellished with all the virtues and merits that one can imagine and with the fruits of grace that the church militant receives every day."[376]

M. Pulidoro replied: "This showing one thing and meaning another should never happen, because the Cross alone, simply represented, will carry these meanings and many others. One can make much fuller interpretations of the simple truth than of the fictional and adulterated. Christ our Savior was not crucified on flowering wood but on dry wood. If this really is its actual form and wood really is its actual material, why should it not be kept in its pure state?[377] And I would say further that in terms of devotion, a wooden cross in a hermitage, cave, or desert place moves me more than one found in a city made of silver or gold and decorated with jewels. Because in the former case I think about the simple truth, while in the latter I think about richness and ornament, about the nobility of the materials and the excellence of the craftsman.[378] **[98]** If I pick up

375. Genesis 2:9 describes two trees growing in the Garden of Eden: the tree of life and the tree of knowledge. Revelation 22:2 describes the tree of life "bearing twelve fruits, yielded its fruits every month, and the leaves of the tree were for the healing of the nations." Schiller, *Iconography,* 134, notes that Bonaventura in the thirteenth century had reactivated an earlier identification of the Cross and the Tree of Life.

376. The reference is to the campanili of the Basilica of Sant'Antonio at Padua. The basilica is known as the Santo.

377. On the preference for the literal over the metaphorical, see Gilio, this volume, 179–80.

378. Baronius, in his letters to his father, 1564, about the crucifix for the church of San Bartolomeo at Sora, writes that it should be placed on a "simple cross of chestnut wood, because the more natural, the greater the strength of devotion" (croce di castagna alla semplice, perché tanto più è di devotione quanto più si accosta al naturale). The crucifix was made by a disciple of Daniele da Volterra, for the love of God ("l'ha fatto un discepolo di Daniele per amor di Dio, essendo egli persona spirituale"). Baronius also says that he has never seen such fine workmanship ("non ho visto niuno di tanto bello artificio"). But he will not divulge the name of the maker in order not to subvert the merit of the work; see Luigi Gulia, "Premessa," in *Baronio e l'arte: Atti del Convegno Internazionale di Studi, Sora, 10–13 ottobre 1984,* ed. Romeo De Maio et al. (Sora: Centro di Studi Sorani Vincenzo Patriarca, 1985), xx. It is a contemporary example of the complex relationship between art and devotion: for Baronius, the highest artistry was desirable but it must be for the benefit of the devout. See Vincenzo Patriarca, *Il Crocifisso del Baronio nella storia e nell'arte* (Sora: La Moderna Grafica, 1947). Baronius's thoughts are very close to those articulated by M. Pulidoro.

Fig. 28.
Taddeo Gaddi (Florentine, active from ca. 1330, d. 1366).
Tree of Life (Arbor Vitae), 1330s, fresco, 1170 × 1120 cm (whole wall). Florence, Santa Croce, Refectory.

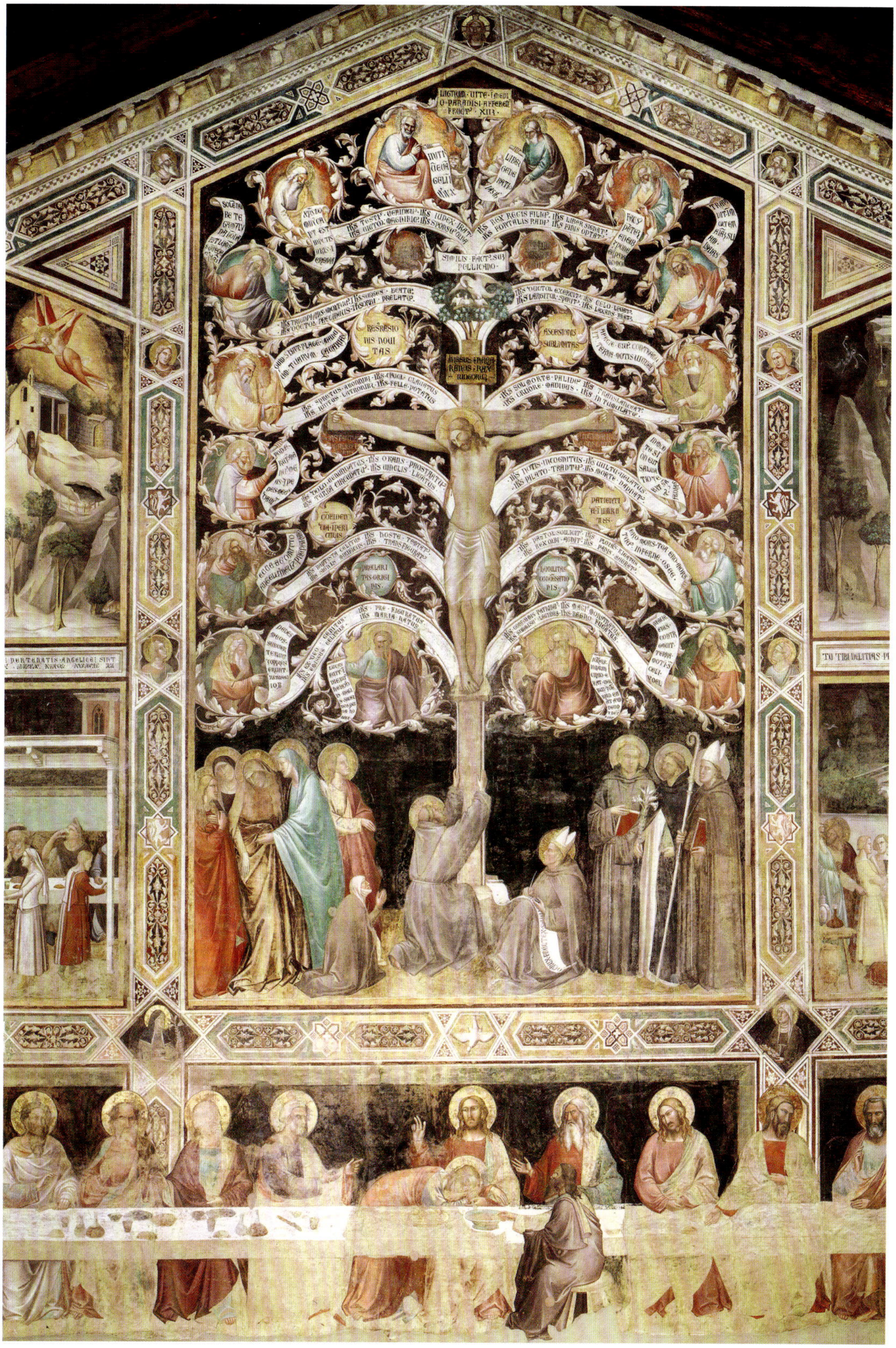

a golden cross and a wooden one, with the latter I feel contrition and become contemplative, while with the former I am like a miser who, in a thousand deluded ways, covets the value of the metal; and I sin more through avarice than I win merit from devotion, because the one is accompanied by humility, while avarice and pride swell the other. I think no one swells with pride when it is a matter of dry wood, while they do with gold; and no one humbles himself when it is a matter of gold, silver, or gems, but he does with poor materials. However, everything made for the glory of God is well made, because he too wished to be glorified with gold, silver, and gems, as it is written in the Old Testament.[379] But I'm talking about the power and efficacy that truth has in itself."

M. Vincenso said: "What do you say about the figures that Cardinal Farnese had painted in the hall of the Cancelleria, M. Pulidoro [fig. 29; see fig. 5]? Have you ever seen them?"

M. Pulidoro replied: "I have seen them and read about them in Doni's *Zucca,* where he writes a commentary on the whole of that mixed history.[380] I would say that they are well arranged, well understood, and well executed. Here and there, however, there are some in which fiction far outweighs truth so that to understand them one needs either the Sphinx or an interpreter or a commentary. To know that this is true, think about the fact that if ten people look at [the figures], they will give ten interpretations with no agreement between them."

M. Vincenso said: "We are not talking about ignorant people, because if one had to provide a commentary on every figure it would be such a business; and it would be too ridiculous to assume such ignorance, because these things are done for the educated and for gentlemen, not for ignorant plebeians, since these are not sacred images."

M. Pulidoro replied: "One thing I judge, M. Vincenso, is that God gave man a tongue so that he could express his thoughts in words and be understood. And if that had not been the case, that good man Averroes would never have sweat so much over expounding Aristotle, nor would Donatus and Servius have done the same with Virgil, nor would any of the others who expounded other philosophers, doctors, orators, poets, and historians.[381] **[99]** Saint Jerome discarded

379. Durandus, *Rationale divinorum officiorum,* 1.3.46 and 1.1.12, citing Exodus 25.

380. Anton Francesco Doni, *Foglie della Zucca* (Venice: Francesco Marcolini, 1552), 133–49. In his letter to Lelio Torelli in the *Zucca,* Doni describes in detail Vasari's frescoes in the Sala of the Palazzo della Cancelleria (the so-called Sala dei Cento Giorni), in which real and allegorical figures are used together so that history can be made to exemplify the moral virtues of the pope; Kliemann, *Gesta Dipinte,* 43. The frescoes were executed in 1546, commissioned by Alessandro Farnese, who, as vice-chancellor of the Church, occupied the Cancelleria as his official residence. See Gilio, this volume, 102–4.

381. Averroes (1126–98) was an Islamic philosopher from Andalusia who defended Aristotelian thought; Aelius Donatus was a fourth-century Roman grammarian who wrote a

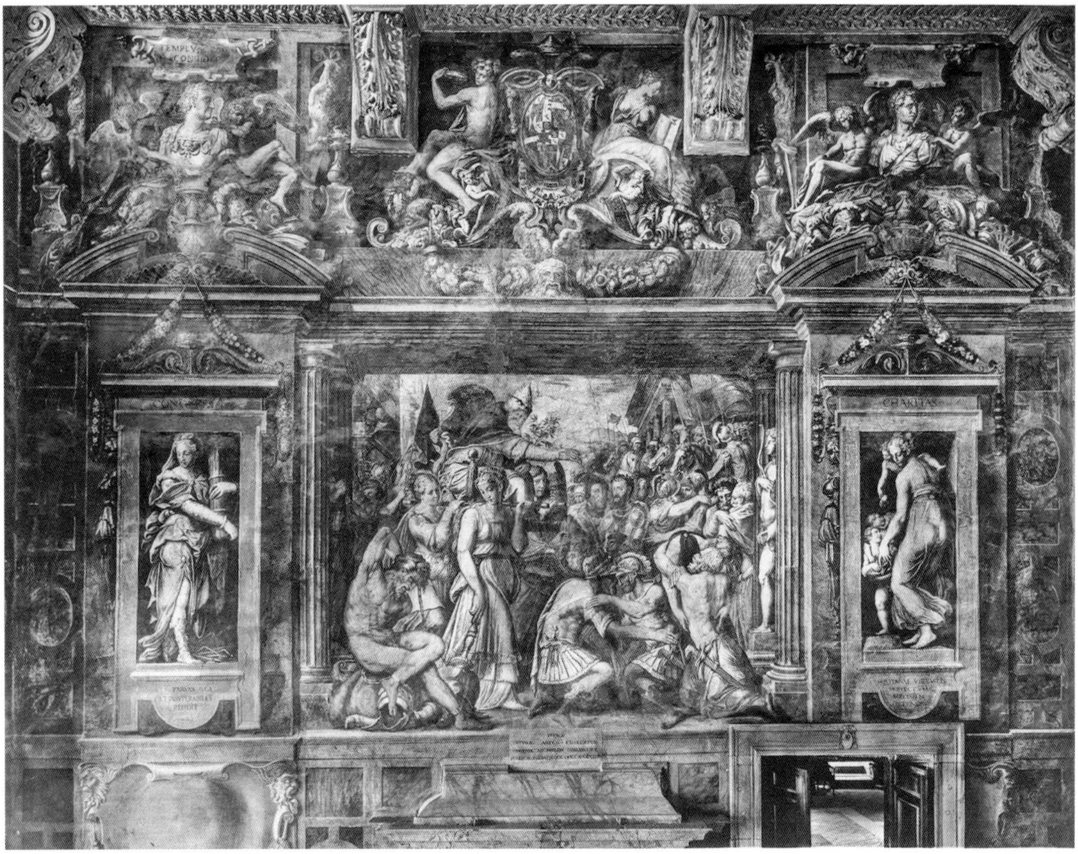

Persius because he did not understand him.[382] Gellius severely rebukes a young man who endlessly spoke to other men about the Twelve Tablets in order not to be understood.[383] Why did your own Bartolus, Baldus, and many other learned men labor, if not to expound the laws?[384] Why did Augustine, Jerome, Gregory, Ambrose, and others labor, if not to make the Scriptures accessible and

commentary on Virgil. Servius, also a fourth-century grammarian, wrote a commentary on Virgil that relied heavily on the work of Donatus.

382. Aulus Persius Flaccus, the Stoic satirist. This story about Jerome, current in the sixteenth century, may not have an ancient source; see J. G. F. Powell, "Persius' First Satire: A Re-examination," in *Author and Audience in Latin Literature,* ed. Tony Woodman and Jonathan Powell (Cambridge: Cambridge University Press, 1992), 150. Jerome actually made a great deal of use of Persius, often quoting him. Dolce, *L'Aretino* in Barocchi, *Trattati,* 1:191 (Roskill, *Dolce's "Aretino,"* 166–67), tells the story of the rejection of Persius on the grounds of his obscurity, but attributes this action to a "learned and saintly man," without mention of Jerome.

383. The *Duodecim tabularum;* there is a discussion of the obscurity of the twelve tables in Aulus Gellius, *Attic Nights* [*Noctes Atticae*], vol. 3, *Books 14–20,* trans. J. C. Rolfe, Loeb Classical Library 212 (Cambridge, MA: Harvard University Press, 1927), 406–7 (20.1.4).

384. These were the famous jurists Bartolo da Sassoferrato (1313–57) and Baldo degli Ubaldi (1327–1400).

Fig. 29.
Giorgio Vasari (Italian, 1511–74).
Paul III as Peacemaker, 1546, fresco. Rome, Palazzo della Cancelleria, Sala dei Cento Giorni.

available? Have your laws not ordained that agreements between men are worthless, if [those men] do not understand one another? If you want to dream, read the *Hypnerotomachia* of Poliphilus, and you will see the difference between the easily understood and the obscure.[385] There is nothing for which Cicero and Virgil are so highly praised as for their fluency and their learning. For me to see a picture and not understand what it means is like listening to a barbarian and not understanding what he says, or reading a book and not knowing what it is about. What is not understood cannot be reflected on, and what is not reflected on cannot be judged. It would be like an ignorant person with an illustrated [*istoriato*] book, who, because he cannot read, just looks at the pictures. The clearer and more accessible the thing, the more beautiful it is. If you were to read a story that was confused, obscure, and tangled, would you not be obliged to do as Saint Jerome did with Persius? Fictions must be infrequent and well arranged in order to give pleasure, in histories I mean. Because if these things are done solely to please the eye, then nothing more need be said, but if they are also done to convey meaning, then they must be arranged so that they can be understood.[386] There are some who, having written a sonnet or something else incomprehensible, believe they've renewed Pegasus's spring.[387] They seem not to realize that if there had not been all the other delights that made him immortal, Petrarch would have been Fra Baldassarre Olimpo's companion for the song 'Mai non vo' più cantar,' since had he wanted to be understood, he would never have written it.[388] The same can be said, I think, of those who create a work and, having done so, only risk showing it on days of ill omen to the few people who would venture to come out, since they are afraid that sunshine and air might steal it from them.[389] **[100]** What is the point of hiding away a treasure that might enrich many, here on Earth, without profit or honor to oneself? To return to our subject I say that these things should be easily understood and clear; I do not praise the painter who introduces among his mixtures [*misture*] such fabulous things that they swallow up truth and take away dignity and beauty from the story, reducing it to fiction or fable."

---

385. Francesco Colonna, *Hypnerotomachia Poliphili* (Venice: Aldo Manuzio, 1499).

386. The blending of fact and fiction echoes Horace, *Ars Poetica,* 462–63 (lines 151–52). On these lines, see also Gilio, this volume, 131–32, 156, 199–200. That poetry and thus painting can instruct or delight, or do both (profit and delight—"aut prodesse . . . aut delectare"), concluding that he who can do both appeals to everyone, is laid out by Horace; see *Ars Poetica,* 478–79 (lines 333–46).

387. The winged Pegasus, striking a rock on Mount Helicon, gave birth to the Hippocrene Spring; the spring became a symbol of poetic inspiration.

388. Petrarch, *Canzoniere* (1996), 160–61, poem 105, "I never want to sing the way I used to . . ."; and Petrarch, *Canzoniere* (1958), 140 (see Barocchi, *Trattati,* 2:608, n3 to Gilio p. 99). It is especially complex and difficult. On Baldassarre Olimpo, see note 187.

389. The phrase "days of ill omen" is a translation of "dì egizziaci" (*dies Aegyptiaci*), the evil or unlucky days of the medieval calendar.

M. Ruggiero asked: "What difference do you think there is between the fictional and the fabulous?"

M. Pulidoro replied: "A great difference. The fictional is that which is not part of the event [*atto*] being represented, but which could be. And note at this point that where the true cannot have a place, the fictional cannot be, for the fictional is nothing other than the mask of the true.[390] The fabulous is that which neither is nor can be; we will explain that in the remainder of this conversation."[391]

M. Troilo said: "Tell me something, how should painters organize their works so as to harmonize the fictional and the true?"[392]

M. Pulidoro replied: "What the true is you can discover for yourself. Virgil teaches us how one should mix in the fictional when he tells the story of Aeneas's journey to Italy. He imagined that fortune carried Aeneas to the shores of Africa where Dido had built Carthage, and that Dido, being in love with him, organized the hunts and the other events that followed, and finally killed herself on account of her love. Yet this is not true, for, according to some, Carthage was built more than 140 years after Aeneas's arrival in Italy and more than 60 years before Rome was built. And Dido killed herself not out of love for Aeneas, whom she could never have known, but to escape the troublesome Iarbas, king of Libya, who wished to take her as his wife while the Carthaginians put pressure on her to accept. This and a great number of other things that Virgil wrote are types of mixture [*mistura*]. As for fabulous things, they are imagined when a form is given to something that does not exist, as when the same poet imagines the figure of Fury.[393] For this is nothing other than an emotion excited in a man's heart as a result of some injury received for which he wants revenge. Because of its unbridled and bestial quality, [Fury] was given the form of a monstrous rather than a natural man. **[101]** In order to show he was the antithesis of peace and quiet, he was represented tied up with great iron chains, with his arms behind him and seated on different types of weapons and instruments

390. The idea that fiction has a place only where truth has a place ("quod ibi demum habet locum fictio, ubi est possibile quod habeat locum veritas") had been asserted by Baldus in his commentary on the *Digest* of Justinian. It was predicated on the idea that the law imitated nature; see Ernst H. Kantorowicz, *The King's Two Bodies: A Study in Medieval Political Theology* (Princeton, NJ: Princeton University Press, 1957), 306, 306–7n81. Augustine had argued that a fiction could be understood as a "figura veritatis"; Augustine, *Quaestionum Evangeliorum libri duo,* in *S. Augustini Tomi Tertii pars altera,* Patrologia Latina, series prima 35, ed. Jacques-Paul Migne (Paris: Migne, 1845), 1362 (2.51). See Gilio, this volume, 110.

391. On Gilio's distinctions between the true, the fictional, and the fabulous, see note 46.

392. See Gilio, this volume, 199–200.

393. On the figure of Fury (Furor), see Virgil, *Aeneid, Books 1–6,* 282–83 (1.293–96). The description that follows suggests that Gilio consulted Vincenzo Cartari, *Le imagini con la spositione de i dei de gli antichi* (Venice: Francesco Marcolini, 1556), 79r.

of war; the kinds of things appropriate to fury, anger, and the desire for revenge. Along with Fury are often found Horror, Fear, Discord, War, Hate, and other such things converted into human form, each with its appropriate qualities. We also read of another kind of thing: fabulous and fictional together. For example, when Aeneas went down into hell in the company of the sibyl, holding the golden bough; passed over the Styx on Charon's boat; placated Cerberus, the three-headed dog; spoke to his father in the Elysian Fields; and saw the Romans who would descend from his blood.[394] Also when, in order to prevent the building of Rome, Juno took from hell the fury Allecto, who wrapped a snake around the neck of Lavinia's mother, Amata, infecting her with such rage that in her fury and madness she ran all over the city and into the forest.[395] Another example is when Allecto, in the form of an old woman, appeared to Turnus, provoking him to take up arms against Aeneas in order to stop the marriage.[396] Or when Venus made Vulcan forge an enchanted shield that showed images of Roman deeds up to the time of Augustus (it certainly must have been a large shield to contain so many things).[397] Many other fictions, discovered by Greek and Latin poets, are included in this [sort of] mixture [*mistura*], and indeed you can recognize them, provided you are familiar with whatever story it is. Examples of the purely fabulous, when it remains true to its nature, are the ships of Aeneas changed into sea nymphs, or men transformed into animals, birds, fish, trees, plants, rocks, and other such things.[398] Discovered and represented by poets, these are things that not only do not exist but never could."

M. Francesco said: "The painters before Michelangelo understood little or nothing of such mixtures, I think; for the art of painting was almost lost to human knowledge. As a person of vigorous intellect [*ingegno vivo*], Michelangelo always worked to restore the art to exactly what it had been among the famous ancient painters and sculptors. So he found new ways that delighted people so much that they have been taken up and used as much in pure histories as in poetic and mixed compositions. **[102]** Then Raphael with his celebrated school bestowed a great deal on the art, and if he had lived one could have expected great things from his marvelous intellect [*ingegno*] [fig. 30].[399]

394. Virgil, *Aeneid, Books 1–6,* 548–97 (6.236–901).
395. Virgil, *Aeneid, Books 7–12,* 24–31 (7.323–405).
396. Virgil, *Aeneid, Books 7–12,* 30–35 (7.406–74).
397. Virgil, *Aeneid, Books 7–12,* 104–13 (8.626–731).
398. Virgil, *Aeneid, Books 7–12,* 122–23 (9.114–22); Bade gave the metamorphosis of Aeneas's ships into nymphs as an example of the fabulous. For Gilio's definition of the fabulous, see Gilio, this volume, 100–102.
399. M. Francesco, picking up what M. Vincenso said earlier about Michelangelo's contribution to painting as a branch of knowledge, abandons the term *scienza* and subsumes it within his praise for Michelangelo's restoration of the art of painting; see note 345. Dempsey notes

Other famous painters have helped to raise up this beautiful art and restore it to its earlier state. So now, if the ancient rules were observed, painting has been restored to a healthy state and has a higher reputation than it has had for many centuries. With the revival of the memory of ancient [practices], artists have borrowed inventions from the poets. For example, when wanting to portray war they have painted the temple of Janus open and then closed for peace, because that is what happened in fact among the Romans. Inside they have painted Fury chained above a pile of arms, and Romulus and Remus united together as Virgil imagined them, using examples and figures that have given spectators great pleasure [see fig. 29].[400] Now this is how painters can make use of metaphors and metonymies in an attractive way, and many other [rhetorical] figures too; so if one of them understands how to arrange and compose [the figures] properly, he will create a fine and beautiful mixture."[401]

M. Pulidoro said: "They have found another fiction, which I think will last forever: giving human form to Honor and Virtue, to which Marcus [Claudius] Marcellus once built temples; and Servius Tullius did the same for Fear and Terror, giving male form to those with masculine names, and female form to those with feminine names.[402] Such things were invented by the ancients in order to eulogize emperors, kings, and great captains as a sign of their glorious deeds. But such inventions seem to me more suitable on triumphal arches than on walls, although nowadays they are put on both."

M. Silvio said: "Before arches were introduced, the ancients used to set up what was taken from their vanquished enemies as trophies; among the Latins, Romulus did so, and for this purpose he built the temple of Jupiter Feretrius on the spot where an oak grew on the Capitoline. Here he hung the arms of Acron, captain of the men of Caenina; and these were called 'spoils of honor.'[403] **[103]** After him, only Cornelius Cossus and Marcus Marcellus raised spoils of

Raphael's use of the mixed mode—what Dempsey calls the ornamented epic style—in the Vatican, especially in Raphael's *Battle of the Milvian Bridge* in the Sala di Costantino (see fig. 30); Dempsey, "Mythic Inventions," 70.

400. Virgil, *Aeneid, Books 1–6,* 282–83 (1:291–96). Gilio may have been alluding to Vasari's fresco of Peace ("Storia della Pace") in the Cancelleria. According to Doni (*Foglie della Zucca,* 134–49, esp. 145–47; see note 380), this fresco shows Paul III being carried away from the closed temple of Janus and also the chained figure of Fury (Furor) seated on a pile of arms; see also Kliemann, *Gesta Dipinte,* in note 52 above.

401. See Gilio, *Topica poetica,* 59v–63v (metaphor), and 67v–69v (metonymy).

402. On the temples of Honos and Virtus, see Plutarch's *Marcellus,* in idem, *Lives,* vol. 5, *Agesilaus and Pompey; Pelopidas and Marcellus,* trans. Bernadotte Perrin, Loeb Classical Library 87 (Cambridge, MA: Harvard University Press, 1917), 512–13 (§28). On the temples of Pallor and Pavor, founded by Tullus Hostilius (not Servius Tullius), see Livy, *History of Rome,* vol. 1, *Books 1–2,* trans. B. O. Foster, Loeb Classical Library 114 (Cambridge, MA: Harvard University Press, 1919), 98–99 (1.27.7).

403. Livy, *History of Rome,* 1:38–41 (1.10): "spolia opime."

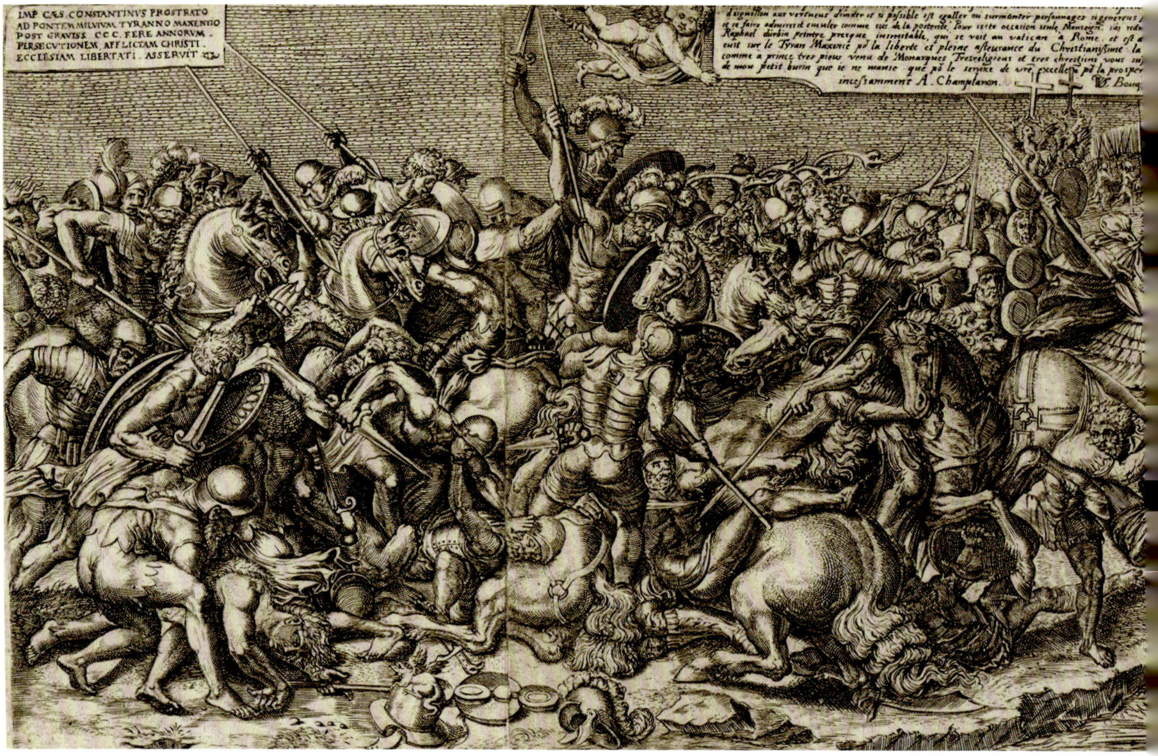

Fig. 30.
Pierre Woeiriot (French, active 1555–96), after Raphael (Italian, 1483–1520).
Battle of Constantine against Maxentius, engraving, 15.1 × 49.9 cm. London, British Museum.

honor as trophies.[404] Over time, other trophies were made in other places, such as those of Claudius Marius on the Esquiline hill, which can still be seen today in Rome [fig. 31].[405] Other consuls did the same, I think, but it has not been recorded. The Greeks also did the same and frequently set up trophies on the precise site of their victory, like Agathocles did.[406] This practice continued until the reign of Emperor Titus, when, instead of trophies being displayed, a triumphal arch was built, which was carved with scenes from the Jewish Wars [fig. 32]. Pliny says that this was the first arch built to mark a triumph in Rome and that all the others were modeled on it.[407] Carvings on the arches showed images of Victory holding a palm, as well as images of Rome, Peace,

404. On Cossus, see Livy, *History of Rome,* 2:320–21 (4.20). On Marcus Claudius Marcellus, see Livy, *History of Rome,* 4:560–61 (20); and Plutarch, *Marcellus,* 5:454–55 (§8).

405. The trophies of Marius were on the Esquiline in Gilio's time and were subsequently moved to the Capitoline; see Bober and Rubinstein, *Renaissance Artists and Antique Sculpture,* 205 (no. 174).

406. Agathocles set up a trophy after his victory over the Macedonians at Corcyra; see Diodorus Siculus, *Library of History,* vol. 11, *Books 21–32,* trans. Francis R. Walton, Loeb Classical Library 409 (Cambridge, MA: Harvard University Press, 1957), 8–11 (21.2.3).

407. Pliny, who dedicated his *Natural History* to Titus, mentions the recently introduced practice of building such arches but does not comment on individual ones; see *NH,* 9:148–49 (book 34, §27). Gilio is mistaken when he claims Pliny's authority for the idea that the arch of Titus was the earliest triumphal arch.

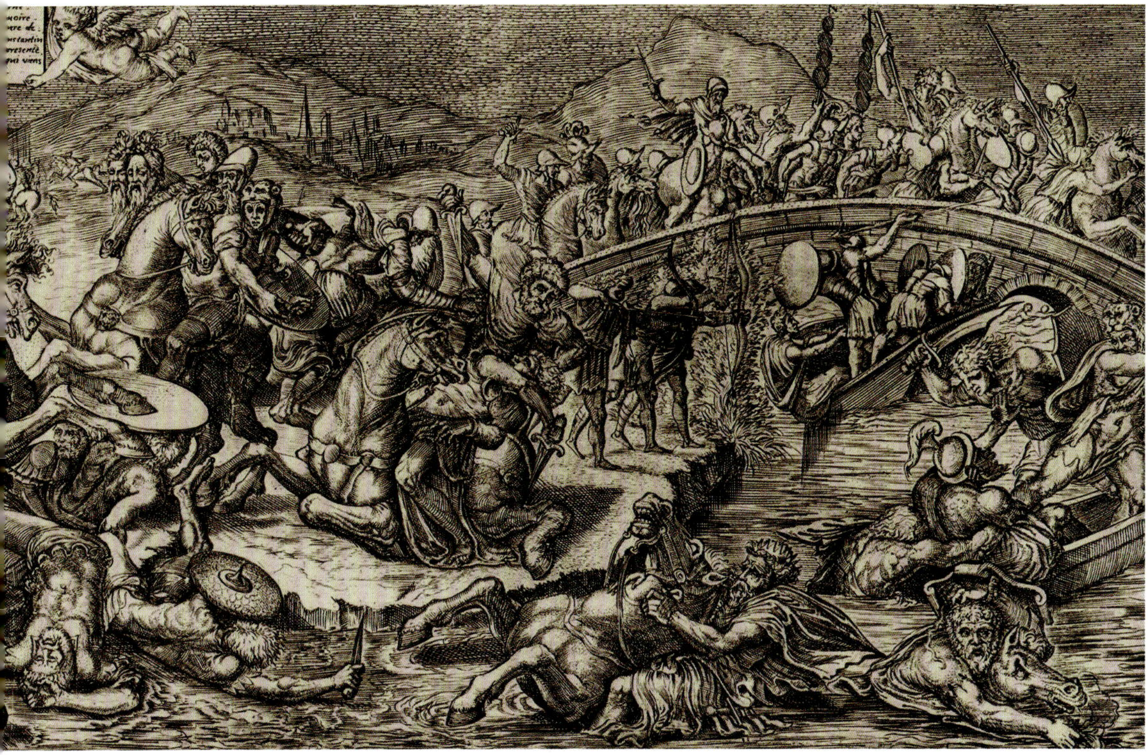

and other such figures, as you described earlier. The use of such figures was, I think, copied by the Romans from the Greeks, for that was the way Apelles painted Castor and Pollux on a panel with Alexander the Great and the image of Victory. The same artist also painted Alexander the Great in another panel, with an image of War being paraded in front of the chariot with his hands tied, while Nicomachus, Aristodemus's son, painted Victory snatching up a quadriga.[408] But what am I doing enumerating things that are known to the most ordinary people? One can also read how temples were dedicated to such fictions; they were worshiped as gods and goddesses, as in the case of Fear and Terror, Honor and Virtue, Concord, Youth, Fever, Fortune under many names, Peace, Tranquility, Piety, Modesty divided into patrician and plebeian forms, Health, Hope, Good Fortune, and many such others."

M. Pulidoro replied: "This sort of paganism will always exist, since it is now too well founded in people's minds. So Christians, prompted by these examples, have learned to give human form to Religion, to Faith, to Hope, to Charity, and to other virtues, which, along with those, are mixed up with sacred matters and are known as theological virtues. And they are classified with sacred things only

408. Pliny, *NH,* 9:330–31, 340–41 (book 35, §93 and §108). In modern editions of Pliny, the name of Nicomachus's father is given as Aristides.

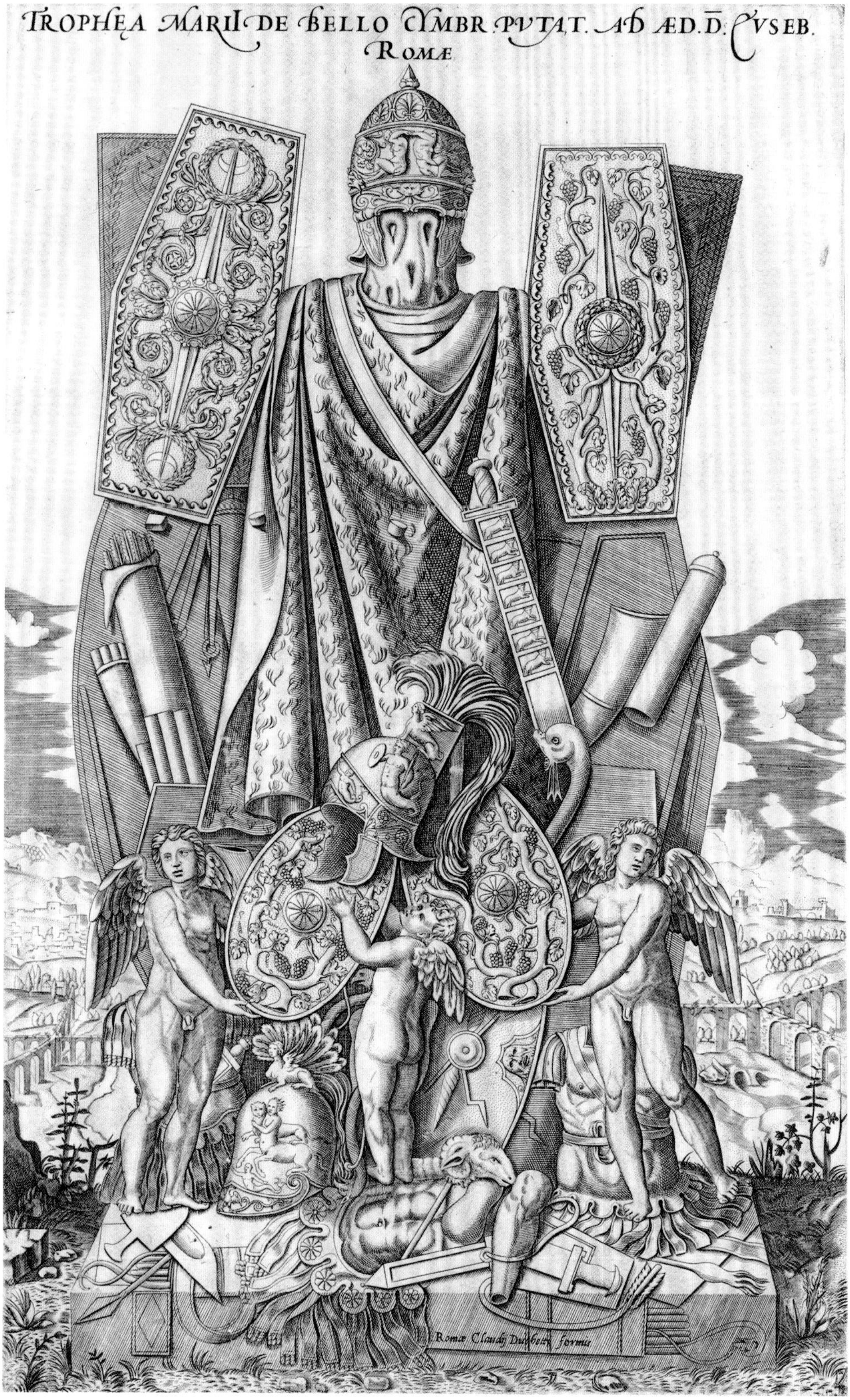
TROPHEA MARII DE BELLO CYMBR. PUTAT. AD AED. D. EUSEB. ROMAE
Romae Claudij Duchetti formis

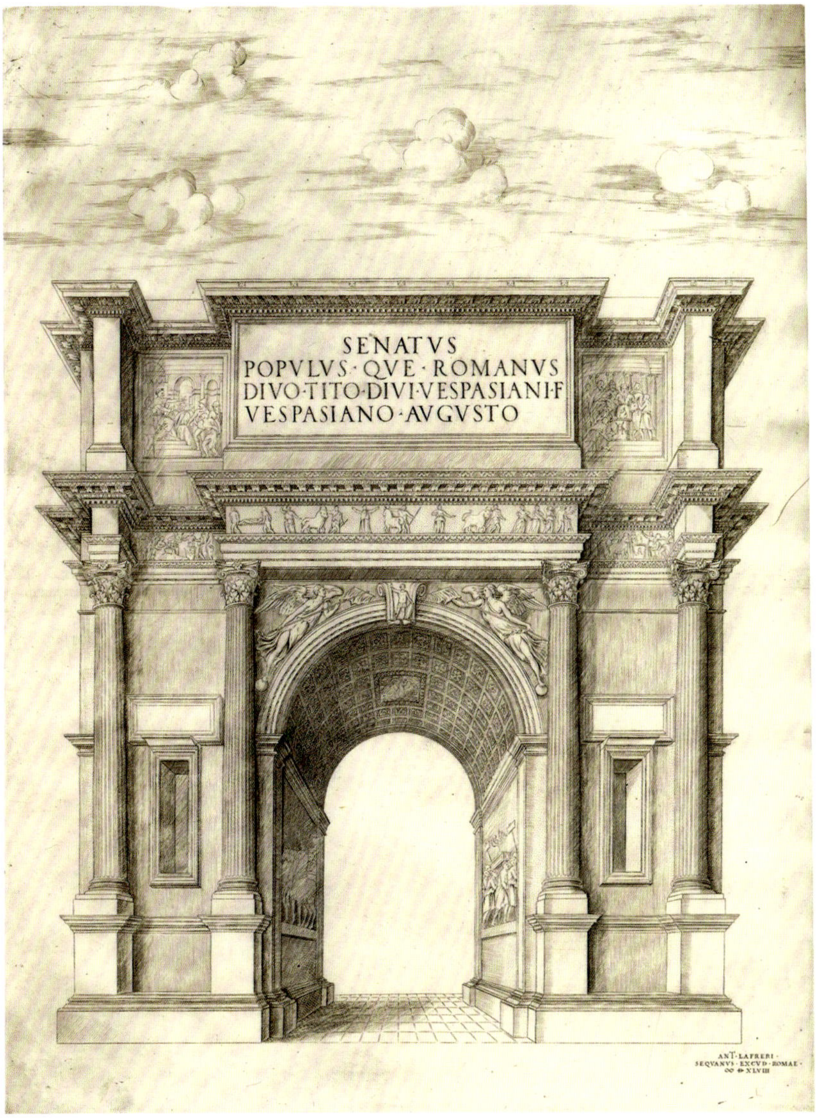

Fig. 31.
Anonymous, published by Claude Duchet (French, active in Italy 1565–85).
Trophies of Marius, 1545–60, engraving, 38 × 24 cm. London, British Museum.

Fig. 32.
Anonymous, published by Antoine Lafréry (French, 1512–77, active in Italy).
Arch of Titus, front view, 1549, engraving, 50 × 38.4 cm. London, British Museum.

because they are virtues, seeing that the pure spirit of religion does not require anything but virtuous things, and especially these. **[104]** Many add them as ornaments for arches and other such things; but I don't approve of their use for profane purposes, unless they represent worthy memories of great men, as in the case of Cardinal Farnese, who arranged them in a pleasing manner, with the most beautiful order and admirable meanings. But I would like these mixtures [*misture*] always to be presented in such a way that they can be understood without great racking of one's brains."[409]

---

409. Gilio is again referring to Vasari's paintings in the Cancelleria, where personifications of Religion and of some of the theological virtues are to be found. See Gilio, this volume, 212, for M. Pulidoro's earlier, similar comments on the Cancelleria frescoes. See also note 52.

M. Francesco said: "I think that the ancients taught the moderns the practice of giving female form to the virtues that are called liberal, like Geometry, Philosophy, Astrology, Music, Rhetoric, Grammar, Arithmetic, not to mention Theology.[410] And today these are most frequently placed on pyramids and tombs erected to dead princes and to gentlemen whom the world celebrates for their fame, excellence, and greatness."

M. Pulidoro said: "I think that, in order to show the different qualities of men, [the moderns] have learned to use different animals and birds as symbols: a snake biting its tail is used for the representation of time, the parrot for loquacity, the hippopotamus for cruelty, the stork for piety, the cockerel for the dawn, the owl and the bat for the night, the eel for envy, the dolphin for speed, and for a fickle, weak-minded person, the chameleon and the octopus. These and other such things are done in imitation of the Egyptians and can be found in abundance on the small obelisks that came from Egypt, they say."

M. Vincenso said: "I don't know what else to say, except that these things have something charming and ingenious about them, allowing important meanings to be conveyed in a small image. And if this had not had something worthy about it, the world would not have accepted it nor continued to use it over so many years; and now more than ever it is in use all over the world.[411] For one cannot do to such figures what the famous painter Pauson of Sicily did. He was asked to paint a horse rolling in the dust, but instead he showed it galloping, in a cloud of dust. Seeing this, the patron who had commissioned the work refused to pay him, because he had not respected the agreement. **[105]** Pauson laughed, saying: 'Just turn the painting the other way up, and you'll see that it is what you asked for.' The patron did so and saw that the painting was as he wished, so he paid the artist in full.[412] The things we are talking about cannot be turned like this, because the symbols always carry the same meaning. But tell me one thing, M. Pulidoro: is it a modern or an ancient practice to paint episodes from one's own life, as the Duke of Urbino did, or from the lives of others, as Cardinal Farnese did?" [fig. 33].[413]

---

410. These are the seven liberal arts plus theology. See Durandus, *Rationale divinorum officiorum,* 1.3.22, for personifications of the virtues.

411. As evidence of contemporary interest in hieroglyphics, Barocchi (*Trattati,* 2:610, n4 to Gilio p. 104) cites Piero Valeriano, *Hieroglyphica: sive; De sacris Aegyptiorum literis commentarii* (Basel: Palma Ising, 1556). Gilio claims that the conventional character of these symbols avoids the ambiguities of paintings that imitate nature.

412. Aelian, *Historical Miscellany,* ed. and trans. N. G. Wilson, Loeb Classical Library 486 (Cambridge, MA: Harvard University Press, 1997), 464–65 (14.15).

413. The Duke of Urbino at the Villa Imperiale at Pesaro. For the episodes of the life of Francesco Maria della Rovere, see Antonio Pinelli and Orietta Rossi, *Genga Architetto: Aspetti della cultura urbinate del primo 500* (Rome: Bulzoni, 1971), 128, 188n36 (e.g., Sala

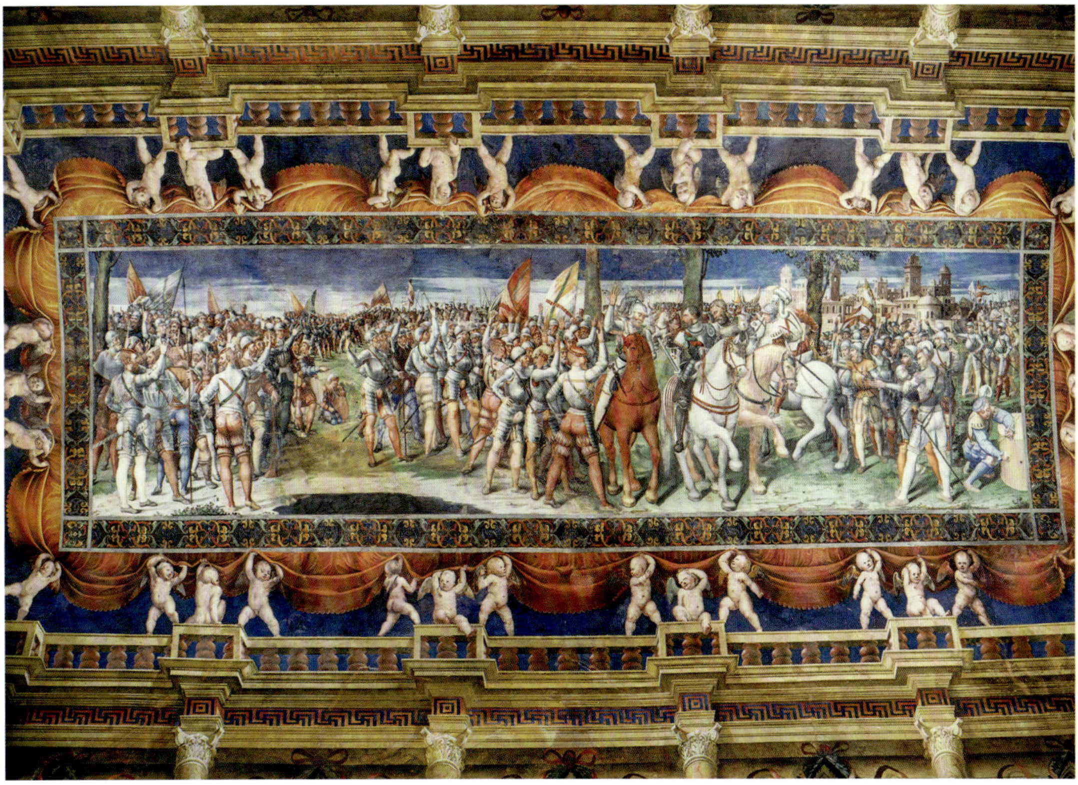

M. Pulidoro replied: "It is undoubtedly a very ancient custom. Pliny tells us that the painter Bularchus, who lived at the time of Romulus, painted the wars of the Magnetes, while Pamphilus painted the victory of the Athenians at Filemonte, Aristides of Thebes the wars of Alexander the Great against the Persians, Nealces the naval battle between the Persians and the Egyptians (and to show that it was fought on the Nile, he painted a donkey drinking and a crocodile lying in wait to seize it), and, lastly, Teodoro the Trojan War.[414] Many Romans commissioned paintings in various places in order to leave a

del Giuramento, with the vault fresco of the oath sworn by the soldiers before the victory on the colle dell'Imperiale); also Kliemann, *Gesta Dipinte,* 21–28. Gilio had dedicated his *Trattato de la emulatione che il demonio ha fatto a Dio,* printed at Venice in 1563, to the Duchess of Urbino, Vittoria Farnese, who was Cardinal Alessandro Farnese's sister. For a further reference to Vasari's frescoes for Alessandro Farnese (representing acts of Paul III at the Cancelleria) and to Salviati's in the Palazzo Farnese, see note 52 and fig. 6.

414. On Bularchus, see Pliny, *NH,* 9:300–303 (book 35, §55); on Pamphilus, see Pliny, *NH,* 9:316–17 (book 35, §76); on Aristides, see Pliny, *NH,* 9:332–35 (book 35, §98–99); and on Nealces, see Pliny, *NH,* 9:364–65 (book 35, §142). The name of the place given as Filemonte by Gilio is now read as Phlius, and the name he gives as Teodoro is now read as Theorus; see Pliny, *NH,* 316–17, 366–67 (book 35, §76 and §144). On the question of the texts of Pliny available to Gilio, see Barocchi, *Trattati,* 2:610, n3 to Gilio p. 105.

Fig. 33.
Girolamo Genga (Italian, 1476–1551).
The Oath, 1528, fresco on the ceiling of the Sala del Giuramento. Pesaro, Villa Imperiale.

record of their glorious deeds to future generations. Messala princeps placed a panel—a work by Manlius Valerius, featuring the wars he had waged against the Carthaginians in Sicily, when he defeated Hieron—in the Curia Hostilia. Lucius Scipio commissioned a representation of the wars he had fought in Asia against Antiochus (which greatly upset Scipio the Elder, since his son was taken prisoner); L. Ostilius Mancinus commissioned the destruction of Carthage to show that he had been the first to breach the walls.[415] Others commemorated their deeds in more lasting monuments, like the triumphal arches, which were made for Titus, Severus, and Constantine; others, like Trajan and M. Antoninus Pius, made beautiful, tall columns. Caracalla ordered all the wars that his father had fought, and his triumphs, to be painted in a portico, as Spartianus writes.[416] Maximinus, the first emperor to bear the name, had the wars he waged against the Germans portrayed on panels that he placed in the Curia.[417] Many years later, this custom passed to the Greeks and thus Emperor Justinian ordered fine representations of the wars that he had fought, through Belisarius, against the Persians, the Goths, and the Vandals, both on land and sea, and he had this done not on panels or canvas, but in his Augustaeum, as Procopius has it.[418] **[106]** In these representations, the imperial navies were beautifully shown fighting on the sea, vanquishing their enemies, seizing their ships, routing armies on the land, and taking prisoner the Gothic king Vitiges, in Ravenna, and the king of the Vandals, Gelimer, in Africa. Belisarius, who had undertaken these campaigns, was shown triumphant, entering Constantinople and presenting Justinian with those kings and other noble barons. A long time later, and with more lasting renown, Pope Eugenius IV ordered portrayed, on the bronze doors of St. Peter's at Rome, records of the many peoples who had been reconciled with the Church by his doing, as [Flavio] Biondo writes.[419] So, to conclude, I

415. These references are all from Pliny, *NH*, 9:276–77 (book 35, §22–23). The names Messala and Valerius seem to be derived from Manius Valerius Maximus Messala, who had his victory over the Carthaginians painted on a wall in the Senate-house at Rome.

416. Aelius Spartianus, *Antoninus Caracallus*, in *Historia Augusta: Volume II*, trans. David Magie, Loeb Classical Library 140 (Cambridge, MA: Harvard University Press, 1924), 2:24–25 (9.6).

417. Julius Capitolinus, *The Two Maximini*, in *Historia Augusta: Volume II*, trans. David Magie, Loeb Classical Library 140 (Cambridge, MA: Harvard University Press, 1924), 338–39 (12.10–11).

418. Procopius describes the vestibule of the palace of Justinian at Constantinople, which had a mosaic ceiling decorated with scenes of victories and of Belisarius presenting the emperor with the spoils; see Procopius of Caesarea, *Constructions de Justinien Ier: Peri ktismaton = De aedificiis*, with introduction, translation, commentary, and index by Denis Roques, posthumous publication ed. Eugenio Amato and Jacques Schamp (Alessandria: Edizioni dell'Orso, 2011), 1.10.15–19.

419. Flavio Biondo, *Roma ristaurata et Italia illustrata, tradotta in lingua volgare per Lucio Fauno* (Venice: Michele Tramezzino, 1542), 13r. The deeds of Eugenius IV on Filarete's bronze doors include representations of the pope's reception of Emperor John Paleologus in

maintain that this custom has always existed and, although it may have fallen into disuse, Francesco Maria, Duke of Urbino, ordered excellent painters to portray his worthy military deeds in several rooms of the Villa Imperiale outside Pesaro (so that he would be remembered by future generations).[420] I think this is what provided the model for Cardinal Farnese's portrayal of the deeds of Pope Paul [III] in the hall of the palace of the Cancelleria and in the Palazzo Farnese at Campo de' Fiori [see figs. 5, 6].[421] That it was customary among the ancients is recorded by Virgil, who imagined that there were paintings of the Trojan wars in Juno's temple at Carthage."[422]

M. Troilo said: "I would like to hear whether you think the custom of painting temples is ancient or modern."

M. Pulidoro replied: "As I said, Virgil tells us that it was ancient.[423] This is also borne out by the works of various artists dedicated in different temples. Pliny writes that Polygnotus, an ancient and most excellent artist, painted the temple of Apollo at Delphi, and Protogenes the temple of Minerva.[424] This custom was then brought to Rome where Fabius the painter, from the noble Fabii family, painted the temple of Health and Pacuvius the poet painted the temple of Hercules on the Forum Boarium.[425] Besides paintings, many statues were also dedicated in temples: the most noble statues of the Amazons at the temple of Diana at Ephesus, made by Polycleitus, Phidias, Cresilas, and Cydon, to be judged and compared by the very best artists;[426] at the temple of Lacinian Juno,

Ferrara, of the Council of Florence, and of the Abbot Andrew receiving the decree for the unification of Eastern and Western churches; also of the arrival at Rome of the Ethiopian Jacobite delegation (1441); see John Pope-Hennessy, *Italian Renaissance Sculpture* (London: Phaidon, 1996), 398–99.

420. Kliemann, *Gesta Dipinte*, 21–28; and Giorgio Vasari, "Vite di Girolamo e di Bartolomeo Genga," in Vasari, *Le vite de' più eccellenti pittori, scultori, e architettori: Nelle redazioni del 1550 e 1568*, vol. 5, ed. Rosanna Bettarini and Paola Barocchi (Florence: S.P.E.S., 1984), 348–49. Note that in Gilio, *Topica poetica*, 7v–8r, some of these same examples are used to illustrate the idea of imitation—namely, Francesco Maria della Rovere imitated Justinian and Cardinal Farnese imitated Francesco Maria. See note 413.

421. Another reference to Vasari's Sala dei Cento Giorni in the Cancelleria and Salviati's Sala dei Fasti Farnesiani in the Palazzo Farnese (see note 52 and fig. 6).

422. The subject of the mixed painter, which M. Pulidoro had been asked to speak about, has been forgotten. After this digression on the subject of the history of paintings representing episodes from the lives of individuals, further digressions follow: evidence about the history of painting temples and the history of painting churches, and finally a statement about how sacred pictures should be painted. It is only at the very end (Gilio, this volume, 237–39) that M. Pulidoro resumes his discussion of the mixed painter.

423. Barocchi notes that Braun used the same example; see Braun, *De imaginibus*, 144 (in Barocchi, *Trattati*, 2:611, n3 to Gilio p. 106). This is true; however, Braun uses it as an example of what to avoid—that is to say, secular history in a temple, which is not Gilio's purpose.

424. Pliny, *NH*, 9:304–7, 334–37 (book 35, §59 and §101).

425. Pliny, *NH*, 9:274–75 (book 35, §19).

426. Pliny, *NH*, 9:166–67 (book 34, §53).

the famous Venus by Zeuxis, portrayed from the five maidens of Croton, as Cicero, Pliny, and other writers recorded, but this was not a statue but a painting.[427] **[107]** At the temple of Juno in Rome, there was a bronze statue of a dog licking its wound, which was of such excellence that the temple guardians committed their lives and belongings to ensuring its safety and preservation.[428] In the temple of his father, [Julius] Caesar, Octavius Augustus dedicated the famous Venus emerging from the sea by Apelles. A work, as Pliny tells us, that was never equaled.[429] Vespasian dedicated the Ialysus by Protogenes in the temple of Peace, a work whose excellence had led Demetrius to pardon the Rhodians.[430] *The Rape of Proserpine,* a work by Nicomachus, son of Aristodemus, was dedicated in the temple of Minerva on the Capitoline.[431] Cornelius Pinus and Attius Priscus painted the temples of Honor and Virtue, which were restored by Vespasian because they had become dilapidated with age.[432] The poet Ludius painted the temple of the people of Ardea, for which he was made a citizen.[433] The orator Hortensius built a temple specially for the purpose of dedicating a painting of the Argonauts by Cydias that he had purchased for 144 talents.[434] The image of Bacchus was dedicated in the temple of Concord.[435] Caesar dedicated the Ajax and Medea of Timomachus of Byzantium, purchased for the sum of 80 talents, in the temple of Venus Genitrix.[436] In Augustus's temple, Emperor Tiberius dedicated [the painting] of Hyacinthus, which had earlier been brought by Augustus from Alexandria.[437] Nicias painted Phylarchus in the temple of Ceres at Eleusis.[438] Aristoclides painted the temple of Apollo at Delphi, but what the subjects were I have not read.[439] It would take me too long

427. Pliny, *NH,* 9:308–9 (book 35, §64); and Cicero, *On Invention,* in Cicero, *On Invention; The Best Kind of Orator; Topics,* trans. H. M. Hubbell, Loeb Classical Library 386 (Cambridge, MA: Harvard University Press, 1949), 166–69 (2.1.1–3).
428. Pliny, *NH,* 9:156–57 (book 34, §38).
429. Pliny, *NH,* 9:328–29 (book 35, §91).
430. Pliny, *NH,* 9:336–41 (book 35, §102–5).
431. Pliny, *NH,* 9:340–41 (book 35, §108). According to the modern reading of Pliny's text, his father was Aristides, not Aristodemus as in Gilio's text.
432. Pliny, *NH,* 9:348–51 (book 35, §120).
433. Pliny, *NH,* 9:346–47 (book 35, §115); Pliny actually ascribes the work to the painter Marcus Plautius Lycon.
434. Pliny, *NH,* 9:356–57 (book 35, §130).
435. Pliny, *NH,* 9:356–57 (book 35, §131).
436. Pliny, *NH,* 9:360–61 (book 35, §136).
437. Pliny, *NH,* 9:356–57 (book 35, §132); Tiberius had built the temple of Augustus in the Forum at Rome.
438. Gilio read Pliny to mean that Nicias painted a portrait of Phylarchus, while the word *phylarchum* in the text means, according to modern authorities, a cavalry captain; see Pliny, *NH,* 9:358–59 (book 35, §134).
439. Pliny, *NH,* 9:360–63 (book 35, §138).

if you wanted me to tell you about all the temples that were painted and which works were dedicated in them."

M. Ruggiero said: "When was the custom of painting our churches first introduced?"

M. Pulidoro replied: "I think that this happened right from the beginning, and I start from the argument that, since the new Christians were not yet well established in their faith, this holy custom was initiated to make them forget paganism and firmly root the new religion in their minds; by seeing the image of our Lord and the saints, they would forget their gods. This is also confirmed by the fact that at the Second Council of Nicaea and the Sixth Council of Constantinople there are some indications that painting began to be used in churches from the time of the most holy Apostles."[440] **[108]**

M. Vincenso said: "What do you think was painted?"

M. Pulidoro replied: "I think that the Old and New Testaments were painted, as can be seen in St. Peter's, although those figures look like *baronci,* or were made by Goths.[441] The aim of those early Fathers was simply to eradicate idolatry, erasing the memory of the false and profane gods whose figures filled their temples; and to plant the new faith, rooted in the concordance of the new and old Scriptures.[442] For those who could not read, it was easy to learn the sacred mysteries of both the Old and the New Testaments by seeing the holy stories. And to prove it was only for that purpose that pictures were permitted in churches, Pope Gregory said:

440. Barocchi points out that Braun, *De imaginibus,* 120–26, was even more radical, given his insistence that the early use of painting in churches had not human but divine and apostolic foundation; Barocchi, *Trattati,* 2:611, n2 to Gilio p. 107. She also corrects the reference to the Sixth Council of Constantinople: it should be the Fourth. See Norman Tanner, ed. and trans., *Decrees of the Ecumenical Councils* (Washington, D.C.: Georgetown University Press, 1990), 1:opening 168; and for the Second Council of Nicaea (AD 787), see 1:openings 133–37.

441. For the biblical cycles in old St. Peter's, see Giacomo Grimaldi, *Descrizione della basilica antica di S. Pietro in Vaticano: Codice Barberini latino 2733,* ed. Reto Niggl (Vatican City: Biblioteca Apostolica Vaticana, 1972), 140–43, 148–49. The Baronci were a proverbially ugly family. See Giovanni Boccaccio, *The Decameron,* trans. Guido Waldman, ed. Jonathan Usher (Oxford: Oxford University Press, 2008), 6.6, where the story is told of how it was demonstrated that the Baronci were the most ancient family of Florence: "when God made the Baronci, He was but a novice in His art . . . their faces resemble those that children make when they begin to learn to draw." Vasari, in the 1550 preface to his *Lives,* describing the pitiful state to which the arts of painting and sculpture had been reduced in Italy before 1250, writes that not knowing better, people admired "Greek" works, even though they were *baroncesche* ("ancora che baroncesche fossero"); Vasari, *Le vite . . . 1550,* 99.

442. Carmelo Occhipinti sees M. Pulidoro as excusing the lack of art by claiming that the early painters were exclusively preoccupied with extirpating paganism; see Occhipinti, *Pirro Ligorio e la storia cristiana di Roma: Da Costantino all'Umanesimo* (Pisa: Edizioni della Normale, 2007), 412.

> For the worship of a picture is one thing but learning what should be worshipped through the story in a picture is another. For what writing provides for readers, this a picture provides for uneducated people looking at it, for in it the ignorant see what they should follow and the illiterate read the same from it.[443]

So this is why paintings were allowed; it is an extremely powerful reason. And, besides what is ordinarily admitted, at times one can learn more from a painting than from a book, because a painting shows the story with all its circumstances and details at a single glance, especially when it is done by an excellent master, while the book reveals the story successively, little by little.[444] Who would deny that painting has its own affective power [*energia*], as was described earlier about Gregory of Nyssa, who was utterly moved to tears by seeing Isaac ready to be sacrificed on the altar?[445] [Pope] Gregory wrote that one man, called Secundinus, always wanted to have before him the image of Christ on the Cross, so that he would have the opportunity to repent more often.[446] To demonstrate the potency of painting, its affective strength, and the reason why it was permitted, John of Damascus said: "the Fathers deemed it fit that these events should be depicted as a sort of memorial and terse reminder. It certainly happens

443. See Gregory the Great, *Letters,* 3:744–46. For the original Latin, see Pope Gregory, *S. Gregorii Magni opera,* 874. See also note 89.

444. Horace, *Ars Poetica,* 464–65 (lines 180–82), had commented on the mind being stirred more slowly by what is heard than by what is seen. Leonardo had developed the idea of the single glance as a proof of the superiority of painting in his *paragone* between painter and poet; see, for example, *Trattato* 19, in Jean Paul Richter, *The Literary Works of Leonardo da Vinci* (London: Low, Marston, Seale, & Rivington, 1883), 1:61 (no. 27).

445. For the argument that the image moves men more ("plus movet"), see Gilio, this volume, 136–37; and Durandus, *Rationale divinorum officiorum,* 1.3.4.

446. Attributed to Pope Gregory, letter to Secundinus: Pope Gregory, Appendix to *S. Gregorii Magni opera: Registrum epistolarum; Libri VIII–XIV,* 1110–11. John K. G. Shearman discusses *energia* as a term used by Dolce, *L'Aretino,* in Barocchi, *Trattati,* 1:171 (Roskill, *Dolce's "Aretino,"* 128–290); John K. G. Shearman, *Only Connect: Art and the Spectator in the Italian Renaissance* (Princeton, NJ: Princeton University Press, 1992), 209–12. Gilio, in *Topica poetica,* 73r–v, defines it thus: "*Energia* is a rhetorical figure by means of which the form, portrait, and image of a thing is described so as to bring it before the eyes of the reader or the listener in such a way that it quickly moves him to anguish, or anger, or happiness, or tearfulness, depending on the subject being discussed" (Energia è una figura per lo cui mezzo la forma, il ritratto, e l'imagine della cosa in modo col dire si spiega, che a gli occhi del lettore, o del auditore si rappresenta, che tosto si muove o al cordoglio, o all'ira, o a l'allegrezza, o alle lagrime, secondo il soggetto del quale si ragiona). He mentions various poets, from Petrarch to Ariosto, in whose work it may be found: "some say that painting too has its *Energia* as, according to what Cicero, Pliny, and many others wrote, was to be seen in the Sacrifice of Iphigenia painted by Timanthes" (Però dicono alcuni, che anco la pittura ha la sua Energia, come per le parole di Cicerone e di Plinio, e di molti altri si vedeva nel Sacrificio di Iffigenia, dipinto da Timante). On the painting by Timanthes, see Pliny, *NH,* 9:314–15 (book 35, §73); and Cicero, *Orator,* 360–61 (§74).

frequently that at times when we do not have the Lord's Passion in mind we may see the image of His crucifixion and, being thus reminded of His saving Passion, fall down and adore."[447] **[109]** Therefore you can see how careful, diligent, and honest, how truthful and chaste [*onesto*] the painter must be. If a man causes serious scandal by reading out and teaching false doctrine, can we say that a painter whose work displays false doctrine is edifying?"[448]

M. Silvio said: "Indeed the painter has much more impact than the teacher, because the latter teaches a hundred, while the [work of the] former is seen by ten thousand. The latter can be corrected whenever he is revealed as wrong, while the former's work cannot be amended without erasing it from the wall. Who could be so obstinate (unless he be a Lutheran) that, on seeing the image of our Lord crucified, scourged, and bleeding, he would not feel some remorse in his conscience and would not wish to honor him and pay him reverence?"

"That shows," said M. Vincenso, "how saintly, holy, and necessary the work of the Church has been in allowing paintings, by means of which both learned and ignorant men are aroused to devotion, challenged to imitation, and provoked into penitence every time they see them."

"Now," said M. Francesco, "consider what Lutheran churches must be without paintings. And indeed all Lutherans have shown how they have erased completely from their hearts the memory that they stripped from the churches."[449]

"So," said M. Ruggiero, "the painter should endeavor to make his figures chaste and devout; and on this subject, please note the well-expressed opinion of Konrad Braun, which I pointed out earlier. How well he teaches the painter to paint sacred images:

> Thus the usage of sacred images is to be regulated so that people are offered holy not profane things, true histories, not the fables and dreams of inquisitive men. Many vain things, over a long period, have been heard preached and seen painted in churches, not without great offense to Christ's faithful. Just as ecclesiastical writings should be true and not false,

447. Saint John of Damascus, *An Exact Exposition of the Orthodox Faith* [*De Fide Orthodoxa*], in *St. John of Damascus: Writings,* trans. Frederic H. Chase Jr. (Washington, D.C.: Catholic University of America Press, 1958), 372 (book 4, ch. 16).

448. What M. Pulidoro lays out in his answer to M. Vincenso are the three functions of Christian images, as defined from at least the thirteenth century: to teach the truth, to excite devotion, and to activate our memories of God's purposes; see Michael Baxandall, *Painting and Experience in Fifteenth-Century Italy: A Primer in the Social History of Pictorial Style* (Oxford: Oxford University Press, 1972), 40–41. It is essential that painters do not subvert these functions by teaching what is false and arousing unedifying emotions. What M. Pulidoro says is then endorsed by M. Ruggiero quoting Braun.

449. Braun, *De imaginibus,* letter to Alessandro Farnese, *v recto, describes the difference in the behavior of worshippers, after the sermon, in churches stripped of images and in those that retain their images.

> should teach and not deceive, and confirm rather than weaken and discourage piety in the minds of their readers, so painted images are not to be vacuously frivolous, but true, not shamefully lascivious, but chaste, and altogether so arranged that the dispensation of Christ made man and the pious deeds of the saints, are restored to memory. So that when placed before the eyes of the beholders, they may incite their minds to piety and a more holy life, not corrupt them with anything obscene.[450] **[110]**

Piously and well this learned man has spoken, and it all comes as a further argument against Michelangelo's personal inventions [*capricci*]."

"Now," said M. Troilo, "I would very much like to know how sacred images should be painted, and what Michelangelo has strayed away from."

M. Pulidoro replied: "That is a matter for men of religion, but M. Ruggiero, who reads the sacred texts, will be able to tell you."

"What you say is right," replied M. Francesco. "Now, tell us, M. Ruggiero, how the sacred images should be painted."[451]

M. Ruggiero replied: "It is a difficult matter to construct a correct and infallible argument that it should be like this and could not be otherwise, since we have no law or rule about this matter, except the evidence of what was the custom of painters prior to Michelangelo (which, as you lawyers know, is law), and except what Gulielmus Durandus wrote about it in his *Rationale divinorum officiorum*.[452] I will therefore outline his opinion and we can discuss it among ourselves. Many painters think that it does not matter how religious paintings should be done, provided that they are painted and, having been painted in whatever manner, that they are seen; but [those painters] are very wrong, because, when figures were permitted, each painter was not allowed to paint them according to his own judgment, for that would have been a mistake. I think painters were given rules or methods of procedure, but, in the same way that many, many books have perished, so too these [rules] have been lost. But custom is enough for us, since, as I mentioned, it has the force of law, given that it lasted for so many years before being altered and ruined by the subjective conceptions [*capricci*] of modern painters. What has been even worse is the mixing-in of fables with the Gospel stories; the majority of painters, like unbridled horses, gallop across this holy ground without respect or consideration." **[111]**

450. Braun, *De imaginibus*, 144. The opening words had been already cited in Gilio, this volume, 196. The passage from Braun was later quoted by Borghini, *Il Riposo*, 119–20 (Borghini, *Raffaello Borghini's "Il Riposo,"* 100).
451. On the title page of the *Dialogo* it is announced that the text included a "statement of how sacred images should be painted" (dechiarazione come vogliono essere dipinte le sacre imagini). It was presumably to this section that reference is being made.
452. Durandus, *Rationale divinorum officiorum*, 1.3.

"What is this ancient custom?" said M. Troilo.

M. Ruggiero added: "Painting chaste and devout sacred images, using the symbols that the ancients gave them by privilege of their holiness, which to modern [painters] have seemed base, uncouth, plebeian, old-fashioned, and humble, lacking in both intellect and art [*ingegno ed arte*] [fig. 34]. For this reason, [modern painters], giving the art of painting precedence over decency, abandoned the practice of painting clothed figures and painted them naked, as they still do. And abandoning the practice of making figures devout, they gave them strained [*sforzato*] poses, since it seemed more impressive to twist heads, arms, and legs so as to make them look like people dancing and being active rather than people in states of contemplation. And they have so degraded that holy practice with this new invention [*invenzione*] of theirs that figures could not be painted more indecently, even if they were in public bath houses [*stufe*] or taverns."[453]

M. Silvio added: "Unless they painted the orgies of Tiberius and Heliogabalus.[454] Now go on."

M. Ruggiero continued his argument and said: "The zeal of those early fathers was such that, in order not to scandalize either the learned or the ignorant, they thought it best to paint the crucified Christ clothed. When they did paint him naked, they did it with the greatest possible modesty [*onestà*]. And in addition to the figures of our Lord, which we have discussed from the start, they were allowed to paint the angels (notwithstanding they are spirits) in the form in which they made themselves visible to men.[455] In this too, Michelangelo has wanted to find a new way, and that is to paint them without wings."

M. Vincenso said: "But angels don't have wings. As they don't have them, this cannot be said to be wrong."

---

453. Aretino, in his letter to Alessandro Corvino, had written of the *Last Judgment* that "[t]he freedom with which he [Michelangelo] has proceeded is required on the walls of a voluptuous bathhouse, not on those of a celestial chapel" (Ne le mura d'un bagno delitioso, et non in le facciate d'un choro superno si richiedeva la libertà del far suo). Aretino, *Il quarto libro,* 83r–84v; see also note 202. Both the word *stufa* in Gilio and *bagno* in Aretino imply a brothel.

454. On the *spintriae* of Tiberius, see Suetonius, *Lives of the Caesars: Tiberius,* in idem, *Suetonius: Volume I,* trans. J. C. Rolfe, Loeb Classical Library 31 (Cambridge, MA: Harvard University Press, 1914), 1:370–71 (3.43). In the sixteenth century the word could mean "obscene sexual behavior, the place where it was practiced, or the persons performing it"; Bette Talvacchia, *Taking Positions* (Princeton, NJ: Princeton University Press, 1999), 56. See also John Florio, *Queen Anna's New World of Words; or, Dictionarie of the Italian and English Tongues* (London: Edw. Blount and William Barret, 1611), 524: "places where were practised or men which devised all manner of beastly and unnaturall or monstrous lust and letcherie not to be spoken of."

455. Braun, *De imaginibus,* 36, justified the representation of angels in churches; they were to have wings. See note 326.

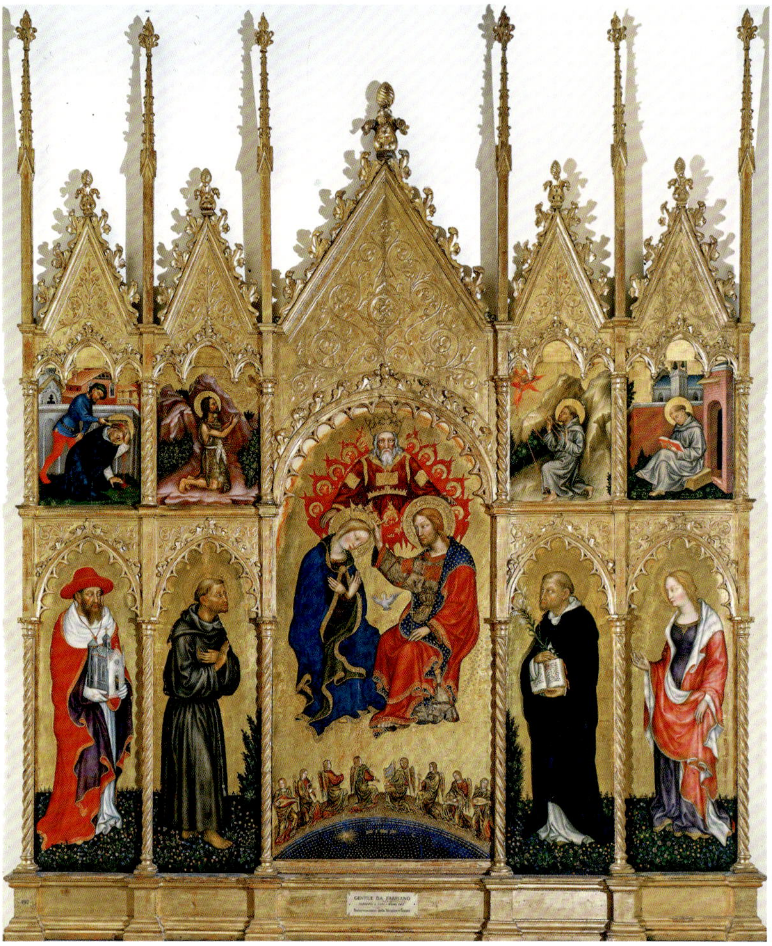

M. Ruggiero replied: "The ancient custom was to paint them with wings in order to show their speed and the swiftness with which they executed God's orders; and this is how they are described in the Scriptures. And so that you don't think I am expressing an idiosyncratic view, listen to what Isaiah says: 'In the year that Ozias died, I saw the Lord sitting upon a throne high and elevated: [and the house was filled with his majesty], and his train filled the temple. Upon it stood the seraphims: the one had six wings and the other had six wings; with two they covered his face, and with two they covered his feet, and with two they flew.'[456] **[112]** A little further on, in the same chapter, he says: 'And one

Fig. 34.
Gentile da Fabriano (Italian, ca. 1370–1427).
Valle Romita Polyptych, ca. 1410–12, tempera and gold on panel, 280 × 250 cm. Milan, Pinacoteca di Brera.

456. The translation follows Douay-Rheims, Isaiah 6:1–2. Gilio was perhaps working from memory and, although he quotes Isaiah in Latin, there are differences from the Vulgate; he included an additional passage, indicated here by the square brackets. Isaiah's words had been cited by Durandus, *Rationale divinorum officiorum*, 1.3.7. See Gilio, this volume, 192–93. Braun gathered this and many other biblical accounts of angels; see idem, *De imaginibus*, 32–36.

of the seraphims flew to me.'[457] Ezekiel, talking about the cherubim whom he saw in his vision, says: 'And the house was filled with the cloud, and the court was filled with the brightness of the glory of the Lord. And the sound of the wings of the cherubims was heard even to the outward court.' Further on, in the same chapter, he says: 'And when the cherubims lifted up their wings.'[458] And not wishing to quote all the many authoritative passages in Scripture, found especially in Revelation, it may be concluded that from every point of view angels must be given wings: both so that they do not resemble mere men and also to show their speed. Also they must be painted as beautiful young men, because this is how they manifested themselves, and this is what differentiated them from devils, who have to be extremely ugly so that they arouse fear, just as angels impart consolation.[459] Furthermore, it seems to me to be an abuse to paint the cherubim and seraphim as little dolls, namely a head alone with wings, which cannot be the case, as we read in the chapters and authoritative passages quoted above, which describe the whole body and not just the head. Likewise it seems to me an abuse to paint Saint John the Baptist wearing an animal's skin that barely covers his buttocks, since I believe that the skin was long, like the garments worn by all the Jews; and it would not have been appropriate for him, as a model of chasteness and modesty, to show his naked thighs.[460] It would not be appropriate for him to wear short garments, when the others wear long robes, and even less for him to wear another cloak over the animal's skin, as he is usually depicted. The figures of the prophets must be painted holding scrolls, not books as painters do today. This is to show that at that time, the law was written on stone tablets and also to show that it was wrapped in shadow, obscured in figurative language. In contrast, the Apostles must be represented with books to show that the authority of the Gospels had already been written down in books and that [the Apostles] had been ordered to preach it. Therefore, because the law of the gospel is clear, open, easily understood, and mild, the books must be open. And when the prophets are given books, [those books] must be closed to show the obscurity of the old law, which was hidden, secret, and locked up in figurative language. By this means they can demonstrate the difference between the [old law] and the law of the gospel.[461] **[113]** However, ancient usage has been retained for many figures, like the Evangelists shown

457. Isaiah 6:6.

458. Ezekiel 10:4–5 and 10:16.

459. Durandus, *Rationale divinorum officiorum,* 1.3.7–8. M. Ruggiero had commented on Michelangelo's failure to distinguish adequately between angels and devils in his *Last Judgment;* see Gilio, this volume, 193.

460. For an earlier comment on this aspect of the dress of John the Baptist, see Gilio, this volume, 124.

461. Durandus, *Rationale divinorum officiorum,* 1.3.11.

as the four animals seen in Ezekiel's vision.[462] The apostle Peter is shown with the keys and Paul [is shown] with a sword, in order to demonstrate how, when [Paul] was complicit in Jewish obstinacy, he wanted to defend that with a physical sword, and then, once he converted to Christianity and became the chosen vessel, he defended the law of the gospel with a spiritual sword, which is the Word of God, as he said.[463] Saint John is painted in the cauldron of boiling oil, or holding the poisoned chalice. Saint Andrew is painted with his cross, Saint Stephen with stones, Saint Lawrence with the gridiron, Saint Blaise with combs, Saint Sebastian with arrows, and many other martyrs with the instruments of their martyrdom. Indeed, they must be painted like this to show that they resisted tyrants even unto loss of life and limb; ultimately through their torments they gave God clear testimony of their faith, having placed their souls with Christ.[464] Martyrs were also painted holding a palm as a token of their glorious victory, as we read in the Psalms that the righteous shall flourish like the palm tree and, as John wrote in his book of Revelation, they shall hold palms in their hands.[465] Virgins who were not martyrs were painted holding a lily as a sign of their virginity. Confessors were painted in the same way, as a token of their chastity. Bishops were painted with their miters and crosiers to show that they had carried out their pontifical office well.[466] Saints were also painted with halos, which Michelangelo removed, as have many modern painters, perhaps feeling that they signified something ignoble. But you should know that this was not done accidentally, nor were saints given that mark in order to make them appear despicable; on the contrary, it was given as a token of their sanctity, since it is written in the Scriptures that 'Therefore shall they receive a kingdom of glory, and a crown of beauty at the hand of the Lord.'[467] And you should note that the custom of the Latin Church was to give no halo to the Old Testament saints, in order to distinguish them from the New Testament saints, for [the Latin Church] only celebrates the feast days of those saints who went straight to heaven as soon as they died, with no impediment whatsoever. **[114]**

---

462. Durandus, *Rationale divinorum officiorum,* 1.3.9.

463. On Saint Paul as the "vaso d'elezione" (*vas electionis*), see Acts 9:15; see Ephesians 6:17 for the spiritual sword.

464. Gilio, this volume, 187–92. M. Ruggiero had allowed the inclusion of the attributes of the martyrs only for the ignorant: "in order that their minds may take in whatever little they can." The context had been the narrative history of the Last Judgment. Here M. Ruggiero is explicitly expounding the ideas of Durandus and envisages figures that are not part of a narrative.

465. Psalms 91:13 (see Durandus, *Rationale divinorum officiorum,* 1.3.14); Revelation 7:9. See also Braun, *De imaginibus,* 105–7, for his opinions about the images of saints and their attributes.

466. Durandus, *Rationale divinorum officiorum,* 1.3.15.

467. *Liber Sapientiae* (Wisdom of Solomon) 5:17; Durandus, *Rationale divinorum officiorum,* 1.3.19; and Braun, *De imaginibus,* 108.

"But those ancient Fathers, although they were saints, did not enter heaven immediately but remained in Limbo until Christ led them up to heaven. The Greek Church did not make this distinction; rather, it celebrated the saints of the Old and New Testaments with equal honor, and this was imitated by the Venetians.[468] So here you have, as far as I have been able to understand them, the rules concerning the way sacred images of the saints should be painted."

M. Pulidoro replied: "You have spoken extremely well and when it should happen that painters want to paint images with figures in strained poses, then they must give them the kinds of movements that will not hinder devotion."

M. Vincenso said: "Whoever wants to see an awkward movement should look at the Madonna that Cardinal Cesi commissioned to be painted in his chapel at Santa Maria della Pace [figs. 35, 36]. Receiving the annunciation from the angel, she makes a movement turning round that makes me laugh whenever I see her.[469]

"So that most illustrious lord must be careful not to allow such graceless and indecent figures to be painted in the chapel he recently had built in Santa Maria Maggiore.[470] The Cardinal Santa Fiore should act to achieve the same in the chapel he is building there now, and not allow it to be sullied by false and fabulous figures, because there is no conformity whatsoever between Christ and Belial nor between what is true and what is false.[471] We have had sufficient

---

468. Venetian devotion to Old Testament figures is attested by churches dedicated to Job (Giobbe), Moses (Moisè), and so on.

469. Michelangelo designed the *Annunciation* for Cardinal Federico Cesi, for his chapel in Santa Maria della Pace at Rome; it was painted by Marcello Venusti. The chapel was begun circa 1524 for Angelo Cesi, continued for his son Ottavio, and was still not complete in 1546, by which time responsibility for it had fallen to Cardinal Federico Cesi. See Federica Kappler, "Una nota di cronologia sui disegni di Michelangelo per la pala Cesi di Santa Maria della Pace," *Mitteilungen des kunsthistorischen Institutes in Florenz* 56, no. 3 (2014): 355–60. Her attempt to date the *Annunciation* before 1546 is not convincing. The engraving by the Master of the Die (see fig. 36) shows the Virgin with an altered pose, eliminating some of the awkwardness identified in Gilio's text.

470. The Cesi Chapel in Santa Maria Maggiore had been founded by Cardinal Paolo Emilio Cesi (d. 1537). When Gilio was writing, Cardinal Federico Cesi (d. 1565) was overseeing its construction and decoration; see Francesco Colalucci, "Le pitture della cappella di S. Caterina in S. Maria Maggiore: i Cesi, Vasari, Siciolante e la controriforma," *Bollettino dei Monumenti, Musei e Gallerie Pontificie* 14 (1994): 113–61, esp. 114. Carmelo Occhipinti has argued that Gilio was criticizing the altarpiece of the Martyrdom of Saint Catherine by Girolamo Siciolante da Sermoneta (1521–75); see Occhipinti, *Pirro Ligorio,* 91. But it seems likely that the altarpiece was not begun until circa 1566; see John Hunter, *Girolamo Siciolante pittore da Sermoneta (1521–1575)* (Rome: L'Erma di Bretschneider, 1996), 174 (no. 31).

471. Adjacent to the Cesi Chapel, the Sforza Chapel in Santa Maria Maggiore was dedicated to Saints Flora and Lucilla. It had been founded by Guido Ascanio Sforza, cardinal of Santa Fiore, who died on 6 October 1564. The design had been commissioned from Michelangelo circa 1560; see Giulio Carlo Argan and Bruno Contardi, *Michelangelo Architect,* trans.

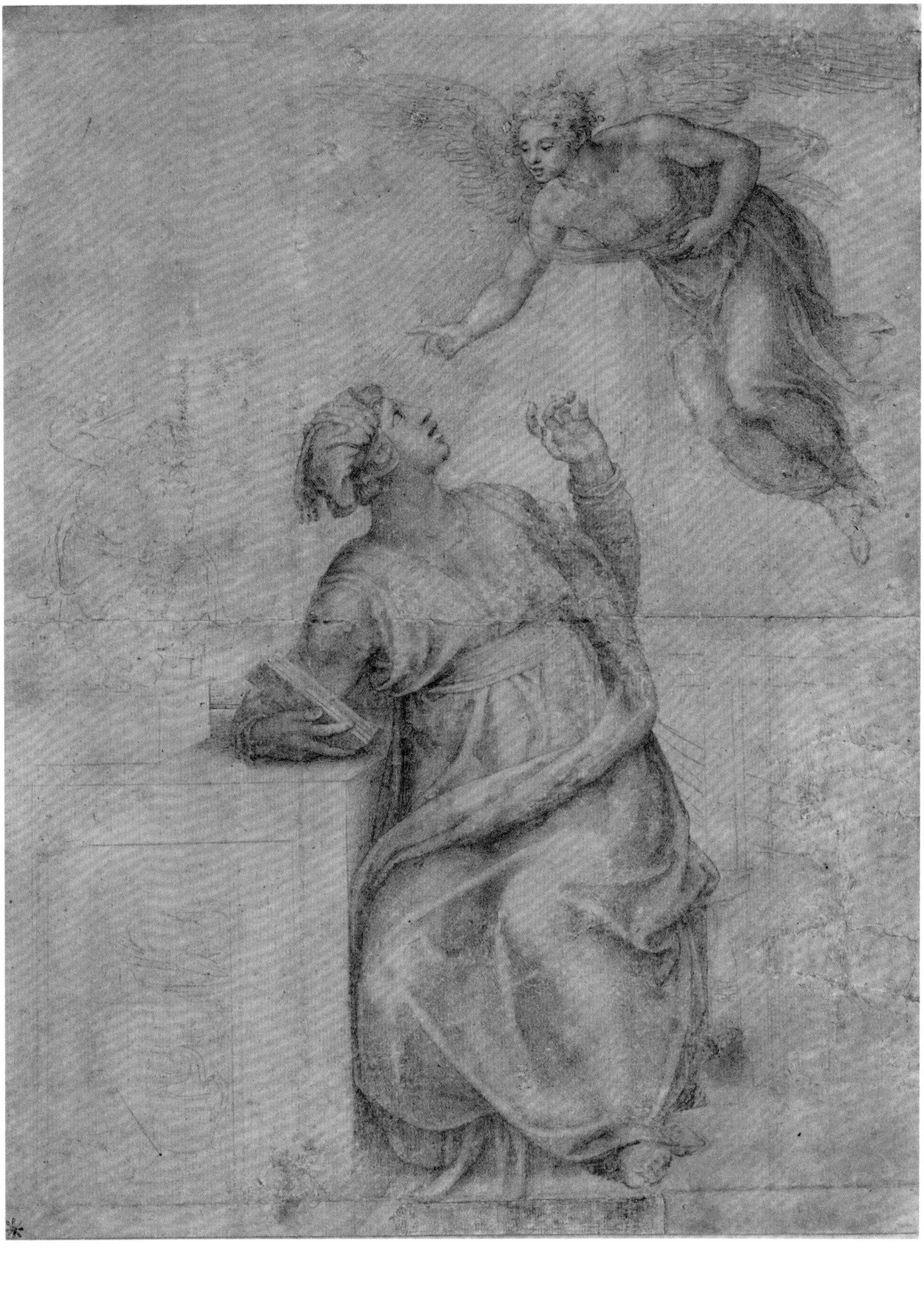

discussions from the start about the figures of God the Father, our Lord Jesus Christ, the Holy Spirit, and the glorious Virgin, and therefore I will say no more now.[472] So, M. Pulidoro, do finish your discussion of the mixed painter."[473]

M. Pulidoro started to speak again and said: "In truth, mixed paintings should not be placed in churches, or among sacred things, and I wholeheartedly praise our pope, Pius IV, who—in the public hall of the two chapels, begun by Paul III—instead of subjects from the Roman wars, commissioned paintings of Catholic emperors who did great service to the Roman Church, to the pope, or to the Christian religion [fig. 37].[474] These are the stories that should be painted in the halls of cardinals and the pope: the proceedings of general councils, and especially the four principal ones, so that those who bestowed benefits on the Church may be known and others be encouraged and motivated to imitate them, to praise them, and to exalt them. **[115]** Moreover, the mixed painter should not treat everything, whether sacred or profane, in this mixed mode, because it is not appropriate to pure histories, nor to the fabulous either. If the painter does really know how to arrange his mix, he will make it pleasing, delightful, and beautiful, but if he doesn't, it will be just risible. Therefore, an ignorant painter should not trust his own personal conceptions [*capriccio*], thinking it sufficient to know how to handle colors and use his brush well, since this is not enough. Instead, if a good result is wanted, some intelligent and well-educated person [*letterato*] should be asked to expound the story and arrange the mixture [*mistura*] desired,

Marion L. Grayson (New York: Harry N. Abrams, 1993), 348 (no. 29). The reference to Belial and Christ is from 2 Corinthians 6:14–15.

472. See Gilio, this volume, 126–28, 185, 208–9.

473. The discussion of the mixed painter now resumes, after a long interruption that began in Gilio, this volume, 222.

474. Although the text identifies the pope as Pius III, Gilio meant Pius IV, whose reign (1559–65) corresponded with the period when he was writing his treatise. The hall of the two chapels is now usually called the Sala Regia, off of which opened the Sistine and the Pauline Chapels. Pius IV, elected in December 1559, seems to have moved quickly to have the decoration, left unfinished at the death of Paul III, completed; there are payment documents dated 1561 showing that work had begun. See Loren Partridge and Randolph Starn, "Triumphalism and the Sala Regia in the Vatican," in *"All the world's a stage . . . ": Art and Pageantry in the Renaissance and Baroque,* vol. 1, ed. Barbara Wisch and Susan Scott Munshower (University Park: Pennsylvania State University Press, 1990), 57. There is no independent evidence to support Gilio's suggestion that Roman wars were ever proposed as the subject for the wall paintings. Vasari recorded Daniele's scheme for the walls of the Sala Regia in the last years of the reign of Paul III as the representation of kings who had defended or otherwise brought benefit to the papacy; see Giorgio Vasari, "Vita di Daniello Ricciarelli da Volterra," in Vasari, *Le vite de' più eccellenti pittori, scultori, e architettori: Nelle redazioni del 1550 e 1568,* vol. 5, ed. Rosanna Bettarini and Paola Barocchi (Florence: S.P.E.S., 1984), 543. For a discussion of the themes proposed for the decoration, see Clare Robertson, "Phoenix Romanus," in *Rome,* ed. Marcia B. Hall (Cambridge: Cambridge University Press, 2005), 198.

Fig. 35.
Michelangelo Buonarroti (Italian, 1475–1564).
Annunciation to the Virgin, late 1540s, black chalk, outlines indented, 38.3 × 29.7 cm.
New York, The Morgan Library and Museum.

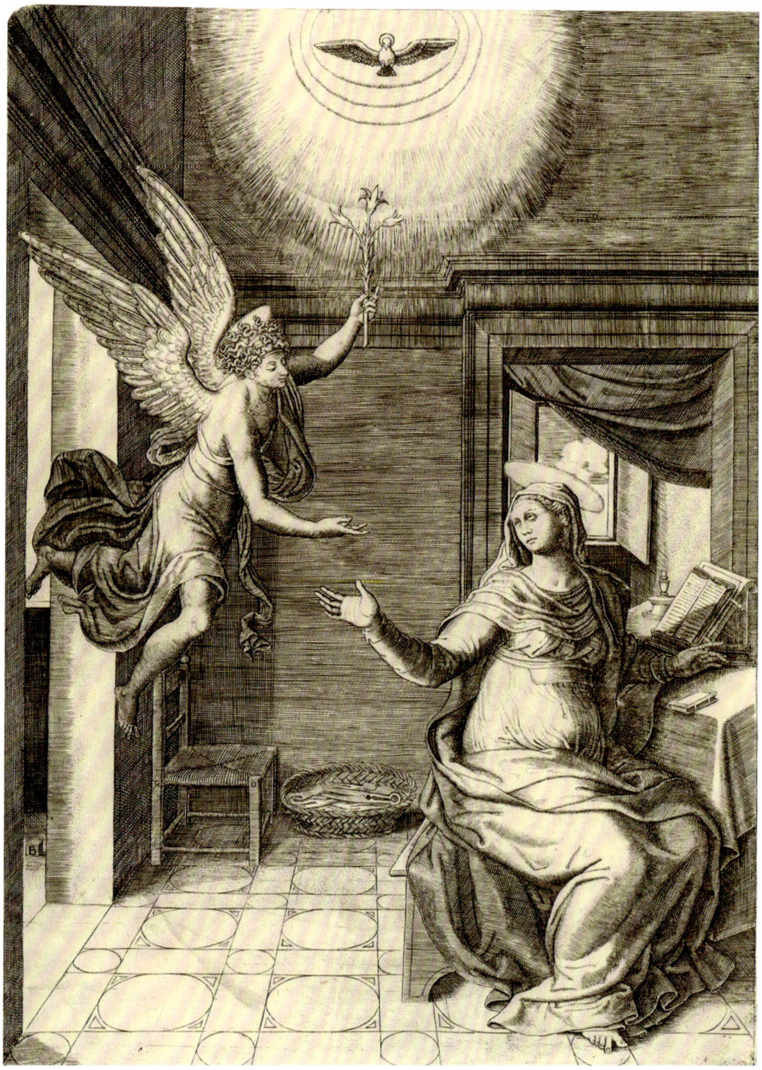

or to invent a poetic one.[475] Within this [mixed] genre we can also include all those who make *imprese,* whether chivalrous or amorous, or of any other kind; they should ensure that the meanings correspond to what they are intended and designed to mean.[476] In this way painters will acquire praise and honor. But if our M. Francesco Agostini publishes the work on painting that he has written,

475. Such a person as Annibale Caro; see Clare Robertson, "Annibal Caro as Iconographer: Sources and Method," *Journal of the Warburg and Courtauld Institutes* 45 (1982): 160–81.

476. An impresa was a personal device or emblem, consisting of an image and a motto. Learned and often witty, the meaning of an impresa was not intended to be easily understood. The first treatise on the subject was Paolo Giovio's *Dialogo dell'imprese militari et amorose* (Rome: Antonio Barré, 1555). See John Manning, *The Emblem* (London: Reaktion, 2002), 73–79.

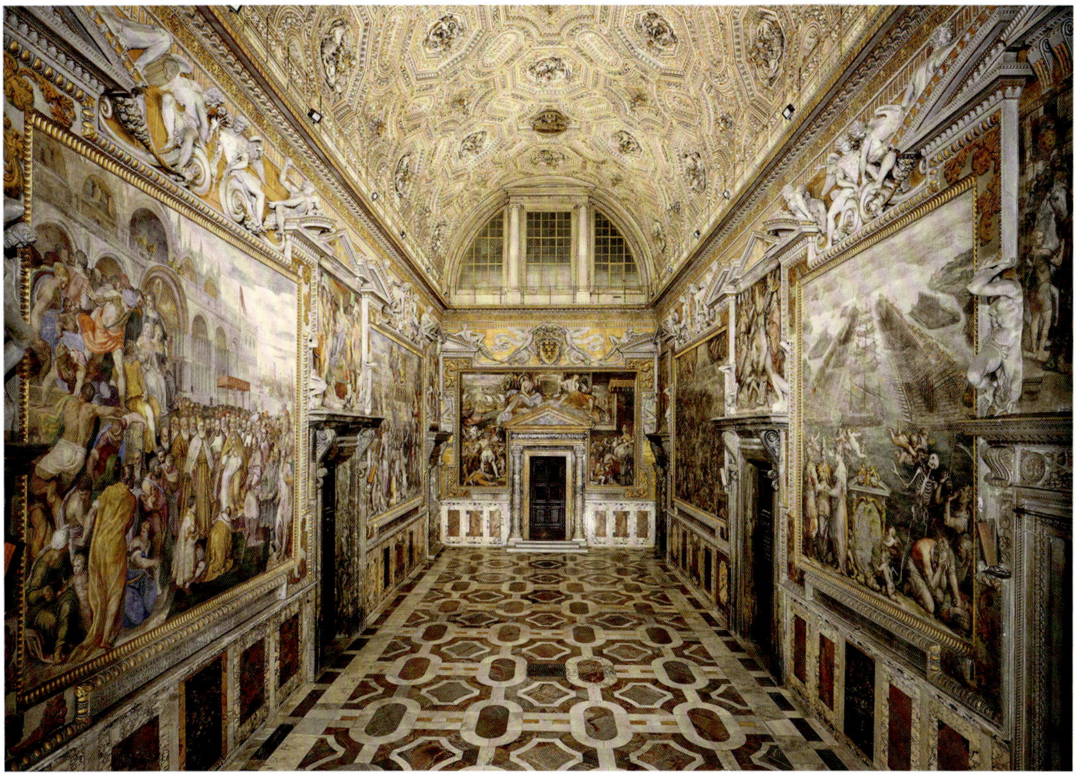

then we won't need to ask for anything more; because in it we will see in full all the qualities, all the virtues, and all the vices of the art of painting and of those who practice it."[477]

THE END OF THE DIALOGUE CONCERNING THE ERRORS OF PAINTERS WITH REGARD TO HISTORIES, BY M. GIOVANNI ANDREA GILIO, FOR THE MOST ILLUSTRIOUS CARDINAL FARNESE.

477. Agostini also appears in the first dialogue of Gilio's *Due dialogi* (1564, 2v) as "our M. Francesco Agostini," where he is described as having made a fine model of an ancient theater.

According to the entry by Antonio Pinelli in Saur's *Allgemeines Künstlerlexikon,* Agostini was a painter and sculptor, born between 1490 and 1500 at Fabriano, and active at Fabriano and Rome. He was last recorded in 1566, at Rome, when he acted as an expert adviser on the statue of Paul IV of Giacomo da Cassignola in Santa Maria sopra Minerva; see Antonino Bertolotti, *Artisti subalpini in Roma nei secoli XV, XVI e XVII: Ricerche e studi negli archivi romani* (Mantua: Tip. lit. Mondovì, 1884), 100–101. There is a record of a painting of Saint Jerome, after Dürer, signed and dated Rome 1565. See also Anon., "Agostini, Francesco," *DBI,* 1 (1960); Agostini built and restored, at his own expense, two fountains in Fabriano: one in the marketplace (1519), the other in front of San Antonio (1559), as was recorded by inscriptions that no longer exist.

Fig. 36.
Master of the Die (Italian or German, active from 1530s), variant of Marcello Venusti (Italian, ca. 1512–79) and Michelangelo Buonarroti (Italian, 1475–1564).
Annunciation to the Virgin, 1550–60, engraving, 42.6 × 31 cm. London, British Museum.

Fig. 37.
View of the Sala Regia.
Vatican City, Vatican Apostolic Palace.

GLOSSARY

accidenti
The nonessential qualities of a thing (in the Aristotelian sense), as opposed to the substance (*sostanza*) of a thing.

anima
Soul.

arte
The skills and techniques of an art or craft (here, usually the art of painting) that can be taught and learned. Also the command of those; namely, artistry. Often used in contrast to *ingegno,* which means the qualities of mind or intellect that are innate.

artefice
Artist; painter; maker. Connotes an artisan, rather than an artist as in the modern sense of the word.

atto
Action; event; sometimes movement, as in *atto sforzato.*

capriccio,* pl. *capricci
A personal idea or invention; a subjective or personal conception; flight of imagination; fancy; whim.

convenevole
Proper; appropriate. See also *decoro.*

debita proporzione,* pl. *debite proporzioni
In proper proportion; often used to describe the proper balance or correspondence between type of subject matter and its treatment in a painting.

decoro
Decorum; appropriateness; dignity. Especially applied to the appropriate representation of people. See also *convenevole.*

energia
Affective power.

favola,* pl. *favole
A pagan myth; legend; fable.

favoloso
Fabulous, in the sense of "derived from fable." Not meant in the sense of "marvelous," as often used in modern English.

fingere/fingendo
To invent, simulate, or make up.

finto
Fictional; fanciful. Often carries the implication of being truth-like or lifelike (*verisimile*) as opposed to being either really true (*vero*) or fabulous (*favoloso*). See *pittore poetico.*

finzione
An invention; a fiction (as in *poetiche finzioni* [poetic fictions]).

forza dell'arte
The forceful power of the art of painting.

garbo
Grace; graceful, as in a well-mannered, decorous way.

Gentili
Pagans (not Gentiles in the biblical sense).

gesto,* pl. *gesti
Action; movement; gesture.

gravità
Dignity; gravity.

ignorante
Illiterate in the sense of not educated, unable to read Latin; not a man of letters (*letterato*); not learned (*dotto*).

ingegnioso
Ingenious; brilliant.

ingegno
Mind, intellect, talent. The innate qualities of mind as opposed to acquired skills (*arte*).

ingegno vivo
Vigorous intellect; inventive mind.

invenzione
Invention, with the sense of finding, discovering. (From the Latin, *inventio.*)

istoria
Story, history; a painting with narrative subject matter.

istoriato
Illustrated.

istorie mondane
Secular stories or histories.

letterato
A man of letters; a well-educated person who reads Latin (not *ignorante*).

mistura*, pl. *misture
A painting of mixed subject matter: mixtures of the true (*vero*), the fictional (*finto*), and/or the fabulous (*favoloso*).

***onestà* (adj. *onesto*)**
Modesty; decency; chasteness; chastity.

ordine
Method; disposition; order.

pittore istorico
A historical painter who paints historically true subjects (e.g., events from history or the Bible). See also *vero*.

pittore misto
A painter of subjects that are a mixture (*mistura*) of the true (*vero*), the fictional (*finto*), and/or the fabulous (*favoloso*).

pittore poetico
A painter who paints fictional (*finto*) or fabulous (*favoloso*) subjects. Contrasted with *pittore istorico*.

pitture sacre
Religious pictures.

prosopopeia
Affectation.

prudente
Wise; prudent.

regola*, pl. *regole
A norm; a model; a rule; a set of rules.

regolata mescolanza
A regulated mixture; a balance between truth on the one hand and intellect (*ingegno*) and artistry (in the sense of "skill") on the other.

scienza
Knowledge; branch of knowledge.

***sforzato* (*atto sforzato*)**
Strained (movement or pose).

sforzo*, pl. *sforzi
Movement.

sostanza
Substance, in the Aristotelian sense: the essential quality of a thing, as opposed to its accidents (*accidenti*).

stufe
Public bath houses. Frequently used to denote a brothel.

***vaghezza* (adj. *vago*)**
Allure or appeal; attractiveness; beauty.

verisimile
Lifelike or truth-like; verisimilitude; not true, but having the appearance of truth.

vero
True, historically true; real. As opposed to fictional (*finto*) and fabulous (*favoloso*). See *pittore istorico*.

BIBLIOGRAPHY

Acidini Luchinat, Cristina. *Taddeo e Federico Zuccari: Fratelli pittori del Cinquecento.* 2 vols. Milan: Jandi Sapi Editori, 1998.

Aelian. *Historical Miscellany.* Edited and translated by N. G. Wilson. Loeb Classical Library 486. Cambridge, MA: Harvard University Press, 1997.

Aelius Lampridius. *Severus Alexander.* In *Historia Augusta: Volume II,* translated by David Magie, 178–313. Loeb Classical Library 140. Cambridge, MA: Harvard University Press, 1924.

Aelius Spartianus. *Antoninus Caracallus.* In *Historia Augusta: Volume II,* translated by David Magie, 2–31. Loeb Classical Library 140. Cambridge, MA: Harvard University Press, 1924.

Agrippa von Nettesheim, Heinrich Cornelius. *Dell'incertitudine e della vanità delle scienze* [Venice, 1548]. Edited by Tiziana Provvidera. Turin: Nino Aragno, 2004.

Alberti, Leandro. *Descrittione di tutta Italia.* Venice: Giovanni Maria Bonelli, 1553.

Alberti, Leon Battista. *Della pittura.* Edited by Luigi Mallé. Florence: Sansoni, 1950.

———. *De pictura.* Basel: Westheimer, 1540.

———. *On Painting and On Sculpture: The Latin Texts of "De pictura" and "De statua."* Edited and translated by Cecil Grayson. London: Phaidon, 1972.

———. *La pittura.* Translated by Lodovico Domenichi. Venice: Giolito, 1547.

Alciati, Andrea. *Parergon Iuris Libri VII Posteriores.* Lyon: Sebastianus Gryphius, 1544.

Aldrovandi, Ulisse. *Delle statue antiche.* In Lucio Mauro, *Le antichità della città di Roma,* 115–316. Venice: Giordano Ziletti, 1556.

Aleandri, Vittorio Emanuele. *La stampa degli statuti di Camerino e il tipografo Antonio Gioioso.* Camerino: Tipografia Savini, 1902.

Allgemeines Künstlerlexikon Online: Internationale Künstlerdatenbank. Berlin: K. G. Saur, 2009.

Alpers, Svetlana. "*Ekphrasis* and Aesthetic Attitudes in Vasari's *Lives.*" *Journal of the Warburg and Courtauld Institutes* 23, nos. 3/4 (1960): 190–215.

Ammianus Marcellinus. *History.* Vol. 3, *Books 27–31; Excerpta Valesiana.* Translated by J. C. Rolfe. Loeb Classical Library 331. Cambridge, MA: Harvard University Press, 1939.

Andaloro, Maria. *La pittura medievale a Roma, 312–1431: Atlante percorsi visivi.* Vol. 1, *Suburbio, Vaticano, Rione Monti.* Viterbo: Università della Tuscia, 2006.

Antoninus of Florence. *Summa theologica moralis.* Venice: Nicolaus Jenson, 1477.

Apollonj Ghetti, Bruno Maria. *Santa Prassede.* Rome: Marietti, 1961.

"Appendix: The Assumption of the Virgin, 3. Latin, A. *The Narrative of Pseudo-Melito.*" In *The Apocryphal New Testament: A Collection of Apocryphal Christian Literature in an English Translation,* edited and translated by James K. Elliott, 708–16. Oxford: Oxford University Press, 1993.

Aquinas, Thomas. *Summa contra Gentiles (Liber de veritate catholicae fidei contra errores infidelium).* 4 books in 5 vols. *Book 1, God,* translated by Anton C. Pegis. *Book 2, Creation,* translated by J. F. Anderson. *Book 3, Providence,* translated by Vernon J. Bourke. *Book 4, Salvation,* translated by C. J. O'Neil. Notre Dame, IN: University of Notre Dame Press, 1975.

———. *Summa theologiae.* Vol. 45, *Prophecy and Other Charisms (2a2ae. 171–78).* Edited and translated by Roland Potter. London: Blackfriars in conjunction with Eyre & Spottiswoode, 1975.

Aretino, Pietro. *Opera nova del fecundissimo Giovene Pietro Pictore Aretino.* Venice: Zoppino, 1512.

———. *Il quarto libro de le lettere.* Venice: Bartolomeo Cesano, 1550.

Argan, Giulio Carlo, and Bruno Contardi. *Michelangelo Architect.* Translated by Marion L. Grayson. New York: Harry N. Abrams, 1993.

Aristotle. *De Anima.* In Aristotle, *On the Soul; Parva Naturalia; On Breath,* translated by W. S. Hett, 8–203. Loeb Classical Library 288. Cambridge, MA: Harvard University Press, 1957.

———. *Meteorologica.* Translated by H. D. P. Lee. Loeb Classical Library 397. Cambridge, MA: Harvard University Press, 1952.

———. *Poetics.* Translated by Stephen Halliwell. In Aristotle, *Poetics;* Longinus, *On the Sublime;* Demetrius, *On Style,* translated by Stephen Halliwell, W. H. Fyfe, Doreen C. Innes, and

W. Rhys Roberts, 28–141. Loeb Classical Library 199. Cambridge, MA: Harvard University Press, 1995.
Armenini, Giovanni Battista. *De' veri precetti della pittura.* Edited by Marina Gorreri. Turin: G. Einaudi, 1988.
———. *On the True Precepts of the Art of Painting.* Translated by Edward J. Olszewski. New York: Burt Franklin, 1977.
Arriaga Florez, Mercedes. "Le scrittrici marchigiane: Un giallo letterario." *Studi umanistici piceni* 28 (2008): 161–66.
Augenio, Orazio. *Epistolarum et consultationum medicinalium.* 2 vols. in 1. Venice: Damianum Zenarium, 1592.
Augustine. *De civitate Dei: Libri XXII.* In *S. Augustini Tomus Septimus.* Patrologia Latina, series prima 41, edited by Jacques-Paul Migne, cols. 13–804. Paris: Migne, 1845.
———. *De doctrina Christiana.* Edited and translated by R. P. H. Green. Oxford: Clarendon, 1995.
———. *De Trinitate libri XV.* In *S. Aurelii Augustini tomus octavus.* Patrologia Latina, series prima 42, edited by Jacques-Paul Migne, cols. 819–1098. Paris: Migne, 1845.
———. *Quaestionum Evangeliorum libri duo.* In *S. Augustini Tomi Tertii pars altera.* Patrologia Latina, series prima 35, edited by Jacques-Paul Migne, cols. 1321–63. Paris: Migne, 1845.
———. *St. Augustine on the Psalms.* Edited and translated by Scholastica Hebgin and Felicitas Corrigan. 2 vols. Westminster, MD: Newman, 1960–61.
———. *The Works of St. Augustine: A Translation for the 21st Century; Part 3: Sermons.* Vol. 5, *On the New Testament (148–183).* Edited by John E. Rotelle. Translated by Edmund Hill. New York: New City, 1990–92.
Aulus Gellius. *Attic Nights* [*Noctes Atticae*]. Vol. 1, *Books 1–5.* Translated by J. C. Rolfe. Loeb Classical Library 195. Cambridge, MA: Harvard University Press, 1927.
———. *Attic Nights* [*Noctes Atticae*]. Vol. 2, *Books 6–13.* Translated by J. C. Rolfe. Loeb Classical Library 200. Cambridge, MA: Harvard University Press, 1927.
———. *Attic Nights* [*Noctes Atticae*]. Vol. 3, *Books 14–20.* Translated by J. C. Rolfe. Loeb Classical Library 212. Cambridge, MA: Harvard University Press, 1927.
Azkoul, Michael. *St. Gregory of Nyssa and the Tradition of the Fathers.* Lewiston, NY: Edwin Mellen Press, 1995.
Bade, Josse Q. [Iodocus Badius Ascensius], ed. *De arte poetica libellus.* Paris: Jean Petit and Denis Roce, 1503.
Baldinucci, Filippo. *Vocabolario toscano dell'arte del disegno.* Florence: Franchi, 1681.
Barnes, Bernadine. *Michelangelo in Print: Reproductions as Response in the Sixteenth Century.* Aldershot: Ashgate, 2010.
Barocchi, Paola. "Nota filologica." In *Trattati d'arte del Cinquecento: Fra manierismo e controriforma,* vol. 2, edited by Paola Barocchi, 544–48. Bari: Laterza, 1961.
———. "Schizzo di una storia della critica cinquecentesca sulla Sistina." *Atti dell'Accademia Toscana di Scienze e Lettere "La Colombaria"* 21 (1956): 194–212.
———, ed. *Trattati d'arte del Cinquecento: Fra manierismo e controriforma.* 3 vols. Bari: Laterza, 1960–62.
———. *Vasari pittore.* Florence: Barbèra, 1964.
Baronio, Cesare. *Annales Ecclesiastici.* Vol. 1. Antwerp: Plantin, 1589.
Bartsch, Adam von. *The Illustrated Bartsch.* Vols. 28–31, *Italian Masters of the Sixteenth Century.* Edited by Suzanne Boorsch and John T. Spike. New York: Abaris, 1982–86.
———. *Le peintre graveur.* 21 vols. Vienna: J. V. Degen, 1802–21.
Battaglia, Salvatore, and Giorgio Bárberi Squarotti, eds. *Grande Dizionario della Lingua Italiana.* 21 vols. Turin: Unione tipografico-editrice torinese, 1961–.
Battisti, Eugenio. *Rinascimento e Barocco.* Turin: Einaudi, 1960.
Bauer, Stefan. *The Censorship and Fortuna of Platina's "Lives of the Popes" in the Sixteenth Century.* Turnhout: Brepols, 2006.
Baxandall, Michael. *Painting and Experience in Fifteenth-Century Italy: A Primer in the Social History of Pictorial Style.* Oxford: Oxford University Press, 1972.
Bellini, Paolo, ed. *L'Opera incisa di Adamo e Diana Scultori.* Vicenza: Pozza, 1991.
Belting, Hans. *Likeness and Presence: A History of the Image before the Era of Art.* Chicago: University of Chicago Press, 1994.

Bernard of Clairvaux. "From *An Apologia for Abbot William*." In *The Cistercian World: Monastic Writings of the Twelfth Century*, translated and edited by Pauline Matarasso, 42–58. Harmondsworth: Penguin, 1993.
Bertolotti, Antonino. *Artisti subalpini in Roma nei secoli XV, XVI e XVII: Ricerche e studi negli archivi romani.* Mantua: Tip. lit. Mondovì, 1884. Facsimile reprint, Bologna: Arnoldo Forni, 1965.
Bibliotheca Hagiographica Latina antiquae et mediae aetatis. Brussels: Socii Bollandiani, 1898–1901, 1911 (supplement).
Biferali, Fabrizio. *Battista Franco "pittore viniziano" nella cultura artistica e nella vita religiosa del Cinquecento.* Pisa: Edizioni della Normale, 2007.
Biondo, Flavio. *Roma ristaurata et Italia illustrata, tradotta in lingua volgare per Lucio Fauno.* Venice: Michele Tramezzino, 1542.
Bober, Phyllis Pray, and Ruth Rubinstein. *Renaissance Artists and Antique Sculpture: A Handbook of Sources.* London: Harvey Miller, 1986.
Boccaccio, Giovanni. *The Decameron.* Translated by Guido Waldman. Edited by Jonathan Usher. Oxford: Oxford University Press, 2008.
Boethius. *Theological Tractates; The Consolation of Philosophy.* Translated by H. F. Stewart, E. K. Rand, and S. J. Tester. Loeb Classical Library 74. Cambridge, MA: Harvard University Press, 1973.
Boorsch, Suzanne, Michal Lewis, and R. E. Lewis. *The Engravings of Giorgio Ghisi.* Exh. cat. New York: Metropolitan Museum of Art, 1985.
Borea, Evelina. "Stampe da modelli fiorentini del Cinquecento." In *Firenze e la Toscana dei Medici nell'Europa del Cinquecento: Il primato del disegno,* edited by Luciano Berti, 225–86. Florence: Edizioni Medicee, 1980.
Borghini, Raffaello. *Il Riposo.* Florence: Marescotti, 1584. Reprint with introduction and analytical index by Mario Rosci. Milan: Edizioni Labor, 1967. Published in English as *Raffaello Borghini's "Il Riposo."* Edited and translated by Lloyd H. Ellis. Toronto: University of Toronto Press, 2007.
Borromeo, Federico. *Sacred Painting, Museum.* Edited and translated by Kenneth S. Rothwell. Introduction and notes by Pamela M. Jones. Cambridge, MA: Harvard University Press, 2010.
Boschloo, Anton W. A. *The Limits of Artistic Freedom: Criticism of Art in Italy from 1500 to 1800.* Leiden: Primavera Pers, 2008.
Brandolini, Aurelio. *De ratione scribendi.* Basel: R. Winter, 1543.
Braun, Konrad [Conradus Brunus]. *Adversus novam historiam ecclesiasticam quam Mathias Illyricus et eius Collegae Magdeburgici per centurias nuper ediderunt . . . admonitio Catholica.* Dillingen: Sebald Mayer, 1565.
———. *De imaginibus.* In idem, *Opera Tria.* Mainz: Franz Behem, 1548.
Bruni, Francesco. "Nota linguistica." In Giovanni Andrea Gilio, *Dialogo del letterato cortigiano,* edited by Paolo Cherchi, 23–35. Ravenna: Longo, 2002.
Buchowiecki, Walther. *Handbuch der Kirchen Roms: Der römische Sakralbau in Geschichte und Kunst von der altchristlichen Zeit bis zur Gegenwart.* 4 vols. Vienna: Hollinek, 1967–97.
Bull, Malcolm. *The Mirror of the Gods.* London: Allen Lane, 2005.
Buranelli, Fabrizio, Paolo Ballirano, Fabrizio Mancinelli, Gianluigi Colalucci, Nazzareno Gabrielli, and Fabio Morresi. *The Last Judgement: I, The Restoration.* New York: Rizzoli, 1999.
Bury, Michael. "Mannerism." In *The Oxford Companion to Western Art,* edited by Hugh Brigstocke, 446–47. Oxford: Oxford University Press, 2001.
———. "Niccolò della Casa's *Last Judgement* Dissected." *Print Quarterly* 27 (2010): 3–10.
———. *The Print in Italy, 1550–1620.* London: British Museum Press, 2001.
———. "The 'Triumph of Christ,' after Titian." *The Burlington Magazine* 131, no. 1032 (1989): 188–97.
Camuffo, Dario, and Silvia Enzi. "Reconstructing the Climate of Northern Italy from Archive Sources." In *Climate since A.D. 1500,* edited by Raymond S. Bradley and Philip D. Jones, 143–54. London: Routledge, 1995.
Caputo, Vincenzo. "Ragionando di pittura tra artisti e letterati." *Quaderni di italianistica* 31 (2010): 43–60.
Caro, Annibale. *De le lettere familiari del commendatore Annibal Caro.* Venice: Bernardo Giunti, 1581.

Carruthers, Mary. *The Craft of Thought: Meditation, Rhetoric, and the Making of Images, 400–1200.* Cambridge: Cambridge University Press, 1998.

Cartari, Vincenzo. *Le imagini con la spositione de i dei de gli antichi.* Venice: Francesco Marcolini, 1556.

"Catalogus codicum hagiographicorum bibliothecae civitatis Carnotensis." *Analecta Bollandiana* 8 (1889): 86–208.

Catarino, Ambrogio [Politi]. *De certa Gloria.* In idem, *Opuscula.* Lyon: M. Bonhomme, 1542.

———. *Disputatio . . . de cultu et adoratione imaginum.* [Rome, 1551.] In idem, *Enarrationes.* Rome: A. Blado, 1552.

Cattaneo, Enrico. "La singolare fortuna degli 'Acta Ecclesiae Mediolanensis,'" *La Scuola Cattolica* 111 (1983): 191–217.

Cesareo, Francesco C. "The Episcopacy in Sixteenth-Century Italy." In *Early Modern Catholicism: Essays in Honour of John W. O'Malley, S.J.,* edited by Kathleen M. Comerford and Hilmar M. Pabel, 67–83. Toronto: University of Toronto Press, 2001.

Chazelle, Celia. "Memory, Instruction, Worship: 'Gregory's' Influence on Early Medieval Doctrines of the Artistic Image." In *Gregory the Great: A Symposium,* edited by John C. Cavadini, 181–215. Notre Dame, IN: University of Notre Dame Press, 1995.

Christian, Kathleen W. *Empire without End: Antiquities Collections in Renaissance Rome, c. 1350–1527.* New Haven, CT: Yale University Press, 2010.

Christin, Olivier. "L'iconoclasme huguenot: 'Praxis pietatis' et geste révolutionnaire." In "Usages de l'image," special issue, *Ethnologie française* 24, no. 2 (1994): 216–25.

Chrysostom, Saint John. *The Homilies of Saint John Chrysostom on the Gospel of Saint Matthew.* London: Aeterna, 2015.

Cicero. *Brutus; Orator.* Translated by G. L. Hendrickson and H. M. Hubbell. Loeb Classical Library 342. Cambridge, MA: Harvard University Press, 1939.

———. *On Invention; The Best Kind of Orator; Topics.* Translated by H. M. Hubbell. Loeb Classical Library 386. Cambridge, MA: Harvard University Press, 1949.

———. *On the Orator [De Oratore]: Books 1–2.* Translated by E. W. Sutton and H. Rackham. Loeb Classical Library 348. Cambridge, MA: Harvard University Press, 1942.

[Cicero]. *Rhetorica ad Herennium.* Translated by Harry Caplan. Loeb Classical Library 403. Cambridge, MA: Harvard University Press, 1954.

Clark, Mary T. "De Trinitate." In *The Cambridge Companion to Augustine,* edited by Eleanore Stump and Norman Kretzmann, 91–102. Cambridge: Cambridge University Press, 2001.

Cleri, Bonita, and Giampiero Donnini, eds. *La Cattedrale di Fabriano.* Fabriano: Cassa di Risparmio, 2003.

Clicthove, Josse. *Sermones Judoci Clichtovei Neoportuen . . .* Cologne: Quentel, 1535.

Cochrane, Eric W. *Historians and Historiography in the Italian Renaissance.* Chicago: University of Chicago Press, 1981.

Colalucci, Francesco. "Le pitture della cappella di S. Caterina in S. Maria Maggiore: i Cesi, Vasari, Siciolante e la controriforma." *Bollettino dei Monumenti, Musei e Gallerie Pontificie* 14 (1994): 113–61.

Cole, Michael W. *Leonardo, Michelangelo, and the Art of the Figure.* New Haven: Yale University Press, 2014.

Colonna, Francesco. *Hypnerotomachia Poliphili.* Venice: Aldo Manuzio, 1499. Published in English as *Hypnerotomachia Poliphili: The Strife of Love in a Dream.* Translated by Jocelyn Godwin. London: Thames and Hudson, 1999.

Colucci, Giuseppe. *Antichità picene dell'abate Giuseppe Colucci patrizio camerinese,* vol. 17, *Delle antichità del Medio e dell Infimo Evo,* vol. 2. Fermo: Dai torchi dell'autore, 1792.

Comanini, Gregorio. *Il Figino: Overo del fine della pittura.* Mantua, 1591. In *Trattati d'arte del Cinquecento: Fra manierismo e controriforma,* vol. 3, edited by Paola Barocchi, 237–379. Bari: Laterza, 1962. Published in English as *The Figino; or, On the Purpose of Painting: Art Theory in the Late Renaissance.* Translated by Ann Doyle-Anderson and Giancarlo Maiorini. Toronto: University of Toronto Press, 2001.

Condivi, Ascanio. *Vita di Michelangelo Buonarroti.* Edited by Giovanni Nencioni. Florence: S.P.E.S., 1998. Published in English as *The Life of Michelangelo.* Translated by Alice Sedgwick Wohl. Edited by Hellmut Wohl. University Park: Pennsylvania State University Press, 1999.

Corthell, Ronald. "Robert Persons and the Writer's Mission." In *Catholicism and Anti-Catholicism in Early Modern English Texts,* edited by Arthur F. Marotti, 35–62. London: Macmillan, 1999.

Cox-Rearick, Janet. *La collection de François Ier.* Paris: Éditions des Musées Nationaux, 1972.

Crawford, Michael H. *Roman Republican Coinage.* 2 vols. Cambridge: Cambridge University Press, 1975.

Curran, Brian A., Anthony Grafton, Pamela O. Long, and Benjamin Weiss. *Obelisk: A History.* Cambridge, MA: MIT Press, 2009.

Dacos, Nicole, and Caterina Furlan. *Giovanni da Udine 1487–1561.* Udine: Casamassima, 1987.

Da Feltre, Bernardino. *Sermoni di Beato Bernardino Tomitano da Feltre: Nella redazione di fra Bernardino Bulgarino da Brescia M. O.* Edited by Carlo Varischi da Milano. 3 vols. Milan: Cassa di Risparmio delle Provincie Lombarde e Banca Del Monte, 1964.

Dandolo, Francesco, and Gaetano Sabatini. *Lo stato feudale dei Carafa di Maddaloni.* Naples: Giannini, 2009.

Daniello da Lucca, Bernardino. *Della Poetica.* Venice: Nicolini da Sabio, 1536. In *Trattati di poetica e retorica del Cinquecento,* edited by Bernard Weinberg, 1:227–318. Bari: Laterza, 1970.

Dante Alighieri. *The Divine Comedy: 1. Inferno.* Translated by John D. Sinclair. New York: Oxford University Press, 1939.

———. *The Divine Comedy: 2. Purgatorio.* Translated by John D. Sinclair. New York: Oxford University Press, 1939.

Danti, Vincenzo. *Trattato delle perfette proporzioni.* [Florence: Eredi di Lorenzo Torrentino, 1567.] In *Trattati d'arte del Cinquecento: Fra manierismo e controriforma,* vol. 1, edited by Paola Barocchi, 207–69. Bari: Laterza, 1960.

De Bujanda, J. Martinez. *Index des livres interdits.* Vol. 8, *Index de Rome 1557, 1559, 1564: Les premiers index romains et l'index du Concile de Trente.* Quebec: Centre d'Études de la Renaissance, 1990.

De Luca, Maurizio. "Il Restauro della Cappella Paolina." In Maurizio De Luca, Arnold Nesselrath, Antonio Paolucci, and Ulderico Santamaria, *La Cappella Paolina,* 43–50. Vatican City: Musei Vaticani, 2013.

De Maio, Romeo, Agostino Borromeo, Luigi Golia, Georg Lutz, and Aldo Mazzacane, eds. *Baronio e l'arte: Atti del Convegno Internazionale di Studi, Sora, 10–13 ottobre 1984.* Sora: Centro di Studi Sorani Vincenzo Patriarca, 1985.

———. *Michelangelo e la Controriforma.* Florence: Sansoni, 1990.

Dempsey, Charles. *Inventing the Renaissance Putto.* Chapel Hill: University of North Carolina Press, 2001.

———. "Mythic Inventions in Counter-Reformation Painting." In *Rome in the Renaissance: The City and the Myth; Papers of the Thirteenth Annual Conference of the Center of Medieval & Early Renaissance Studies,* edited by P. A. Ramsey, 55–75. Binghamton: State University of New York at Binghamton, Center for Medieval & Early Renaissance Studies, 1982.

Dio Cassius. *Roman History.* Vol. 8, *Books 61–70.* Translated by Earnest Cary and Herbert B. Foster. Loeb Classical Library 176. Cambridge, MA: Harvard University Press, 1925.

———. *Roman History.* Vol. 9, *Books 71–80.* Translated by Earnest Cary and Herbert B. Foster. Loeb Classical Library 177. Cambridge, MA: Harvard University Press, 1927.

Diodorus Siculus. *Library of History.* Vol. 1, *Books 1–2.34.* Translated by C. H. Oldfather. Loeb Classical Library 279. Cambridge, MA: Harvard University Press, 1933, 1954, 1957.

———. *Library of History.* Vol. 10, *Books 19.66–20.* Translated by Russel M. Geer. Loeb Classical Library 390. Cambridge, MA: Harvard University Press, 1954.

———. *Library of History.* Vol. 11, *Books 21–32.* Translated by Francis R. Walton. Loeb Classical Library 409. Cambridge, MA: Harvard University Press, 1957.

Dionysius of Halicarnassus. *Roman Antiquities.* Vol. 1, *Books 1–2.* Translated by Earnest Cary. Loeb Classical Library 319. Cambridge, MA: Harvard University Press, 1937.

Ditchfield, Simon. "'Historia Magistra Sanctitatis'? The Relationship between Historiography and Hagiography in Italy after the Council of Trent (ca. 1564–1742)." *Studies in Medieval and Renaissance History* 3 (2006): 159–84.

———. *Liturgy, Sanctity, and History in Tridentine Italy: Pietro Maria Campi and the Preservation of the Particular.* Cambridge: Cambridge University Press, 1995.

———. "Of Dancing Cardinals and Mestizo Madonnas: Reconfiguring the History of Roman Catholicism in the Early Modern Period." *Journal of Early Modern History* 8, no. 3 (2004): 386–408.

———. "Thinking with Saints: Sanctity and Society in the Early Modern World." *Critical Inquiry* 35, no. 3 (2009): 552–84.

———. "Trent Revisited." In *La fede degli italiani: Per Adriano Prosperi,* edited by Guido Dall'Olio, Adelisa Malena, and Pierroderto Scaramella, 1:357–70. Pisa: Edizioni della Normale, 2011.

———. "What Was Sacred History? (Mostly Roman) Catholic Uses of the Christian Past after Trent." In *Sacred History: Uses of the Christian Past in the Renaissance World,* edited by Katherine Van Liere, Simon Ditchfield, and Howard Louthan, 72–97. Oxford: Oxford University Press, 2012.

Dizionario Biografico degli Italiani. http://www.treccani.it/biografie/.

Dobschütz, Ernst von. *Christusbilder: Untersuchungen zur christlichen Legende.* Vol. 2 (supplements). Leipzig: J. C. Hinrichs, 1899.

Dolce, Lodovico. *Dialogo della pittura intitolato l'Aretino.* Venice: G. Giolito de' Ferrari, 1557. In *Trattati d'arte del Cinquecento: Fra manierismo e controriforma,* vol. 1, edited by Paola Barocchi, 141–206. Bari: Laterza, 1960.

———, trans. *La poetica d'Horatio tradotta per Messer Lodovico Dolce.* Venice, 1535.

Doni, Anton Francesco. *Foglie della Zucca.* Venice: Francesco Marcolini, 1552.

D'Ovidio, Francesco, and Wilhelm Meyer-Lübke. *Grammatica storica della lingua e dei dialetti italiani.* Translated by Eugenio Polcari. Milan: Tipografia Umberto Allegretti, 1906.

Dummett, Michael. *The Game of Tarot: From Ferrara to Salt Lake City.* London: Gerald Duckworth, 1980.

Durandus, Guillaume [Gulielmus Durandus]. *Rationale divinorum officiorum.* Vol. 1, books 1–4. Edited by Anselme Davril and Timothy M. Thibodeau. Turnhout: Brepols, 1995.

Durandus, William [Gulielmus Durandus]. *The Symbolism of Churches and Church Ornaments: A Translation of the First Book of the "Rationale Divinorum Officiorum" Written by William Durandus.* Edited and translated by John Mason Neale and Benjamin Webb. Leeds: T. W. Green, 1843.

Ehrman, Bart D., and Zlatko Plese. *The Apocryphal Gospels.* Oxford: Oxford University Press, 2011.

Elliott, James K., ed. and trans. *The Apocryphal New Testament: A Collection of Apocryphal Christian Literature in an English Translation.* Oxford: Oxford University Press, 1993.

Emser, Hieronymus. *Das man der heyligen bilder in den kirchen nit abthon, noch unehren soll.* Dresden, 1522. In *A Reformation Debate: Karlstadt, Emser, and Eck on Sacred Images; Three Treatises in Translation,* edited and translated by Bryan D. Mangrum and Giuseppe Scavizzi. Toronto: Centre for Renaissance and Reformation Studies, 1991.

Everson, Jane E., Lorenza Gianfrancesco, Denis V. Reidy, Lisa Sampson, and Simone Testa, *The Italian Academies 1525–1700: A Themed Collection Database,* London, British Library, 2009–. http://www.bl.uk/catalogues/ItalianAcademies/Default.aspx

Excerptiones patrum, Collectanea. In *Venerabilis Bedae.* Patrologia Latina, series secunda 94, edited by Jacques-Paul Migne. Paris: Migne, 1850.

Finocchiaro, Maurice A. *The Routledge Guidebook to Galileo's Dialogue.* New York: Routledge, 2014.

Florio, John. *Queen Anna's New World of Words; or, Dictionarie of the Italian and English Tongues.* London: Printed by Melch. Bradwood, for Edw. Blount and William Barret, 1611.

———. *A Worlde of Wordes: A Critical Edition.* Edited by Hermann W. Haller. Toronto: University of Toronto Press, 2013. First published as *A Worlde of Wordes; or, Most Copious and Exact Dictionarie in Italian and English.* London: Printed by Arnold Hatfield for Edw. Blount, 1598.

Foster, Brett. "Gregory Martin's 'Holy Latinate Jerusalem': Roman English, Romanist Values, and the Rheims New Testament (1582)." *Prose Studies: History, Theory, Criticism* 28 (2006): 130–49.

Fracastoro, Girolamo. *De temperatura vini sententia.* Camerino: Antonio Gioioso, 1553.

Frazier, Alison K. *Possible Lives: Authors and Saints in Renaissance Italy.* New York: Columbia University Press, 2005.

Fuchs, Leonhart. *De historia stirpium commentarii insignes.* Basel: Michael Isengrin, 1542. English translation in *The Great Herbal of Leonhart Fuchs.* Translated by Frederick Meyer, Emily Trueblood, and John Heller. 2 vols. Stanford, CA: Stanford University Press, 1999.

Gaillardetz, Richard R. "The Reception of Doctrine: New Perspectives." In *Authority in the Roman Catholic Church: Theory and Practice,* edited by Bernard Hoose, 95–114. Aldershot: Ashgate, 2002.

Gardner, Julian. Review of *Federico Borromeo and the Ambrosiana,* by Pamela Jones. *Journal of Ecclesiastical History* 45, no. 1 (1994): 179–80.

Gaston, Robert W. "How Words Control Images: The Rhetoric of Decorum in Counter-Reformation Italy." In *The Sensuous in the Counter-Reformation Church,* edited by Marcia B. Hall and Tracey E. Cooper, 74–90. Cambridge: Cambridge University Press, 2013.

Gauthier, Roland. "Saint Joseph d'après deux series d'homélies latines du Vie siècle sur S. Matthieu." In "Saint Joseph durant les quinze premiers siècles de l'Église," special issue, *Cahiers de Joséphologie* 19 (1971): 161–82.

Gerson, Jean. *Oeuvres complètes.* Vol. 5, *L'oeuvre oratoire.* Edited by Palémon Glorieux. Paris: Desclée Paris: 1963.

Gilbert, Creighton. "The Archbishop on the Painters of Florence." *Art Bulletin* 41 (1959): 75–87.

Gilio, Giovanni Andrea. *Dialogo del letterato cortigiano.* Edited by Paolo Cherchi. Ravenna: Longo, 2002.

———. *Discorso sopre la Città, l'Urbe, Colonia, Municipio, etc.* In idem, *Due dialogi,* 123r–144r. Camerino: Antonio Gioioso, 1564. Facsimile reprint, Florence: S.P.E.S., 1986.

———. *Due dialogi. Nel primo de' quali si ragiona de le parti morali e civili appertenenti a' letterati cortigiani, et ad ogni gentil'huomo, e l'utile che i prencipi cavano dai letterati. Nel secondo si ragiona degli errori de' pittori circa l'historie.* Camerino: Antonio Gioioso, 1564. Facsimile reprint, Florence: S.P.E.S., 1986.

———. *Le persecuzioni della Chiesa.* Venice: Gabriele Giolito de' Ferrari, 1573.

———. *Topica poetica.* Venice: Oratio de' Gobbi, 1580. Facsimile reprint, Munich: W. Fink, 1970.

———. *Trattato de la emulatione che il demonio ha fatto a Dio . . .* Venice: Francesco de' Franceschi, 1563.

———. *La vita di S. Atanasio patriarca di Alessandria. . . .* Venice: Pietro Bosello, 1559.

Giovio, Paolo. *Dialogo dell'imprese militari et amorose.* Rome: Antonio Barré, 1555.

———. *Scritti d'arte: Lessico ed ecfrasi.* Edited by Sonia Maffei. Pisa: Scuola Normale Superiore, 1999.

Giraldi, Giovanbattista Cinzio. *Discorso intorno a quello che si conviene a giovane nobile et ben creato nel servire un gran principe.* Pavia: Girolamo Bartoli, 1569.

Gombrich, Ernst H. "The Leaven of Criticism in Renaissance Art: Texts and Episodes." In idem, *Studies in the Art of the Renaissance,* vol. 3, *The Heritage of Apelles,* 111–31. Oxford: Phaidon, 1976.

Grafton, Anthony. "The Identities of History in Early Modern Europe." In *Historia: Empiricism and Erudition in Early Modern Europe,* edited by Gianna Pomata and Nancy G. Siraisi, 41–74. Cambridge, MA: MIT Press, 2005.

Gregorius, Magister. *The Marvels of Rome.* Edited and translated by John Osborne. Medieval Sources in Translation 31. Toronto: Pontifical Institute of Mediaeval Studies, 1987.

———. *Narracio de mirabilibus urbis Rome.* Edited by R. B. C. Huygens. Leiden: E. J. Brill, 1970.

Gregory the Great [Pope Gregory]. *The Letters of Gregory the Great.* Translated by John R. C. Martyn. 3 vols. Toronto: Pontifical Institute of Mediaeval Studies, 2004.

———. *S. Gregorii Magni opera: Registrum epistolarum; Libri VIII–XIV.* Edited by Dag Ludwig Norberg. Turnhout: Brepols, 1982.

Grimaldi, Giacomo. *Descrizione della basilica antica di S. Pietro in Vaticano: Codice Barberini latino 2733.* Edited by Reto Niggl. Vatican City: Biblioteca Apostolica Vaticana, 1972.

Gulia, Luigi. "Premessa." In *Baronio e l'arte: Atti del Convegno Internazionale di Studi, Sora, 10–13 ottobre 1984,* edited by Romeo De Maio et al., xvii–xxiii. Sora: Centro di Studi Sorani Vincenzo Patriarca, 1985.

Hall, Marcia B. *After Raphael: Painting in Central Italy in the Sixteenth Century.* Cambridge: Cambridge University Press, 2001.

———, ed. *Michelangelo's "Last Judgment."* Cambridge: Cambridge University Press, 2005.

———. "Michelangelo's *Last Judgment:* Resurrection of the Body and Predestination." *Art Bulletin* 58, no. 1 (1976): 85–92.

———. *The Sacred Image in the Age of Art: Titian, Tintoretto, Barocci, El Greco, Caravaggio.* New Haven, CT: Yale University Press, 2011.

Hall, Marcia B., and Tracey E. Cooper, eds. *The Sensuous in the Counter-Reformation Church.* Cambridge: Cambridge University Press, 2013.

Hansen, Morten Steen. *In Michelangelo's Mirror: Perino del Vaga, Daniele da Volterra, Pellegrino Tibaldi.* University Park: Pennsylvania State University Press, 2013.

Herklotz, Ingo. "*Historia sacra* und mittelalterliche Kunst während der zweiten Hälfte des 16. Jahrhunderts in Rom." In *Baronio e l'arte: Atti del Convegno Internazionale di Studi, Sora, 10–13 ottobre 1984,* edited by Romeo De Maio et al., 21–72. Sora: Centro di Studi Sorani Vincenzo Patriarca, 1985.

Herodotus. *The Persian Wars.* Vol. 2, *Books 3–4.* Translated by A. D. Godley. Loeb Classical Library 118. Cambridge, MA: Harvard University Press, 1921.

Hilhorst, Anthony. "The Chapter on Clement in Jacobus de Voragine's *Golden Legend.*" In *The Pseudo-Clementines,* edited by Jan N. Bremmer, 285–306. Leuven: Peeters, 2010.

Hirst, Michael. *Sebastiano del Piombo.* Oxford: Clarendon, 1981.

Homer. *Odyssey.* Vol. 1, *Books 1–12.* Translated by A. T. Murray. Revised by George E. Dimock. Loeb Classical Library 104. Cambridge, MA: Harvard University Press, 1919.

Hope, Charles. *Titian.* London: Jupiter, 1980.

Horace. *Ars Poetica.* In *Satires; Epistles; The Art of Poetry,* translated by H. Rushton Fairclough, 450–89. Loeb Classical Library 194. Cambridge, MA: Harvard University Press, 1926.

Hülsen, Christian. "Das Speculum Romanae Magnificentiae des Antonio Lafreri." In *Collectanea variae doctrinae Leoni S. Olschki,* 121–70. Munich: Jacques Rosenthal, 1921.

Hunter, John. *Girolamo Siciolante pittore da Sermoneta (1521–1575).* Rome: L'Erma di Bretschneider, 1996.

Isidore of Seville. *The Etymologies of Isidore of Seville.* Edited and translated by Stephen A. Barney, W. J. Lewis, J. A. Beach, and Oliver Berghof. Cambridge: Cambridge University Press, 2006.

Jacobilli, Lodovico. *Discorso della Città di Foligno.* Foligno: Agostino Alterii, 1646.

Jedin, Hubert. *Crisis and Closure of the Council of Trent: A Retrospective View from the Second Vatican Council.* Translated by N. D. Smith. London: Sheed & Ward, 1967.

———. *Geschichte des Konzils von Trent.* Vol. 4. Freiburg: Herder, 1975.

———. *A History of the Council of Trent.* Vol. 2, *The First Sessions at Trent 1545–47.* Translated by Dom Ernest Graf. St. Louis, MO: B. Herder Book Co., 1961.

Jerome. "Letter LVII to Pammachius on the Best Method of Translating." Translated by William H. Freemantle. In *A Select Library of Nicene and Post-Nicene Fathers of the Christian Church,* 2nd ser., vol. 6, *The Principal Works of Jerome,* edited by Philip Schaff and Henry Wace. New York: Christian Literature Company, 1893.

———. Letter 127 to Principia. In *Jerome,* edited and translated by Stefan Rebenich, 119–29. London: Routledge, 2002.

———. *Liber de optimo genere interpretandi (Epistula 57).* Edited by G. J. M. Bartelink. Leiden: E. J. Brill, 1980.

John of Damascus. *An Exact Exposition of the Orthodox Faith* [*De Fide Orthodoxa*]. In *St. John of Damascus: Writings,* translated by Frederic H. Chase Jr., 165–406. Washington, D.C.: Catholic University of America Press, 1958.

Jones, Pamela. *Federico Borromeo and the Ambrosiana: Art Patronage and Reform in Seventeenth-Century Milan.* Cambridge: Cambridge University Press, 1993.

Josephus. *The Jewish War.* Vol. 3, *Books 5–7.* Translated by Henry St. John Thackeray. Loeb Classical Library 210. Cambridge, MA: Harvard University Press, 1928.

Julius Capitolinus. *The Two Maximini.* In *Historia Augusta, Volume II,* translated by David Magie, 314–79. Loeb Classical Library 140. Cambridge, MA: Harvard University Press, 1924.

Kantorowicz, Ernst H. *The King's Two Bodies: A Study in Medieval Political Theology.* Princeton, NJ: Princeton University Press, 1957.

Kanz, Roland. "Der Capriccio-Begriff bei Vasari und Gilio in der Kontroverse um Michelangelos *Jüngstes Gericht.*" In *Künste und Natur in Diskursen der frühen Neuzeit,* edited by Hartmut Laufhütte, 1:497–513. Wiesbaden: Harrasowitz, 2000.

Kappler, Federica. "Una nota di cronologia sui disegni di Michelangelo per la pala Cesi di Santa Maria della Pace." *Mitteilungen des kunsthistorischen Institutes in Florenz* 56, no. 3 (2014): 355–60.

Kirkham, Victoria. "Creative Partners: The Marriage of Laura Battiferra and Bartolomeo Ammannati." *Renaissance Quarterly* 55 (2002): 498–559.

Kliemann, Julian. *Gesta Dipinte: La grande decorazione nelle dimore italiane dal Quattrocento al Seicento.* Milan: Silvana Editoriale, 1993.

Krey, Philip D. W., and Lesley Smith, eds. *Nicholas of Lyra: The Senses of Scripture.* Leiden: E. J. Brill, 2000.

Kristeller, Paul Oskar. *Iter italicum: Accedunt alia itinera; A Finding List of Uncatalogued or Incompletely Catalogued Humanistic Manuscripts of the Renaissance in Italian and Other Libraries.* Vol. 6, *(Italy 3 and alia itinera 4), Supplement to Italy (G–V), Supplement to Vatican and Austria to Spain.* London: Warburg Institute, 1992.

Kuntz, Margaret. "Designed for Ceremony: The Cappella Paolina at the Vatican Palace." *Journal of the Society of Architectural Historians* 62, no. 2 (2003): 228–55.

Kusukawa, Sachiko. *Philosophy in the Sixteenth and Seventeenth Centuries: Conversations with Aristotle.* Aldershot: Ashgate, 1999.

———. *Picturing the Book of Nature: Image, Text, and Argument in Sixteenth-Century Human Anatomy and Medical Botany.* Chicago: University of Chicago Press, 2012.

Lanciani, Rodolfo. *Storia degli scavi di Roma e notizie intorno le collezioni romane di antichità.* Vol. 4, *Dalla elezione di Pio V alla morte di Clemente VIII (7 gennaio 1566–3 marzo 1605).* Edited by Paolo Liverani. Rome: Quasar, 1992.

Langer, Ulrich. "Invention." In *The Cambridge History of Literary Criticism,* vol. 3, *The Renaissance,* edited by Glyn P. Norton, 136–44. Cambridge: Cambridge University Press, 1999.

Lawrence, Hugh. "Spiritual Authority and Governance: A Historical Perspective." In *Authority in the Roman Catholic Church: Theory and Practice,* edited by Bernard Hoose, 37–57. Aldershot: Ashgate, 2002.

Lee, Rensselaer W. "*Ut pictura poesis*": *The Humanistic Theory of Painting.* New York: Norton, 1967. First published in *Art Bulletin* 22, no. 4 (1940): 197–269.

Lingo, Stuart. *Federico Barocci: Allure and Devotion in Late Renaissance Painting.* New Haven, CT: Yale University Press, 2008.

Lionardi, Alessandro. *Dialogi dell'invenzione poetica.* Venice: Plinio Pietrasanta, 1554. Facsimile reprint, Munich: Wilhelm Fink, 1970.

Livy. *History of Rome.* Vol. 1, *Books 1–2.* Translated by B. O. Foster. Loeb Classical Library 114. Cambridge, MA: Harvard University Press, 1919.

———. *History of Rome.* Vol. 2, *Books 3–4.* Translated by B. O. Foster. Loeb Classical Library 133. Cambridge, MA: Harvard University Press, 1922.

Lomazzo, Giovanni Paolo. *Il libro dei sogni* [ca. 1563]. In *Scritti sulle arti,* edited by Roberto Paolo Ciardi, 1:1–240. Florence: Marchi and Bertolli, 1973–74.

Macrobius. *Commentary on the Dream of Scipio.* Edited and translated by William Harris Stahl. New York: Columbia University Press, 1952.

Maffei, Sonia. "La fama di Laocoonte nei testi del Cinquecento." In *Laocoonte, fama e stile,* edited by Salvatore Settis, 85–214. Rome: Donzelli Editore, 1999.

Mâle, Emile. *L'art religieux de la fin du moyen âge en France: Étude sur l'iconographie du moyen âge et sur ses sources d'inspiration.* Paris: Hérissey, 1922.

Mancinelli, Fabrizio. "The History, Execution Technique, First Censorship and Restoration Intervention." In *The Last Judgement: I, The Restoration,* Francesco Buranelli, Paolo Ballirano, Fabrizio Mancinelli, Gianluigi Colalucci, Nazzareno Gabrielli, and Fabio Morresi, 7–36. Milan: Rizzoli, 1999.

Mancini, Matteo. *Tiziano e le corti d'Asburgo: Nei documenti degli archivi spagnoli.* Venice: Istituto Veneto di Scienze, Lettere ed Arti, 1998.

Mangrum, Bryan D., and Giuseppe Scavizzi, eds. and trans. *A Reformation Debate: Karlstadt, Emser, and Eck on Sacred Images: Three Treatises in Translation.* Toronto: Centre for Renaissance and Reformation Studies, 1991.

Manning, John. *The Emblem.* London: Reaktion, 2002.

Marcucci, Marcello. "Accademia Senese degli Intronati." In Marcello Marcucci and Natalina Crevani, *Accademie e istituzioni culturali in Toscana,* edited by Francesco Adorno, 454–61. Accademia toscana di scienze e lettere "La Colombaria," Serie Studi 92. Florence: Leo S. Olschki, 1988.

Marucci, Valerio, Antonio Marzo, and Angelo Romano, eds. *Pasquinate romane del Cinquecento.* 2 vols. Rome: Salerno, 1983.

Massari, Stefania. *Giulio Bonasone.* Exh. cat. 2 vols. Rome: Quasar, 1983.

Masséna, Victor (Prince d'Essling). *Les livres à figures vénitiens de la fin du XVe siècle et du commencement du XVIe.* 6 vols. in 3 parts. Florence: Olschki, 1907–14.

Mattioli, Pietro Andrea. *Commentarii in libros sex Pedacii Dioscoridis Anazarbei De materia medica . . .* Venice: V. Valgrisi, 1554.

McMullin, Ernan. "Galileo on Science and Scripture." In *The Cambridge Companion to Galileo,* edited by Peter Machamer, 271–347. Cambridge: Cambridge University Press, 1998.

Mejía, Jorge María, Arnold Nesselrath, Pier Nicola Pagliara, and Maurizio De Luca. *The Fifteenth-Century Frescoes in the Sistine Chapel.* Vatican City: Musei Vaticani, 2003.

Meyer zur Capellen, Jürg. *Raphael: A Critical Catalogue of His Paintings.* 3 vols. Landshut: Arcos-Veri, 2001–15.

Michelangelo e la Sistina: La tecnica, il restauro, il mito. Exh. cat. Rome: Fratelli Palombi, 1990.

Miedema, Hessel. "On Mannerism and *maniera.*" *Simiolus: Netherlands Quarterly for the History of Art* 10, no. 1 (1978–79): 19–45.

Migliorini, Bruno. *Storia della lingua italiana.* Florence: Sansoni, 1960.

Minnich, Nelson. "Prophecy and the Fifth Lateran Council 1512–1517." In *Prophetic Rome in the High Renaissance Period,* edited by Marjorie Reeves, 63–88. Oxford: Clarendon, 1992.

Moltedo, Alida, ed. *La Sistina Riprodotta.* Exh. cat. Rome: Fratelli Palombi, 1991.

Mortari, Luisa. *Francesco Salviati.* Rome: Leonardo-De Luca, 1992.

Moss, Ann. "Horace in the Sixteenth Century: Commentators into Critics." In *The Cambridge History of Literary Criticism,* vol. 3, *The Renaissance,* edited by Glyn P. Norton, 66–76. Cambridge: Cambridge University Press, 1999.

Mouren, Raphaële. "La Bibliothèque du Palais Farnèse avant Fulvio Orsini." *Mélanges de l'École française de Rome: Italie et Méditerranée* 107, no. 1 (1995): 7–14.

Murphy, James J. "Saint Augustine and the Debate about a Christian Rhetoric." In *The Rhetoric of St. Augustine of Hippo: "De Doctrina Christiana" and the Search for a Distinctly Christian Rhetoric,* edited by Richard Leo Enos and Roger Thompson, 205–18. Waco, TX: Baylor University Press, 2008. First published in *Quarterly Journal of Speech* 46 (1960): 400–410.

Nagel, Alexander. "Art as Gift: Art and Religious Reform in the Renaissance." In *Negotiating the Gift: Pre-Modern Figurations of Exchange,* edited by Gadi Alzazi, Valentin Groebner, and Bernhard Jussen, 319–60. Göttingen: Vandehoeck & Rupprecht, 2003.

———. *The Controversy of Renaissance Art.* Chicago: University of Chicago Press, 2011.

———. *Michelangelo and the Reform of Art.* Cambridge: Cambridge University Press, 2000.

Natali, Pietro de'. *Catalogus sanctorum et gestorum eorum.* Lyon: E. Gueynard, 1519.

Newman, John Henry. *Apologia pro vita sua.* London: Longmans, Green & Co., 1929.

———. *A Letter Addressed to His Grace the Duke of Norfolk on Occasion of Mr. Gladstone's Recent Expostulation.* London: B. M. Pickering, 1875.

Nicolas of Lyra. *Postillae perpetuae in universam S. Scripturam.* Rome: Sweynheym and Pannartz, 1471–72.

Noble, Thomas F. X. *Images, Iconoclasm, and the Carolingians.* Philadelphia: University of Pennsylvania Press, 2009.

Nogara, Bartolomeo. "Per la storia della Cappella Sistina." *Monatshefte für Kunstwissenschaft* 3 (1910): 160–62.

Nova, Alessandro. *The Artistic Patronage of Pope Julius III (1550–1555): Profane Imagery and Buildings for the De Monte Family in Rome.* New York: Garland, 1988.

Oberhuber, Konrad, and Achim Gnann. *Roma e lo stile classico di Raffaello (1515–1527).* Exh. cat. Milan: Electa, 1999.

Occhipinti, Carmelo. *Pirro Ligorio e la storia cristiana di Roma: Da Costantino all'Umanesimo.* Pisa: Edizioni della Normale, 2007.

O'Malley, John W. "Content and Rhetorical Forms in Sixteenth-Century Treatises on Preaching." In *Renaissance Eloquence: Studies in the Theory and Practice of Renaissance Rhetoric,* edited by James J. Murphy, 238–52. Berkeley: University of California Press, 1983.

———. "Patronage, Spirituality, and the Power of the Beautiful: Some Historiographical Considerations." In *Federico Borromeo Principe e Mecenate: Atti delle giornate di studio 21–22 novembre 2003,* edited by Cesare Mozzarelli, 23–30. Milan: Biblioteca Ambrosiana, 2004.

———. "The Theology behind Michelangelo's Ceiling." In *The Sistine Chapel: The Art, the History, and the Restoration,* edited by Carlo Pietrangeli, 92–148. New York: Harmony, 1986.

———. "Trent, Sacred Images, and Catholics' Senses of the Sensuous." In *The Sensuous in the Counter-Reformation Church,* edited by Marcia B. Hall and Tracey E. Cooper, 28–48. Cambridge: Cambridge University Press, 2013.

———. *Trent: What Happened at the Council.* Cambridge, MA: Belknap, 2013.

Ossola, Carlo. "La 'Topica Poetica' di G. A. Gilio da Fabriano." In *Retorica e poetica: Atti del III Convegno Italo-Tedesco,* edited by Daniela Goldin and Gianfranco Folena, 259–83. Padua: Liviana, 1979.

Ovid. *Fasti.* Translated by James G. Frazer. Loeb Classical Library 253. Cambridge, MA: Harvard University Press, 1931.

Ovid. *Metamorphoses.* Vol. 1, *Books 1–8.* Translated by Frank Justus Miller. Revised by G. P. Goold. Loeb Classical Library 42. Cambridge, MA: Harvard University Press, 1916.

———. *Metamorphoses.* Vol. 2, *Books 9–15.* Translated by Frank Justus Miller. Revised by G. P. Goold. Loeb Classical Library 43. Cambridge, MA: Harvard University Press, 1916.

Paleotti, Gabriele. *Discorso intorno alle imagini sacre e profane.* [Bologna, 1582.] In *Trattati d'arte del Cinquecento: Fra manierismo e controriforma,* vol. 2, edited by Paola Barocchi, 117–509. Bari: Laterza, 1961. Published in English as *Discourse on Sacred and Profane Images.* Translated by William McCuaig. Los Angeles: Getty Research Institute, 2012.

Panigarola, Francesco. *Il compendio de gli Annales ecclesiastici del Padre Cesare Baronio.* Rome: Gigliotto, 1590.

Parks, George B. *The English Traveller to Italy.* Vol. 1, *The Middle Ages (to 1525).* Rome: Edizioni di Storia e Letteratura, 1954.

Parma Baudille, Rita. "L'ultimo lavoro romano di Battista Franco: La cappella Gabrielli in Santa Maria sopra Minerva." *Arte/Documento* 6 (1992): 183–96.

Partridge, Loren, and Randolph Starn. "Triumphalism and the Sala Regia in the Vatican." In *"All the world's a stage . . .": Art and Pageantry in the Renaissance and Baroque,* vol. 1, edited by Barbara Wisch and Susan Scott Munshower, 23–81. University Park: Pennsylvania State University Press, 1990.

Parvis, Paul. "Guardian Angels and Carrotburgers: Two Views of the Role of the Magisterium." *New Blackfriars* 71, no. 841 (1990): 368–76.

Passavant, Johann David. *Le peintre-graveur.* 6 vols. Leipzig: Weigel, 1860–64.

Pastor, Ludwig von. *The History of the Popes from the Close of the Middle Ages: Drawn from the Secret Archives of the Vatican and Other Original Sources.* Vol. 12, *Paul III (1534–1549).* Edited by Ralph Francis Kerr. London: Kegan Paul, Trench, Trubner, 1923.

———. *The History of the Popes from the Close of the Middle Ages: Drawn from the Secret Archives of the Vatican and Other Original Sources.* Vol. 14, *Marcellus II (1555); Paul IV (1555–1559).* Edited by Ralph Francis Kerr. London: Kegan Paul, Trench, Trubner, 1924.

Patriarca, Vincenzo. *Il Crocifisso del Baronio nella storia e nell'arte.* Sora: La Moderna Grafica, 1947.

Pecci, Giovanni Antonio. *Memorie Storico-Critiche della Città di Siena.* 4 vols. Siena: Pazzini Carli, 1755–60. Facsimile reprint, edited by Mario Pavolini and Ennio Innocenti. 2 vols. Siena: Cantagalli, 1988.

Persius Flaccus, Aulus. *Satires.* In *Juvenal and Persius,* edited and translated by Susanna Morton Braund, 41–125. Loeb Classical Library 91. Cambridge, MA: Harvard University Press, 2004.

Pertile, Fidenzio, and Ettore Camesasca. *Lettere sull'arte di Pietro Aretino.* Vol. 2. Milan: Edizioni del Milione, 1957.

Petrarch, Francesco. *The Canzoniere; or, Rerum vulgarium fragmenta.* Translated and edited by Mark Musa. Bloomington: Indiana University Press, 1996.

———. *Canzoniere, Trionfi, Rime Varie e una scelta di versi Latini.* Edited by Carlo Muscetta and Daniele Ponchiroli. Turin: Einaudi, 1958.

Pinelli, Antonio, and Orietta Rossi. *Genga Architetto: Aspetti della cultura urbinate del primo 500.* Rome: Bulzoni, 1971.

Pino, Paolo. *Dialogo di pittura.* [Venice: Paolo Gherardo, 1548.] In *Trattati d'arte del Cinquecento: Fra manierismo e controriforma,* vol. 1, edited by Paola Barocchi, 93–139. Bari: Laterza, 1960.

Platina, Bartolomeo. *Historia de vitis pontificum Romanorum, a D.N. Iesu Christo usque ad Paulum papam II longè quàm antea emendatior; cui Onuphrii Panuinii Veronensis fratris eremitae Augustiniani opera, reliquorum quoque pontificum uitae usque ad Pium IIII pontificem maximum adiunctae sunt; Et totum opus uariis annotationibus illustratum.* Edited by Onofrio Panvinio. Venice: Michele Tramezzino, 1562.

Pliny the Elder. *Natural History.* Translated by H. Rackman, W. H. S. Jones, and D. E. Eichholz. 10 vols. Loeb Classical Library 330, 352–53, 370–71, 392–94, 418–19. Cambridge, MA: Harvard University Press, 1938–63.

Plutarch. *Lives.* Translated by Bernadotte Perrin. Vol. 1. Loeb Classical Library 46. Cambridge, MA: Harvard University Press, 1914.

———. *Lives.* Translated by Bernadotte Perrin. Vol. 5. Loeb Classical Library 87. Cambridge, MA: Harvard University Press, 1917.

———. *Lives.* Translated by Bernadotte Perrin. Vol. 9. Loeb Classical Library 101. Cambridge, MA: Harvard University Press, 1920.

———. "Were the Athenians More Famous in War or in Wisdom?" In *Moralia: Volume IV,* translated by Frank Cole Babbitt, 489–527. Loeb Classical Library 305. Cambridge, MA: Harvard University Press, 1936.

Poggi, Giovanni, Paola Barocchi, and Renzo Ristori, eds. *Il Carteggio di Michelangelo,* vol. 4, *1533–1552.* Florence: Sansoni, 1979.

Pollmann, Judith. "Countering the Reformation in France and the Netherlands: Clerical Leadership and Catholic Violence 1560–1585." *Past & Present,* no. 190 (2006): 83–120.

Pope-Hennessy, John. *Italian Renaissance Sculpture.* London: Phaidon, 1996.

Possevino, Antonio. *Bibliotheca selecta.* 2 vols. Rome: Domenico Basa, 1593.

Powell, J. G. F. "Persius' First Satire: A Re-examination." In *Author and Audience in Latin Literature,* edited by Tony Woodman and Jonathan Powell. Cambridge: Cambridge University Press, 1992.

Procopius of Caesarea. *Constructions de Justinien Ier: Peri ktismaton = De aedificiis.* Introduction, translation, commentary, and index by Denis Roques. Posthumous publication edited by Eugenio Amato and Jacques Schamp. Alessandria: Edizioni dell'Orso, 2011.

Prodi, Paolo. *Il Cardinale Gabriele Paleotti (1522–1597).* 2 vols. Rome: Edizioni di Storia e Letteratura, 1959, 1967.

———. *Ricerca sulla teorica delle arti figurative nella Riforma Cattolica.* 2nd ed. Bologna: Nuova Alfa, 1984. First published in *Archivio italiano per la storia della pietà* 3 (1965): 121–212.

Pseudo-Bonaventura. *Meditations on the Life of Christ.* Translated and edited by Isa Ragusa and Rosalie B. Green. Princeton NJ: Princeton University Press, 1961.

Pullapilly, Cyriac K. *Caesar Baronius: Counter-Reformation Historian.* Notre Dame, IN: University of Notre Dame Press, 1975.

Puterbach, Joseph. "'Truth Hath the Victory': Dialogue and Disputation in John Foxe's *Actes and Monuments.*" In *Printed Voices: The Renaissance Culture of Dialogue,* edited by Dorothea Heitsch and Jean-François Vallée, 137–56. Toronto: University of Toronto Press, 2004.

Quintilian. *The Orator's Education.* Vol. 1, *Books 1–2.* Edited and translated by Donald A. Russell. Loeb Classical Library 124. Cambridge, MA: Harvard University Press, 2002.

———. *The Orator's Education.* Vol. 3, *Books 6–8.* Edited and translated by Donald A. Russell. Loeb Classical Library 126. Cambridge, MA: Harvard University Press, 2002.

———. *The Orator's Education.* Vol. 5, *Books 11–12.* Edited and translated by Donald A. Russell. Loeb Classical Library 494. Cambridge, MA: Harvard University Press, 2002.

Ramelli, Camillo. *Di Francesco Agostini, pittore fabrianese.* Fabriano: Crocetti, 1854.

Ratzinger, Joseph. "On the Interpretation of the Tridentine Decree on Tradition." In Karl Rahner and Joseph Ratzinger, *Revelation and Tradition,* translated by W. J. O'Hara, 50–66. Freiburg: Herder, 1966.

Rhodes, Dennis E. "Notable Acquisitions 1975–1985: Italian Books 1501–1600." *The British Library Journal* 12, no. 1 (1986): 86–101.

Richardson, Brian. "The Concept of a *Lingua Comune* in Renaissance Italy." In *Languages of Italy: Histories and Dictionaries,* edited by Anna Laura Lepschy and Arturo Tosi, 11–28. Ravenna: Longo, 2007.

———. *Manuscript Culture in Renaissance Italy.* Cambridge: Cambridge University Press, 2014.

Richardson, Carol M. *Reclaiming Rome: Cardinals in the Fifteenth Century.* Leiden: E. J. Brill, 2009.

Richter, Jean Paul. *The Literary Works of Leonardo da Vinci.* 2 vols. London: Low, Marston, Seale, & Rivington, 1883.

Rigoni, Erice. "Appunti e documenti sul pittore Girolamo dal Santo." *Atti e memorie dell R. Accademia di Scienze, Lettere, ed Arti in Padova,* n.s., 57 (1940–41): 35–58. Reprinted in Erice Rigoni, *L'arte rinascimentale a Padova,* 187–200. Padua: Antenore, 1970.

Robertson, Clare. "Annibal Caro as Iconographer: Sources and Method." *Journal of the Warburg and Courtauld Institutes* 45 (1982): 160–81.

———. *"Il gran cardinale": Alessandro Farnese, Patron of the Arts.* New Haven, CT: Yale University Press, 1992.

———. "Phoenix Romanus." In *Rome,* edited by Marcia B. Hall, 184–245. Cambridge: Cambridge University Press, 2005.

Robinson, Howard. "Substance." In *The Stanford Encyclopedia of Philosophy,* edited by Edward N. Zalta. Stanford University, Spring 2014 edition. http://plato.stanford.edu/archives/spr2014/entries/substance/.

Rosand, David, and Michelangelo Muraro. *Titian and the Venetian Woodcut: A Loan Exhibition.* Exh. cat. Washington, D.C.: The Foundation, 1976.

Roskill, Mark W., ed. and trans. *Dolce's "Aretino" and Venetian Art Theory of the Cinquecento.* Toronto: University of Toronto Press in association with the Renaissance Society of America, 2000.

Rothlände, Stefanie, ed., and Doris Mueller-Ziem, trans. "Giovanni Andrea Gilio, *Degli errori de' pittori circa l'istorie* (1564)." In *Historienmalerei,* edited by Thomas W. Gaehtgens and Uwe Fleckner, 99–105. Berlin: Reimer, 1996.

Rotili, Mario, ed. *Fortuna di Michelangelo nell'incisione.* Exh. cat. Benevento: A.B.E.T.E., 1964.

Rowland, Ingrid D. *The Culture of the High Renaissance.* Cambridge: Cambridge University Press, 1998.

Rufinus of Aquileia. *Historia Ecclesiastica.* In *The Church History of Rufinus of Aquileia: Books 10 and 11,* translated by Philip R. Amidon. Oxford: Oxford University Press, 1997.

Russell, Donald Andrew, and Michael Winterbottom, eds. *Classical Literary Criticism.* Oxford: Oxford University Press, 1972.

Sacrorum conciliorum nova et amplissima collectio. Edited by Gian Domenico Mansi. Vols. 1–31. Florence: Zatta, 1759–98.

Sacrorum conciliorum nova et amplissima collectio continuata curantibus J. B. Martin et L. Petit. Edited by Jean Baptiste Martin, Gabriel Cossart, and Louis Petit. Vols. 32–53. Paris: Hubert Welter, 1901–27.

Sacrorum conciliorum nova et amplissima collectio . . . Edited by Gian Domenico Mansi, Jean Baptiste Martin, Gabriel Cossart, and Louis Petit. 53 vols. in 59 books. Graz: Akademische Druck- und Verlagsanstalt, 1960–62. Reprint of the editions of 1759–98 and 1901–27.

Sansovino, Francesco. *Della origine et de' fatti delle famiglie illustri d'Italia.* Venice: Altobello Salicato, 1609.

Santoni, Michele. "L'arte della stampa in Camerino: Appendice a Bibliografia storica marchigiana." *Atti e memorie della R. Deputazione di storia patria per le provincie delle Marche* 6 (1903): 95–102.

Saslow, James M. *The Poetry of Michelangelo: An Annotated Translation.* New Haven, CT: Yale University Press, 1991.

Sassi, Romualdo. *Le chiese di Fabriano.* Fabriano: Arti grafiche "Gentile," 1961.

———. "Sonetti di poeti fabrianesi in onore di Gentile da Fabriano." *Rassegna marchigiana* 2 (1923–24): 273–82.

Scavizzi, Giuseppe. *Arte e architettura sacra: Cronache e documenti sulla controversia tra riformati e cattolici (1500–1550)*. Reggio Calabria: Casa Editrice del Libro, 1982.

———. *The Controversy on Images from Calvin to Baronius.* New York: Peter Lang, 1992.

Scevolini, Giovanni Domenico. "Dell'istorie di Fabriano." In *Antichità picene dell'abate Giuseppe Colucci patrizio camerinese.* Vol. 17, *Delle antichita del Medio e dell Infimo Evo*, vol. 2, edited by Giuseppe Colucci, 5–151. Fermo: Dai torchi dell'autore, 1792.

Schiller, Gertrud. *Iconography of Christian Art.* Vol. 2, *The Passion of Christ.* London: Lund Humphries, 1972.

Schlitt, Melinda. "Painting, Criticism and Michelangelo's *Last Judgment* in the Age of the Counter-Reformation." In *Michelangelo's "Last Judgment,"* edited by Marcia B. Hall, 113–49. Cambridge: Cambridge University Press, 2005.

Schlosser, Julius von. *La letteratura artistica: Manuale delle fonti della storia dell'arte moderna.* Translated by Filippo Rossi. Edited by Otto Kurz. Florence: Nuova Italia, 1964. First published as Julius von Schlosser, *Die kunstliteratur: Ein Handbuch zur Quellenkunde der neueren Kunstgeschichte.* Vienna: Anton Schroll, 1924.

Schneemelcher, Wilhelm, and Robert McLachlan Wilson, eds. *New Testament Apocrypha.* Vol. 1, *Gospels and Related Writings.* Cambridge: James Clarke, 1991.

Segni, Bernardo. *Rettorica e poetica d'Aristotele.* Florence: Torrentino, 1549.

Seneca. *Natural Questions.* Vol. 1, *Books 1–3.* Translated by Thomas H. Corcoran. Loeb Classical Library 450. Cambridge, MA: Harvard University Press, 1971.

———. *Natural Questions.* Vol. 2, *Books 4–7.* Translated by Thomas H. Corcoran. Loeb Classical Library 457. Cambridge, MA: Harvard University Press, 1972.

Sénécal, Robert. "Carlo Borromeo's *Instructiones fabricae et supellectilis ecclesiasticae* and Its Origins in the Rome of the Time." *Papers of the British School at Rome* 68 (2000): 241–67.

S. Gelasius I Papa / S. Avitus / S. Faustinus . . . Patrologia Latina, series prima 59, edited by Jacques-Paul Migne. Paris: Migne, 1847.

Shea, William. "Galileo's Copernicanism." In *The Cambridge Companion to Galileo,* edited by Peter Machamer, 211–43. Cambridge: Cambridge University Press, 1998.

Shearman. John K. G. *Mannerism.* Harmondsworth: Penguin, 1967.

———. *Only Connect: Art and the Spectator in the Italian Renaissance.* Princeton, NJ: Princeton University Press, 1992.

———. *Raphael's Cartoons in the Collection of Her Majesty the Queen, and the Tapestries for the Sistine Chapel.* London: Phaidon, 1972.

Shuger, Debora K. *Sacred Rhetoric: The Christian Grand Style in the English Renaissance.* Princeton, NJ: Princeton University Press, 1988.

Sicard of Cremona. *Mitrale, sive De officiis ecclesiasticis summa.* In *Sicardus Cremonensis Episcopus, Petrus Sarnensis, Anonymi saeculi XII.* Vol. 1. Patrologia Latina series secunda 213, 14–434. Paris: Migne, 1855.

Steele, Robert. "A Notice of the *Ludus Triumphorum* and Some Early Italian Card Games." *Archaeologia* 57 (1900): 185–200.

Stumpel, Jeroen. "Speaking of Manner." *Word and Image* 4, no. 1 (1988): 246–64.

Suetonius. *Suetonius: Volume I.* Translated by J. C. Rolfe. Loeb Classical Library 31. Cambridge, MA: Harvard University Press, 1914.

———. *Suetonius: Volume II.* Translated by J. C. Rolfe. Loeb Classical Library 38. Cambridge, MA: Harvard University Press, 1914.

Summers, David. *Michelangelo and the Language of Art.* Princeton, NJ: Princeton University Press, 1981.

Talvacchia, Bette. *Taking Positions.* Princeton, NJ: Princeton University Press, 1999.

———. "The Word Made Flesh: Spiritual Subjects and Carnal Depictions in Renaissance Art." In *The Sensuous in the Counter-Reformation Church,* edited by Marcia B. Hall and Tracey E. Cooper, 49–73. Cambridge: Cambridge University Press, 2013.

Tanner, Norman, ed. and trans. *Decrees of the Ecumenical Councils.* 2 vols. Washington, D.C.: Georgetown University Press, 1990.

Titi, Filippo. *Studio di pittura, scoltura, et architettura, nelle chiese di Roma (1674–1763).* Edited by Bruno Contardi and Serena Romano. Florence: Centro Di, 1987.

Tolnay, Charles de. *The Sistine Chapel.* Princeton, NJ: Princeton University Press, 1945.

Tolomei, Claudio. *Delle lettere libri sette.* Naples: Albergo de' poveri, 1829.

Tommaseo, Niccolò, and Bernardo Bellini. *Dizionario della lingua italiana.* 8 vols. Turin: L'Unione, 1861–74. http://www.tommaseobellini.it/.

Trexler, Richard C. *The Journey of the Magi: Meanings in History of a Christian Story.* Princeton, NJ: Princeton University Press, 1997.

Ughelli, Ferdinando. *Italia Sacra, sive de Episcopis Italiae, et insularum adjacentium, rebusque ab iis praeclare gestis. . . .* Venice: Sebastiano Coleti, 1720.

Uginet, François-Charles, François Fossier, Bertrand Jestaz, Michel Hochmann, and Philippe Sénéchal. *Le Palais Farnèse.* 3 vols. in 6 parts. Rome: École française de Rome, 1981–94.

Valeriano, Piero. *Hieroglyphica: sive; De sacris Aegyptiorum literis commentarii.* Basel: Palma Ising, 1556.

Varchi, Benedetto. *Lezzione nella quale si disputa della maggioranza delle arti e qual sia più nobile, la scultura o la pittura . . .* [Florence: Lorenzo Torrentino, 1549.] In *Trattati d'arte del Cinquecento: Fra manierismo e controriforma,* vol. 1, edited by Paola Barocchi, 1–82. Bari: Laterza, 1960.

Vasaeus, Johannes. *Chronici rerum memorabilium Hispaniae: Tomus prior.* Salamanca: Ioannes Iunta, 1552.

Vasari, Giorgio. *Le opere di Giorgio Vasari.* Edited by Gaetano Milanesi and Paola Barocchi. 9 vols. Florence: Sansoni, 1973.

———. *Le vite de' più eccellenti architetti, pittori, et scultori Italiani . . . nell'edizione per i tipi di Lorenzo Torrentino, Firenze 1550.* Edited by Luciano Bellosi and Aldo Rossi. Turin: Einaudi, 1986.

———. *Le vite de' più eccellenti pittori, scultori, e architettori: Nelle redazioni del 1550 e 1568.* Edited by Rosanna Bettarini and Paola Barocchi. 6 vols. Florence: S.P.E.S., 1966–87.

Vecchietti, Filippo, and Tommaso Moro. *Biblioteca picena, o sia notizie istoriche delle opere e degli scrittori piceni . . .* 5 vols. Osimo: D. A. Quercetti, 1790–96.

Vickers, Brian. *In Defence of Rhetoric.* Oxford: Clarendon, 1998.

Virgil. *Aeneid, Books 1–6.* In *Eclogues; Georgics; Aeneid, Books 1–6,* translated by H. Rushton Fairclough, revised by G. P. Goold, 261–597. Loeb Classical Library 63. Cambridge, MA: Harvard University Press, 1999.

———. *Aeneid, Books 7–12; Appendix Vergiliana.* Translated by H. Rushton Fairclough. Revised by G. P. Goold, 2–367. Loeb Classical Library 64. Cambridge, MA: Harvard University Press, 2001.

Vitruvius. *On Architecture.* Vol. 1, *Books 1–5.* Translated by Frank Granger. Loeb Classical Library 251. Cambridge, MA: Harvard University Press, 1931.

———. *On Architecture.* Vol. 2, *Books 6–10.* Translated by Frank Granger. Loeb Classical Library 280. Cambridge, MA: Harvard University Press, 1934.

Voragine, Jacobus de. *The Golden Legend: Readings on the Saints.* Translated by William Granger Ryan. Princeton, NJ: Princeton University Press, 1993.

Weber, Christoph, ed. *Legati e governatori dello Stato pontificio 1550–1809.* Rome: Ufficio Centrale per i Beni archivistici, 1994.

Weinberg, Bernard. *A History of Literary Criticism in the Italian Renaissance.* 2 vols. Chicago: University of Chicago Press, 1961.

White, Paul. *Jodocus Badius Ascensius: Commentary, Commerce, and Print in the Renaissance.* Oxford: Oxford University Press, 2013.

Wilde, Johannes. *Italian Drawings in the Department of Prints and Drawings in the British Museum: Michelangelo and His Studio.* London: British Museum, 1953.

Williams, Megan Hale. *The Monk and the Book: Jerome and the Making of Christian Scholarship.* Chicago: University of Chicago Press, 2006.

Wind, Edgar. *The Religious Symbolism of Michelangelo: The Sistine Chapel.* Edited by Elizabeth Sears. Oxford: Oxford University Press, 2000.

Winfrid, Paul [Paulus Winfridus Diaconus]. "Homiliarius." In Venerabilis Bedae, *Opera Omnia,* vol. 6, and Paul Winfrid, *Opera Historica, sive opera eius omnium pars prima.* Patrologia Latina series secunda 95, edited by Jacques-Paul Migne, 1159–1582. Paris: Migne, 1851.

Witcombe, Christopher L. C. E. *Print Publishing in Sixteenth-Century Rome: Growth and Expansion, Rivalry and Murder.* London: Harvey Miller, 2008.

Wohl, Hellmut. *The Aesthetics of Italian Renaissance Art: A Reconsideration of Style.* Cambridge: Cambridge University Press, 1999.

Wright, D. R. Edward. "Structure and Significance in Dolce's *L'Aretino.*" *Journal of Aesthetics and Art Criticism* 45, no. 3 (1987): 273–78.

Zeri, Federico. "L'Angelo con la barba: L'Annunziazione del transito della Vergine (e un errore di Giovanni Andrea Gilio)." In *Hommage à Michel Laclotte: Études sur la peinture du Moyen Âge et de la Renaissance,* edited by Pierre Rosenberg, Cécile Scailliérez, and Dominique Thiébaut, 304–10. Milan: Electa, 1994.

———. *Pittura e Controriforma: L'arte senza tempo di Scipione da Gaeta.* Turin: Einaudi, 1957.

ACKNOWLEDGMENTS

In the 1980s, when Michael Bury started teaching a course on sixteenth-century Roman art, there were few secondary texts available in English, never mind translated primary sources. To fill this gap and to provide students with an important insight into the period's values and debates, Michael translated the sections where Gilio's interlocutors discuss particular works of art in Rome—Michelangelo's *Last Judgment* in particular—amounting to approximately one-third of the *Dialogo*. When Carol M. Richardson moved to the University of Edinburgh and started to teach a course on Catholic Reform art in Rome, she turned to the by-then-ragged photocopied pages of Michael's translation. Only then did the extraordinary effort that Michael put into the original translation become apparent. Lucinda Byatt, a professional translator and a historian with expertise in sixteenth-century reform debates, joined Michael in what was initially intended to be a checking and tidying-up of the translation. At that stage it was realized that it would be worthwhile to translate more of the *Dialogo*. Michael and Lucinda therefore set to that work, while Carol looked after the project management.

We are grateful to numerous people and institutions that have supported us over these years of work. First, our thanks go to the Edinburgh College of Art at the University of Edinburgh for supporting the costs of the Gilio project and for providing the kind of scholarly community that makes such collaborative enterprises possible. We have received invaluable assistance from librarians and archivists at many institutions, among them the Archivio di Stato di Napoli, the Biblioteca Nazionale Centrale di Firenze, and the Biblioteca Casanatense in Rome. We are especially grateful to the scholars with whom we have worked directly on this project and whose work has proved such an inspiration: Stephen Bowd, Abigail Brundin, Jill Burke, Elizabeth Cowling, Simon Ditchfield, Pamela Jones, Davide Messina, Brian Richardson, Clare Robertson, Jeremy Taylor, and Arno Witte. The staff at Getty Research Institute Publications, including Gail Feigenbaum and Janelle Gatchalian, have been immensely helpful and supportive in bringing this project to fruition. Laura Santiago in particular has worked patiently and tirelessly to ensure that the whole is greater than its parts.

—Michael Bury, Lucinda Byatt, and Carol M. Richardson

BIOGRAPHICAL NOTES ON CONTRIBUTORS

MICHAEL BURY is honorary fellow in history of art at the University of Edinburgh. His books include *Art and Identity in Early Modern Rome* (2008), edited with Jill Burke, and *The Print in Italy, 1550–1620* (2001), which won the Eric Mitchell Prize. Bury has also published articles on many aspects of Italian art from the fifteenth to the seventeenth century. He has held visiting curatorships, fellowships, and professorships at various institutions, including the British Museum, Smith College, the Courtauld Institute of Art, and the British School at Rome. Bury is a member of the editorial board of *Print Quarterly*.

LUCINDA BYATT has worked as a professional translator since 1990. She obtained a doctorate at the European University Institute, Florence, and now teaches history courses on Renaissance Italy and early modern Europe at the University of Edinburgh. Her most recent translations include Marzio Barbagli, *Farewell to the World: A History of Suicide* (2015); Antonio Forcellino, *Raphael: A Passionate Life* (2012); and Antonio Foscari, *Andrea Palladio: Unbuilt Venice* (2010). Her own publications include entries for *Dizionario Biografico degli Italiani* and articles on the finances and households of cardinals in sixteenth-century Rome.

CAROL M. RICHARDSON is senior lecturer in history of art at the University of Edinburgh, where she lectures on Renaissance and early modern topics. Her research has always been driven by a passionate curiosity for Rome and for the ways in which religious institutions represent individuals. Recent publications include the monograph *Reclaiming Rome: Cardinals in the Fifteenth Century* (2009); edited collections *Old Saint Peter's, Rome* (2013) and *The Possessions of a Cardinal: Politics, Piety, and Art, 1450–1700* (2010); and teaching texts published with The Open University. Richardson is currently working on a monograph about English Catholic art and history.

ILLUSTRATION CREDITS

Every effort has been made to identify and contact the copyright holders of images published in this book. Should you discover what you consider to be a photo by a known photographer, please contact the publisher. The following sources have granted additional permission to reproduce illustrations in this volume.

Figs. 1, 2, 5, 33, 37. © 2016. Photo Scala, Florence.

Figs. 3, 14, 26. Vatican Museums, all rights reserved.

Figs. 4, 7, 9, 11, 13, 15, 18, 25, 27, 30–32, 36. © Trustees of the British Museum.

Fig. 6. De Agostini Picture Library / P. Carrieri / Bridgeman Images.

Figs. 8, 29. Fratelli Alinari.

Fig. 10. Vatican Museums and Galleries, Vatican City / De Agostini Picture Library / Bridgeman Images.

Fig. 12. San Pietro in Montorio, Rome, Italy / Bridgeman Images.

Fig. 16. Photo: Carol M. Richardson.

Fig. 17. jozef sedmak / Alamy Stock Photo.

Fig. 19. Vatican Museums and Galleries, Vatican City / Artothek / Bridgeman Images.

Fig. 20. New York, Metropolitan Museum of Art.

Figs. 21, 22. New York, Metropolitan Museum of Art. The Elisha Whittelsey Collection, The Elisha Whittelsey Fund, 1959.

Figs. 23a–e. New York Public Library.

Fig. 24. Musei e Galleria Pontificie, Musei Vaticani, Vatican City / Mondadori Portfolio / Bridgeman Images.

Fig. 28. Opera di Santa Croce, Florence, Italy / Bridgeman Images.

Fig. 34. Pinacoteca di Brera, Milan, Italy, Alinari / Bridgeman Images.

Fig. 35. The Morgan Library and Museum. IV, 7. Purchased by Pierpont Morgan (1837–1913) in 1909.

INDEX

Other translations published in the TEXTS & DOCUMENTS Series by the Getty Research Institute

Jusepe Martínez, *Practical Discourses on the Most Noble Art of Painting* (ca. 1672)
Edited by Zahira Véliz
Translated by David McGrath and Zahira Véliz
ISBN 978-1-60606-528-0 (paper)

Umberto Boccioni, *Futurist Painting Sculpture (Plastic Dynamism)* (1914)
Introduction by Maria Elena Versari
Translation by Richard Shane Agin and Maria Elena Versari
ISBN 978-1-60606-475-7 (paper)

Heinrich Wölfflin, *Principles of Art History: The Problem of the Development of Style in Early Modern Art* (1915)
Essays by Evonne Levy and Tristan Weddigen
Translation by Jonathan Blower
ISBN 978-1-60606-452-8 (paper)

The First Treatise on Museums: Samuel Quiccheberg's Inscriptiones, *1565*
Introduction by Mark A. Meadow
Translation by Mark A. Meadow and Bruce Robertson
ISBN 978-1-60606-149-7 (paper)

Gabriele Paleotti, *Discourse on Sacred and Profane Images* (1592)
Introduction by Paolo Prodi
Translation by William McCuaig
ISBN 978-1-60606-116-9 (paper)

Antoine Quatremère de Quincy, *Letters to Miranda and Canova on the Abduction of Antiquities from Rome and Athens* (1796, 1815)
Introduction by Dominique Poulot
Translation by Chris Miller and David Gilks
ISBN 978-1-60606-099-5 (paper)

Alois Riegl, *The Origins of Baroque Art in Rome* (1908)
Edited by Andrew Hopkins and Arnold Witte
Essays by Alina Payne, Arnold Witte, and Andrew Hopkins
Translation by Andrew Hopkins and Arnold Witte
ISBN 978-1-60606-041-4 (paper)

Le Corbusier, *Toward an Architecture* (1924)
Introduction by Jean-Louis Cohen
Translation by John Goodman
ISBN 978-0-89236-899-0 (hardcover), ISBN 978-0-89236-822-8 (paper)

Johann Joachim Winckelmann, *History of the Art of Antiquity* (1764)
Introduction by Alex Potts
Translation by Harry Francis Mallgrave
ISBN 978-0-89236-668-2 (paper)

Jacob Burckhardt, *Italian Renaissance Painting according to Genres* (1885–93)
Introduction by Maurizio Ghelardi
Translation by David Britt and Caroline Beamish
ISBN 978-0-89236-736-8 (paper)

Gottfried Semper, *Style in the Technical and Tectonic Arts; or, Practical Aesthetics* (1860–63)
Introduction by Harry Francis Mallgrave
Translation by Michael Robinson and Harry Francis Mallgrave
ISBN 978-0-89236-597-5 (hardcover)

Julien-David Le Roy, *The Ruins of the Most Beautiful Monuments of Greece* (1770)
Introduction by Robin Middleton
Translation by David Britt
ISBN 978-0-89236-669-9 (paper)

Giovanni Battista Piranesi, *Observations on the Letter of Monsieur Mariette; with Opinions on Architecture, and a Preface to a New Treatise on the Introduction and Progress of the Fine Arts in Europe in Ancient Times* (1765)
Introduction by John Wilton-Ely
Translation by David Britt and Caroline Beamish
ISBN 978-0-89236-636-1 (paper)

Carl Gustav Carus, *Nine Letters on Landscape Painting, Written in the Years 1815–1824; with a Letter from Goethe by Way of Introduction* (1831)
Introduction by Oskar Bätschmann
Translation by David Britt
ISBN 978-0-89236-674-3 (paper)

Walter Curt Behrendt, *The Victory of the New Building Style* (1927)
Introduction by Detlef Mertins
Translation by Harry Francis Mallgrave
ISBN 978-0-89236-563-0 (paper)

Aby Warburg, *The Renewal of Pagan Antiquity: Contributions to the Cultural History of the European Renaissance* (1932)
Introduction by Kurt W. Forster
Translation by David Britt
ISBN 978-0-89236-537-1 (hardcover)

Friedrich Gilly: Essays on Architecture, 1796–1799
Introduction by Fritz Neumeyer
Translation by David Britt
ISBN 978-0-89236-281-3 (paper)

Heinrich Hübsch, Rudolf Wiegmann, Carl Albert Rosenthal, Johann Heinrich Wolff, and Carl Gottlieb Wilhelm Bötticher, *In What Style Should We Build? The German Debate on Architectural Style* (1828–47)
Introduction and translation by Wolfgang Herrmann
ISBN 978-0-89236-198-4 (paper)

Otto Wagner, *Modern Architecture: A Guidebook for His Students to This Field of Art* (1902)
Introduction and translation by Harry Francis Mallgrave
ISBN 978-0-22686-939-1 (paper)